Indian Society
Institutions and Change

RAJENDRA K. SHARMA

ATLANTIC
PUBLISHERS & DISTRIBUTORS (P) LTD

Published by
ATLANTIC
PUBLISHERS & DISTRIBUTORS (P) LTD
7/22, Ansari Road, Darya Ganj, New Delhi-110002
Phones : +91-11-40775252, 40775214, 23273880, 23275880
Fax: +91-11-23285873
Web: www.atlanticbooks.com
E-mail: orders@atlanticbooks.com

Reprint 2016, 2018, 2020, 2021, 2022, 2023

Printed & bound in India by Atlantic Print Services

Preface

This book covers the following papers presented at Undergraduate and Post Graduate levels in Sociology in Indian Universities:

Indian Society, Indian Society and Culture, Indian Society and Social Institutions, Social Change in India, Indian Social Institutions and Contemporary Indian Society and Culture.

Based on latest published material the book includes latest data on every subject. While the subject has been presented in an analytical style with central, side and running headings, integral and holistic view has been adopted, in matters having different opinions. The language is easy and free of technical jargon as far as possible. At the end of each chapter, questions actually asked at University examinations have been given for preparation for examination. Thus, the author has tried to present an ideal textbook on the subject.

Starting with characteristics of Indian Society, the book deals with Hindu, Muslim, Christian, Rural, Tribal and Urban social systems and institutions. It describes major Religious Groups in India. After summarization of social changes in India it discusses various trends in contemporary social changes such as Industrialization, Urbanization, Labour Problems, Secularization, Tradition and Modernity, Sanskritization, Westernization, Modernization, Politicization and Democratization. In the end, it points out need and methods of realization of national and emotional integration in India.

Thus, the author has tried to solve the student's problems of what, how and why about the subject. However, suggestions for improvement are most cordially invited for further improvement.

RAJENDRA K. SHARMA

Contents

		Page Nos.
	Preface	*iii*
1.	Characteristics of the Indian Society	1
2.	The Hindu Varna System	11
3.	The Hindu Ashram System: Rinas, Karma and Sanskaras	27
4.	The Hindu Concept of Purusharthas	47
5.	Caste and Casteism among Hindus and Muslims	61
6.	The Untouchability	77
7.	Backward Classes and Minorities	88
8.	The Hindu Family: Joint Family	99
9.	The Hindu Marriage	107
10.	The Status of Hindu Women	123
11.	Muslim Social System and Institutions	129
12.	Christian Social System and Institutions	139
13.	Tribal Social System and Institutions	145
14.	Rural Social System and Institutions	171
15.	Urbanization and Urban Communities in India	235
16.	Major Religious Groups in India	260
17.	Contemporary Social Change	282
18.	Industrialization and Labour Problems in India	289
19.	Secularization	302
20.	Socio-Religious Movements in India	309
21.	Tradition and Modernity	323

22.	Sanskritization	337
23.	Westernization	345
24.	Modernization	355
25.	Politicization	360
26.	Democratization	363
27.	National Emotional Integration	369
	Bibliography	375

1

Characteristics of the Indian Society

DEMOGRAPHIC CHARACTERISTICS

According to latest census of India in March 1991, the demographic characteristics of Indian population at present are as follows:

Total Population	843,930,861
Male Population	437,597,929
Female Population	406,332,932
Decennial Increase (1981-1991)	160,601,764 or 23.50 per cent
Density of Population	267 persons per K.M.
Male-Female Ratio	929 females per thousand males
Literacy Rate Total	52.11%
Literacy Rate Male	63.86%
Literacy Rate Female	39.42%
Birth Rate per ten thousand	27.4
Death Rate per ten thousand	9.4
Biggest State, U P.	138.6 crores
Densest State, West Bengal	800 per sq.km.
Highest Literacy Rate, Kerala	90.59%
Lowest Literacy Rate, Haryana	38.54%
Maximum Population Increase State, Nagaland	56.9%
Indian Percentage in Total World Population	16%
Decennial Density Increase	51 persons per sq.km.
Percentage of U P., Population of India	16%

Table 1: *Demographic Characteristics*

UNITY AND DIVERSITY IN INDIAN CULTURE

One finds a fundamental unity in Indian culture that can possibly elude one, if one concerns himself only with the external aspects of it. Such a man fails to find unity in diversity, the simple in the complex, the individual in the typical or common.

It is, however, fallacious to think that India lacked all cultural unity in the past, and that this phenomenon is the outcome of recent events, the British rule among them. The ideal of cultural unity is not new to India, it is a concept which has been common to Indians of the past. The seers who gave birth to Indian culture were perfectly aware of the unity in India, the unity that derives from many common and uniform elements. The unity can be comprehended easily by understanding the unity that exists in various fields.

1. Geographical Unity. India, like every other country, has its own fixed boundaries that are natural. India is limited within boundaries that are evidence of a geographical unity, a unity which baffles the scholars who themselves live in small European countries and find it difficult to comprehend how such a large country with so much variety of nature can be united.

The very name Bharatvarsha implies a historical significance that symbolizes unity. The name is not born of geographical necessity, but is concerned with the ideal of *Chakravarti.* This name, the chief characteristic of which is unit, has always occupied an important place in the minds of religious thinkers, political philosophers and poets since each has conceived of the country as a single expanse from the Himalayas to Cape Comorin, a country ruled by one king. It is for this unified entity that they have expressed admiration and love. Much of the literature of the past has praise for those kings and emperors who had tried to extend their respective empires from the Himalayas to Cape Comorin and from the Brahamputra in the East to the Indus in the West. Some of them achieved success in their endeavours. Even in the medieval period, each successive ruler treated the country as a geographical unit and tried to extend his rule over the entire expanse of land. Even today when we address our country as Mother India it includes the realization of a geographical unity. Bankim Chandra Chatterjee's patriotic hymn *Bande Matram* exudes the feeling of this Indian unity.

2. Religious Unity. Although the various religious groups in India present elements of external difference, it is not impossible to trace elements common to all. Each religious group exhibits one single feeling, each accepts the truth of immortality of soul, temporary nature of world, rebirth; the law of Karma, monism, salvation, nirvana, contemplation and all the other things that go to make up the religious paraphernalia. There are differences in the way these elements are treated but each religion preaches a fundamentally single religious faith and shares a belief in the purity and value of life, faith in an invisible power, benevolence, piety, honesty and liberality, with every other religious system. The rituals are almost common to every form of religion in the country. If one were to look no further than the followers of Shiva and Vishnu one would find that although they pray to different gods, they are spread out all over the country and they have erected temples wherever they have gone. These temples are to be found not only in the ice-bound breaches of the Himalayas and fertile plains of the Ganges but also in the deltas of Tungbhadra, Cauvery and Krishna. Ramayana and Mahabharata, the epics, are read as avidly in the Punjab and Kashmir as they are in the South. The legends of Rama and

Krishna are sung and repeated with equal fervour among people who speak Hindi and among those who speak such language as Tamil, Telugu and the rest. Equal respect is given everywhere to the Gita, the Vedas, Puranas and other scriptures in India.

This respect is given because these religious texts provide much satisfaction and solace to the people. Religious unity in India finds its expression through the places of worship scattered all over the country. Such religious places of the Hindus as Badrinath in the North, Dwarika in the West, Rameshwar in the South and Puri in the East represent the religious unity of this vast country . It has been considered obligatory for every Indian to visit each of these holy places. But this pilgrimage comprehends the feeling of patriotism and a feeling for the unity of the country also. When the Hindu prays during his bath, he recounts the name of every major river in the country such as Ganges, Jamuna, Godavari, Sarasvati, Narbada, Indus and the Cauvery. The prayer is intended not merely to remind the mortal of the vast size of the country but also of the religious and cultural unity that exists between Indians belonging to different parts.

3. Cultural Unity. Indian culture possesses a fundamental unity, a unity the impress of which can be found on the literature and thought of different communities, despite the obvious difference in customs and traditions. The fundamental approach to literature, philosophy, traditions and customs is typically Indian. The basis of the social and cultural unity of the country is common to every group. One finds this common element lurking out from behind the apparent differences of social intercourse, religious rites, ceremonies and the rest of it. All groups and communities unanimously accept the inviolable nature of family, sanctity of sanskaras and of the kitchen are commonly accepted. Many of the festivals are celebrated all over the country in one and the same manner. This is possible only because a cultural unity does exist.

4. Unity of Emotion. It has been difficult to discover why the South Indian languages have remained confined to that area. A large number of languages make it difficult to promote a national unity, while a large number of races make this even more difficult. Both these elements are present in India, but since Sanskrit was the common base of the Indian languages, the problem of linguistic multiplicity has been solved. People of the North as well as of the South accepted Sanskrit. At the same time Sanskrit became the language of Hindu culture and all classics were composed in this language. It was in the protective atmosphere of Hindu culture and Sanskrit that this land of many languages became one nation.

Sanskrit was the ancient language of India, used in common converse many centuries before Christ, but in three or four centuries B.C. Prakrat language spread in the country, a language which resembles Sanskrit. At that time Sanskrit was the language of the scholars and Prakrat that of the common people. In the dramas produced during the first century B.C., a mixture of Sanskrit and Prakrat is found in the works of Kalidas and Ashvaghosh. In these dramas it was the convention for the educated person to speak Sanskrit and for uneducated to converse in Prakrat. This is clear evidence of the fact that Prakrat was the language of the uneducated masses of India. Ashok promoted the spread of religion on a door to door basis through Buddhist monks, the language being Prakrat. Later on Pali replaced Prakrat. Much literature was produced in Pali, Buddhist philosophical and religious texts known as Jataka and Tripitaka were composed in Pali. Jain literature was also composed in the same language.

In spite of the literature in Pali and Prakrat, Sanskrit was invariably chosen by all groups and religions as the language of all classical compositions which demanded reverence and respect. Sanskrit was the root of Pali and Prakrat. This accounts for the overt similarity between these three languages. Besides, all the modern Indian languages have been derived from Sanskrit. Even Tamil and Telugu have been influenced by Sanskrit, for Sanskrit is the only language in which the entire ancient literature and philosophy of the past is recorded and available. Through its influence on all the other languages Sanskrit has played an important part in creating and maintaining unity in the country.

5. Political Unity. The political unity of the country is, in fact, an offshoot of the religious and cultural unity that has characterised India in the past. It cannot be denied that in moments of heat and controversy the various territorial princes rebelled against the central authority, but each one realized the value of the ideal of universal overlord. Kings released horses to be called universal overlords (Chakravarti) and Vedic literature contains numerous instances in which kings did achieve this position. Some of these kings are Prathu, Dilip, Aj, Dashrath, Sagar, Yayaati, Mandhata and Yudhistira. At times it was observed that kings declared war on other kings for no purpose other than to gain the title of universal overlord. But in all such conflicts the motive was not of material or psychological advantage but the desire to unite the entire country under a central authority. Never has any Indian ruler transcended the natural boundaries of the country to attack any external power, with any expansionist ambition. But one of the marked tendencies of all political sovereigns within the country has been to bring the largest tract of land under their control and to establish as large a political unit as possible. Chandra Gupta, Ashok and Samudra Gupta, among other emperors, claimed the title of universal overlord by performing what is known as the ashvamedha yagya. This notion of universal overlordship is very old. The presence of various terms synonymous with universal overlordship in Vedic literature and the fact that religious practices such as the ashvamedha yagya indicates that even the most ancient ruler in India was fired with an ambition of ruling over the entire nation. Many of them wanted to create political unity and some of them did succeed to some extent.

From the earliest times India has been invaded by different races such as the Aryans, Shaka, Huns, etc., but they merged so completely in the local population and culture that they lost all traces of their original nature and cannot be distinguished today. They came to India and became Indians. Today, many of the Indians and Christians who live in India are born of Indian parents who adopted these alien religions. With the passage of time these tribes and races established a physical identification with Indian culture and civilization. Before the advent of the Muslims; but before and after the downfall of Maurya empire many tribes and races came to India, but, when the Muslims arrived the, only people living here were the Hindus, Negroes, Dravidians, Aryans, the Mongols, the Greeks, the Yuchi, Shak, Aabhir, the Turks, the Hunas have failed to retain their individual character, and have been completely assimilated into the four varnas of Indian society. Indian culture is an amalgam of the various racial cultures which have been imported into the country, so much so that today it is impossible to discover the extent to which any one race has left its mark. It were the Aryans who succeeded in introducing unity in Indian culture, and for that reason Indian culture is also known as Aryan culture. Even the Muslims could not avoid being assimilated into the Indian cultural tradition, with the result that the Muslims of India differ considerably from the Muslims of Arabia, Iran and other Middle East countries.

Even in the most ancient and dark periods the Hindus have always been proponents of a fundamental unity in spite of surface dissimilarities. This basic trait inherent in Hindu culture has influenced every Hindu. There has never been any conflict between the proponents of different religions and each has continued to blow his own trumpet without interference from any other. All these saints have evinced the feeling of belonging to each other, a sense of identity of purpose and emotion. The interest that many Muslims have taken in Indian religion, philosophy, science and culture is evidence of the fact that cultural unity has always marked the Indian life.

It becomes quite obvious from the above account that India is a fine example of unity in diversity, despite the external differences. Indian cultural unity transcends birth, caste, creed, social customs and religious groupings to establish a unity in diversity.

IMPORTANT AND PERMANENT ELEMENTS IN INDIAN CULTURE

The following are the important and permanent elements in Indian culture:

1. Indian Culture is Religion-oriented. Indian culture is founded on religion but the obvious question is, what is religion? 'Dharma' has been liberally interpreted in the Indian context for it does not coincide with the English term religion, the latter denoting the external rites and performances. In Indian culture the word 'Dharma' includes the performances of rites, but it further comprehends cultural organization and spirituality. It is so comprehensive that it is placed above other aims in life. It is the thread which ties the Indians together, and according to Indian culture, it is the element that distinguishes man from beast.

It is the opinion of some people that the religiosity of Indian culture is turned towards a hereafter that has nothing to do with the present world, and is, therefore, an escapist approach. This conception is false. Indian seers believed that the relation between the present world and the hereafter is a deep one, that nothing can be of value if one rejects the existing world and turns to the unseen universe, that material and the spiritual are perfectly blended, and it is dharma which achieves this blend.

2. Indian Culture is Spiritual. The basic aim of Indian culture is self-knowledge. The originators of Indian culture, the seers and the mendicants came to the conclusion that man should know himself because that is the only way in which the truths of the world can be known with any fullness. It is for this reason that Indian religion is more introverted than extroverted, more tendencious towards the spiritual than towards the material. Sri Aurobindo has rightly stated that spirituality is the key to the Indian mind. It is this spirituality which has helped Indian culture to retain its novelty among all the other cultures. Spirituality is one sphere in which Indian culture has led all the rest. All the theistic and atheistic philosophies that go to make up Indian culture are imbued with the idea of spirituality. Religion and Philosophy are important elements in Indian culture, and both these have influenced Indian culture and civilization greatly. Everything carries a tinge of religion and philosophy in India.

3. Religious Tolerance. Religious tolerance has been a common feature of the Indian culture. Religion was preached and propagated but it never became a source of conflict and violence. People tried to appreciate common elements of different religions and thus understood essential unity of religions.

4. Synthetic Spirit. Since its very beginning Indian culture had been synthetic in its spirit. Aryans, the founders of Indian culture, gave it a capacity to assimilate the foreign elements which came in India from time to time. Even the inner revolts as that of Buddhism which arose within it gradually subsided and merged in it. Hinduism, the essence of Indian culture, has accepted many different religions into its fold and has only gained thereby. Even the Muslim religion could not escape the synthesizing tendency of Hindu culture.

5. Power of Adaptation. Darwin argued that only the fittest could survive in this universe, and that species who are weak are eliminated by circumstances. Those who are powerful change the circumstances to suit their own convenience. The fact that Indian culture is alive today proves that it has greater power than the other cultures. Innumerable social upheavals and political changes have taken place in India since the Vedic age to the present day, but Indian culture has always managed to adapt circumstances to its own requirements.

6. Comprehensive Viewpoint. The viewpoint of Indian culture has never been one-sided; instead it has always been integral in its approach to life. It stresses the importance of both the material and the spiritual aspects and advocates the advances and development of literature, music, art, science and the other disciplines. This is a clear evidence of the comprehensive viewpoint. Indian culture has accepted four primary values, and in this scale earning and sex have been placed on an equal footing with duty and salvation. Cultural development is incomplete without economic freedom from want, that is what

Table 2: *Population in India*

	Place in 1991	Population 1991	Percentage of Total 1991	Percentage of Total 1981	Place in 1981
1	2	3	4	5	6
1.	U.P.	13,91,12,287	16.44	16.22	1
2.	Bihar	8,63,74,465	10.21	10.23	2
3.	Maharashtra	7,89,37,187	9.33	9.19	3
4.	West Bengal	6,80,77,965	8.04	7.99	4
5.	A.P.	6,65,08,008	7.86	7.84	5
6.	M.P.	6,61,81,170	7.82	7.64	6
7.	Tamil Nadu	5,58,58,946	6.60	7.08	7
8.	Karnataka	4,49,77,201	5.31	5.43	8
9.	Rajasthan	4,40,05,990	5.20	5.01	9
10.	Gujarat	4,13,09,582	4.88	4.99	10
11.	Orissa	3,16,59,736	3.74	3.86	11
12.	Kerala	2,90,98,518	3.44	3.72	12
13.	Assam	2,24,14,322	2.65	2.64	13
14.	Punjab	2,02,81,969	2.40	2.46	14
15.	Haryana	1,64,63,648	1.94	1.89	15
16.	Delhi	94,20,644	1.11	0.91	16
17.	J & K	77,18,700	0.91	0.88	17
18.	Himachal Pradesh	51,70,877	0.61	0.63	18
19.	Tripura	27,57,205	0.33	0.30	19
20.	Manipur	18,37,149	0.22	0.21	20
21.	Meghalaya	17,74,778	0.21	0.19	21
22.	Nagaland	12,09,546	0.14	0.11	23
23.	Goa	11,69,793	0.14	0.15	22
24.	Arunachal Pradesh	8,64,558	0.10	0.09	24
25.	Pondicherry	8,07,785	0.09	0.09	25
26.	Mizoram	6,89,756	0.08	0.07	26
27.	Chandigarh	6,42,015	0.08	0.07	27
28.	Sikkim	4,06,457	0.05	0.05	28
29.	Andaman & Nicobar	2,80,661	0.03	0.03	29
30.	Dadra & Nagar Haveli	1,38,447	0.02	0.01	30
31.	Daman & Diu	1,01,586	0.01	0.01	31
32.	Lakshadweep	51,707	0.01	0.01	32

Table 3: *Density of Population*

Place in 1991	State/UT	Density 1981	Density 1991
1	2	3	4
1.	Delhi	4,194	6,352
2.	Chandigarh	3,961	5,632
3.	Lakshadweep	1,258	1,616
4.	Pondicherry	1,229	1,642
5.	Daman and Diu	705	907
6.	West Bengal	615	767
7.	Kerala	655	749
8.	Bihar	402	497
9.	U.P.	377	473
10.	Tamil Nadu	372	429
11.	Punjab	333	403
12.	Haryana	292	372
13.	Goa	272	316
14.	Assam	230	296
15.	Dadra & Nagar Haveli	211	282
	India	230	273
16.	Tripura	196	263
17.	Maharashtra	204	257
18.	A.P.	195	242
19.	Karnataka	194	235
20.	Gujarat	174	211
21.	Orissa	169	203
22.	M.P.	118	149
23.	Rajasthan	100	129
24.	Himachal Pradesh	77	93
25.	Manipur	64	82
26.	Meghalaya	60	79
27.	J & K	59	76

Table 4: *Male-Female Ratio: India (1901-1991)*

Census Year	Females per 1000 Males
1	2
1901	972
1911	964
1921	955
1931	950
1941	945
1951	946
1961	941
1971	930
1981	934
1991	927

Table 5: *Age Structure*

(Percentage)

Age Group	1980	1985	1990	2000
0-4	14.18	13.91	12.85	10.66
5-14	25.54	24.34	23.15	20.95
15-59	54.07	55.51	57.51	60.80
More than 60	6.21	6.24	6.49	7.59
Total	100.00	100.00	100.00	100.00

Table 6: *Population According to Language*

Languages	Population (Crores)		Percentage	
	1971	1981	1971	1981
Hindi	208.5	264.5	38.0	42.9
Bengali	44.8	51.3	8.2	8.3
Telugu	44.8	50.6	8.2	8.2
Marathi	41.8	49.5	7.6	8.0
Tamil	37.7	3.8	6.9	0.6
Urdu	28.6	34.9	5.2	5.7
Gujrati	25.9	33.1	4.7	5.4
Malyalam	21.9	25.7	4.0	4.2
Kannade	21.7	25.7	4.0	4.2
Oriya	19.9	23.0	3.6	3.7
Punjabi	14.1	19.6	2.6	3.2
Assamia	9.0	0.1	1.6	0.01
Sindhi	1.7	2.0	0.3	0.3
Kashmiri	2.5	3.2	0.5	0.5

Indian culture has always believed. Its aim has always been the integral development of man. India has allowed the simultaneous development of religion, economic theory and varieties of sex practices.

7. Freedom of Thought. It is necessary to have freedom in the sphere of thought because the cultural development of any country depends upon the independent thought of its intellectuals. Indian culture has always valued independence of thought. It is because of this independence that India has been the birth place of such varied philosophies as Hindu Vedanta, Buddhism, Jainism and Charvaka, monism, qualified monism and all the rest of the philosophic traditions. Every individual in India possessed the right to think for himself, and as a consequence different ideologies flourished here without any rancour and discord, in a mood of harmony.

QUESTIONS FOR EXERCISE

1. Explain and discuss unity and diversity in Indian culture.
2. What are the important and permanent elements in Indian culture?

2

The Hindu Varna System

Meaning of Varna

According to Sanskrit Hindi Dictionary by Varnana Shivarama Apte, the term varna means colour, description, explanation, interpretation, praise, extension, observation, perception, form, beauty, caste, race, type, genus, etc.[1] According to *Meghdoot* of Kalidas, Varna means complexion, form and beauty.[2] According to *Raghuvansha* of Kalidas, Varna means human class, tribe or clan.[3] In most of the passages of *Rigveda* the word Varna means colour or light.[4] However, in some of its verses the word Varna is associated with groups of people having a skin of a dark or fair colour. For example, according to *Rigveda.* Indra placed the dasa colour in a cave of darkness.[5] Similar passages may be found in so many places in *Rigveda.* The Arya Varna (colour of the skin) was white. In contrast, the colour of the skin of the dasas or dasyus was dark. This contrast has been pointed out at so many places in *Rigveda.* These passages make it clear that both the Aryas and Dasas were designated as Varna on account of colour of their skin.

Similar references may be traced in Brahmana scriptures. The Taittariya. Brahmana says, "The Brahmana is the divine varna and Sudra is the Asurya."[6] The Sudras were called Asur mainly because of their dark complexion. In *Rigveda* words, "Asuryam Varnam" means Sudra tribe. The Aryan's always kept Aryas and Dasas quite distinct and belonging to antagonistic camps due to the distinctions in their complexion. The earliest meaning of the term varna was colour, in the context of Aryas and Dasas. According to P.V. Kane, "Though the words brahmana and kshatriya occur frequently in the *Rigveda*, the word varna is not used in connection with them. Even in the Purusa sukta *(Rigveda* X.90) where

1 Apte, V.S., *Sanskrit-Hindi Dictionary*, p. 901.
2 *Meghdoot*, 46.
3 *Raghuvansh*, 5.19.
4 *Rig Veda*, I.73.7, II. 3.5, IX.97.15, IX.104. 4. IX.105.4, X.124.7.
5 *Ibid.*, II. 12.4.
6 *Taitt. Bra.* 1.2.6.

the words brahmana, rajanya, vaisya and sudra occur, the word Varna is not used. Hence, one may reasonably say that the only watertight groups that are positively or expressly vouch safed by the Rigveda are arya and dasa or dasyu."[1]

Thus though the word Varna in Dharmasastras means social classes, it was not the original meaning of the term. It may be noted that the Dharmasastras traced the origin of Varna system to Purusa sukta. However, as has been pointed out above, the word Brahmana in *Rigveda* does not mean caste. P.V. Kane, including some other scholars, points out that Purusa sukta is a much later hymn than most of the hymns of the *Rigveda.* According to him, "In the whole of the *Rigveda* the words vaisya and sudra do not occur except in the Purusa sukta, though both of them occur in the *Atharvaveda.*"[2] It may be conceded that the four varnas may have come into existence at the time of the opposite of Purusa sukta. Dr. G.S. Ghurye thinks that the reference in Rg.X, 71.9 to a false claim for being regarded as a Brahmana points to the conclusion that Brahmins had become a caste.[3] This claim, however, has been refuted P.V. Kane by various examples. Similarly, Dr. Ghurye's claim about the existence of other varnas in Vedic times has been also refuted by Prof. P.V. Kane. According to the latter's conclusion, "The position of the three varnas *inter se* (called collectively arya) now requires consideration. It is clear that the Samhitas other than the Rigveda and Brahmana works show that the three classes of Brahmins, Kshatriya and Vaisyas had become differentiated and their privileges, duties and liabilities had become more or less fixed in those times."[4]

SIGNIFICANCE OF THE VARNA SYSTEM IN PERSONAL LIFE

Whatever may be the discussion about the nature of man, one thing has been generally accepted, that man is not a simple unit but a complex whole consisting of several constituents. Social harmony demands that each of these constituents should get its due. Thus, all should act in harmony. In Indian terminology, there should be balance between *Sattva, Rajas* and *Tamas* elements within the man. None of these should be completely eradicated all should get their due. He should get a fair dealing in society. He may be allowed to follow his vocation, leanings, urges, etc. He may be allowed to live a life according to himself. Of course, this freedom cannot be unlimited. While one has a right for personal development and satisfaction, there is a corresponding duty that one should not become a hindrance in the fulfilment of the identical rights of others. Social justice, therefore, is based upon a harmony between rights and duties. The Indian thinkers have gone even further in emphasizing duties more than rights. It is so since man is naturally selfish in nature. No training is required for seeking self-satisfaction. On the other hand, a constant emphasis on duties is a must to remind him of his share in social justice.

1 Kane, P.V., *History of Dharmasastra,* Vol. II, Part I, p. 27.

2 *Ibid.*

3 Ghurye, G.S., *Caste and Race in India*, p. 42.

4 Kane, P.V., *History of Dharmasastras* Vol. II, Part I, p. 36.

The Varna system presents a structure of values and functions which provide both the social and personal justice. It is based upon the moral principle of *Karma.* It is believed that every one is born with peculiar leanings, temperament and abilities due to his past *karmas.* The future birth may be changed by practicing the duties attached to the Varna of the present life. Therefore, each one was asked to follow the social duties and functions characteristic to his Varna.

Swabhava and Swadharma

In personal life Varna is based upon the twin ideals of psychological and social aspects of the same phenomena. The social duties of a person are relative to his psychological make-up. Each one should follow his own psychological make-up, since by that alone he can make his contribution to the social whole. Thus, within the person *Swabhava* is the guiding principle. One who acts on *Swabhava* acts spontaneously. Spontaneity is the result of totality. Thus, following *Swabhava* results in harmony. It gives justice to each part of man. And the result is happiness, since psychologically speaking, happiness is the outcome of total satisfaction which involves satisfaction of each aspect. *Swadharma* means one's duties in society. These duties should not be imposed from outside. In order to be natural, spontaneous and divine the duties must be based on *Swabhava.* Thus, *Swadharma* and *Swabhava* should be identical. *Swabhava* should decide *Swadharma.* It may be noted here that according to Western psychology of vocational and educational guidance also *Swabhava* is the basis of choice in education and vocation. Again, from the point of view of national progress also this alone is the golden principle. If everyone is allowed to follow education and vocation according to his *Swabhava,* the total result of national achievement will be obviously maximum. Thus, Varna system provides a solid basis for personal harmony and happiness.

The above interpretation of the close relationship between *Swabhava* and *Swadharma* requires an understanding of the inner meaning of the beliefs behind Varna system. Varna system has a Divine sanction at its back. It has been generally believed in India that one is born in particular Varna due to Divine will. This Divine will, however, does not contradict but affirm Nature's Laws. Indian metaphysics does not distinguish between man, Nature and God. The trinity is essentially based upon the Unity known as Brahman. Therefore, if Varna system is ordained by Divine, it only means the realization of the natural principle. And since man is a part of Nature it is a human principle. Further, since humanity and the individuality are just two names of the same phenomena, the Varna system is the individual principle. Therefore, in order to achieve harmony either within the man or within the society, in order to achieve maximum national progress and the happiness one should follow a vocation according to his innate leanings, temperament and abilities, which was the essential meaning of Varna system applied to the individual. This shows the significance of the Varna system in a society.

DUTIES OF THE VARNAS

Dharmasastras have described in details the duties of the varnas. This description was in keeping with the ancient tradition starting right from the *Vedas*. Thus the propositions with which the Dharmasastras start were borrowed from the *Vedas*, the *Brahmanas*, the *Upanisads* and the *Bhagvadgita*. After an elaborate discussion of varna system in all these before the advent of Dharmasastras, P.V. Kane arrives at the following conclusions:[1]

(1) that in the earliest times about which we have literary records there were only two varnas, the aryas and their opponents the dasyus or dasas; that the difference between the two was based on difference of colour and culture and was thus more or less racial and cultural;

(2) that centuries before the samhita period closed, the dasyus had been conquered and were given a position subservient to the aryas;

(3) that the sudras were the dasyus so subjugated and made subservient;

(4) that the spirit of exclusiveness and pride of superiority existing among the aryas with reference to dasyus soon extended to groups among the aryas themselves;

(5) that by the time of the *Brahmana* Literature, brahmins (men supposed to be devoted to learning and priesthood), kshatriyas (kings, noblemen and some warriors) and vaisyas (the artisans and common people) had become separated into groups more or less dependent on birth and that the brahmin had come to be regarded as superior to the kshatriya by the fact of birth.

(6) that even such low castes as chandalas and paulkasas had been evolved long before the end of the Vedic period;

(7) that owing to cultural advance, division of labour arose and numerous arts and crafts had been developed and they were in the process of contributory to the complexity of the system by creating numerous sub-castes based upon occupations;

(8) that besides the four varnas, intermediate castes like the *rathakara* had been evolved;

(9) that there were certain non-Arya tribes which were supposed to have been originally kshatriya but fallen later on.

The writers on Dharmasastra start with the proposition that the four varnas *viz.*, brahmin, kshatriya, vaisya and sudra, are arranged in a descending scale of social status with duties peculiar to them. The duties and privileges of varnas occupy a prominent place in Dharmasastras. The peculiar duties were the principle means of livelihood of these varnas. According to *Manu Smriti*, the basic social ideal is the division of society into four sections: Brahmins, Kshatriyas, Vaisyas, and Sudras. These divisions are of divine origin. The Brahmin was created from the mouth of Brahma; the Kshatriya from his arms; the Vaisya from his thighs and the Sudra from the Lord's feet. [2] The ethical implication of the divine origin of Varna is that it is an integral part of a divine

1 *Ibid.*, p. 48.

2 *Manu*, I. 87.

pattern, "for the sake of the prosperity of the world,"[1] and, therefore, it is morally incumbent that one obediently accepts his role in compliance with the "sacred law."[2] The study of the Vedas, offering sacrifices and giving gifts are said to be the duties absolutely enjoined on the brahmana, kshatriya and vaisaya,[3] while each of these three varnas has certain peculiar privileges, which are its principle means of livelihood. Teaching Vedas, officiating at sacrifices and receiving gifts — these are the, privileges of Brahmins; the profession of warfare and protection of the people are the peculiar privileges of kshatriyas, agriculture, rearing cattle, trade and money-lending are the peculiar privileges of vaisyas. The first three *viz.*, study, sacrifices and liberality are said to be the dharmas of all dvijas and the other actions such as teaching the Veda are said to be the vrtti or jivika (means of livelihood) of the dvijas. According to P.V. Kane, "The consequence of this bifurcation is that if the first three are not performed or are neglected, the person concerned was dreamed to incur sin, while a brahmin is not bound necessarily to earn his livelihood by all or anyone of the three *viz.*, teaching, officiating at a sacrifice or receiving gifts."[4]

Duties of the Brahmin

According to *Manu Smriti,* to the Brahmin is assigned the role of "teaching and studying (the *Veda),* sacrificing for their own benefit and for others, giving and accepting (of alms)."[5] By virtue of his birth from Brahma's mouth, being first born and possessing the Veda, the Brahmin is considered, "the Lord of this whole creation."[6] No created being can surpass him "through whose mouth the gods continually consume the sacrificial viands and the manes the offerings of the dead."[7] "A Brahmin who dutifully performs his dharma is the most excellent of created beings."[8] "The very birth of a Brahmana is an eternal incarnation of the sacred law: for he is born to (fulfil) the sacred law, and becomes one with Brahman."[9] Thus, in brief, the duties of the Brahmin and the vocation open for his livelihood as prescribed by Dharmasastras are as follows:

1. Study of Vedas. According to Manu, a Brahmin should always and assiduously study the Veda alone; that *(Veda* study) is his highest dharma: everything else is inferior to dharma.[10] According to Yajnavalkya smriti, "the Creator created Brahmins for the preservation of the *Vedas,* for the satisfaction of the gods and pitra, for the safeguarding of dharma."[11]

1 *Ibid.*
2 *Ibid.*, I. 98.
3 *Gautam,* Dh. S . X. 1-3, 7, 50; *Baud. Dh. S.* I.10, 2-5: *Vas.* II. 13-19:, *Manu* I. 88-90, X. 75-79; *Yaj.* I. 118-119: *Vishnu Dh. S.* II. 10-15.
4 Kane, P.V., *History of Dharmasastras.*, p. 105.
5 *Manu Smriti*, I, 88.
6 *Ibid.*, I. 93.
7 *Ibid.*, I. 95.
8 *Ibid.*
9 *Ibid.*, I. 98.
10 *Ibid.*, IV. 147.
11 Yajnavalkya *Smriti*, I. 198.

2. Teaching the Vedas. According to Apastamba Dharmasastra, the brahmin alone can be the teacher of a brahmin, but in distress *i.e.,* in the absence of a brahmin teacher, a brahmin may learn from a kshatriya or vaisya, but the only service which as a pupil he should render to a kshatriya or vaisya teacher is to go after him and not shampooing his feet, etc., and after the brahmin finishes his study, the brahmin may go in front of his kshatriya teacher. Gautam and Manu lay down the same rules.[1] Manu adds that a perpetual student *naisthika brahmachari* should not stay as a pupil with a teacher who is not a brahmin and that brahmin may learn even from a sudra a useful or efficacious craft.[2] The profession of teaching the Veda could not have brought much money or wealth to brahmin, since very great emphasis was laid, on teaching without any prior agreement about payment.

3. Officiating as a Priest. It was the privilege of a brahmin alone to officiate as a priest. According to Manu, a devalaka *i.e.,* a brahmin who took remuneration to perform service before the image in a temple for three years continuously was unfit to be invited at a sraddha or to officiate in a sacrifice for gods.[3]

4. Receiving Gifts from Worthy Persons. As a means of livelihood the Brahmin was permitted to receive gifts from a worthy person of the three higher varnas. This was known as *pratigraha.* According to Manu, *pratigraha* from an unworthy person or a sudra is worse than the act of teaching him or officiating as a priest for him.[4] Very elaborate rules were laid down about gifts *i.e.,* who should receive gifts, from whom gifts may be received and on what occasions and what things were proper subjects of gift.

Duties of Kshatriya

According to Manu, the duties of Kshatriya may be summed up thus when he fights with his foes in battle, let him not strike with weapons concealed (in wood), nor with (such as are) barbed, poisoned, or the points of which are blazing with fire. Let him not strike one who (in fight) has climbed on an eminence, nor an eunuch, nor one who joins the palms of his hands (in supplication), nor one who (flees), with flying hair, nor one who sits down, nor one who says, "I am thine", nor one who sleeps, nor one who has lost his coat of mail, nor one who is naked, nor one who is disarmed, nor one who looks on without taking part in the fight, nor one who is fighting with another (foe); now one whose weapons are broken, nor one afflicted (with sorrow), nor one who has been grievously wounded, nor one who is in fear, nor one who has turned to flight (but in all these cases let him remember the duty of honourable warriors).[5] The ethics of war was closely connected with the status and role of kshatriya in society. Some exceptions were allowed in the case of war.

1 *Ap. Dh.* S., II, 2. 4. 25-28: *Gau. Dh. S.* VII. 1-3: *Manu. Dh. S.X.* 1, II. 241.
2 *Manu Smriti,* II. 242. II. 238.
3 *Ibid.,* III. 152.
4 *Ibid., X.* 109-111.
5 *Ibid.,* VII. 90-93.

Duties of the Vaisyas

The duties of Vaisyas were particularly those concerning with trade, commerce, agriculture, animal husbandry, etc. As has been already pointed out, teaching of *Vedas* was equally the duty of Brahmins, Kshatriyas and Vaisyas, but gradually due to Brahmanism, particularly in *Manu Smriti,* the distance between the brahmins and kshatriyas on the one hand and vaisyas on the other, increased so much so that sometimes vaisyas were bracketed with sudras. According to S. Cromwell Crawford, "The chief cause for this ignominious descent was not even remotely connected with moral consideration but with externalities of professionalism. The Brahmins had developed a positive antipathy towards some Vaisya occupations such as trade, agriculture, and cattle-breeding. So despised were these professions that under no circumstances could a Brahmin personally engage in them. Baudhayana states the penalty for any infraction of the law: Let him treat Brahmins who tend cattle, those who live by trade, (and) those who are artisans, actors (and bards), servants or usurers like Sudras.[1]

Evidence of the Vaishya's humiliation was apparent in several discriminatory ways.[2] For instance, a Vaisya guest was to be treated on par with a Sudra in respect to all items of hospitality.[3]

Duties of Sudra

According to almost all Dharmashastras, the special duty of the Sudra was to render service to the twice-born classes, to obtain his livelihood from them. Serving brahmin conferred greater happiness or benefit on the sudra than serving a kshatriya and serving a kshatriya conferred greater good than serving a vaisya. According to Gautama, Manu and others the Sudra was to wear the old or cast-off cloths, umbrellas, sandals, mattress, etc., of his patron and leavings of food (uchhista) were to be given to him.[4] If he became old and unable to do work while serving any one of the higher varnas he was to be fed by him whom he had formerly served.[5] In course of time the position of the sudra improved. According to Yajnavalkya, if unable to maintain himself by the service of dvijas, the Sudra may carry on the profession of a vaisya or may take to the various crafts.[6]

Devala, quoted in the Mistakshara,[7] prescribes that the sudra should serve the twice-born and may engage in agriculture, rearing cattle, carrying loads, sale of commodities, drawing and painting, dancing, singing and playing on musical instruments like the flute, drums and tabors.[8] The foregoing will show that the Sudra gradually rose in social status so far as occupation was concerned and could

---

1 *Baud.,* 1.5.10.24.
2 *Gaut.,* V. 41-42.
3 *Ibid.* V. 45.
4 *Gaut.,* X. 60-61; *Manu.* X. 124-25.
5 *Gaut.,* X. 63.
6 *Yaj.,* I. 120.
7 *Ibid.*
8 *Manu.,* IV. 61.

follow all occupations except those specially reserved for the Brahmin so much so that sudras became even kings and Manu had expressly to enjoin upon Brahmins not to dwell in the kingdom of a sudra.[1] The Smiritis, however, did not like that wealth should be accumulated in the hands of the sudra. They did not like that kshatriyas and vaisyas should command all wealth. According to Gautama, the sudra's accumulation of wealth should be for the support and benefit of the other varnas.[2] According to Manu, a sudra even though able to accumulate wealth should not do so, as on account of pride of his wealth, and his ignorance, he may cause obstructions and trouble to the brahmins.[3]

ASCENDING ORDER OF RESPONSIBILITIES

In the above mentioned fourfold classification of duties according to Dharmashastras, there was an ascending order of responsibilities. While brahmin was given the highest position he was also entrusted with maximum responsibilities so much so that in penal system he was given maximum punishment for lapses. Like the philosopher king of *The Republic* of Plato, the Brahmin had to study and achieve scholarship and guide to other varnas in the society. Therefore, the entire task of preserving Dharma was mainly the responsibility of the Brahmin. The next social status in varna hierarchy was given to the Kshatriya. It was he who had the responsibility of defending the nation in times of war and administering law and order in the society. He provided social justice with the help of the scholar Brahmin. Thus, the power of the mind and the soul united with the power of arms to maintain Dharma in society. This responsibility of the Brahmin and the Kshatriya was sacrosanct. It has been prescribed as the absolute unconditional responsibility of the varnas. It is so since, as the author of the *Bhagvadgita* points out, it results in absolute familial and social disorganization. According to *Gita,* "In the ruin of a family, its moral laws perish: and when the laws perish, the whole family is overcome by lawlessness. And when lawlessness prevails, O Krishna! the women of the family are corrupted, O Varshneya! a mixture of caste arises. And this confusion brings the family itself to hell and those who have destroyed it; for their ancestors fall, deprived of their offerings of rice and water. By the sins of those who destroy a family and create a mixture of caste, the eternal laws of the caste and the family are destroyed. The men of the families whose laws are destroyed, O Janardana! assuredly will dwell in hell; so we have heard."[4]

Thus, both Kshatriya and Brahmin were entrusted with heavy responsibilities. The ideal laid before Brahmin was one of poverty, of plain living and high thinking, of forsaking the active pursuit of riches and cherishing cultural preservation and advancement. Manu lays down the general rule that when not in distress a brahmin

1 *Ibid.*

2 *Gaut., X.* 64-65.

3 *Manu., X.* 129.

4 Deutsch. E. (Tr). *The Bhagavadgita* (New York) Holt. Rinehart and Winston (1968). I. 40-42.

should acquire wealth only sufficient to maintain himself and his family, and to enable him to perform his religious duties without causing any harm to others or by as little harm to others as possible and without unduly worrying his own body and than Manu says[1] that a Brahmin householder may either accumulate so much grain but not more as would fill a kusula a granary, or a kumbhi or he may have as much com as would satisfy all his needs for his family.

Thus, it is clear, that there was an ascending order of responsibilities along with an ascending order of privileges and rights. Above this social order, P.V. Kane rightly points out, "It raised the Brahmin to the highest pinnacle of reverence, but at the same time it placed before him the ideal of not hankering after temporal power, of leading a life of comparative poverty and of making his knowledge available to the other classes for a scanty and precarious return. It made the military caste feel that they were not all-in-all but had to look up to some other class as superior to themselves."[2] This is also clear from a summary of the privileges enjoyed by the Brahmins. These privileges were as follows:

(1) The brahmin was to be gum, object of reverence to all varnas by the mere fact of birth.[3]

(2) The brahmin was to expound the duties of all other classes, to indicate to them proper conduct and their means of livelihood and they were to abide by his directions and the king was to rule in accordance with such directions.[4]

(3) The king was the ruler of all, except brahmins.[5]

(4) The king should exonerate the brahmin in the six matters, *viz.*, a brahmin should not be beaten or whipped, he should not have fetters put on him, he should not be loaded in fines of money, he should not be driven out of the villages of country, he should not be censured, he should not be abandoned.[6]

(5) Most smritis lay down that a srotriya, a brahmin, learned in the *Veda*, was to be free from taxes.[7]

(6) In the matter of treasure trove the brahmin was more favourably treated than members of other classes.[8]

(7) The general rule about the property of one dying hairless is that it eschews to the king, but there was an exception in the case of hairless brahmin.[9]

(8) The rule of the road was in favour of brahmin even as against the king.[10]

(9) The person of the brahmin was regarded as very sacred from ancient times and so brahmahatya or killing a brahmin was looked upon as the greatest sin.[11]

1 Manu, IV. 7-8.
2 Kane, P.V., *History of Dharmasastras*, p. 137.
3 *Vas. Dh. S.* IV. I: *Manu.* I. 31 and 94.
4 *Vas. Dh. S.* I. 39-41: *Manu,* VII. 37. X. 2.
5 *Gautama.* XI. 1.
6 *Gaut.,* VIII. 12-13.
7 Ap. Dh. S. II. 10. 26. 10.: Vas. Dh. S. 8. 19. 23: *Manu,* 133.
8 *Vas. Dh. S.* III. 13-14: Manu, VIII. 37-38: Yaj. II. 34-35.
9 Manu, IX. 188-189: *Baud, Dh. S.* I. 5. 118-122.
10 *Visnu* Dh. S. V. 91.
11 Manu. XI. 54.

(10) Even threatening a brahmin with assault, or striking him or drawing blood from his body drew the severest condemnation from very ancient times.[1]

(11) For certain offences a brahmin received lesser punishment than members of other classes.[2]

(12) A brahmin could not be cited as a witness by a litigant who was not a brahmin and the king would not summon him, provided he, the brahmin, was not an attesting witness on a document.[3]

(13) Only certain brahmins were to be invited for dinner in sraddhas and in rites for gods.[4]

(14) Certain sacrifices could be performed only by brahmin.[5]

(15) The periods of mourning were less in the case of brahmin.[6]

From the above survey it is clear that the Hindu Dharmasastras provided highest social status to the Brahmin. But, at the same time, they were entrusted with the highest social responsibilities. Conversely, the Sudra was given the lowest social status along with minimum privileges but at the same time his responsibilities were also minimum. Both in the matter of privileges and responsibilities he was the lowest in the social order. This will be clear by a survey of the disabilities and the corresponding absence of responsibilities of the sudra given below:

(1) He was not allowed to study the Vedas.

(2) The Sudras were not to consecrate sacred fires and to perform the solemn Vedic sacrifices.

(3) As to Samskaras, there is some apparent conflict among the authorities. Allowing him the freedom from many restrictions in the absence of high Samskaras, Manu said, "The sudra incurs no sin by eating forbidden articles like onions and garlic, he is not fit for samskaras, he has no adhikara or authority to perform dharma, nor he be forbidden from performing dharma."[7]

(4) Liability to higher punishment for certain offences.

(5) In the matter of the period for impurity on death or birth the sudra was held to be impure for a month, while a brahmin had to observe ten days period only.

(6) A sudra could not be a judge or propound what dharma was. Katyayana says that when a brahmin is not available as a judge the king may appoint as judge a kshatriya or a vaisya who is proficient in dharmasastra, but he should carefully avoid appointing a sudra as judge.[8]

---

1 *Gaut.*, 22. 20-22.
2 Ibid.
3 *Ibid.*, XIII. 4.
4 *Manu*, III. 124. *Jay.* I. 217.
5 *Manu*, V, 83.; *Yaj* III. 22.
6 *Manu*, X. 126.
7 *Manu*, X. 126.
8 Katyayana, quoted in the *Mit. on the Yaj.* I. 3.

(7) A brahmin was not allowed to receive gifts from a sudra except under great restrictions.

(8) A brahmin could not take food from a sudra except when the sudra was his own cowherd, or tilled his field or was a hereditary friend of the family, or his own barber or his dasa.

(9) The sudra gradually came to be so much looked down upon that he could not touch a brahmin, though at one time he could be a cook in a brahmin household and a brahmin could eat food from their houses.

(10) As the sudra could not be initiated into Vedic study, the only ashram, out of the four, that he was entitled to, was that of the household.

(11) The life of a sudra was esteemed rather low.

As has been already pointed out, the Varna social order connected privileges with responsibilities. Now, since the disabilities of sudra were the greatest he was exonerated from so many social responsibilities. He was free from the round of countless daily rites. He was free from all samskaras, except marriage. In the absence of samskaras, he could indulge in any kind of food or drink such as wine. As disallowed from the study of *Vedas*, he had to undergo no penances for lapses from the rules of the shastras. Similarly, while the dwij varnas has to follow so many restrictions, the sudra was free from all restrictions of gotra and pravara in marriages. In the case of profession he was equally free. He could follow almost any profession except the few particularly reserved for brahmins and kshatriyas. It may be noted here that these special professions were linked with heavy responsibilities, high moral character and great physical and mental abilities. Therefore, P.V. Kane has rightly pointed out, "If the sudra laboured under certain grave disabilities, he had certain compensating advantages.[1]

INTERDEPENDENCE OF VARNAS

1. Religious Duties. The fourfold division of society, according to the Varna system, was based upon the scientific idea of division of labour. In the words of P.V. Kane, "The theory of varnas, as conceived by Manu and other smritikaras, was based upon the idea of division of labour, on the idea of balancing the rival claims of various sections of the community; it laid greatest emphasis upon the duties of the varnas rather than upon their rights and privileges."[2]

Therefore, all the varnas were interdependent. The entire social order depended upon a close co-operation between the brahmin and the kshatriya. According to *Satapatha Brahmana*, "A brahmin must certainly be approached by a kshatriya who is about to perform some acts, for indeed that act of a kshatriya which is shed on by brahmin succeeds."[3] This co-operation was, firstly, in the matters concerning Dharma. The purohita of a kshatriya occupied a very high position, may, the purohit was indispensable to even by the vaisya. The purohits

1 Kane P.V., *History of Dharmashastras*, p. 164.

2 Ibid., p. 137.

3 *Satapatha, S.B.E.*, Vol. 26. pp. 270-271.

were brahmins. Therefore, it has been said that, "a brahmin may remain without a king, but a king should not be without a brahmin."[1] Again, "the purohita is half the soul of the kshatriya." Similarly, "for indeed the gods do not eat the food of a king who has no purohita; therefore, a king when about to offer a sacrifice should have a brahmin as his purohita with the idea, 'may the gods eat my food'. "[2] Therefore, it was concluded that the combination of the brahmin and the rajanya is the most desirable and conducive to the eminence of both.

2. Caste Mobility. This interdependence of the different varnas was not only limited in the field of religious duties but extended to the field of vocations and professions, education, marriage and statecraft. There was a constant upward and downward social mobility between the different varnas, at least in theory. Yajnavalkya speaks of two kinds of such mobility. When a lower Varna changed into a higher varna, it was known as *jatyutkarsa* or uplift of the caste. On the other hand, if a person belonging to a higher Varna gradually descended into a lower Varna, it was known as *jatyapakarsa* or the degeneration of the caste. Provisions for both these processes of social mobility in stratification were laid by different Dharmasastras with minor distinctions about the conditions. It was particularly based upon two conditions, firstly, upon the following of the vocation of some other Varna for five to six generations and secondly, marrying into different varnas for as much period. It may be easily guessed that in practice such mobility happened only in exception, since the process had to be covered for several generations, but it is clear that the Dharmasastras did prescribe change of varnas by means of interactions between the varnas both upwards and downwards.

3. Marriage. Another important source of interaction was marriage. Since love between man and woman knows no rules and transcends all bounds, it was natural that males and females belonging to different varnas met and even married against social conventions. Such marriages were known by the names of anuloma and pratiloma marriages.

4. Education. Similarly, in the field of education there was interdependence in the varnas. Normally, brahmin was the educator and the other varnas depended upon him for education. Again, in the matter of gifts (dana) the varnas were interdependent. The brahmacharis of the first three varnas used to depend upon the householders of these varnas for their physical needs. The best recipient of gifts was, of course, brahmin and that too because of his character and responsibility, but there was more emphasis on the criteria of the qualities of the recipient rather than the varnas. The gifts were given generally to the brahmins since they were forbidden to earn much money or gather wealth. Thus, by the institution of gifts or dana the other three varnas kept the brahmins, the teacher and the priests free from the worries of earning his bread so that he may devote all his time in spiritual persuit. Similar arrangements were made by Plato in his *The Republic.* It must be conceded here that if a certain section of society has to develop moral and

1 *Ibid.,* p. 270.

2 *Ait. Br.* Chap. 40.1.

spiritual values, the other sections must help in this effort since ultimately it is in the collective good. Such was the practice in India due to the prescription of Dharmasastras. In the words of P.V. Kane, "Even in the 20th century rural India has villages with a considerable populations of brahmins w here many srotriyas, learned in the Veda, and pandits (those who study shastras like grammar, logic, mimamsa) are still found who arc content with what little part partimony they have got, who engage in the profession of teaching the Veda and Shastras in accordance with ancient rules and who do not go about seeking gifts nor accept invitations for dinner at sraddhas."[1]

APAD DHARMA

The Indian Varna system was not a rigid scheme, since no scheme meant for human society should be rigid. It should allow sufficient scope for social mobility and the remedies in emergencies and exceptions. Apad means distress or troublesome circumstances. While Varna dharma had to be followed in normal circumstances, in abnormal circumstances the Dharmasastras prescribe what is known as Apad Dharma or that which is worthy of following in exceptional circumstances. Thus, Manu enumerate ten means of maintaining oneself in apad (distress) *viz.*, learning, arts and crafts, work for wages, service *i.e.*, carrying out another's orders, rearing cattle, sale of commodities, agriculture, contentment, alms, money-lending."[2] Out of these some cannot be followed by brahmin or a kshatriya when there is no distress *e.g.*, a brahmin cannot engage in service. Yajnavalkya enumerates seven of these and adds some more apad dharma. These are driving carts for hire, subsisting on the price of grass and fuel taken from hills, resorting to begging from a king and residing in a country full of water, trees and shrubs. According to Narad Smriti, three modes of acquiring wealth are common to all varns. These are: inheritance, a gift of friendliness or affection and what comes to a man with a wife. Besides, each of the three varnas has three special modes of acquiring wealth. These are: receiving gifts, fees as priest and fees for teaching in the case of brahmins. In the case of kshatriyas it is booty in war, taxes and fines in judicial trials. In the case of vaisyas it is agriculture, rearing cattle and selling commodities.[3]

However, not all types of jobs were permitted even in the time of troubles. The Dharmasastras maintained that brahmin doing certain things are to be treated as sudras. According to Baud. Dh. Sutra, a religious king should employ brahmins who do not perform the morning and evening adoration, in doing work appropriate to sudras.[4] According to Manu, a brahmin, who without studying the Veda, works hard to master something else is quickly reduced while still living to the status of a sudra together with his family.[5] Manu further points out that those brahmins who do not study Vedas and give up the rules are killed by death before

1 Kane., P.V., *History of Dharmasastras*, p. 115.
2 *Manu, Dharmasastra*. X. 116.
3 Yaj., III. 42
4 Narad. Rnadana Sutra. 50-55.
5 Baud., Dh. S. III. 4.20

the allotted span of human life.[1] Thus, Apad Dharma does not mean the licence to do whatever one likes to do in the times of trouble. There are numerous cases of so many notable persons who refused to change their allotted duties even in the face of extremely adverse circumstance. Again, even while such a change was permitted, it was always looked down and never appreciated. Exceptions to varna dharma were tolerated so far as human failings are a part of social life. However, as a general rule, the Dharmasastras insist that everyone should follow the duties allotted to him. In the words of P.V. Kane, "The Brahmins were the creators and custodians of the vast literature that had grow n up, they were the guardians of the culture of ages, they were expected to shoulder the burdens of teaching and preserving the vast literature on such gifts as were voluntarily made. Though, many among them did not live up to the high ideas set up for their order, there must have been not a few who made as near an approach to the fulfilment of the ideal as possible. It was the greatness of these latter that led to the glorification of the whole order to which they belonged."[2]

CRITICAL EVALUATION

Social Harmony

The Dharmasastras prescribed the varna system on the basis of the cultural heritage of the Vedas and the Upanisads. Thus, they only tried to continue the traditions already established in Aryan society. They only codified the rules and regulations which were already established by customs and traditions. As a part of Aryan ethics, the varna system was value based. The central value was harmony or unity in diversity. It is what is known in western societies as division of labour. Division of labour has been the characteristics of all the well developed societies. It leads to an ordering of the status and roles in social stratification. It makes them complimentary to each other, so that all the classes may act in co-operation for the betterment of society. This is clear by the interdependence of varnas.

Balance of Privileges and Responsibilities

According to the criteria of ethics justice involves fairness, equality, humanity, mutuality, freedom and harmony of various constituents. As a general rule, all these characteristics, may be seen in our discussion of social duties among various varnas. We have already pointed out that if brahmins were given maximum privileges they were also to shoulder maximum responsibility. Conversely, if the sudras were deprived of certain privileges and had to undergo so many disabilities they were also free from almost all the social responsibilities. The burden of maintaining the Dharma in society was mainly on the shoulder of the first two varnas, *viz.*, the brahmin and the kshatriyas. If, like Plato in *The Republic*, these classes were given special privileges, it was quite in keeping with the principle of

1 *Manu*, II. 168.

2 *Ibid.*, V. 4.

social justice. It is very important that the brahmin was forbidden from amassing wealth. He had to depend on the next two varnas even for his livelihood, in exchange to the goods he delivered to the society. Therefore, his life was full of sacrifices in spite of so many privileges. And if he shirks from the sacrifices, the authors of Dharmasastras have only derogatory remarks for him, so much so that people were asked to treat him as sudra. Thus, social respect was connected with social responsibility and not with money and political power. The political power was subordinated to the spiritual power and the power of money occupied only the third place. Therefore, the system of reward and punishment aimed at hierarchy of values in which the spiritual values were foremost, the virile virtues and skill in arms were next and the economic values occupied the third place.

Freedoms to Sudra

The most controversial issue in the Varna system was the status of sudra. This, however, was not dependent upon birth but upon abilities and skills. As he has been already pointed out, any member of the first three varnas, who failed to fulfil his social duties, was counted among sudras Then, there is mention of possibility of the change of varnas through marriage and change of vocation for several generations. The reason for insisting upon a period of several generations was to get the change established so that there may be no disorder. Therefore, those who wanted to rise in the social ladder were allowed to do so. And since the sudra was allowed so many freedoms along with the capacity to fulfil so many responsibilities, it can be easily understood that they did not feel exploited by the social status given to them.

The Dynamic Aspect

In fact, most of the criticisms of the varna system are based upon misunderstanding of contemporary situations. As has been already pointed out, there were sudra kings in the time of Manu, and they were notorious for their international activities. Therefore, prescriptions against them by *Manu Smriti* were only natural. *Yajnavalkya Smriti,* an equally important Dharmasastra removes all imbalances in Varna system prescribed by Manu. It restores a suitable social status for women and sudras and treats them as equal in almost all the matters. *Manu Smriti* alone does not represent Dharmasastras. *Yajnavalkya Smriti is a better representative from the point of view of social justice.* This must be remembered while evaluating social justice among varnas as prescribed by Dharmasastras. Finally, this social system was based upon centimes of actual experience which in fact is the surest criteria of social justice.

The Dharamasastras have clearly and elaborately laid down the daily duties, the social duties and all other types of duties of different varnas. These duties were complementary. There was an ascending order of responsibilities corresponding with a descending order of freedom. Thus, while brahmin was the most responsible, sudra was the most free. However, Brahmins enjoyed maximum social respect while no respect was shown towards sudra. Such a system could have been justified were it actually based on individual differences. However, in practice the distinction among different varnas was always based upon distinction of birth. Therefore, the entire system was converted into a tyranny on the sudras. The bonds were further strengthened by the Law of Karma, an eschatological principles admirably converted into an instrument of exploitation by the high caste Hindus. This again, explains why Indian society never witnessed the revolt of the downtrodden.

QUESTIONS FOR EXERCISE

1. What were the main principles of social stratification in Varna system?
2. What is Varna? Describe Hindu Varna System.

3

The Hindu Ashram System: Rinas, Karma and Sanskaras

Meaning of Ashrama

According to *Sanskrit Hindi Dictionary* of V.S. Apte, the term Ashram means stages, monastery, duties etc.[1] Writing in *Encyclopaedia of Religion and Ethics,* the German scholar, Paul Deussen gives two meanings to the word ashram: (1) That place where people labour or make effort, (2) To labour or make effort. The word ashrama comes from the Sanskrit root srama giving the meaning of 'making an effort.' In this way ashrama literally means a step in the journey of life. In the words of P.V. Kane, "The word asrama is derived from srama, to exert, to labour and etymologically means a stage in which one exerts oneself."[2] According to Hindu ethics, the final aim of life is liberation. And every ashrama is a step in the long journey to that aim. "The whole of the life of a human individual is for the Hindu," says P.H. Valvalker, "a kind of schooling and self-discipline."[3] In the Shanti Parva of Mahabharata, Saint Vedavyasa has described ashrama as a four rung ladder which takes one in the direction of Brahman. Vedavyas says, *Chatushpadi hi nihsreni brahman yesha Pratishthita, etamaruhya ninshreni brahmaloke mahiyate.*"[4] In this way, in each ashrama the person prepares himself for every succeeding ashrama state. Literally, an Ashrama is a halting place. The ashrama system is a means of systematic development for the better life. Dr. P.M. Modi has tried to prove that in the beginning there were only three ashramas and that Vanprastha and Sanyasa were considered as one ashrama.[5] He has cited instances in his favour

1 Apte, V.S., *Sanskrit Hindi Dictionary*, p. 65.

2 Kane, P.V., *History of Dharmasastras,* Vol. I. Part II. p. 415.

3 Valvalkar, P.H , *Hindu Social Institutions,* p. 65.

4 *Mahabharata Santi Parva*, 242, 15.

5 Modi, P.M. Art, on Development of the System of Ashramas in *Proceedings of Seventh All India Oriental Conference,* Baroda, December, 1933.

from Chandogya Upanisad and Manusmriti.[1] It is in Jabala Upanisad that one finds the mention of four ashrams for the first time. This scheme of the stages of life during the period preceding Dharmasastras was rather indefinite. They were made definite for the first time by Dharmasastras. The Dharmasastras maintained clearly that each individual should normally pass through the four stages of life known as Asharmas. In the 2nd chapter of Manusmriti, the author has described in details the characteristics and the activities of Brahmacharaya Ashrama. The 3rd chapter describes the duties of Grihastha Ashrama. The fourth chapter describes this Ashrama in four varnas. Then Vanprastha Ashrama has been discussed in chapter sixth. This chapter also discusses the last Ashrama known as Sanyasa. Thus, according to Dharmasastras the stages of human individual's life are four: Brahmacharya, Grihastha, Vanprastha and Sanyasa. Of these, at least three have been described by Upanisads before Dharmasastras. According to P.V. Kane, "The word asrama does not occur in the Samhitas or Brahmanas. But this cannot be stretched to mean that the stages of life denoted by this word in the sutras were unknown throughout the Vedic period."[2]

Number of Ashramas

From the times of the most ancient dharmasutras the number of ashramas has been four, though there are slight differences in the nomenclature and in their sequence. According to Ap. Dh. Sutra, "there are four ashramas, *viz.* (staying in) the teacher's house, the stage of householder, stage of being a muni, the stage of being a forest dweller."[3] According to Gaut. Dharmasutra, there are four ashramas, brahmachari, grahastha, bhiksu and vaikhanasa.[4] According to Vas. Dh. Sutra, there are four ashramas, brahmachari, grhastha, vanaprastha and parivrajaka.[5] According to Manu smriti, there are four ashramas, the last being called Yati and also sanyasa.[6] According to Manu smriti the span of human life is 100 years though all do not live to that age. In fact, it is the maximum age one can expect to reach. This has been divided into four parts so that one may lead an alround integral life. It is not necessary that each of these stages should be lived for 25 years, it may be more or less. However, normally the span of each Ashrama was prescribed as 25 years. According to Manu smriti, the first part of man's life is brahmacharya in which he learns at his teacher's house and after he has finished his study, in the second part of his life he marries and becomes an householder, discharges his debts to his ancestors by begetting sons and to the gods by performing yajnas.[7] Then, when he sees that his head has grey hair and that there are wrinkles on his body he resorts to the forest, *i.e.* becomes a vanaprastha.[8] After spending the

1 *Chandogya* Up., II. 23, 25. *Manu*, II. 230.
2 Kane, P.V., *History of Dharmasastra*, Vol. I. Part II. p. 418.
3 *Ap. Dh. S.* II, 9, 21, 1.
4 *Gautama Dharmasutra*, II. 1.
5 *Vas. Dh. S.* VII. 1-2.
6 *Manu smriti*, VI. 87, 96.
7 Ibid., IV. 1
8 *Ibid.*, V. 169.

third part of his life in the forest for some time he spends the rest of his life as a sanyasin.[1] Similar rules have been laid down by other Dharmasastras, with, of coarse, minor differences here and there. For example, according to Baudhayana Dharmasastra, the stage of sanyasa starts after the 70th year.

Interpretation of this Scheme

The above mentioned scheme of four ashramas was interpreted from three different points of view, as follows:

1. Samuccaya (orderly co-ordination). According to this view, a person can resort to the four asramas one after another in order and that he may not drop any one or more and pass on to the next nor may he resort to the householder's life after becoming a sanyasin.[2] This view was primarily supported by Manu. This view lays emphasis upon the householder since the other ashramas depend upon it. Most of the Dharmasastras push the last two ashramas in the background so much so that according to some of them these are forbidden in the Kali age.

2. Vikalpa (Option). According to this view, there is an option after brahmacharya, *i.e.* a man may become a parivrajaka immediately after he finishes his study or immediately after the householder's way of life. This view has been supported by Vasistha Dharmasastra, Yajnavalkya smriti and others.[3]

3. Badha (annulment or contradiction). According to this view, there is really one Ashrama and that is that of the householder. The first stage is a mere preparation for this Ashrama while the other last two Ashramas are inferior to it. This view was supported by Gautama and Baudhayana. According to Gautama, there is only one Ashrama.[4] According to Baudhayana, the ashramas other than that of householder do not beget offspring and are therefore not much important.[5] It was due to the influence of this viewpoint that almost all the dharmasastras praise the ashrama of householder as the highest. This is, particularly important from the point of view of provision for social development, progress, stability and justice.

In spite of the above three views about the following of the Ashrama system, the general view believes that all the four ashramas have their value and details about the activities and duties of all these ashramas have been prescribed by Dharmasastras. Some have clearly pointed out that there is no distinction due to superiority of anyone among the four ashramas.[6] Others maintained that the householder's life was the rule and other ashramas were for the blind and other incapable persons. This view has been vehemently opposed by others.[7]

1 *Ibid.*, V. 169.

2 *Ibid.*, VI. 1-2.

3 *Ibid.*, VI, 33.

4 *Gautama Dharmasutra*, III. 1 and 35.

5 *Baud. Dh. S.* II. 6. 29.

6 *Ap. Dh. S.* II. 9. 21. 2.

7 *Mit.* on Yaj. III. 56.

BRAHMACHARYA ASHRAMA

Objectives of this Ashrama

The first of the four ashramas is Brahmacharya ashrama. It starts with the Upanayana ceremony.[1] Brahmacharya means the leading of the life according to Brahman. In this Ashram, the student or Brahmachari spent 25 years with his teacher studying the Vedas and leading a life of self-control. The education and control of the Brahmacharya prepared a person for future life. Certain rules and observances are prescribed for all brahmacharins. They are of two kinds, some are prescribed for a very short time and some have to be observed for all the years of studenthood. The first kind of observances were generally concerned with studies. The second kind of observances, *i.e.*, those which have to be observed throughout this period were concerned with the daily routine and general discipline of the persons in this stage of life. Of the two, the later were definitely more important. These are principally acamana, gurususrusa, vaksamyama (silence), samidadhana. The smritis have laid down detailed rules about these observences. The rules centre principally around agniparicarya (worshiping fire), bhiksa (begging for food), samdhyopasana, study of Veda and its methods and duration, avoidance of certain foods and drinks and other matters like singing etc., gurususrusa (including honouring him and his family and other elders), and the special vratas of the brahmachari. The rules about different aspects of the student's life also fall in the category of the rules about brahmacharya ashrama.

Classification of Brahmacharins

The Brahmacharins were further divided into two types upakurvana and naisthika. The former meant those who offered some return to the teacher. These were celibates for a certain period. There were, however, some students who remained so till their death. These were, known as naisthika. According to Yajnavalkya smriti, naisthika has been derived from nistha.[2] Therefore, it includes Brahmacharins who determined to lead a life of celibacy till death. The word naisthika occurs in Vishnu Dharmasastra, Yajnavalkya smiriti, and Mahabharata.[3] In Chandogya upanisad, it has been said that the third branch of Dharma is the status of a student who stays with his teacher's family and who wears out his body to the end in the family of his teacher.[4] According to Manu smriti and Yajnavalkya smriti, if the student likes so, he may stay with his teacher till his death, serve his teacher and study the Vedas.[5] He has to perform throughout his life the duties of offering fuel sticks, Veda study, begging for food, sleeping on the ground (not on a cot), and of self-restraint,

1 *Grh Sutra*, 11.

2 Mil. on Yaj. I. 49.

3 *Vishnu Dh. S.* 28. 46, *Yaj.* I. 49, *Veda-Vyasa* I. 41.

4 *Chandogya Up.* II. 23. 1.

5 *Manu.*, II. 243, 247-249, *Yaj.* I. 49-50.

If the teacher be dead he may stay with and serve the teacher's son if he is worthy or the teacher's wife or he may worship the fire kindled by his deceased guru; he should thus wear out his body; he obtains the highest worlds of bliss and is not born again.

Duties of Brahmacharins: Scope of Study

The Dharmasastras have prescribed details about the duties of the Brahmacharin. It appears from certain passages of the Upanisads that the usual duration of brahmacharya was 12 years. The main function of the Brahmacharin was to study the Vedas. The study of the Veda means the study of the Mantras and the Brahmana portion of the particular sakha or stsakhas. According to Yajnavalkya smriti, the student should study every day according to his ability also Vakovakya, Purana, Narasamsi, gathas, itihasa, vidyas if he desired to please the gods and manes. Yajnavalkya smriti further enumerates 14 vidyas, Vayu Purana, Vrdha-Gautama and other works, *viz.* four vedas, 6 angas, puranas, nyaya (logic), mimamsa and dharmasastra. Some added four more to these, *viz.* the Upavedas of Ayurveda, Dhanurveda, Gandharvaveda and Arthasastra (which were affiliated respectively to the four Vedas) and thus the vidyas are also spoken of as 18.

Duties in Guru's Ashrama

According to Chandogya Upanisad, the student had to serve the teacher by tending his cattle, had to beg for food and announce it to the teacher, and to look after his sacred fires and to learn the Veda only in the time that would be left after doing work for the guru.[1] Besides these, the rules concerning his conduct towards the teacher, the teacher's wife and son, concerning the method of salutation and showing respect, the food, drinks and actions allowed or prohibited to students are too numerous to be set out in detail. Both Manu smriti and Yajnavalkya smriti, along with some other notable Dharmasutras, lay down the following rules for the Brahmacharin. The student should speak the truth, bathe everyday, should not look at the sun; should avoid honey, flesh, perfumes, the wearing of flowers, sleeping by day, rubbing oil on the body, putting collyrium in the eyes, going in a cart, wearing shoes and holding an umbrella, love affairs, anger, covetousness, infatuation, vain discussions, playing on musical instruments, luxurious baths with hot water, meticulous cleansing of the teeth, ecstatic states of mind, dancing, singing, calumny of others, dangerous places, gazing at women or touching young women, gambling, serving a low person (or doing very low work), injury to animals, obsence or harsh talk, and wine. Manu prescribes that he should not sleep on a cot and should observe complete celibacy, but if he suffers from night emissions he should bathe, worship the sun and repeat thrice the mantra 'punar mam.'[2] The Apastamba Dharma Sutra contains similar rules of conduct. According to it the student should not wash his limbs with hot water (generally), but he may

1 *Chandogya* IV. 4.5; 3.5; VII. 15. 1.

2 *Manu,* II. 198; 180-181.

do so if they are smeared with dirty and impure matter provided he does it out of the sight of the teacher and that he should not bathe in water in a sportive manner, but should bathe in it motionless like a stick.[1] It also not only prohibits him sexual intercourse but ordains that he should speak with women only as much as is absolutely necessary. The student was not to laugh, but if he could not help laughing he should do so covering his face with his hands.

Duties Towards Teachers

According to Gautama and Baudhayana Dharma Sutra, the student is to serve his teacher by following after him when he goes anywhere, he should help the teacher in his toilet and bath and should shampoo his body and take food left by him (ucchista)[2], he should be diligent in doing work that would be pleasing and beneficial to the teacher; he was to study when the teacher called him, he was not to cover his throat with a piece of cloth, or was not to sit in the presence of his teacher with his feet on his lap, was not to stretch his feet, he was not to clear loudly his throat, nor to laugh, yawn or crack the knuckles when called by the teacher to reply at once leaving his seat or bed and was to approach the teacher even when he called from a distance; he should always occupy a seat lower than that of his teacher and should go to sleep after his teacher and rise before him. Similar rules have been prescribed by other Dharmasastras.[3] According to Manu smriti, a pupil should not mimic the gait, the manner of speech and the actions of the teacher.[4] It calls upon the pupil to close his ears with his hands or fingers or to leave the place where somebody indulges in calumnies about the teacher or points out the faults in him, and states that if the pupil himself finds fault with his teacher or caluminates him, the pupil in the next life is born as an ass or a dog.[5] One of the rules for the student was that he was not to pronounce the name of his teacher even when the teacher was not present without prefixing or affixing an honorific addition such as sri, bhatta, acharya etc. The student should not speak of his teacher, the teacher's son or wife or of a man who has been initiated for a srauta sacrifice by their bare names.[6] When it is absolutely necessary to refer to these by name the student should not pronounce the name and gotra of his teacher as they are, but by means of a synonym. According to Ap. Sutra, even after returning home a snataka should avoid touching his former teacher with his fingers to call his attention, frequent muttering of something in his ears, laughing into his face, calling him out loudly, speaking his name, ordering him about.[7] According to Manu smriti a man who has been initiated for a srauta sacrifice should not be addressed by his name, even

1 *Ap. Dh. S.* I. 1. 3. 11-24; I. 1. 2. 28-30; I. 1.2. 26.

2 *Baud. Dh. S.* 37, *Gautama.* I. 1.2. 34.

3 *Manu.* II. 194-198; *Ap. Dh. S.* I. 2. 5. 26; *Gautama.* II. 20-21, 30-32.

4 *Manu.* II. 199.

5 *Ibid.*, 200-201.

6 *Ibid.*, 199.

7 Ap. Dh. S., 1 2 8. 15.

though he may be younger than the person addressing, but that one should use the words "bhoh" and "bhavat" when addressing him or speaking about him and may refer to him by words like diksita, etc.[1] Very detailed rules were laid down about pratuthana or rising from one's seat to receive a person, *abhivadana* or saluting a man *upasamgrahana* or saluting by clasping the feet of the teacher or another with one's hands, *pratyabhivadana* or returning a salutation, and *namaskara* or bowing with the word *namah.* According to Ap. Dh. Sutra, the student must clasp his teacher's feet when he meets his teacher after sunrise, and also beginning the day's lesson of Vedic study and even after finishing it. This has been corroborated by Manu.[2]

5. Salutations. According to Dharmasastras, Abhivadana is of three types, viz., nitya or obligatory everyday, naimittika to be done only on certain occasions and kamya to be done only if a person has certain rewards in view. The manner of abhivadana was as follows: A brahmana shall salute stretching forward his right arm on a level with ear, a kshatriya holding it on a level with the cheek, a vaisya holding it on a level with the waist and a sudra holding it low upto his feet and that the salutation shall be done by joining one's hands.[3] There were other rules about honouring the one's elders in the presence of one's teacher or honoring the teacher's teacher or about one's behaviour when a gentleman comes to see one's acharya and leaves him.[4] In the case of certain persons one was to show honour only by rising from his seat and not by abhivadana. The works on Dharmashastra give very interesting rules about the grounds on which respect was to be shown to a person.

6. Brahmacharin Dharmah. Certain rules and observances were prescribed for all brahmacharins by the Dharmasastras. These were known as brahmacharin-dharmah. They were of two kinds. Some were prescribed for very short time and some had to be observed during the entire period of this ashrama. Thus, according to the Asv. gr. Sutra, "for three nights, or twelve nights or a year after upanayana the brahmachari should not eat ksara and lavana and should sleep on the ground."[5] Milk had to be avoided for three days, along with the avoidance of ksara, of lavana and vegetables, and the duty of sleeping on the ground, of not drinking out of an earthen vessel, of not giving the remnants of his food to sudras and several other observances which he has to continue throughout the period of studenthood. These later are briefly indicated by many as, offering samidha into fire, begging for food, not using a cot, working for the teacher, daily bath, tarpana of gods, sages and pitra etc.[6]

7. Regular Observances. Thus, there were observances that last throughout the period of studenthood. These are principally achamana, gurususrusa, vaksamyama

1 *Manu,* II. 128
2 *Ap. Dh. S.,* 1. 2. 5. 19; 1. 3 10. 17.
3 *Manu.* II. 71
4 *AP. Dh. S.,* 1 2. 6. 29-32.
5 *Asv. gr.,* I. 22. 17
6 *Manu,* II. 108 and 176.

(silence), samidadhana. These rules centre principally round agniparicharya (worshipping fire), bhiksha (begging for food), samdhyopasana. study of Veda and its methods and duration, avoidance of certain foods and drinks and other matters like singing etc., gurususrusa (including honouring him and his family and other elders), and the special vratas of the brahmachari. The principal constituents of samdhyopasana are these: achamanas (sipping of water), pranayama, marjana thrice (sprinkling himself with water to the accompaniment of several mantras), aghamarsana, offering of water to the sun (arghya), japa of Gayatri, and upasthana (reciting mantras by way of worship of the sun in the morning and generally of varuna in the evening).

8. Qualification of the Aspirant. The Dharmasastras have laid qualifications of the student who deserved to be taught. According to Manu, 10 persons deserved to be taught *viz.,* the son of the teacher, a student who served his guru, one who gives some knowledge in exchange, one who knows dharma or who is pure (in body and mind), who is truthful, who is able to study and retain it, who gives money (for teaching), who is well disposed and who is one's near relative (agnate).[1] According to Yajnavalkya Smriti, besides all these, the student must be grateful, not inclined to hate or prove false to the teacher, healthy and not disposed to find fault.[2] The student should always be dependent on and under the control of the teacher and should stay with no one but the teacher.

GRAHASTHA ASHRAMA

Value of Grihastha Asthrama

According to Dharamasastra, as has been already pointed out, of the four ashramas, the Grihastha Asthrama is the most important. This was due to several reasons. First, as Gautama points out, the Grihastha ashrama is the source of the other ashramas "because the others do not produce offspring."[3] Second, Yajnavalkya correctly observes that this was the only stage in which all of the purusarthas were jointly realized.[4] Thirdly, it is the opinion of all the writers that the family was basic to the Varna system. It provided the regulatory machinery for the strict enforcement of varna informing its members of their duties, and imbuing them with the varna spirit. These are some of the reasons why the householder stage was given a central place, and why the ethical codes governing it were invested unequivocally with divine authority. Thus, after spending 25 years as a Brahmachari and finishing his education, a man married and entered the Grihastha Ashrama. According to the Gautama Dharmasutra the Grihastha Ashrama is the foundation of all the ashramas, because the other three do not produce offspring.[5] According to Manu smriti, as ail creatures live by receiving support from the air, so other ashramas

1 *Manu,* II. 109 and 112.

2 *Yaj.,* 1. 28.

3 *Gaut.,* III. 3: also *Manu,* III. 78.

4 *Yaj.,* I. V. 115; also *Gaut.,* IX. 46.

5 *Gaut.,* III. 3.

subsist by relying for support on the householder and that as men belonging to all the three other orders (ashramas) are supported from day to day by the householder alone with (gifts of) food and sacred knowledge, the householder's is therefore the most excellent ashrama.[1] Manu reiterates the same sentiments under a different figure "just as all big and small rivers find a resting place in the ocean, so men of all ashramas find support in the householder and the householder is declared to be the most excellent of all the ashramas by the precepts of the Veda and smritis, since he supports the other three."[2] According to Mahabharata, as all beings live on the support given by their mothers, so other ashramas subsist on the support of the order of householder.[3]

Types of Grahasthas

The Dharmasastras divide householders into several varieties such as salina and yayavara. The salina is one who dwells in a house, is possessed of servants and cattle, has a fixed place and a fixed village and has grain and wealth and follows the life of worldly people; the yayavara is one who subsists by the best of livelihood, *viz.* picking up grains that fall down when the com that is reaped is taken to the house or thrashing floor by the owner and who does not accumulate wealth or who does not earn his livelihood by officiating as priest, or by teaching or by accepting gifts.[4] According to Manu, the householder may be divided into four varieties, *viz.* one who possesses enough to fill a granary or store filling a corn jar, one who collects as much as will satisfy his needs for three days, or one who makes no provision for the morrow. According to Yajnavalkya smriti salina is of four varieties, *viz.* (1) one who maintains himself by officiating as a priest, teaching Veda, accepting gifts, agriculture, trade and breeding cattle, (2) one who subsists by the first three out of the above six, (3) one who subsists by officiating as a priest and by teaching, (4) one who subsists by teaching alone. Manu has also referred to these four varieties.[5] Again Vaik. Dh. Sutra divides householders into four classes. The first class (called vartavrtti) maintains itself by agriculture, cattle-rearing and trade; the second (salina) observes various niyamas, offers pakayajnas (sacrifices of cooked food), kindles the srauta fires, offers the darsa and purnamasa sacrifices each half month, offers caturmasyas, in each half year offers an animal sacrifice and each year the soma sacrifice; the third (yayavara) is engaged in the six actions, *viz.* offering sacrifices of havis and soma, officiating as priest at such sacrifices, studying the Veda and teaching it, making gifts and receiving them, constantly attends his fires srauta and smarta, and gives food to guests that come to him; the fourth called ghoracarika, one whose rules are awfully difficult to observe, is observant of niyamas, offers sacrifices but does not officiate at others' sacrifices,

1 *Manu.* III. 77-78.
2 *Ibid.*, VI. 89-90.
3 *Mahabharat, Santi,* 270, 6-7.
4 *Mit.* on *Yaj.*, I. 128.
5 *Manu.* IV. 7.

studies the Veda but does not teach it, makes gifts but does not receive them, maintains himself on com fallen in the fields etc., is absorbed in Narayana, performs agnihotra in the morning and evening.[1]

Daily Duties

The Dharmasastras have described in details, the nityakarma or the daily duties, the naimittika karma or duties on purpose and kamya karma or duties desired along with duties peculiar to one's own Varna etc. in details. They generally divide day time in eight parts and describe in details the proper routine to be carried out according to scriptures at different times of the day. Yajnavalkya Smriti prescribes the following duties for the householder. A householder should perform every day a Smriti rite (*i.e.*, a domestic rite prescribed by the Sacred Law, Smriti) on the nuptial fire or on the fire brought in at the time of the partition of ancestral property. He should perform a Vedic rite on the sacred fires. Having attended to the bodily calls, having performed the purificatory rites, and after having first washed the teeth, a twice-born (Aryan) man should offer the morning prayer. Having offered oblations to the sacred fires, becoming spiritually composed he should murmur the sacred verses addressed to the sun god. He should also learn the meaning of the Veda and various sciences. He should then go to his lord for securing the means of maintenance and progress. Thereafter having bathed he should worship the gods and also offer libations of water to the manes. He should study according to his capacity the three Vedas, the Atharva Veda, the Puranas, together with the Itihasas (legendary histories), as also the law relating to the knowledge of the self, with a view to accomplishing successfully the sacrifice of muttering prayers. Offering of the food oblation, offering with the proper utterance, performance of Vedic sacrifices, study of the sacred texts, and honouring of guests, these constitute the five great daily sacrifices dedicated respectively to the spirits, the manes the gods, the Brahmans and men. He should offer the food oblations to the spirits (by throwing it in the air) out of the remnant of the food offered to the gods. He should also cast food on the ground for dogs, untouchables and crows. Food, as also water, should be offered by the householder to the manes and men day after day. He should continuously carry on his study. He should never cook for himself only. Children, married daughters living in the father's house, pregnant women, sick persons, girls, as also guests and servants only after having fed these should the householder and his wife eat the food that has remained. Having risen before dawn the householder should ponder over what is good for the Self. He should not, as far as possible, neglect his duties in respect of the three ends of man, namely, virtue, material gain and pleasure, at their proper times. Learning, religious performances, age, family relations and wealth — on account of these and in the order mentioned are men honoured in society. By means of these if possessed in profusion, even a sudra deserves respect in old age.[2]

1 *Vaik,* VIII. 5.

2 *Yaj.*, I. 97-116, Passim, in *Sources of Indian Tradition*, W.T. Bary, ed. New York: Columbia University Press, 1966, Vol. I. pp. 231-232.

Purposive and Desired Duties

From the above description of the routine of the householder it is clear that his duties were mainly concerned with rituals, procreation, conjugal functions and social duties. The mention of the five daily sacrifices shows a broadening of ethical awareness. The institution of gifts (dana) and the warm reception to the guest shows that the main virtue of the householder was social. His values were concerned with three cardinal aims: Dharma, Art ha and Kama. While Manusmriti overlooks Kama.[1] Yajnavalkya Smriti gives it equal value along with Dharma and Artha.[2] Thus, it presents a more integral outlook. Among the values which added to the respect of the householder, learning, including both intellectual and ethical knowledge, stood first. It was followed by performance of religious duties, age, family relations and wealth. It may be noted here, that several Dharmasastras proclaimed Artha as the highest value for the householder, while some other give place to learning. It may be agreed that of these two views, the later was more popular. However, it should be conceded that Artha was never devalued. Even Dharma at every stage required Artha, at least for social purposes. Dharma involving spiritual values was given the highest position. It was the most necessary requirement for acquiring highest social status.

Duties towards Wife

Yajnavalkya Smriti has given a detailed description of the householder's duties to his wife. He must be solely devoted to her, having become one through sacramental bonds; he must satisfy her sensuous yearning, only refraining from sexual intercourse on inauspicious days. Care of the wife is essential because through her the householder begets sons whereby the family is continued both in time and in eternity.[3]

Social Duties

Thus, the Dharmasastras prescribe to the householder, the actions to be done on getting from bed till going to bed. Rules were prescribed about answering calls of nature, sauca or cleanliness of body and mind, Acamana or sipping water, Dantadhavana or brushing the teeth, snan or bath or general cleanliness of the both, tarpana, clothes to be worn on different occasions, making marks on the forehead after bathing, samdhya, homa, japa, etc. Among Mahayajnas were included Nryajna or Manusya Yajna meaning honouring of guests. Thus, yajna had a humanistic meaning. Universal kindliness was the general attitude towards the guest. Another significant prescription was concerning dana or gifts. It was a special feature of grahasthasrama. The Dharmasastras give a detailed description about the types of gifts, difference between dana, yag and homa, persons fit and

1 *Manu*, IV. 92.

2 *Yaj.*, I. 115.

3 *Ibid.*, I. 111, 78-81

unfit to be donees, types of donations etc. Gifts of land was not favoured. Gifts of horses was censured in some works. All could make gifts including women and sudras. Gifts could be of three kinds: nitya or daily gifts, naimittika or purposive gifts and kamya or desired gifts. Making gifts in secret was eulogised. Certain gifts were forbidden. Proper times for making gifts were specified. Generally, gifts were not made at night. Gifts at time of eclipses, samkranti, on *ayana* days were specially recommended, proper places for gifts were specified. Various articles of gifts were connected with different presiding deities. The general procedure of making gifts was laid down. Kings were required to make various kinds of gifts to brahmanas. Spending money for marriages of brahmanas and settling them in houses was highly eulogised. Temples and brahmanas were particularly recommended for gifts. Sixteen Mahadanas were prescribed. Gifts of cow was highly extoled. Other types of gifts included those of edible things, grains, books, hospitals etc. Kinds of invalid gifts were specified along with expiations for accepting such gifts. One some occasions gifts became irrevocable. Detailed rules were given about founding of temples and dedication of wells and other charitable work. Charity was considered more meritorious than sacrifices.

The Dharmasastras prescribe detailed rules about food and meals concerning their kinds, occasions, preliminaries, postures, procedures, types etc. Besides, equally detailed rules were prescribed about steeping, sexual intercourse, period of menstruation and the duties of the king in 24 hours. Thus, it is clear that the Dharmasastras have prescribed rules for the householder in great details.

VANAPRASTHA ASH RAMA

Objectives of Vanaprastha

In the various stages of life, according to Dharmasastras, the third is the Vanaprastha Ashrama. According to Manu Smriti, when a householder sees his skin wrinkled, and his hair white, and the sons of his sons, then he may resort to the forest. Abandoning all food raised by cultivation, and all his belongings, he may depart into the forest either, committing his wife to his sons, or accompanied by her. Taking with him the sacred fire and the implements required for domestic sacrifices, he may go forth from the village into the forest and reside there, duly controlling his sense.[1] The ancient word for vanaprastha was Vaikhanasa. If a person suffered from an incurable disease, he was allowed to start on the great journey till the body falls to rise no more. Members of all varnas except sudras could become vanaprasthas. This was also applicable to princely houses. Most of the duties prescribed for vanaprastha ashrama were similar to those of the next ashrama called Sanyas. It was so since vanaprastha was a preparation for sanyas. It was a transitional period between the two opposite types of stages, that of the householder and of the recluce.

1 *Manu Smriti*, VI. 2-8.

Duties of Vanaprastha

About the activities of the vanaprastha ashrama, Manu smriti prescribes: Let him offer those five great sacrifices according to the rules, with various kinds of pure food fit for ascetics, or with herbs, roots, and fruits. Let him wear a skin or a tattered garment; let him bathe in the evening or in the morning: and let him always wear his hair in braids, the hair on his body, his beard, and his nails being undipped. Let him perform the Bali — offering with such food as he eats, and give alms according to his ability; let him honour those who come to his hermitage with alms consisting of water, roots, and fruit. Let him always be industrious in privately reciting the Veda; let him be patient of hardships, friendly toward all, of collected mind, ever liberal and never a receiver of gifts, and compassionate towards all living creatures.[1]

From the above description it is clear that the ideal of this stage of life was liberation. Therefore, rules about it should be evaluated from the point of view of spiritual evolution. The asceticism characteristic of this stage of life was not an end in itself but a means for achieving self-control and spiritual power, the two essential pre-requisites for realisation of the goal of liberation. Secondly, it was a stage of ethical activity. The activity in this ashrama is prompted solely by Brahman. The individual in this stage of life had an attitude of friendship, liberality, wisdom and compassion towards all living beings, even plants. He was absolutely devoid of any motives of personal gain and pleasure, Artha and Kama. In spite of all, asceticism, Dharmasastras do not prescribe mortification of the flesh. The antinomy between the body and the spirit, so much characteristic of the Buddhist philosophy, was not the trait of Hinduism. The Indian philosophers, from the Vedas to Sri Aurobindo, treat both body and spirit in the individual, as equal expressions of the Divine. Therefore, in spite of all asceticism, the Vanaprastha Ashrama aimed more on positive individual and social virtues.

SANYAS ASHRAMA

Objectives of Sanyasa

Describing the fourth stage of life, Manusmriti prescribes "Having thus passed the third part of a man's natural term of life in the forest, he may live as an ascetic during the fourth part of his existence, after abandoning all attachment to worldly objects.[2] The goal of this stage of life was liberation.

Duties of Sanyasa

Therefore, it has been prescribed that the recluse should always wander alone without a companion. He should be "indifferent to everything, firm of purpose, meditating and concentrating his mind on Brahman." He should be free of all desire, whether to live or to die, and must wait for his appointed time "as a servant

1 *Ibid.*
2 *Ibid.*, VI. 33.

waits for the payment of his wages." Though a reduce is aiming at liberation, a goal transcending ethics, yet he treads the path of good. In the words of Manu smriti, again, "Let him put down his foot purified by his sight, let him drink water purified by straining with a cloth, let him utter speech purified by truth, let him keep his heart pure. Let him patiently bear hardships, let him not insult anybody, and let him not become anybody's enemy for the sake of this perishable body. Against an angry man let him not in return show anger, let him bless when he is cursed, and let him not utter speech, devoid of truth, scattered at the seven gates."[1]

The entire purpose of the prescription by Dharmasastras about this stage of life was to help in the achievement of the liberation, to make an individual fit for immortality. Therefore, it was proclaimed, "A twice-born man who becomes an ascetic after the successive performance of the above-mentioned acts, shakes off sin here below and reaches the highest Brahman."[2] In this process the reduce, through a life of duty and discipline, contributed his share to the welfare of the community, not in terms of Artha and Kama but in terms of Dharma. As Kevala Motwani rightly points out that the life of a Sanyasin was "an example of fulfilment and a promise of the future of all."[3]

CRITICAL EVALUATION

Integral Approach

From the above discussion of the prescriptions of the Dharmasastras about various stages of life, it is clear that the ashrama system is indicative of an integral approach to human life. By it a complete development of human power, physical, mental and spiritual, takes place and their proper satisfaction leads to an integral development of man. It maintains the balance of social and individual development. It is the most unique system in human social history and has eternal value. The ashrama system was prescribed for the achievement of the values included in the concept of purusarthas. The idea of Purusharthas is the fundamental principle of Indian social ethics. According to it, the aim of every person in the world is to attain the four purusharthas-Dharma, Artha, Kama and Moksha. Kama or sex is a natural tendency in every person. Artha or wealth is the means of fulfilment of sex and other needs and the life system of society. Dharma implies the laws or principles on which society is based. According to the Vaisesika philosophy, Dharma is that which leads to improvement in this world and to liberation in the next. Dharma, Artha and Kama relate to objects of this world. These are, in brief, called the Trivarga. Duty, wealth or sex indicate respectively ethical ideals, physical means and physical mental and vital desires of man. It is man's duty to fulfil all the three.

Besides trivargas, liberation is just as important in human life. At one time the Hindus interpreted trivarga as a means to liberation though generally all the four

---

1 *Ibid.*, 46-48.

2 *Ibid.*, 850.

3 Motwani, K., *Manu Dharma Sastra*, Madras, Ganesh and Co., 1958, p. 61.

Purushart has have been stressed. Vatsyayana has written, "A man in hundred years of age should gain knowledge in childhood, sex satisfaction in youth and attend to duty and liberation in old age."[1] Manu stated clearly, "Some people attribute more importance to duty, some to wealth and some to sex. Actually, all the three are equally important and creditable."[2] Manu had gone to the extent of saying that one should try for liberation only after he has passed through the Ashramas to fulfil duty, attain wealth and enjoy sex, and has rid himself of the three debts to God, ancestors and teachers because a person not doing so will find himself in trouble. In this way, it is clear that with regard to the aim of life, Indian social ethics emphasizes an integral approach.

Connected to Rinas

The system of Ashramas was also closely connected to the concept of rinas. Four types of debts have been enumerated in the Shatpath Brahamana: (1) to gods, (2) to seers, (3) to ancestors, and (4) to fellow beings. Ordinarily, Indian thinkers have accepted three types of debts: (1) Paternal debt, (2) Debt towards teachers, and (3) Debt towards gods. Debt to parents is the highest because they look after a person in his infancy, suffering much pain themselves in the process. According to the Indian commentators, the way of repaying parental debts is to have children oneself and look after them in the same way. Besides the parents, the seers and teachers impart knowledge to a person and make him capable of doing all work efficiently in the world. As for the repayment of this debt the means are to study the Vedas and to obey the laws of the Brahmacharya Ashrama. The debts to gods is paid off by performing different yajnas. A person owns these debts the moment he is born and he cannot hope for liberation unless he clears the debt. In Brahmacharya Ashrama the individual clears his debt to his ancestors, seers, gods and fellow beings. The same is true about the Grahastha Ashrama as well. After repayment of the debts in these two ashramas a person may enter Vanaprastha Ashrama, followed by Sanyas. However, in these two Ashramas as well the person remained concerned with his fellow beings though he was no more under any obligation.

Growth of Integral Man

The ashrama system aimed at the establishment of an order in which different aspects of man's personality may achieve satisfaction, growth and evolution. It is generally accepted that the main urges of men are biological and innate. Freud called it 'Id' while other psychologists have given it different names but did not refuse to accept it. Similarly, the social aspect of personality called ego by Freud, has been also generally accepted. Most of the psychologists have called it self and self-psychology is a branch devoted to researches in this field. The socialization of self or ego leads to a further bifurcation known as super ego in Freudean terms.

1 Vatsyayana, *Kamasutra*, II.
2 Manu, *Dharmasastra*, III.

This super ego carries on the mechanism of social control. It is developed by the family, neighbourhood, educational institutions and social institutions. It includes the sentiments of self-regard, the basis of human character. It is also the basis of the system of values as well as the dynamics of personality. Indian thinkers knew these different facets of human personality. Analysing the different stages of human life, keeping in mind all the time their continuity, the authors of Dharmasastras have given detailed rules and principles to realise maximum harmony, integrity, satisfaction, happiness, growth and development, in every stage of life. Thus, each ashrama was an order to realise these ends in that particular stage of life.

Value of Brahmacharya Ashrama

The stage of life corresponding to brahmacharya ashrama is a stage involving all types of physical and mental growth. Therefore, the chief aims of this stage of life are study, physical development and fulfilment of Dharma. The Indian thinkers never accepted a philosophy of *Laissez Faire* in human life, because they were convinced that whether in cosmos or in human life there is a law of causation based upon certain eternal principles. For example, it is a physiological rule that the physical development of a person is completed by the age of youth and any deficiency in this stage cannot be completely recouped in later age. Again, it has been generally accepted that the different organs of human body grow to their maturity during this period. Similarly, it is a psychological principle that the period of study requires maximum concentration and minimum distraction. Distractions include the urban environment, hetro-sexual relationships and most of the matters concerning household life. Therefore, the authors of Dharmasastras decided that the males and females should devote all their energies to physical and mental development upto the age of 25 years, ignorant of the world around them. Some Western thinkers have recently laid a strong emphasis on sex education. But the Indian thinkers have refused to accept its necessity during the period of celibacy. Since, the Western woman wonders as to how can a woman be happy in a marriage decided entirely by the choice of the parents, premarital love for her is a necessary requirement for the solid foundation of marriage. In India, on the other hand, even now in majority of the cases, the mates are selected by the parents and they have not been found in any way less satisfactory than love marriages. Even in the West so many thinkers have come out with arguments against love marriages. Therefore, the prescriptions of the brahmacharya ashrama are based upon psychological, physiological and sociological facts. With minor modifications it can be carried on even today. Therefore, all the contemporary Indian thinkers have supported it. Again, it is the basis of justice towards physical and mental growth. It is admitted that a life in this ashrama alone could be one-sided. It may be noted that in spite of the prescriptions for a life long celibate life by the authors of Dharmasastras, it was practiced only in exceptions. Usually, almost all the persons entered grahastha ashrama after the period of celibacy.

Value of Grahastha Ashrama

After achieving all round physical and mental development the individual used to enter grahastha ashrama. By so many experiments on learning, psychologists have found out that it is closely linked with maturity and training is not very much helpful in so many of the cases. This is also true about sexual behaviour. It is a result of maturity and generally males and females learn it by individual private experiments without much difficulty since Nature is the best guide in these matters. However, the Indian thinkers developed a whole science and art of sex in the form of the tradition of Kamasastras. The *Kamasutra* of Vatsyayana is a monument on this aspect of human knowledge. It can be very favourably compared with even the best classic on sex produced by the West. It has discussed in details the different activities concerned with sexual behaviour between male and female. Besides the sexual aspects of the householder's life, the authors of Dharmasastras have equally emphasised the importance of children in the family, so much so that the primary aim of marriage in India was not sex enjoyment but birth of suitable progeny. Again, the social responsibilities of the householder have been so much emphasised that the Dharmasastras call grahastha ashrama the basis of all ashramas. Thus, the prescriptions of this ashrama are based upon the principle of equal justice to the three constituents of the family, the parents, the husband and wife and the children. With the addition of hospitability towards guests at all costs, it has emphasised the social aspect of the householder's life. It goes without saying that the evaluation of Hindu family and Hindu marriage is also the evaluation of grahastha ashrama.

Value of Vanaprastha and Sanyas

The most significant contribution made by Indian thinkers to the world of human knowledge is about the rules of mental hygiene in different stages of life. The vanaprastha ashrama prescribes remedies to the problems of old age and even death. In the entire psychological wisdom gathered by humanity in East and West, there is no parallel to the concept of vanaprastha ashrama so far as the challenges of old age and death are concerned. While youth was considered the stage of enjoyment of life, old age in India was considered the age of renunciation and liberation. The Vanaprasthi used to roam from village to village, forest to forest, not staying at one place for a long time. This was the stage of preparation for the final liberation in sanyas ashrama. And it was provided a period equal to any other, a whole span of 25 years so that there may be a complete mental and psychical transformation of the human individual. It was so because the spiritual values have been given the highest status in Indian Axiology. Therefore, H.H. Allport has rightly pointed out that Hindu psychology is much more mature and integrated as compared to modern Western psychology. While the later has made significant breakthrough about the matters concerning childhood and youth, it has only touched the surface of the problems of old age. Some existentialist psychologists have tried to analyse the consciousness of death and also searched for some solutions but they have not been useful to normal individuals. In fact, while Indian psychology is firmly routed in axiology, the Western psychology is valueless. While Indian psychology is geared around the hierarchy of values, with spiritual values at the apex, the Western psychology is naturalistic, statistical and even mechanist. Any solution of human problems without any reference to individual and social values, and purely based upon mechanical and material models, is bound to fail in the end. Knowing this fact very well, the Indian psychologists developed psychological prescriptions upon the spiritual model of the individual and society. And since, on the spiritual plane, the contradictories naturally become complimentaries, therefore, it is the only solid basis for providing individual and social justice. Thus, the Ashrama system avoids both the extremes of unrestrained enjoyment and unprincipled asceticism, the two extremes which have plagued human cultures everywhere and had been the major cause of their degeneration and death. This is again, the secret of longevity and vitality of Indian culture. It may be noted here that the ashrama system is the general form or structure of the actual functioning of the social institutions in Indian society. It was the principle of order and harmony in individual and social life.

THE CONCEPT OF RINAS

The Indian social organization paid attention to the idea of Rinas or debts along with the four ashrama and purusharthas. Four types of debts have been enumerated in the Shatpath Brahmana:

(1) to god, (2) to seers, (3) to ancestors, and (4) to fellow beings. Ordinarily, Indian thinkers have accepted three types of debts: (1) Paternal debt, (2) Debt towards teachers, and (3) Debt towards gods. Debt to parents is the highest because they look after a person in his infancy, suffering much pain themselves in the process. According to the Indian commentators, the way of repaying parental debt is to have children oneself and look after them in the same way. Besides the parents, the seers and teachers impart knowledge to a person and make him capable of doing all work efficiently in the world. As for the repayment of this debt the means are to study the Vedas and to obey the laws of the Brahmacharya ashrama. The debt to gods is paid off by performing different yajnas. A person owns these debts the moment he is born and he cannot hope for liberation unless he clears the debt. The idea of debts conveys the lesson of unselfish fulfilment of duty and responsibility to man.

THE DOCTRINE OF KARMA

The doctrine of karma is the ethical background of Indian social organization. There are three major elements in the doctrine of Karma — (1) Every human activity entails results which may take any of the following forms — physical, mental or ethical. It effects the person's nature, character and tendencies. Man reaps the harvest of past life in the form of lust and sanskaras. (2) Karma necessitates another life because man cannot reap the reward of his actions in one life.

(3) The diversities, *i.e.* poor or rich, happy or sorrowful, intelligent or foolish etc., are all result of the actions of previous births. (4) The doctrine of Karma makes indispensable a belief in the immortality of the self. To reap the reward of actions of this life the jiva should be reborn just as the karmas of this life prove the previous existence of jiva.

The doctrine of karma prevents people from bad actions, it does not encourage fatalism. AB. Keith holds that it encourages fatalism and hinders moral progress, and this criticism is valid for the present distorted form of the doctrine. But in its pure philosophical form it preaches purushartha instead of fatalism and morality in place of immorality. According to this doctrine, although man's present state is due to past actions, his future still depends on him. Every person can improve his future by good actions. Actually, the doctrine is based on real facts and its message to the people is to improve their lives by making use of natural laws.

THE SANSKARAS

Sanskara means to purify. According to Manu, sanskaras purify the body. Starting with Garbhadhana they end with Antyeshti. Every sanskara starts with a yajna. Opinions differ in regard to their number. Whereas Gautama Dharma Sutra details some 48 sanskaras, most sutras put their number at 40. Some of the more important sanskaras are — Garbhadhana, Punsavana, Jatakarma, Namkarana, Upanayana, Samavartana, Vivaha and Antyesthi.

1. Garbhadhana. Garbhadhan is the first sanskara of human life. After marriage, the couple make sacrifices to the fire and promising to lead a life of love they pray to Vishnu, Sinivali, Ashwini, Agni, Indra and other gods, to grant to them the most powerful and innocent children to enable them to follow dharma. The first sanskara performed with this pure feeling is garbhadhana, it being done for the being to come into the womb of woman.

2. Punsavana. The Punsavana sanskara is performed in the third month of the wife's pregnancy. In this the prayer is directed to gods who protect pregnancy. At the time the woman is told that the aim is the desire of a powerful son and the safety and health of the embryo.

3. Jatakarma. The Jatakarma sanskara is performed when the child is born. In this the father touching the child whispers some mantras into his ears expressing the desire that he be intelligent and live to a ripe old age. Following it, OM is inscribed on the child's tongue with a pen of gold. The aim is to create an atmosphere for the complete development of the child's powers right from birth and to remind the parents of their responsibility in his character formation.

4. Namakarana. Ten or twelve days after the child's birth the namakarana sanskara is performed. Following it are performed the niskramana in the fourth month, and annaprashana in the sixth, churakarma in the third year, and the kamavedha sanskara in the fifth year. On the subject of namakarana, Manu opines that the names given should be according to the Varna and ideals.

5. Upanayana. The Upanayana sanskara takes place in the eighth year. Of the two parts of the word, the former 'up' means near while the child was taken to the teacher. In India in the past, the child used to live with the teacher to study after upanayana. The aim of this sanskara is to establish as close a relation between the teacher and the taught, as possible. He is given the sacred thread to wear and told the laws of Brahmacharya.

6. Samavartana. After the person has finished his studies, observing all the laws of Brahmacharya, he comes home and it is the occasion for the samavartana sanskara. At this stage he is shaved for the first time and given cosmetics to use. He is now considered as one possessing the right to spend a domestic life.

7. Vivaha. Vivaha or marriage is an indication of the person's having entered domestic life. According to Valvalkar, the person is thereby socialised because herein reproduction is promised for the furtherance of the race. In the marriage sanskara many rituals like madhuparka, shilaroana etc., are observed, to impress the importance of holy wedlock.

After grahastha ashrama at fifty, the person entered the vanaprastha ashrama and the sanyasa ashrama at 75.

8. Antyesthi. The antyesthi sanskara is performed at the person's death. In this sanskara the tradition is to burn the body on a wooden pyre. Many mantras are chanted as ghee is sprinkled on the fire. Normally it is the eldest son who performs the last rites.

The sanskaras have a great importance from the viewpoint of social ethics. According to Valvalkar the whole system of sanskara points out that some new responsibilities are being put on man for Social and individual good and it is his major duty to respect them. Marriage and other sanskaras are not only for individual good, they also represent one's responsibility to society. Thus the balance and harmony of the individual and society is maintained and both rise to progress.

In this way, the Hindu ethics maintains a proper balance between the individual and the social good, good of this life and the next, means and end, rights and duties. In an integral approach to life all these combine naturally and exist as mutual complements.

QUESTIONS FOR EXERCISE

1. Discuss the Psycho-moral basis of the Ashrama theory.
2. What is Ashrama System? Explain its importance in Hindu life. Can this system be suitable in modern Indian Society?

4

The Hindu Concept of Purusharthas

In the evolution of a world culture, each country has given particular contribution through its culture. This leads us to the conclusion that no culture should be called higher or lower and each adds to the richness of the human culture as a whole. Thus, each culture must grow independently and fully so that it may contribute to the world of human culture. This again, is the principle of the fulfilment of 'Swadharma.' Thus, the Indian culture will contribute to the world culture only that which has been peculiar to it. Secondly, in the realm of thought, only that idea can be effective which, along with being universal, fulfils the local needs as well. Hence, in India, only that ideology can act as a guide which is in tune with the Indian culture and national consciousness provided that it should not be contradictory to world consciousness but complementary to it.

Integral approach has been the Chief characteristic of Indian culture. Indian philosophy has emphasised one ultimate element underlying the multiplicity of the phenomenal world. Leaving aside exceptional philosophies as Charvaka, from the philosophers of the ancient Vedas down to the contemporary Indian thinkers as Rabindranath Tagore, Sri Aurobindo, Swamy Vivekanand, Mahatma Gandhi and others, one finds an integral approach in philosophy. While some philosophers have negated multiplicity from unity, most of the Indian thinkers have considered multiplicity as increasing the richness of unity. Not only in the philosophical fields, but in economic, social, political and all other fields of life, the Indian approach is integral. Hence, Integral Humanism is most suitable to the genius of this country.

In social life, the Indians have everywhere advocated a versatile integral progress as the ideal. Since ancient times, the Indian ideal of four Purusharthas *i.e.*, Dharma, Artha, Kama, and Moksha, has presented an integral view of life. Some maintain that the ideals of renunciation and liberation in Indian thinking exhibit other-worldliness and escapism. Granted that in some philosophical schools, the ideal of liberation has been presented in a way which has no consistency with the terrestrial aims of life, it is however, necessary to go deeper into the meanings of these values before arriving at any final conclusion. In spite of Buddha's ideal of *Nirvan,* his characteristic sympathy for human beings makes it difficult to admit that his philosophy should be called other-worldly. In Hindu social philosophy, the concept of Varna again, shows the same integral approach. While Samkara has emphasised the value of liberation in human life, the sage Vatsyayana has laid emphasis upon the ideal of Kama in his famous treatise *Kamasutra.* In the history of man, wherever any culture too much emphasised some one particular aspect of human personality or life and left the other aspects unfulfilled, it led to cultural degeneration and the birth of reactions. The conflict observed everywhere among man and man, man and society, nation and nation, and even the conflict within the individual himself only exhibits Nature's attempt everywhere to achieve harmony, synthesis, balance and integrality. This tendency is found not in human society alone but even in the animal and plant life. In man it becomes only more conscious. This is proved by the fact that man cannot rest in peace unless he solves his problems and removes his tensions. The integral philosophy of life shows the limitations of every need and value, gives it a sufficient place, leaves none, since the warp and woof of human life has been knitted by all these, and, however one may wish, he cannot remove any element of human personality and life, though by suppressing it one may make his life one-sided, frustrated and full of tensions.

The idea of Purusharthas is a fundamental principle of Indian ethics. According to it, the aim of every person in the world is to attain the four Purusharthas — Dharma, Artha, Kama and Moksha. Kama is a natural tendency in every person. Wealth is the means of fulfilment of kama and other needs and the life system of society. Dharma implies the laws or principles on which society is based. According to the Vaisesika philosophy, Dharma is that which leads to improvement in this world and to moksha in the next. Dharma or duty, wealth and kama relate to objects of this world. These are, in brief, called the Trivarga. Duty, wealth and sex indicate respectively ethical ideals, physical, mental and vital desires of man. In this way it is man's duty to fulfil all the three. Besides trivargas, moksha is just as important in human life. At one time the Hindus interpreted trivarga as a means to Moksha but generally all the four purusharthas have been stressed. Vatsyayan writes, "A man in hundred years of age should gain knowledge in childhood, sex satisfaction in youth and attend to duty and moksha in old age."[1] Manu states clearly, "Some people attribute more importance to duty, some to wealth and some to sex. Actually, all three are equally important and creditable."[2] Manu has gone to the extent of saying that man should try for moksha only after he has passed through the three ashramas to fulfil duty, attain wealth and enjoy sex, and has rid himself of the three rinas, because a person not doing so will find himself in trouble. In this way, it is clear that with regard to the aim of life, Indian ethics emphasizes an integral approach.

1 Vatsyayan, *Kamasutra*, II.

2 Manu, *Dharmashastra*, III.

There are many instances in history of the balance between the society and the individual being lost due to laying of excessive emphasis upon one aspect of life. Buddhists, Christians, among them St. Paul and Tartarian and priests of the middle ages in Europe laid excessive emphasis on abstention with the result that there was a strong reaction in the direction of immorality. Varna Margi Buddhists took women and wine to be an important part of the means. Immortality was conspicuous by its absence in groups like Choli Marga. In Europe in middle ages, the monastries had become centres of corruption. This reaction was manifested in other direction in the form of cruelty and violence. Indian seers were acquainted with these psychological possibilities. They thus, emphasized all the four purusharthas equally. This kept the organisation of society and the individual solid and balanced.

DHARMA

Dharma as Cosmic Principle

Like all other fundamental references in Indian social philosophy, the first references to the universal nature of Dharma have been made in the Vedas. The Vedic term Rta, as has been pointed out earlier, stands for the cosmic principle of Dharma. Varnashrama Dharma, the basis of Vedic social organisation, was the main form of Dharma. The Vedic ethics was based upon Dharma. Thus, Dharma was the cosmic principle expressing as Rta in cosmos and Varnasrama Dharma among human beings. In fact, the Indian social philosophers never distinguish between cosmic, natural, social and individual. All these, according to them, are essentially one and the same. This was known as Brahman in Upanisads. By the identity of Atman and Brahman it was maintained that what is individual is cosmic and *vice versa*. Thus, individual justice can be achieved only by achieving social justice. Social justice, in its turn, can be achieved by following natural law which is only an aspect of universal law.

This cosmic nature of Dharma, however, is more explicit in Upanisads. The Upanisads identify Dharma (Righteousness) with Satya (Truth). The Brahadaranyakopanisad declares, "Verily, that which is righteousness is truth. Therefore, they say of a man who speaks the truth, he speaks righteousness, or of a man who speaks righteousness that he speaks the truth. Verily, both these are the same thing."[1] This Dharma leads to Brahman realisation which is impossible without moral uplift. Hence, Taittiriya Upanisad says, "Having taught the Veda, a teacher further instructs a pupil: 'Speak the Truth (Satyam Vada), practice virtue (Dharmam Chara).....' One should not be negligent of truth. One should not be negligent of virtue. One should not be negligent of welfare. One should not be negligent of prosperity."[2] According the Chandogya Upanisad, Dharma is Yajna or sacrifice. It is soul force. It is the spiritual energy in

1 *Brih.*, II. 5, 11.
2 *Taittiriya Upanisad*, I.

the universe. Besides the Upanisads, the Geeta also treated Dharma as the cosmic principle. Continuing this tradition the Dharmasastras also insisted upon the universal form of Dharma. In the words of P.V. Kane, "The writers on dharmasastra meant by dharma not a creed or religion but a mode of life or a code of conduct, which regulated a man's work and activities as a member of society and as an individual and was intended to bring about the gradual development of a man and to enable him to reach what was deemed to be the goal of human existence."[1] This goal of human existence was liberation. Liberation has been defined as realisation of Brahman. The Upanisadic Mahavakya, "Tattavarnasi", "Ayamatma Brahman", "Atmacha Brahman", "Sarvam khalvidam Brahman", express the universal nature of Brahman which is the same as Dharma.

One of the noblest prayers in all literature occurs in the Brihadaranyaka Upanisad, "Lead me from falsenood unto truth, from darkness lead me into light, from death lead me unto immortality."[2] This is the universal form of Dharma. Dharma has been further described in terms of universal virtues. Its identity with truth has been already pointed out. Dharmasutras have included almost all the moral virtues in it. The Gautama Dharmasutra holds that daya (compassion or love for all beings), ksanti (forebearance), anasuya (freedom from envy), saucha (purity of body, speech and thought), anayasa (absence of painful efforts or ambitions), mangala (doing what is commended), akarpanya (not demeaning oneself before others), asprha (not hankering after sensual pleasures or the possessions of others)[3] are the qualities of the soul. Vasistha says that avoiding backbiting, jealousy, pride, egoism, unbelief, crookedness, self-praise, abuse of others, deceit, covetousness, delusion, anger and envy is the dharma of all asramas and further he delivers a fine exhortation "practise dharma (righteousness) and not adharma; speak the truth and not untruth; look far ahead, not near: look at what is highest, not at what is not highest."[4] The reason for the cultivation of the above mentioned virtues and abstention from the opposite vices is based upon the philosophical principle that there is one universal essence underlying everyone. Thus, the ideal of dharma combines morality and metaphysics. Like Kant, Daksa declares "one who desires happiness should look upon another just as he looks upon himself."[5] In the words of Devala, "The quintessence of dharma is that one should not do to others what would be disliked by one's self."[6] As a universal principle, dharma stands higher than Artha and Kama. The Mahabharata says, "A wise man tries to secure all three, but if all three cannot be attained, he secures dharma and artha or only dharma if he has a choice of only one from among the three. A man of middling discipline

1 Kane, P.V., *History of Dharmasastra*, Vol. II. Part I. Bhandarkar Oriental Research Institute, Pune, 1941. p. 2.

2 *Brih.*, I, 3, 28.

3 *Gautama Dharma Sutra*, VIII. 24-26.

4 *Vasistha Dharma Sutra*, X. 30.

5 *Daksa*, III. 22.

6 Devala, quoted in *Kratyaratanakar*, p. 17.

prefers artha to the other two; dharma is the source of both artha and kama."[1] In the words of Gautama, "One should not allow the morning, midday and evening to remain fruitless so far as dharma, artha and kama are concerned. But among these three one should attach most importance to dharma."[2] According to Yajnavalkya also dharma is the highest among Purusharthas.

Since the moral qualities prescribed for the following of Dharma were common to all, they express the universal nature of Dharma. According to Sankhasmriti, "forbearance, truthfulness, self-restraint and purity are common to all varnas."[3] According to Mahabharata, "there are the best qualities among all beings *viz.*, absence of enmity, truthfulness and freedom from anger."[4] Vasistha says that "truthfulness, freedom from anger, generosity, ahimsa (non-injury) and procreation of offspring are the common dharma of all varnas."[5] According to Gautama, "Even the Sudra has to submit himself to the dharma of truthfulness, freedom from anger and purity of body and mind." Manu says that "ahimsa, truthfulness, no wrongful taking of another's possessions, purity and restraint of senses are in brief the common dharmas of all varnas."[6]

General Characterisations of Dharma

From the above discussion concerning the nature of dharma as cosmic principle some general characteristics can be deduced. The most important among these are as follows:

1. Three Active Modes. According to Chandogya Upanisad, there are three active modes of dharma: yajna, adhyavana and dana (sacrifice, study, and dedication).[7] Yajna or sacrifice is qualified as tapas. The meaning of tapas is soul-force. It refers to the spiritual energy which is generated by bringing one's physical nature under the control of his rational will. The second mode of dharma is adhyayana or study. Related to the study of scriptures is the exposition of the scriptures or pravachana. The third mode of dharma is dana. Commenting on these three modes of dharma. Prof. G. Mukhopadhyaya summarises the inter-relatedness and ethical intentionality of the ideas expressed above: "By yajna or sacrifice one is linked with the world of the gods, through study or adhyayana one is joined with the supreme sphere of Sabda-Brahman, and lastly through dana, self-giving or gift of things one gets connected with the human world. Dharma thus covers all the spheres of life and is not an isolated state of things."[8]

1 *Mahabharata,* Uddyogaparva, 124, 34-38.

2 *Gautama Dharma Sutra*, IX. 46-47.

3 *Sankhasmriti*, 1.5

4 *Vassisthasmriti*, IV. 4

5 *Manusmriti*, X, 63 and I. 62.

6 *Gautamadharma Sutra*, X. 52.

7 *Manusmriti*, IV. 175.

8 G. Mukhopadhyaya, *Studies in the Upanisads,* Calcutta, Oriental Press, 1960, p. 157.

2. Social Principle. In the words of S. Cromwell Crawford, "The key to understanding Brahmanical society is found in the first purusartha, namely. dharma. It is a development of the earlier Rg-Vedic idea of Rta, which have been represented cosmic law operating in all phenomena — natural, religious and moral. In the smriti period this law permeating the whole universe was called dharma. Within the social order, dharma was explicitly defined in terms of certain duties and obligations which were codified in the great Law Books."[9]

3. Criteria of Duty. While Advaita Vedanta has developed dharma as a metaphysical principle, the Mimamsa philosophers develop the concept of dharma as duty. Jaimini starts his sutras with an enquiry regarding the nature of dharma *i.e.*, the nature of Vedic duties, relevant proofs, means of the production of dharma and its fruits.[10] Whatever is enjoined by Vedic injunctions is dharma or duty, (yascondanalaksanah sa dharmah) provided it is not intended to produce any injury to other persons. There are certain sacrifices, such as syena-yaya, which are performed for injuring one's enemy; though there are injunctions regarding such sacrifices, nevertheless, since they produce injury for others, they are not to be regarded as dharma. Dharma cannot be known by any of the other pramanas such as perception, inference or implication; the only way of knowing it is by the Vedic injunction. Dharma is thus, according to the Mimamsa not a quality of the understanding of the self, but is of the nature of the Vedic sacrifices. It means only such prescribed sacrifices of the Vedas as have not been associated with any harmful effects. Dharmas are either enjoined by the Vedas or directed towards beneficial ends. In the words of Surama Das Gupta, "When it is said that Vedic injunctions or prohibitions define the nature of dharma or adharma, the idea is that whether any sacrificial action will produce advantage or disadvantage cannot be known by any other means but the injunction or the prohibition of the Vedas."[11]

4. Practical Principle. Summing up the practical nature of the concept of dharma in Dharmasastras, P.V. Kane writes, "The foregoing discussion establishes that all dharmasastra writers attached the highest importance to moral qualities and enjoined them upon all with all the emphasis they could command; but as their main purpose was a practical one, *viz.*, to guide people to right acts in everyday life, they dealt more elaborately with the acts, rites and ceremonies that each person had to do with reference to his station in society."[12]

5. The Principle of Good. The concept of Dharma seems to be closely associated with that of punya or the good. The Brihadaranyaka Upanisad defines Dharma as shreyah (good). There is nothing greater than Dharma. In Kathopanisad Dharma has been defined as mystic self-knowledge. Thus, the upanisads define Dharma in the sense of good. Adharma therefore means the opposite of good or evil. This has been also elaborated in the Nyaya vaisesika concept of good. The Nyaya Vaisesika

9 S. Cromwell Crawford, *Evolution of Hindu Ethical Ideals*, p. 80.

10 Jaimini, *Sastradipika*, I. 1. 1.

11 Das Gupta, S., *Development of Moral Philosophy in India*, p. 79.

12 Kane, P.V., *History of Dharmasastra*, p. 11.

philosophers define Dharma as merit and Adharma as demerit. Therefore, in order to achieve liberation one must follow Dharma.

6. Differentia of Men. According to Indian thinkers, it is Dharma which distinguishes between man and animal. It is so since it represents the moral law in human society, which is a part of universal divine principle. Dharma, therefore, it is the basis of all values. It is the substratum of Purusarthas. It is the regulative principle. In the words of K.N. Upadhyaya, "The persistence and intensity with which the inquiry into dharma has been pursued in India is mainly on account of the firm conviction of the Indian people that dharma constitutes the differentia of man, whereby he is distinguished from brutes, just as in the West, following Aristotle, rationality is regarded as the distinguishing mark of man. This approach at once reveals...that what is most vital to man's life is not his mental, but his moral and spiritual nature."[1]

7. The Principle of State Craft. But the most important characteristic of dharma is that it is the principle of state craft. In Hindu polity the king was entrusted the responsibility of upholding dharma. According to Manu, government is an extension of the eternal divine order of society, and the king is responsible for upholding dharma.[2] Thus dharma is the principle of state craft. It is the basis of law and order in the state. Prof. Basham reminds us that in ancient and classical India, government, no matter what its shape, was not an end in itself. "The Hegelian concept of the state as an organism of supernatural size and power, transcending all other entities upon earth and mystically linking man with the Absolute, is completely foreign to anything ever thought of in India."[3] The state as protector of dharma comes closer to the Thomistic doctrine of government as the means for promoting salvation.

8. Principle of Law and Order. Therefore, Dharmasastras consider dharma as the principle of law and order. Legislation and the theory of punishment in ancient Indian states was based upon the principle of Dharma. The country observing law and order was known as Dharmarajya. According to Mahabharat kingship was imposed by Divine upon mankind, designed to help people live by the laws of Dharma.[4] Manusmriti regards the king as the repository of all Dharma and responsible for maintaining the order of law. Kamandaka describes the king as the preserver and the maintainer of the duties of varnas and Asramas who should himself also be entirely obedient to the laws relating to them.[5] Thus, the rule according to Dharma not only included legal justice but also social justice.

9. Integral Approach. The most important characteristic of Dharma from the point of view of culture, is the integral standpoint. The principle of following swadharma is the basis of unity in diversity in society. Integral approach has been characteristic to Indian culture. Indian philosophy has emphasised one ultimate

1 Upadhyaya, K.N., *Dharma as a Regulative Principle*, p. 1.
2 *Manu*, VII. 35.
3 A.L. Basham, *Aspects of Ancient Indian Culture* (New York), Asia Publishing House, (1970), p. 5.
4 *Manu*, VIII. 307-316.
5 *Mahabharata*, XII. 59.

element underlying the multiplicity of the phenomenal world. Leaving aside exceptional philosophies as that of Charvaka, from the philosophers of the ancient Vedas down to the contemporary Indian thinkers including Rabindranath Tagore, Sri Aurobindo, Swami Vivekananda, Mahatma Gandhi and others, one finds an integral approach in philosophy. Dharmasastras advocated a multisided integral progress as the ideal. Since, ancient times the Indian ideal of four Purusharthas *i.e.*, Dharma, Artha, Kama, and Moksha has presented an integral view of life.[1] The integral view point does not negate the distinctions but shows unity in diversity and neither emphasises unity nor diversity exclusively but harmonises both in a more integral vision.[2]

10. Characteristics of Indian Culture. One of the meaning of the term Dharma is culture. Therefore, all the characteristics of Indian culture are the characteristics of Dharma in India. The fundamental characteristics of Indian Culture are: religious orientation, spirituality, religious tolerance, synthetic spirit, adaptability', freedom of thought, integral approach and most of all, unity in diversity. All these characteristics are equally the characteristics of Dharma. Dharma is cultural organisation and spirituality. It has been equated with self-knowledge. According to Sri Aurobindo, spirituality is the key to the Indian mind.[3] We can say that spirituality is the key to understand Dharma. Spirituality is spontaneity. It is totality. It is synthesis. It is integrality. It is dynamism and comprehensiveness. It is natural principle. All these features characterise Dharma.

11. Humanism. Another significant characteristic of Dharma is humanism. Humanism is the philosophy in which man occupies the central place. Dharma, the universal principle is basically a moral principle which is essentially human. We have already referred to the humanist interpretation of Atman, Brahman and their identity in chapter III in the conceptions of Upanisads and Bhagwad Gita. Humanism propounds unity in diversity, in individual, national and international affairs. The same has been propounded by Dharma. Each country and each human being in a particular time and place has some specific 'Dharma' and the sole aim of his life is to realize it. Similarly, humanity too has a 'Dharma' and that is the maximum and most comprehensive realisation of human values.

12. Dynamic Approach. The followers of Dharmasastras have generally followed the letter in place of spirit and have been too much conservative. Dharma, on the other hand, has the charateristic of a dynamic principle. Defining Dharma as the dynamic human property Prasastapada has maintained, "It brings about to the agent happiness, means of happiness and final deliverance; it is supersensuous; it is destructible by the experiencing of the last item of happiness; it is produced by the contact of the man with the internal organ, by means of pure thoughts and determinations; and with regard to the different castes and conditions of men there

1 Kamandaka, *Nitisara,* Second sarga, Verse 35.

2 Sharma, R.N., *Indian Society and Social Institutions,* Munshiram Manoharlal, 1981, New Delhi, pp. 31-32.

3 Sri Aurobindo, *The Foundations of Indian Culture*, p. 5.

are distinct means of accomplishing it."[1] In the words of S. Cromwell Crawford, "Hindus call their religion Sanatana Dharma which literally means "Eternal Law". The name should in no wise suggest that the ethical ideals connected with this religion are eternal in the sense of being fixed, static, unchanging substances. To the contrary, Hindu ethics, like the river Ganges, has been in a state of ceaseless flow down the ages, constantly changing its course and currents relative to the hard, intervening realities of Indian history. All of its fundamental presuppositions — karman, samsara, dharma — have evolved from streams of thought originating in earliest times. These elements have survived to the present day, not in spite of change, but because of change. Thus, under the rubric of eternal universal law, Hindu ethics combines continuity with dynamic diversity."[2]

It should be remembered here that the description of the characteristics of Dharma in the Vedas, the Upanisads, the Bhagvadgita, the Dharmasutras, the Dharmasastras, the Six systems and even in the writings of contemporary Indian philosophers is only different in emphasis but same in essentials. Therefore, the above description of the characteristics of Dharma is equally applicable in case of Dharmasastras as in all other cases. The above characteristics however, do not exhaust the list. In fact the list cannot be easily exhausted.

ARTHA

The next Purushartha after Dharma is Artha. It has been given an important place in Indian Culture. Kautilya has defined Artha in his Arthasastra as, "The livelihood of human beings is the Artha." Thus, Artha is the use of Earth for the means of livelihood in human lives. Vatsyayan, in his Kamasutra has defined Artha as including knowledge, land, animals, friends and earned money etc., following one's own Dharma and increasing it.[3] Thus, Artha includes the primary needs of men. As has been pointed out by different Dharmasastras, it was essential for the householder to pursue Artha. According to Kamasutra, "A person who did not achieve learning in the first stage, did not earn the money in the second nor did observe penance in the third cannot do anything in the fourth." Thus, it was obligatory on the part of every person to work for Artha. The stage of the householder has been given a central place in Hindu Ashrama system. The main aim of this stage was the achievement of Artha, not only for himself but for so many others in society. It was said that even the fulfilment of Dharma and kama are based on Artha. According to Vatsyayan every householder must pursue Artha. Arjuna said in Mahabharata, "Whatever is considered Dharma in the world is completely based upon wealth...all the religious activities, all the pleasures, even the heaven can be achieved by means of wealth." In Arthasastra, Kautilya has pointed out that among Dharma, Artha and Kama, Artha is the highest since it is the means for the

1 Prasastapada, *Padarthadharmasamgraha*, Tr. G. Jha, Allahabad, E.J. Lazarus and Co., 1916, VI. 133.
2 S. Cromwell Crawford, *Evolution of Indian Ethical Ideals*, Introduction, p. xi.
3 Vatsyayan, *Kamasutra*, 1. 2. 9.

achievement of Dharma and Kama[1] This has been also supported by Panchtantra and Hitopadesha. However, the Indian thinkers seldom considered Artha without Dharma as desirable. While wealth was many a time considered the highest value, it was insisted that it must be based upon Dharma.

Another extreme is the negation of Artha. Some Indian thinkers have supported fatalism and did not include Artha among Purusarthas. They have insisted that wealth is achieved by fate and does not depend upon efforts. This vein of thinking can be observed in the sayings of so many saints in India including Malukadas, Kabirdasa, Dadu etc. However, this has not been given much importance by most of the thinkers. Hitting hard at the supporters of fate, Vatsyayan, in his Kamasutra, pointed out that success is impossible without efforts since Purusartha is the root cause and substratum of all activities. Even necessary things do not happen without it. Therefore, one should make sustained efforts to attain Artha, without it, it is useless to expect pleasure or welfare. According to a famous Sanskrit verse, Lakshmi, the goddess of wealth smiles on the brave and persevering. Similar quotations can be found in abundance in so many Sanskrit works.

As Dharma was systematically and elaboratory discussed by Dharmasastras, India has a tradition of Arthasastras as systematic and detailed works upon the subject of Artha. Kautilya has considered Artha as the main among trivarga. According to him, in Trivarga Artha is the most important, since both Dharma and Kama depend upon it. According to Vatsyayan one should constantly make efforts to increase his learning, land, gold, animals, wealth, clothes, ornaments and friends. The Arthasastras present a scientific analysis for the achievement of Artha. Among Arthasastras, the Arthasastra of Kautilya is the most important. It includes a summary of earlier Arthasastras. These earlier Arthasastras, however, have not been available. The Arthasastra of Kautilya is not only the first available but also the most important work concerning Artha.

Defining the scope of Artha, Kautilya has pointed out in Arthasastra that Artha means the habitat of human beings or the region in which human beings are established. Arthasastra is the science which discusses the establishment of the state and the rules of its preservation. Kautilya has discussed the subject in great details. His work is considered as one of the most important works not only upon Indian Economics and Hindu Polity but among the most important works on this subject in the world. According to Kautilya, the state is the root of Artha. Therefore, a society can achieve Artha only under favourable state. Since the state aims at Artha, the king should have a tendency in its favour. The king is central in the state and therefore for him Artha should be more important than even Dharma and Kama. It is only when the king leads in this matter that others may follow it. Thus Kautilya has insisted that the king should present ideal conduct and character in the achievement of Artha and [2] should maintain conditions in

1 Vatsyayan, *Kamasutra,* 1. 2. 9.

2 Kautilya, *Arthasastra,* 1. 2. 6.

which the citizens may achieve Artha. Thus, Indian thinking was socialistic and humanistic. No one can achieve Artha alone or acting against the society. Artha should be achieved collectively. According to Gita, all land belongs to God. It has been clearly maintained by Kautilya that the king who fails to do his duties concerning Artha he may be removed.

KAMA

The third purusartha is Kama. Kama has been literally defined as desire. Desire is the motivating power of all activities. Therefore, it is at the root of all actions. This Kama, however, may be of three types. Satvika Kama is according to Dharma. Rajasika Kama is the result of the combination of sense organs and desires. This is pleasant while enjoying but its result is poisonous. Tamasika Kama is born of sleep, ignorance and laziness. It is neither pleasant while enjoying nor its results are pleasant. Of the three types of Kama the first has been universally recommended in India. It appears to be ordinary while enjoying but its results are most pleasant.

Laying emphasis upon the value of Kama in Youth, Vatsyayan has said in Kamasutra that one should enjoy Kama in youth.[1] Dividing the average age of one hundred years from the point of view of achievement of Purusarthas, into three categories, Vatsyayan has maintained that since birth to sixteen years of age one should achieve knowledge, from the age of 17 to 70, one should achieve Artha and Kama and after that one should devote the remaining life to Dharma and liberation. Thus Kama has been considered the chief Purusartha in youth. Pointing out the characteristics of Kama, Vatsyayan has said that Kama is the tendency of the desires of the five sense organs for the achievement of their corresponding objects.[2] It is the pleasure experienced by the self in the fulfilment of the sensual tendencies. Thus Kama includes lust and natural attractions. It is the cause of mutual attractions among different living beings. It is the basis of creation, it leads to procreation. The knowledge of Kama is achieved by imitations of efficient persons as well as by the study of Kamasutra. Just as the Arthasastra aims as systematic exposition of the means to Artha, similarly India has a tradition of Kamasastras discussing the means of enjoyment in minute details. However, this was done in a moral and religious background. Therefore, Yashodhara, in his Sanskrit commentary on Kamasutra, maintains "Kamasutra is a normative sastra. It aims at stating the rules by following which a man can achieve Artha, Dharma and Kama." Thus Kamasutra unravels the rules of enjoyment. This enjoyment may be both worldly and other-worldly. The Kamasutra insists upon the achievement of worldly pleasures upon the earth and spiritual welfare in heaven. Therefore, the Indian thinkers have insisted upon a harmony between Dharma, Artha and Kama. It has been insisted that Kama must be based upon Dharma. Thus while accepting all the facts concerning sex and other innate tendencies in human beings, the Indian thinkers have insisted that no enjoyment should be aimed at

1 Vatsyanyan, *Kama Sutra,* 1. 2. 3.

2 *Ibid.,* 1. 2. II.

which is antisocial. The other extreme tendency found in some Indian works, is the down right condemnation of Kama as undesirable. India has an ancient tradition of control of sense organs and sometimes even of self-repression. Brahmacharya has been explained both positively and negatively. While positively, it is conservation of sex energy for its utilisation and diversion into creative spiritual channels, its negative interpretation is based upon extreme repression of the natural tendencies. Both these interpretations can be found in ancient Indian works. These works abound in examples of the dangers of pursuing Kama. There had been a whole science of systematic repression aiming at complete elimination of the natural tendencies in human beings. However, this was not the only trend. The tradition of Kamasutra in India has been actually very powerful and popular. These authors laid strong emphasis upon the worldly enjoyments and fulfilment of natural tendencies. According to Vatsyayan, the enjoyment of Kama is as much necessary for the body as the food.[1] Just as too much food creates diseases and yet no one leaves it entirely for fear of the disease, similarly though the extremes of Kama may be injurious, no wise person should abstain from it. One should try to achieve all the three Purusarthas of Dharma, Artha and Kama. The Kamasutra of Vatsyayan describes in details, not only the daily routine of the householder, the minutest details of love making and sex enjoyment but even the techniques of pre-marital and extra-marital sex relationships as well as the activities of the prostitutes etc. It evolves a science of enjoyment in the form of sixty four arts required to be mastered for cultural development and worldly enjoyment. Thus, Kama was the most important pursuit of the householder. It can be said without exaggeration that the Kamasutra of Vatsyayan may be favourably compared with any treatise presented by any Western scholar.

It should be remembered here that Indian thinkers have insisted upon a positive attitude towards life. Upanishads, the sources of Indian philosophy have maintained that Anand is the source of creation. In the words of Taittariya Upanisad, "All the beings have their origins in *Anand*, all the things and living beings live by *Anand* and they are dissolved in *Anand*. Therefore, *Anand* is everything." Clarifying the concept of *Anand*, Brahdaranyaka Upanisad has clearly pointed out, "The only seat of *Anand* are the sex organs." Thus, many thinkers have compared Kama with the tendency of sexual intercourse. The Indian thinkers maintain that there is a natural tendency in the cosmos of the multiplication of one into many. The Shaiva sect considers the world as the product of mutual attraction between Brahman and Maya. Similar examples can be given from other philosophical and religious sects. In sum, it may be said that Kama has been given its due importance in Indian culture.

MOKSHA

The ultimate end of human life, according to Indian ethics is moksha or liberation. According to Vivekanand, "Morality is not an end in itself; mukti is its end, it is

1 *Ibid.*, 1. 1. 37.

only a means for the achievement of liberation." From Vedas to Sri Aurobindo, Indian thinkers have always considered moksha as the aim of life. It is, however, wrong to consider liberation as the sole ideal of human life. As has been already pointed out, Indian thinkers aimed at a fourfold scheme of values in which each was valuable. Moksha was the last but not the only value.

Moksha literally means deliverance. Thus, it is deliverance from all types of pains, worldly as well as other-worldly. It is a state devoid of all sufferings. It is pure bliss. It is deliverance from the cycle of rebirth. It is the achievement of other-worldly welfare. It is the unity of the Atman with Brahman. It is the highest aim. It is the highest value. It is the realisation of Ultimate Reality. Indian philosophy maintains a harmony in metaphysics, epistemology and axiology. All these aim as the same reality which is Atman in man, Brahman in cosmos and liberation as value. While all other aims are relative, moksha is the ultimate end. It is the status of identity between Atman and Brahman. This mystic realisation has been explained in the Mahavakyas of the Upanisads such as Tattvarnasi, Aham Brahmasmi etc. The microcosm and macrocosm have the same one underlying reality. Forgetfulness of this truth is ignorance. Ignorance is the cause of bondage. Bondage leads to pains and sufferings. Liberation from this depends upon the realisation of the original truth of the identity of Atman and Brahman.

The concept of liberation has taken several forms in the history of Indian philosophy. Of these the most important are as follows:

1. Positive Interpretations. Positive interpretations of Moksha may be found in the Upanisads, the Bhagvadgita and the Vedanta philosophy and the Jain metaphysics. The Advaita Vedanta defines Moksha as Brahmanhood. The Vishishta advaita defines it as Sarupya, Samipya, Salokya and Sayujya etc., including different types of relationships of man and God. Bhagvadgita has defined liberation as complete surrender and identity with the divine. Devotion has been insisted upon as the most important means for the achievement of Moksha from the positive view point. The other equally important means is knowledge and action.

2. Negative Interpretation. According to negative interpretation, Moksha is nihilistic and negative. The example of nihilism is the Shunyavada of Madhyamika Buddhist philosophers. It aims at absolute elimination of all consciousness. It is absolute negation of pain. According to negativism, as found in Nyaya, Vaishesika and Mimamsa philosophical systems, Moksha is the negation of suffering. According to Vaishesika, philosophy it is the complete elimination of nine characteristics of the self. The negative interpretation of liberation is particularly found in Buddhist thought.

3. Neutral Interpretation. Neutral interpretation may be found in Samkhya and Yoga philosophy. According to Samkhya, Moksha means complete elimination from the three types of pains and a status of absolute detachment of the self. Yoga aimed at the attainment of a consciousness absolutely detached and free from all impulses. The tradition of Yoga started in the Vedas and it has been constantly developed and practiced by Indian Philosophers to our own time. It has been the most significant contribution of Indian culture to the world. It is given what is known as liberation while living, which has been accepted as possible, not only by the orthodox schools of Indian philosophy but also by hetrodox schools of philosophy, the Jainism and Buddhism.

Thus, the most prevalent view in Indian thinking is that moksha may be achieved while living. Nyaya Vaishesika and Samkhya philosophers, however, consider moksha as possible only after death. This view, however, has not been accepted by the majority of Indian thinkers. Besides the distinction between liberation while living and liberation after death, there has been a distinction between individual and collective liberation. While the traditional Indian philosophy normally believes in Individual liberation, the Neo-Vedanta philosophers including Vivekananda, M.K. Gandhi, R.N. Tagore, Bhagwandas and Sri Aurobindo insist upon the necessity and possibility of collective liberation. Thus, it is clear that Moksha cannot be called an individualistic or extraterrestrial goal. Sri Aurobindo, particularly, has interpreted it in the light of the consciousness of the modern man. Even the most recent exponents of Indian Yoga such as Rajneesh, Mahesha and others have given an interpretation of Moksha which is acceptable even to the Western men and women. The popularity which Yoga is receiving these days in the West shows that in it Indian culture has offered something which is valuable in all times and climes.

Our discussion of the four Purusharthas, *viz.* Dharma, Artha, Kama and Moksha. In this chapter shows that Indian culture insists upon a harmoneous, multisided, comprehensive, positive, spontaneous, total and spiritual interpretation of human values. It can be said without exaggeration that this axiology provides a firm foundation for an all-round development of human individual and collectivity.

QUESTIONS FOR EXERCISE

1. Bring out the significance of Purusharthas.
2. Explain the major social values of Indian society and examine their influence on social structure.
3. How does the concept of Purusharthas provide the proper frame of reference for human action?

5

Caste and Casteism among Hindus and Muslims

THEORIES OF THE ORIGIN OF CASTE SYSTEM

Theories about the origin of caste in sociology may be classified as: Political theory, Traditional theory, Economic or Occupational theory, Ethical theory, Ethnic theory, Theory of Manu. The explanation concerning caste theories is as follows:

1. Political Theory. According to political theory of caste system, it is the Brahmin progeny of Indo-Aryan culture which developed in Gangetic plain and spread from there throughout the country. According to G.S. Ghurye, this theory was invented due to the political interests of the Brahmins. In his own words: "I may conclude that caste in India is a Brahminic child of the Indo-Aryan culture, cradled in the land of the Ganges country". Political theory was propounded first of all by the French pontiff Abbe Dubois in twelfth century A.D. In his work on the Brahmins, Denzil Ibbetson has supported Abbe Dubois in pointing out that in caste system the occupations held by the Brahmins and Kshatriyas have been considered as the best and the highest. Against the political theory, as an explanation of the origin of caste system in India, D.N. Majumdar has given the following arguments in his famous work *Races and cultures in India:*

(i) This theory has neglected the racial distinctions found among various social classes in India.

(ii) Looking at the complex Hindu social structure based upon castes it appears impossible that the aim of caste system would have been to maintain the dominancc of the Brahmin priests over Hindu society.

2. Traditional Theory. According to Traditional Theory, the caste system was created by creator Brahma himself. According to Rig Veda, Brahmins are like mouth, Kshatriyas are like the arms, Vaishyas like the stomach and the Sudras like the feet of the social body. This explanation of the origin of caste may be suitable as an explanation of the origin of a Varna System: It cannot explain the origin of thousands of castes in Hindu society.

3. Economic or Occupational Theory. Explaining the origin of caste system in India, Nesfield has said, "The function and function alone is responsible for the origin of caste system." The ancient tradition of the Hindus supports this theory. In Bhagwadgita, Shri Krishna has pointed out that the fourfold Varna system has been created by God himself. In Buddhist literature there is a mention of so many castes according to occupational distinctions, skill in various crafts and industries. It is a fact that the occupations of most of the castes in Hindu society were fixed. The words Lohar, Sonar, Chamar, Julaha etc. signify the economic occupation of these castes. However, the economic or occupational theory about the origin of caste system in India suffers from the following defects:

(i) It does not explain the hierarchy in caste system. It does not explain why some castes are considered higher and other castes lower than others. The function of a lohar or chamar is as much vital for the society as that of any other caste and yet why are these castes considered lower castes? In South India, even the cultivators are held to belong to lower castes, while their function is definitely most important for the society. Thus, no one can deny the political intrigue of the higher castes to maintain their hold on Hindu society through the caste system.

(ii) Why do all the farmers not belong to one caste? About 67% Hindus are busy in agricultural occupations. These farmers, however, belong to all the castes. If occupational theory were true then they should have belonged to one caste on the basis of economic occupation. This, however, is not so. In India, there are not as many occupations as there are castes. The number of castes amounts to several hundreds. Thus, D.N. Majumdar rightly pointed out that though function had been the basis of social stratification in ancient India, but it cannot properly and completely explain the Hindu social structure based upon the caste system.

(iii) It neglects racial elements. It does not accept any caste distinctions on the basis of race. This, however, has been proved wrong by modern discoveries.

4. Ethical Theory. S.C. Roy has propounded ethical theory about the origin of caste system in India, in the class system of Indo-Aryans, the tribal system of Pre-Dravidians and conflicts among various occupations. This theory, while emphasising the philosophical aspects of caste system in India, reflects actual facts.

5. Ethnic Theory. Some scholars have propounded ethnic theory about the origin of caste system. According to this theory, castes place to Dravidians in society. This was because the social index of the Dravidians was different from that of Aryans. The groups resembling the nasal structure of the former were therefore labelled as lower castes. According to G.S. Ghurye, the caste system was a clever scheme of the Aryans to maintain their hold on Indian society. According to D.N. Majumdar, the aim of caste system was to maintain the purity of blood. To quote his words, "Nesfield said that superiority or inferiority of occupation is represented in the hierarchy of the castes. We should think that the status of the caste depends upon the degree of purity of blood and the extent of isolation maintained by the social groups." N.K. Datta also agrees with Risley on this point. However, J.H. Hutton has rejected the ethnic theory about the origin of caste system on the following points:

(i) Why did ethnic distinction not create caste system among Muslims or Christians?

(ii) Though ethnic distinctions are found in most of the countries of the world, the caste system is peculiar to India. Why?

(iii) This theory does not explain untouchability.

This theory is disposed of by facts. In the census report of 1931 by Dr. Guha in India, the Nayars of Malabar, the Pathans of N.W.F.P. and the Brahmins of Bengal have similar ethnic characteristics. They, however, do not belong to the same caste. Such examples may be multiplied.

6. Theory of Manu. According to J.H. Hutton, the caste system was originated in the religious customs and rituals of the non-Aryan group, particularly the theory of Manu. Manu is a mystic power. According to Hutton, the traditions of endogamy, untouchability etc. have their roots in Manu. Criticising this theory of the origin of caste system D.N. Majumdar has pointed out that it is absolutely controversial as to what role may be assigned to Manu in the origin of caste system. This theory does not explain that whereas belief in Manu is found among most of the primitive tribes all over the world, why did it create caste system only in India?

Besides the above mentioned important theories concerning the origin of caste system in India some other scholars have also advanced significant views. According to D.N. Majumdar, caste system was developed to save Aryan Race and culture from intermixing with other races. According to Slater, caste system originated in order to safeguard the professional and occupational secrets. According to Gisbert, the geographical distinctions led to the development of the caste-system. Jackson points out that Hindu kings made it obligatory for everyone to follow his caste occupation. All these various views about the origin of caste system are one-sided explanations. They are true so far as they go but they do not exhaust all the explanations of this complex social institution. Caste system, complex as it is, could not originate in some one circumstance or due to some one factor. The different factors pointed out by the theories mentioned above may be taken together to arrive at a multisided explanation of caste system. In the words of J.H. Hutton, "It is urged emphatically that the Indian caste system is the natural result of the interaction of a number of geographical, social, political, religious and economic factors not elsewhere found in conjunction."

The word 'caste' is used in everyday life and we use it to distinguish one person from another. We say that such and such a person belongs to a particular caste. In saying it we generally mean to convey that he is born of parents or is a member of the family said to belong to a particular caste. In this way caste is a hereditary group. In biology this word is used only for descent or heredity. But this definition is inadequate for the purposes of sociology since, it requires a more comprehensive and clear definition. Caste may be defined as a hereditary endogamous group which decides the individual's status in the social stratification and his profession, etc. Some of the well known definitions of caste are as follows:

> "A caste is an aggregate of persons whose share of obligations and privileges is fixed by birth, sanctioned and supported by magic and or religion."[1]
>
> "A caste is a social group having two characteristics (1) Membership is confirmed to those who are born of members and includes all persons so born. (2) The members are forbidden by an inexorable social law to marry outside the group."[2]
>
> "A caste is a closed class."[3]
>
> "When a class is somewhat strictly hereditary, we may call it a caste."[4]
>
> "When status is wholly predetermined, so that men are born to their lot in life without any hope of changing it, then class takes the form of caste."[5]

Modern thinkers consider it best to enumerate the features of caste in defining it. This is what Hutton, Ghurye, N.K. Dutt[6] and many others have done. Of the predominating characteristics of caste, the following are the most important:

1. Determination by Birth. The membership of caste is determined by birth. A person remains the member of caste into which he is born and his membership does not undergo any change even if change takes place in his status, occupation, education, wealth, etc.

2. Rules and Regulations Concerning Food. Each individual caste has its own laws which govern the good habits of its members. Generally, there are no restrictions against fruit, milk, butter, dry fruit, etc. but kachcha food (bread, etc.) can be accepted only from a member of one's own or of a higher caste.

3. Definite Occupations. In the Hindu scriptures there is a mention of the occupations of all Varnas. According to Manu, the functions of the Brahmins, Kshatriyas, Vaishyas and the Sudras were definite. The functions of the Brahmins were to study, teach, guide and perform religious rituals, and to give and receive alms; that of the Kshatriyas to study, perform religious rituals, give alms, punish the evil and go to war; that of the Vaishyas to study, perform religious rituals, give alms, work in agriculture, trade and animal husbandry; that of the Sudras to do menial work for all the other varnas. Having developed from Varna system the occupations in caste system are definite. In Hindu society, even today, in most cases, the son of a blacksmith pursues the occupation of his father; the son of a carpenter becomes a carpenter, while the son of a shoemaker becomes a shoemaker.

---

1 Martindale and Monachesi, *Elements of Sociology*, p. 529.
2 Ketkar, *History of Caste in India*, p. 15.
3 Majumdar, D.N. & Madan, T.N., *An Introduction to Social Anthropology*; Asia Publishing House, Bombay, (1956), p. 221.
4 Cooley, C.H., *Social Organisation*, p. 11.
5 MacIver & Page.
6 Dutta, N.K., *Origin and Growth of Caste in India* (1931).

4. Endogamous Group. The majority of persons marry only within their own caste. Brahmins, Kshatriyas, Sudras and Vaishyas all marry within their respective castes. Westermarck has considered this to be a chief characteristic of the caste system. Hindu community does not sanctify inter-caste marriage even now.

5. Rules Concerning Status and Touchability. The various castes in the Hindu social organisation are divided into a hierarchy of ascent and descent one above the other. In this hierarchy the Brahmins have the highest and the untouchables the lowest place. This sense of superiority is much exaggerated and manifests in the south. The very touch and sometimes even the shadow of a member of the lower caste is enough to defile an individual of a high caste. In Kerala, a Namboodari Brahmin is defiled by the touch of a Nayar, but in the case of a member of a Tiya caste a distance of 36 feet must be kept to avoid being defiled and in the case of a member of the Pulayana caste the distance must be ninety-six feet. The stringent observation of the system of untouchability has resulted in some low castes of the Hindu society being called untouchables who were, consequently, forbidden to make use of places of worship, cremation grounds, educational institutions, public roads and hotels etc., and were disallowed from living in the cities.

The above-mentioned characteristics of the caste system do not take into account all the numerous variations presently taking place in the caste system. Actually, it is difficult to formulate a definite and permanent definition of caste. The most that can be done is to describe the features of the caste system in a particular context, since, the caste system is undergoing considerable modification and transformation. It would not be surprising if castes were eventually reduced to a word signifying merely a group, since inter-caste marriages are increasing and the restrictions on mutual behaviour, exchange of goodwill and conduct are breaking. Some people are changing their caste on the strength of their monetary wealth, the occupations for the various castes are no longer fixed, a member of any caste takes to any profession that he desires, the Brahmins have been deprived of much of their past glory and respect, very few caste panchayats are to be seen and even they have no control whatsoever over the members. Many people have even started excluding their caste name from the name they use. In this way, caste is continually taking on the shape of class and casteism is growing in the form of classism. On the one hand, some conditions are favouring its existence while on the other they are unfavourable.

CONDITIONS FAVOURING THE CASTE SYSTEM

Among the conditions that have favoured the continued existence of the caste system, the following are the most important:

1. Geographical Isolation. Geographical isolation has a large part to play in rendering a society static and powerless. The absence of adequate means of transport leads to the geographical isolation from others, of people who inhabit distantly situated areas and this fosters old customs, mores, traditions and superstitions all of which encourage the caste system.

2. Static Society. Hindu society is not sufficiently dynamic. There has never been any stupendous change in its political circumstances and economic conditions. Its social mores, customs and traditions have failed to change over the ages as times have marched along. But this does not mean that Hindu society has not changed at all. To say that it is static or changeless is only to indicate to extremely slow rate at which changes and modifications are instituted in it. As a general rule, the caste system was most acceptable in India in those days when the dynamic elements were at a low ebb in the society. Thus, the comparatively static nature of society is a condition favourable to the continued existence of the caste system.

3. Foreign Aggression. A further contribution to the disability and utility of the caste system was made by the foreign aggression. Many scholars hold that the caste system was born in India when the Aryans invaded the country. The Aryans were fair-skinned and victors. The natives of India were black-skinned and the victims. Hence, the society was divided into two classes, the members of the victorius class considered themselves superior to the victimised class and thought it below their dignity to associate themselves with it and to marry into it. Therefore, strict laws regarding conduct, diet, marriage, etc. were formulated. These were the fundamental constituents of the caste system.

4. Rural Social Structure. As compared with the urban social structure the rural social structure is usually unchanging and static. Old traditions are more respected in it. As the rural structure weakens, or, as urbanisation in the country increases, the caste also becomes progressively weaker.

5. Influence of Religion. The influence of religion is the most important factor contributing to the continuation of the caste system. The Hindu caste system is looked upon as a divine ordained institution. People who violate it are considered sinners and it is believed that God will punish them. Due to this reason, people do not have the courage to violate the laws of the caste system.

6. Difference of Races. The existence of many races in the country led to the formulation of many strict laws concerning discrimination. Since, each race savoured to maintain its purity. In the medieval period of Indian History stringent laws concerning caste were laid down to protect Hindu society from the Muslims.

7. Lack of Education. Lack of education occupies an important position among the factors which have encouraged the existence of caste system in Hindu society. An illiterate community is usually static and orthodox. Superstitions, traditions and mores play an important role among uneducated people. In this way, lack of education is a condition which particularly favours the caste system.

CONDITIONS UNFAVOURABLE TO CASTE

The following elements have tended to weaken the caste system in the present age:

1. Modern Education. The major part in the weakening of the caste system is played by the existing system of education. Modern education is negative as regards religion. It emphasizes democratic values such as liberty, equality and fraternity. Modern education bears the stamp of the scientific and independent thinking in the West. It has laid much stress upon the importance of man. Thus, the progress of modern education is proportionately demolishing the ties of caste, etc. Education has encouraged inter-caste marriage. The feelings of superiority and untouchability are being gradually eliminated from the minds of younger generation as children of all castes study in the same school.

2. Industrialization. Industrialization also has led to a decrease in the intensity of caste favour because persons from all castes sought and obtained employment in factories. According to A.W. Green, although the Brahmin has to take a prolonged religious bath in order to purify himself against the defilement caused by the mere shadow of a Sudra, yet it is not possible to avoid the shadow of Sudras in the crowded lanes of city and the busy offices. As a result of industrialization individuals of all castes came into mutual contact in factories, hotels, markets, trains, trams and buses, etc., and the observance of laws concerning touchability became impossible.

3. Increase in the Importance of Wealth. In the modern age, wealth is replacing caste as the basis of social prestige. Now-a-days, a person adopts that occupation which appears to him to be the most profitable. The consideration in the choice of a profession is no longer caste but individual capability and the facility in earning wealth. A wealthy Sudra is more respected than a poor Brahmin. For this reason, the ties of the caste are being loosened in the frantic race after wealth.

4. Movements of Social Emancipation. As a result of the influence of modern education there has been a veritable flood of movements for social emancipation.

5. Means of Communication. Along with the progress of industrialisation in India means of communication also developed. This, put an end to geographical isolation and thoughts, customs, etc. of different places that influenced each other. It became difficult to maintain the rigidity of caste in the whirlwind of communication set into motion by industrialisation through such means as buses, trains, trams, cars, etc. In this connection Risley has rightly pointed out that it is not possible to enquire the caste of the seller while purchasing something from him.

6. Political Agitation. An important part of the aims of the national agitation for a political awakening of the people in India was to end the discriminatory practices on the basis of the caste system. The objective of this national movement was the establishment of a democratic pattern of society in India. For this reason, it made efforts towards weakening the caste consciousness in the people.

7. New Legal Machinery. In the new legal machinery of the British government the members of all castes were similarly punished for the same offences. The establishment of judicial courts deprived the caste-panchayats of their power and they no longer retained the authority to punish a criminal. In this way, the restrictions upon the opponents of the caste system were removed and gradually its laws also lost their meaning and significance.

8. Appearance of New Social Classes. At present new classes are appearing in Indian society. These social classes are replacing the castes. The organisation of castes is vertical while that of classes is horizontal. Therefore, as the class consciousness is increasing, caste consciousness is decreasing.

9. Free Democracy in India. The most severe shock to the caste system was the establishment of a free democracy in India. Para 15 (2) of the Constitution of Indian Republic declared all citizens to be equal. The fortress of the caste system collapsed when foreign rule came to an end. According to the Untouchability Crime Act of 1955, it is a crime to prevent anyone from using a public place. The respect once accorded to the caste system dwindled through the influence of the means of transport, educational facilities, industrialization, the democratic method of government, etc.

In spite of, the presence of so many unfavourable circumstances the caste system continues to exist in an aggravated conditions in the country, and, through being identified with political interests, it has become even more strong at some places. Much in the way of a combined effort must be done to eliminate it from the country.

The disorganisation of the caste system leads people to infer that the caste system will cease to exit in the future. But some scholars have discounted this doubt. According to G.S. Ghurye,[1] there is no fear of the extinction of the caste system in the near future due to the following two conditions:

1. Election. Due to the establishment of a democracy in India administrative machinery is operated by representatives elected by the people. The method of election has done much to encourage the caste system because the candidates want to achieve their support by drumming the cause of casteism among the voters. In this way, people are asked to vote for their caste candidate and this casteism is maintained by the elected leaders after the elections are over. Political parties also sponsor only that candidate for election in a particular area whose caste is the most numerous in that area.

2. Protection of Backward Classes. The Indian Constitution has provided for the protection of the backward and scheduled castes. Some posts are reserved for them in government services. Some seats are also retained for them in the legislative assemblies. They are given all types of facilities and special scholarships for education. All these special rights have very much encouraged casteism in the backward castes since, the caste is proving very beneficial to them because of these prerogatives.

Progress of Class Consciousness

In India, on the one hand the caste is becoming weaker due to the influence of such factors as industrialization, urbanization, increase in the means of transportation, popularity of English education, political and social awakening, democratic government and laws abolishing untouchability, etc., and on the other such new organisations as labour unions, etc., on the basis of occupation, post, capacity, etc., are being established. Due to an increase in the desire for money caused by the

1 Ghurye, G.S., *Caste and Class in India*, Popular Book Depot, Bombay, (1957).

influence of materialistic tendencies, the sense of superiority or inferiority is now based on wealth and social power rather than on caste. The class consciousness, based on occupations, financial status, etc., is replacing the caste consciousness.

Casteism

All these changes lead some people to believe that the caste system will generally take on the form of a class system. But, while on the one hand, class consciousness seems to be progressing, on the other one can see progress in casteism as well. Casteism is a blind group loyalty towards one's own caste or sub-caste which does not care for the interests of other castes and seeks to realise the social, economic, political and other interests of its own group. For people who are specially gifted in a particular occupation, other occupations are very limited in India and the paths to those that are available are closed. Children of those parents who have a small income or who have no wealth only look out for service. It is very common in big business institutions and sometimes even in educational institutions that the persons belonging to the castes of the proprietors, organisers and senior officials mostly get employment. Casteism of a similar type prevails also in government services and political elections. Hence, it cannot be asserted that at the present time the caste is being destroyed and classism is increasing. Actually, in India casteism is being transformed into classism.

Future of Caste System

It is difficult to make an unqualified statement concerning the future of the caste system. It is certainly true that the restrictions on marriage, diet, mode of life etc., based on the caste system are breaking down. But, as has been pointed our earlier, casteism is increasing and caste system is being encouraged by the method of election and the government protection to backward classes. Actually, it seems more or less definite that there is no possibility of the caste system being eliminated from the Indian society in the near future. The root of the caste system goes deep in Hindu society and at its base are the important and beneficial principles of division of labour, specialisation in occupation, etc. Foreign invaders made their best efforts to wipe out the Hindu religion. In spite of all the efforts of the Muslims and the Christians no appreciable change could be brought in the caste system. It has been definitely affected somewhat by the influence of Western education and culture and its form has undergone a vast change. There is no room for doubt that this form of caste system will change further in future, it may even change beyond recognition. It will also be influenced by the development of the sense of democracy and nationalism, industrial progress, and by new political and economic movements.

CASTE AMONG MUSLIMS

Though Islam does not admit any type of distinction among its followers, the Indian Muslims have adopted caste system due to the influence of the Hindu social organisation and because most of the Indian Muslims are converts from Hindu religion. It is hence, that one finds caste system and even casteism prevailing among Indian Muslims. Those Muslims who before conversion, belonged to higher castes in Hindus consider other Muslims lower in social status. Among the more important castes found in Indian Muslims are the following:

1. Ashraf Castes: The word *sharif* in Arabic language means a gentleman. *Ashraf* is the plural of this word. Thus, Asraf are those castes which are respectable and gentle. They are considered ashraf since, their forefathers came from Arabia, Persia, Turkey and Afghanistan. These ashraf castes are four in number — Sayyad, Sheikh, Mughal and Pathan. The ancestors of Sayyad and Sheikh are considered to have come from Mecca and Madina and since, these two places are important in Islam, these castes are considered as highest among Muslims. Mughals were the inhabitants of Mongolia in Central Asia and they ruled over India for a long time. Thus, the present Mughals consider themselves to be higher than other Muslims. The Pathans are considered to be the original inhabitants of Afghanistan. Now, we will discuss these four Ashraf castes in more details.

(i) Sayyad: Just as Brahmins are on the apex in Hindu social organisation, similarly Sayyad are considered to be the highest among Muslims in India. Literally speaking, the word Sayyad means a prince. Persons belonging to this caste use the word Mir or Sayyad before their name. Among Sayyads again, there are many sub-castes such as Askari, Bakri, Hasani, Hussaini, Kazmi, Naqvi, Rizvi, Zaidi, Alvi, Abbasi, Zafari and Hashimi etc.

(ii) Sheikh: Literally Sheikh means the chief or the head. Among Muslims Sheikhs are counted after Sayyads. Generally, the religious teachers are known as Sheikh. Among Sheikhs there are several sub-castes such as Usmani, Siddiqi, Ansari, Farookhi, Khorasani, Milki, Qureshi and Kidwai etc.

(iii) Mughal: Mughals are so called after the country of their origin, Mongolia. They use the surname Mirza after their name. Among Mughals there are several sub-castes such as Uzbeg, Turkman, Tazik, Taimuri, Chugtai and Zilbash etc.

(iv) Pathan: Ancestors of Pathans came to India from Afghanistan. They use Khan surname after their proper names. Among Pathans also there are several sub-castes such as Afridi, Bangash, Barak, Durrani, Khalil, Lodhi, Rohilla and Yusufjai etc.

2. Muslim Rajput Castes: In India, in Rajasthan, the Muslims converted many Rajputs to Islam with the force of sword. Some Rajputs embraced Islam due to greed of money or prestige. Therefore, in Muslim society there is a class of Muslim Rajput castes. Since, among these the idea of higher and lower castes was already deeply imbedded, they maintained the same attitude even after embracing Islam. It is due to this attitude that they do not mix up with lower caste Muslims and do not entertain marriage relations with them. They keep their relations confined to equal or higher castes Muslims. Notable among the Rajput Muslim castes are Tomar, Chandel, Bhatti, Gautam, Chauhan, Panwar, Rathaur and Somavanshi etc.

3. Professional Castes: In this class of Muslim castes as is clear by their name, castes have been distinguished on the basis of professions such as Barhai, Dhobi, Lohar, Hajjam, Kumhar, Teli, and Sunar etc. These are the professional castes which were formerly Hindus and were later on converted into Muslims. Besides these, there are some professional castes which are no more found among Hindus but only among Muslims. Notable among these are Atishbazz, Bavarchi, Bhatiara, Bhand, Gaddi, Faqir, Momin, Julaha, Mirasi, Naubat, Kunjara, Dhunia, Kabaria, Chikwa and Manihar etc.

4. Untouchable Castes: Though the Muslim saints considered all human beings to be equal, but one may find untouchability prevalent among Muslims. For example, the Muslim Bhangi or Chamar may enter a mosque for Namaz and not for any other purpose. This proves that untouchability among Muslims is not religious but social. Thus, it is less rigorous than that found among Hindus. Even the untouchable castes among Muslims have several sub-castes such as Ghazipuri, Rawat, Lal Begi, Patthar Phora, Sheikh, Mehtar, Bansphora, Balmiki, etc.

Casteism in Muslim Marriage

Just as Hindus have caste considerations in matrimonial relationships and do not like intercaste marriages, similarly among Muslims also one finds caste considerations in marriage. Just as among Hindus only Anuloma marriages are permitted and Pratiloma marriages are rather exceptions, similarly among Muslims also Anuloma marriages are generally prevalent and the cases of Pratiloma marriages are rather few. In Anuloma marriage a higher caste male marries a female of lower caste. Referring to this custom among Muslims, it has been pointed out by some authors that the males of Ashraf castes first of all try to get a girl in their own caste and when this is not available they want to marry a girl of equal caste. If even in these one does not get a suitable match one marries with a girl of lower caste. A Sayyad may marry a Sheikh girl but a Sayyad girl cannot marry to Sheikh boy. Similarly, Sheikhs marry among Sayyads but do not give their daughters in marriage to Pathans. Among Rajput Muslims almost the same rules are observed as among Hindu Rajputs. They prefer to many their daughters among Ashraf Muslims though the latter do not like to do so.

An extreme example of casteism among Muslims may be observed in the case of occasional conflict between Shia and Sunni Muslims. These two groups often indulge in violent riots. They do not like inter-marriage. Like Hindus Muslims also like endogamy though their rules concerning exogamy are not as strict as in the case of Hindus. The Muslim social rules prohibit marriage only among very close relatives. Thus, among them marriages between maternal and paternal cousins and other relatives are permitted. Just as one has to face social boycott for violating caste rules among Hindus similarly among Muslims also social control is exercised on marriage relationships.

Caste Panchayats among Muslims

Like the Hindu castes one may find caste panchayats among Muslim castes as well. Just as among the higher caste Hindus the caste panchayats do not wield much authority similarly among high caste Muslims also caste panchayats do not have wide rights Thus, among high caste Hindus and Muslims social control is mostly exercised through the joint families. But among professional castes and untouchable castes one finds organised caste panchayats. For example, among Muslims castes like Manihar, Teli, Dhobi, Bhangi, etc. have organised caste panchayats which apply their rules to their members very strictly. Those who do not follow caste rules are boycotted from society and so long as they do not make up for the social loss and repent for it they are kept out of the caste.

Changes in Muslim Castes

Like Hindu castes, Muslim castes are also constantly changing. Urbanization, industrialization, westernization and secularization are constantly undermining the influence of caste among Hindus and Muslims. Incidence of intercaste marriages is increasing among educated persons. Untouchability, is gradually decreasing. Social intercourse is more influenced by economic status than by the castes. Like Hindus one finds taboos about social intercourse among Muslims. But caste rules among Muslims are not as strict as among Hindus. On festivals and religious occasions one finds fraternal behaviour among members of different castes. This is, due to the reason that caste system among Muslims is more social than religious. Among Hindus, it is based upon religious conceptions. It is, hence, that as compared to the Muslim community casteism has deeper roots among Hindus.

CASTEISM

Casteism is partial or one-sided loyalty in favour of a particular caste. When a mode of thinking assumes the form of an ism, it becomes rigid and partial. The sense of caste, when it implies a specific status in society, does not mean casteism. It is converted into casteism only when the tendency to consider the interest of one's own caste as opposed to the other castes is attached to it. Due to it the members of one caste do not hesitate in dealing fatal blows to the interests of the other castes, if the interests of their own caste are furthered in so doing. *In brief, Casteism is a blind group loyalty towards one's own caste or sub-caste which does not care for the interest of other castes and seeks to realise the social, economic, political and other interests of its own group.* This definition of casteism includes all the important definitions of the concept and tends to clarify further the political aspect of casteism.

Causes of Casteism

Some of the many causes of casteism are as follows:

1. Sense of Caste Prestige. The most important cause of casteism is the desire of people belonging to a particular caste to enhance the prestige of their own caste and in so doing see no wrong in adopting even the most downgraded and deleterious methods. But the prestige of the caste can be maintained only on the ground that every opportunity should be availed of in order to improve the social status of members. In order to achieve this objective every caste provides its members with all possible privileges in order to rise their social status. This tends to increase casteism.

2. Marriage Restrictions. Under the caste system the restrictions that apply to marriage turn every caste into a monogamous group in which each individual looks upon himself as related in some way to all the others and for this reason the solidarity within caste group increases which in its turn encourages casteism.

3. Urbanization. With the advent of the tendency to urbanization, it became possible for all castes to collect in large numbers in towns. At the same time the members of various castes had to face various complex problems as a result of which it became necessary to provide security for them on a communal basis. Casteism is spreading because of the necessity to fulfil this need of security.

4. Increase in the Means of Transport and Propaganda. One factor that has assisted the development of casteism is the increase in the means of transport and propaganda because this improvement has led to the establishment of intimate relationships between members of a caste who were previously separated because of distance. And the feeling of casteism is being rapidly propagated through the medium of newspapers and communal magazines.

Consequences of Casteism

On the one hand, casteism serves to further the interests of a small number of individuals but on the other hand, it is proving harmful to the nation as a whole. Some of the major consequences of casteism are the following:

1. Hindrance to the Growth of Nationalism. Casteism hinders the growth and development of nationalism. On the one hand, casteism has divided Indian society into many compartments while, on the other hand, a lot of tension and conflicts have been created on the basis of casteism between these various groups.

2. Impediment in Democracy. Most of the professional leaders in the political field exploit casteism and at election time ask the people to vote for them on communal considerations and they also succeed in their evil designs. This, sometimes, results in the election of unscrupulous individuals who do not hesitate in neglecting common good in the consideration and promotion of caste. In fact, the glories of casteism are sung even behind the scenes where there is professedly equality. Thus, casteism has been fatal to democracy. As K.M. Panikkar has rightly said, "In fact, no organization of society on the basis of equality is possible so long as the sub-caste and the joint family exist."[1]

3. Corruption. Men inspired by the sense of casteism provide all kinds of facilities to people who belong to their own castes and in doing so they resort to all kinds of immoral and corrupt activities.

1 Panikkar, K.M., *Hindu Society at Cross Roads,* (1950), p. 24.

4. Hindrance in Industrial Efficiency. Because the appointments to Government and private services are made on the basis of caste, there seems to be continuing increase in the number of inefficient and worthless people. On the other hand, the efficient and able individuals do not get the opportunity to find employment. Thus, a great obstacle is placed in the path of the nation's industrial and technological advance.

Remedies of Casteism

The following are some suggestions concerning the solution of the problems arising out of casteism:

1. Proper Education. What is most needed for a solution of the problem of casteism is proper education. The educational institutions should be able to provide an atmosphere in which caste distinctions are not encouraged while at the same time the children are allowed to develop a distaste for this kind of discrimination. A healthy point of view for casteism can thus be generated in the public. Casteism can be destroyed only by the development of new psychological tendencies and behavioural patterns.

2. Inter-caste Marriage. Inter-caste marriage provides an opportunity for two families belonging to different castes to come together. In this way, the seed of casteism is unable to strike root and even if it does so the resulting sapling will be so weak that it will, subsequently, be wiped out.

3. Lesser Use of the Word 'Caste'. One way of solving the problem of casteism is to make less frequent use of the word 'caste' so that there may be no traces of it left in the mind of the impressionable children and they should not be imbued with the idea of caste distinction. In this way, at least it will become possible to destroy the tendency of casteism in the coming generation.

4. Cultural and Economic Equality. Inequality, in the sphere of cultural and economic welfare promotes jealousy and competition among various sections of society which later assumes the form of casteism. Hence, the restoration of cultural and economic equality of various castes is an important step towards the abolition of casteism from the society.

Suggestions for the Abolition of Casteism

Mahatma Gandhi has compared caste in society to the appendix in the human body. As long as, it continues to enjoy health it serves its purpose but when it becomes diseased the only course is to eliminate it because if it is not removed it poses a threat to the existence of the entire organism. Caste cannot be declared illegal and then infringed. It is the foundation of Hindu Society. Nothing less than a revolution is needed to get rid of it. But the artificial simulation of a revolution proves harmful in the long run. Hence, as long as the society is not prepared to change the system and to adopt some other social order in its place, it is best to confine oneself to reformation. In this connection, different scholars have expressed different views and have made various suggestions. Some of the important suggestions are the following:

1. In Dr. M.N. Srinivas's opinion most of the shortcomings of the caste system can be removed and the door opened to democratic equality through adult franchise, five-year plans, the provision of education, constant progress of the backward classes and the influence of the culture of higher castes on the living standards of the lower castes.

2. According to Dr. Ghurye, the conflict originating in casteism can be removed by encouraging inter-caste marriages. Co-education should be introduced at the primary level and boys and girls should be given the opportunity to come together. This will lead to improvement of behaviour between different sexes simultaneously with which casteism will be actively refuted. Inter-caste marriages will be encouraged and the individuals marrying outside their own castes will be instrumental in creating an atmosphere that will be fundamentally opposed to casteism.

3. According to the suggestion put forward by Dr. Rao, in order to put an end to casteism and to deprive it of its very basis, the creation of some optional groups should be encouraged in which the communal tendencies of the individual can be manifested and organised. Casteism will decrease as the number of these groups increases because the individuals will have the opportunity to express their instincts and motives outside the caste.

4. It is suggested by Mrs. Iravati Karve that in order to put an end to the conflict arising out of casteism it is necessary to create economic and cultural equality between the castes.

5. According to P.N. Prabhu, the conflicts created by casteism can be ended only when the internal aspects of conduct are influenced. For this it is necessary to try and develop new attitudes in the people. The cinema can do much towards the creation of these attitudes.

The notion of caste has been existent in Indian society for almost thousands of years. Today, it has become an impediment in the progress of the country. It is necessary to change its form in order to ensure the development of national sentiment and the progress and success of democracy in the country. But, this cannot be achieved in a span of few years. For this, it is necessary to determine the extent to which caste system should be developed and then all governmental and non-governmental sources in the country should be employed for the achievement of that level of development. The first step would be to remove the idea of caste discrimination from the minds of the future generations. Coeducation will encourage inter-caste marriages. Further, the idea of eliminating words that indicate caste from names should also be propagated and made popular. Caste committees and associations should be prevented legally and the Government should prevent appointments being made to posts on the basis of caste, whether in Government or non-government organizations. In this way, it is necessary to make efforts in every direction for the elimination of casteism.

QUESTIONS FOR EXERCISE

1. Define caste and explain its origin and characteristics.
2. Describe the structural features of caste system in India.
3. Examine the structural and functional features of caste in India.

6

The Untouchability

In 1935, the Government of India prepared a list of castes for providing special facilities to the untouchable castes. This list included 429 castes whose total population numbered 5-35 crore. These castes were called scheduled castes by virtue of their inclusion in the list. They were also called untouchables. The problem of untouchability is a serious social problem in the Indian society.

Definition of Untouchability

It is extremely difficult to define untouchability. *In fact, it implies those disabilities which were imposed upon the scheduled castes by the superior castes.* In Untouchability Offences Act, 1955, the word untouchability was given this connotation. According to it, "It is an offence to prevent any person on the ground of untouchability (a) from entering any place of public worship which is open to other persons, professing the same religion, (b) from worshipping or offering prayers or performing any religious service in any place of public worship or bathing in or using the waters of any sacred tank, well, spring or water-course in the same manner as is permissible to other persons professing the same religion; and (c) from access to or use of a shop, hotel, public restaurant or place of public entertainment or public conveyance or hospital, dispensary or educational institution or charitable trust." Dr. Bhim Rao Ambedkar and Mahatma Gandhi have also defined untouchability on the basis of some disabilities. In this way, disabilities are a sign of untouchability. Dr. D.N. Majumdar has written, "The untouchable castes are those who suffer from various social and political disabilities, many of which are traditionally prescribed and socially enforced by higher castes."[1] *In brief, untouchables are those castes which are subject to some disabilities in every walk of life — social, religious, economic and political.* This definition will be further clarified by a detailed description of these disabilities.

Disabilities of Harijans

Untouchables suffer from the following disabilities —

---

1 Majumdar, D.N., *Races and Cultures of India,* Asia Publishing House, Bombay, (1958), p. 326.

(i) *Religious disabilities.* In India, the Harijans were subjected to various religious disabilities in the society. They were prevented from entering temples, monastries and cremation grounds, and could not make use of them because it was believed that these places would become impure by their touching them. In this way, the Harijans could not worship in the temple. Their presence was considered sufficient to defile the gods, let alone their worshippers.

But, the disabilities imposed upon the Harijans in India are pre-eminently social and economic, the removal of which will, in itself, eliminate their backward condition in respect of political status. Actually, the religious disabilities of the Harijans are also their social disabilities.

(ii) *Social disabilities.* In the social sphere the disabilities of the Harijans are the following .

1. Prevention from the use of Public Roads. Hudson has written that the presence of a particular untouchable caste in Tamil Nadu was considered so derogatory that their members were prevented from using the public roads in the day time and consequently, they were obliged to do their work at night. Their shadow was enough to defile the members of the higher castes. Thus, upon seeing the members of the higher castes, the Harijans would adopt a prostrate posture upon the ground so that their shadow may not fall on the members of higher castes.

2. Prevention from the use of Public Wells. In almost, all Indian villages the Harijans were forbidden to use the well for drawing water, and this convention was enforced with a greater or lesser degree of strictness. In Bengal, they were permitted to come near the well but not allowed to draw water from it. Only a higher caste Hindu could draw water for them. In some other states the untouchables were not permitted even to approach the well.

3. Prevention from Entering Schools. The Harijan children did not have the right to enter the schools because if they sat down to study along with other children, it would have defiled the latter. On the other hand, there were no separate schools for the Harijans. Actually, education was not even considered necessary for them. If they insisted upon being taught, they had to sit out in the open sun in order to study. In many religious texts education has been forbidden for the lower castes.

4. Other Social Restrictions. Besides, the foregoing disabilities the Harijans were subjected to many other social restrictions. In marriages, the Harijan bride and bridegroom were not allowed to sit in the palanquin. Among the Chamars, the bridegroom was harassed by the Rajputs if he sat on a horse. The Harijans were not allowed the freedom of adopting a respectable outfit. The hair-dresser would not tend their hair. The washerman would not wash their clothes and the shopkeeper would not supply them with food.

(iii) *Economic disabilities.* The disabilities of the Harijans were not restricted only to the social sphere but extended into the economic sphere too. Due to their social disabilities they could not retain any interest in or enthusiasm for their occupation. They did not have the permission to engage in the professions of the higher castes. Their conventional occupations were dirty and soiled and their means for earning their bread and butter were limited Even now, there is next to no education among the Harijans. They are burdened with debt while poverty and famine conditions prevail among them. They live in dirty slums in which new diseases are always making their life miserable. There is no medical provision for them, since, the high caste doctor becomes defiled merely by touching them.

Caste and Untouchability

There are many racial, religious and social causes of untouchability in India. The major cause is the caste system. The untouchable castes are the most inferior among the numerous castes in Hindu community. To the caste system is attached the sense of high and low, which is the fundamental cause of untouchability. Another cause of untouchability is the prevalence of many taboos in the caste system. Just as there are taboos for the higher castes, intermarrying, eating and mixing with the lower castes, in the same way taboos were created, for preventing touching and even seeing of the lower castes which did the dirty work, as a consequence of the feeling of superiority and inferiority. These castes came to be called the untouchables. In this way, untouchability in India is based upon the caste system. Untouchability is the result of the sense of superiority and inferiority, and social taboos. In *Caste and Class in India,* Ghurye has written that in Poona, during the reign of the Marathas the untouchable castes Mahar and Mang were not allowed to enter the gates of towns between three o'clock in the afternoon and nine in the morning because the shadows are at their longest at this time and there is the fear of the higher Brahmins being defiled. In Maharastra, the Mahar caste could spit only in small containers tied around their neck because were they to spit upon the road, it might defile some superior Hindu by touching his foot. Often, if some Brahmin passed their way the Mahars had to destroy the imprints of their feet with brambles and lie down at a distance in order to protect the Brahmin from their shadow. In Malabar, the Shanar had to keep a distance of twenty-four feet from the Brahmin, the Tiya a distance of thirty-six feet and the Pulayan a distance of more than ninety-six feet. It is obvious that the biggest cause of untouchability is the segregation of relation within the castes.

Causes of Untouchability

But, all this does not mean that untouchability is caused solely by the caste system and the elimination of the latter would mean the automatic eradication of the former. Actually, there are other causes of untouchability besides the caste system. In '*Castes in India*' J.H. Hutton writes, "The origin of the position of superior castes is partly religious and partly a matter of social custom." In this way, the three fundamental causes of untouchability are racial, religious and social factors.

1. Racial Factors. The fundamental causes of untouchability are racial factors. The victor always considers himself superior to the vanquished and wants to be spared the latter's influence. This is no less true in the case of races. In the opinion of some scholars the Aryan invaders designated to some derogatory names the non-Aryan races settled in India and considered them untouchable. In Assam, the Ao branch of the Naga tribe is not allowed to wear ivory ornaments on both arms. According to Hutton, this restriction has been imposed upon the Ao people because they are different from the other Naga tribes from the racial viewpoint. In Garhwal, the bride and bridegroom belonging to the artisan and Harijan castes, which had low social status were not allowed the use of the palanquin or the horse. The cause of this has been explained by some sociologists to be the advent of the higher castes from the plains into the native homeland of the artisans and Harijans. These examples prove that racial distinctions have some hand in the origin of the custom of untouchability. Dr. D.N. Majumdar has written correctly, "The disabilities of the so called, 'depressed' castes are not ceremonial but probably founded on racial and cultural differences."[1]

2. Religious Factors. Religious beliefs and conventions are also causes of untouchability. In religion, much importance is attributed to purity and divinity. Thus, it was considered essential to abstain from the people who engage in impure occupations. In the words of Dr. Ghurye, "Idea of purity, whether occupational or ceremonial, is found to have been a factor in the genesis of caste or the very soul of the idea and practice of untouchability."[2] It was the sense of purity which led to the sweepers and cobblers being designated as untouchables in Hindu society. Besides purity another cause of the origin of untouchability is the social taboos. Intermarriage among castes, consumption of the object of totem, or its disrespect in any way are forbidden. Besides these, there are a number of other taboos prevalent in the castes like avoiding washerman because he washes clothes seeped in secretion of the women's menstrual cycle. Thus, in the Vol. I of Census of India Hutton has written, "There can be little doubt that the idea of untouchability originates in taboo."

3. Social Factors. Social customs and conventions shared the burden of maintaining the untouchability recognised by the religious and racil causes. Social conventions are so influential that even the members of the untouchable castes dare not violate the customs of untouchability. In the "Hindu" of 24th December 1932, it was written about the Puraadavanan caste established in the Tinneveli district of Madras that they are not only considered untouchable but even unpresentable and, they cannot leave their dwelling places in the day time because their is a fear of their defiling the other castes. They wash their clothes at night. When Thakkar Bappa went to meet them they came out only upon extreme entreaty and when they came their entire body was trembling because they were burdened by the social stigma of untouchability.

In this way, the racial, religious and social factors are the major ones among the causes of the origin of untouchability.

Efforts to Eradicate Untouchability

There have been numerous governmental and non-governmental efforts towards

1 *Ibid.*, p. 327.

2 Ghurye, G.S., *Caste and Class in India,* Popular Book Depot. Bombay, (1957), p. 241.

the eradication of untouchability in India and the improvement in the condition of the untouchables. The governmental effort is directed towards the prevention of untouchability on the one hand and improvement in the condition of the untouchables on the other. In the paragraph 46 of the Indian Constitution much emphasis has been laid upon the spread of education among the backward castes and the protection of their economic interest.

The Indian Constitution declares the equality of all citizens of India. The following paragraphs in the Constitution provide for the eradication of untouchability.

Para 15 (1) — The state will not discriminate against any citizen on grounds only of religion, race, caste, sex, place of birth, or any of them.

(2) No citizen shall, on grounds only of religion, race, caste, sex, place of birth or any of them, be subject to any disability, restriction or condition with regard to: —

(a) Access to shops, public restaurants, hotels and places of public entertainment, or

(b) The use of wells, tanks, bathing ghats, roads and places of public resort maintained wholly or partly out of state funds, or dedicated to the use of the general public.

Para 16 (1) — There shall be equality of opportunity for all citizens in matters relating to employment or appointment to any office under the state.

(2) No citizen shall on grounds only of religion, race, caste, sex, descent, place of birth, residence or any of them, be ineligible for or discriminated against in respect of any employment or office under the state.

(3) Nothing in this article shall prevent Parliament from making any law prescribing, in regard to a class or classes of employment or appointment to any office under any state specified in the First Schedule or any local or other authority within its territory, any requirement as to residence within that state prior to such employment or appointment.

Para 17 — 'Untochability' is abolished and its practice in any form forbidden. The enforcement of any disability arising out of 'Untouchability' shall be an offence punishable in accordance with law.

The following provision has been made for the eradication of untochability in the Directive Principles of state policy in the Indian Constitution:—

Chapter 6 — The government will develop the economic and educational interests of the weakest classes, especially scheduled castes and scheduled backward castes, with special precautions and will protect them from social injustice and all kinds of exploitation.

Article 46 — The state shall promote with special care the educational and economic interests of the weaker sections of the people and in particular, of the scheduled castes and the scheduled tribes and shall protect them from social injustice and all forms of exploitation.

Article 164 — Provided that in the State of Bihar, Madhya Pradesh and Orissa, there shall be Minister in charge of tribal welfare who may in addition, be in-charge of welfare of the scheduled castes and backward classes or any other work.

Article 320 (1) — Seats shall be reserved in the house of the people for:

(a) The scheduled castes;

(b) The scheduled tribes except the scheduled tribes in the tribal areas of Assam; and

(c) The scheduled tribes in the autonomous districts of Assam.

(2) The number of seats reserved in any state for the scheduled castes or the scheduled tribes under clause (1) shall bear, of as nearly as may be the same proportion to the total number of seats allotted to that state in the house of the people as the population of the scheduled castes in the state or the scheduled tribes in the state or part of the state as the case may be in respect of which seats are so reserved, bears to the total population of the state.

Article 332 (1) — Seats shall be reserved for these scheduled castes and the scheduled tribes, except the scheduled tribes in the tribal areas of Assam in the Legislative Assembly of every state specified in the Part A or Part B of the First Schedule.

(2) Seats shall be reserved also for the autonomous districts in the Legislative Assembly of Assam.

Article 335 — The claims of the members of the scheduled castes and the scheduled tribes shall be taken into consideration, consistently with the maintenance of efficiency of administration, in the making of appointments to services and posts in connection with the affairs of the Union or of a state.

Article 331 (1) — There shall be a special officer for the scheduled castes and scheduled tribes to be appointed by the President.

(2) It shall be the duty of the special officer to investigate all matters relating to the safeguards provided for the scheduled castes and scheduled tribes under this constitution and report to the President upon the working of those safeguards at such intervals as the President may direct and the President shall cause all such reports to be laid before each House of Parliament.

Article 340 (1) — The President may by order appoint a Commission consisting of such persons as he thinks fit to investigate the conditions of socially and educationally backward classes within the territory of India and the difficulties under which they labour and to make recommendations as to the step that should be taken by the Union or any State to remove such difficulties and to improve their condition and as to the grants that should be made for the purpose by the Union or any state and the condition subject to which such grants should be made, and the order appointing such Commission shall define the procedure to be followed by the Commission.

According to the 17th paragraph of the Indian Constitution, untouchability is a punishable offence. In 1955, the Indian Government passed the Untouchability

Offences Act in which any person forcing the disabilities of untouchability can be sentenced to six months imprisonment or a fine of Rs. 500 or both for his first offence. For every subsequent offence the sentence will include both a term in jail as well as a fine. If considered necessary the punishment can also be increased. According to this Act, the following activities were declared offensive, preventing entrance into public temples or places of worship, preventing the drawing of water from sacred lakes, wells, falls or spring, preventing people from the use of dharamshala, inn, hotel, river bank, cremation ground, water tank, water tap, educational institution, public hospital, public restaurant, preventing the Harijans from pursuing any general occupation, doing a barber's job or any general activities and harassing them or discriminating them on the basis of untouchability at such times as religious festivals and residential houses, business or profession.

Besides enacting laws against untouchability the government of India also initiated propaganda against untouchability throughout the country. All the states observe 'Harijan Weeks' and 'Harijan Day'. In States and districts, advisory committees have been organised which increase contact between untouchables and superior Hindus. Books, handbills, posters and pamphlets are printed in Hindi, English and regional languages and distributed among the public in large number. Films and radio are also used as means of propaganda against untouchability.

Seats in services based upon all India competitions and in services to which selections are made in other ways have been reserved for members of the scheduled castes. When the adequate number of members is not forthcoming from the tribal groups their reserved seats are also made over to the members of the scheduled castes.

Economic Improvement

Realising the financial problems of the Harijans the Government have taken the following steps in the direction of their financial improvement —

(i) In nearly all the States of India laws have been enacted for defending the untouchables from the Mahajans.

(ii) In Bihar and Orissa, the Harijans had to become slaves of the moneylenders in the event of their inability to repay debt. Now, this tradition has come to an end due to new laws.

(iii) In Andhra, Bihar, Orissa, Bombay, Madras, Uttar Pradesh and Saurashtra the Government have turned useless and unoccupied land into cultivable land and distributed it among the Harijans.

(iv) The governments of Andhra, Bihar, Orissa, Assam, Madhya Pradesh, West Bengal and Bhopal have enacted laws by virtue of which the Harijan cultivating the land is to be considered the land-owner and cannot be deprived of it.

(v) The Government are giving financial assistance to the Harijans in order that they may be able to buy agricultural implements, animals, manure, superior seeds, modern tools of agriculture etc.

(vi) Assistance to Agriculture, Cottage Industries and Animal Husbandry is being given. In Assam, Bihar, Bombay, Uttar Pradesh, Hyderabad and West Bengal, the Harijans are being assisted financially as well as otherwise for the development of their cottage industries. Training centres are also being opened for teaching people and making them skilled in cottage industries. Animal husbandry and poultry farming are also being encouraged among the Harijans.

(vii) The Government of India is also providing aid to non-governmental institutions which are exerting effort for the eradication of untouchability. In 1954, the Indian Government aided the State Government, Harijans Sevak Sangh, Indian Depressed Classes League and the Harijan Ashram of Prayag to the extent of four crores of rupees.

(viii) The educational facilities provided by the Government to the Harijans are in the form of free education, scholarships, books, stationery and other educational materials.

(ix) According to the Indian Constitution, candidature had been reserved in government services for untouchables for a period of ten years. Not only in Central Government services but also in state government services these seats are reserved even now. The condition of the untouchables improved due to the 'Admission to Malabar Mandir Act' and 'Prohibition of Public Disability Act' of the Madras government. In order to arrange for the progress of the Harijans, the Madras government appointed a Labour Commissioner and enacted many laws for defending the Harijans from the land-lords and also in order to provide them with land. The governments of other states also followed the lead of Madras government. In Uttar Pradesh, two Parliamentary Secretaries were appointed for improving the condition of the Harijans. Many co-operative societies were also opened for the Harijans. Many Harijan students were given scholarships.

Non-Governmental Efforts

Besides, the programme for political awakening, the Indian Natioanl Congress made efforts for the eradication of untouchability. The attempts made by Gandhiji in this direction are well known. As a result of his efforts the untouchables slowly got rid of their social disabilities. The doors of the universities, temples, public places etc. were opened to them. In the beginning, the superior Hindus opposed these improvements but they later agreed to them. Besides the Congress many other political parties took part in the emancipation of the Harijans. Among them, the work done by the Depressed Class Union. The Social Service League, Depressed Classes League, Andhra Deen Seva Sangh, Depressed Classes Conference and Scheduled Castes Federation deserve mention. But the Harijan Sevak Sangh had made the maximum efforts in this direction. In 1932, this Sangh was started under the leadership of Thakkar Bapa. There are many branches of this Sangh in Andhra, Tamil Nadu, Mysore, Hyderabad, Gujarat, Maharashtra, Karnataka, Uttar Pradesh, Bihar and Delhi. 120 Boarding Houses are being managed by the Harijan Sevak Sangh. As a result of the efforts made by the Tamil Nadu Sangh 100 big temples were opened for the Harijans. The Sangh achieved notable success in opening the public places to the Harijans. Many Harijan students should be thankful to the Sangh for their scholarships which they got mainly due to the efforts of the Sangh. Technological schools have also been opened for imparting training in cottage industries and this too has come about mainly through the efforts of the Sangh. Among these institutions, thc Harijan Audyogik Grah Delhi, Harijan Audyogik School and Hostel Kadambokam, Harijan Ashram Allahabad, Harijan Audyogik School Kanjivaram deserve to be mentioned. Institutions of women include Harijan Balika Vidyalaya Sabarmati, Harijan Balika Sadan Hugh, Anjani Harijan Girls Hostel Bezwada, Kastoorba Balika Ashram Okhla etc.

Suggestions for the Eradication of Untouchability

The methods of eradication of untouchability are now known to all educated people. The following suggestions can be made in this direction —

1. Education should be spread among the Harijans and this should include both general education as well as technical education. Education should be free, coupled with facilities of scholarship, books, stationery, hostels etc.

2. Laws should be formulated for legal protection from interest upon loans and deprivation of land in order to improve the financial condition of the Harijans.

3. The Harijans should be helped in every conceivable way so as to remove their economic disabilities.

4. The Harijans should be provided with land, animals, ploughs, seeds, manure and agricultural tools for agriculture. Financial assistance for cottage industries should be supplemented by technical training.

5. Laws should be formulated for preventing the Harijans from being subjected to social disabilities.

6. Laws removing the religious disabilities which burden the Harijans should also be enforced.

7. Platform speeches, radio, newspaper, the press and other means of communication should assist in the propaganda against untouchability.

8. In spite of the enforcement of all the above mentioned measures, it will take the Harijans a long time to achieve equality with the superior castes. Thus, until they do so, same places should be reserved for them in the government services.

9. It is necessary that seats should be reserved for the Harijans in the legislatures for some time to come. Some people contend that this violates the democratic principle of equality, but the people who have been deprived of equality for hundreds of years need some privileges in order to restore them to the general level. Once, they have become equal to the superior castes the privileges will no longer be necessary.

10. The eradication of the caste system is very essential for the removal of untouchability. Actually, the caste system is the biggest single cause of untouchability even though it is not the sole cause. Thus, the eradication of the caste system will also remove the tradition of untouchability.

11. It is necessary that there should be an ever increasing contact between the Harijans and the caste/Hindus at the same time that all the above measures are being put into practice, so that the tradition of untouchability should be destroyed and the feeling of sheer disgust which the superior Hindus harbour for the untouchables as well as the sense of inferiority of the Harijans should be eliminated. This contact will reduce mutual discrimination and culminate in the untouchables attaining a social status equal to that of caste Hindus.

QUESTIONS FOR EXERCISE

1. What are the disabilities of untouchables? Discuss the efforts made by the Government to remove them.
2. Throw light on the problem of untouchability in Indian society.
3. What are the problems of scheduled castes and tribes? Examine the effects of the statutory steps to remedy them.

Table 7: *Scheduled Castes in India 1981*

State/UT	Population ('000)	Percentage
India	2,04,755	15.8
A.P.	7,962	14.9
Assam	NA	NA
Bihar	10,142	14.5
Gujarat	2,438	7.2
Haryana	2,464	19.2
HP.	2,054	29.6
J & K	497	8.3
Karnataka	5,595	15.2
Kerala	2,549	10.0
M.P.	7,359	14.1
Maharashtra	4,480	7.1
Manipur	18	1.3
Meghalaya	5	0.4
Nagaland	NA	NA
Orissa	3,866	14.7
Punjab	4,512	26.9
Rajasthan	5,839	17.0
Sikkim	18	5.8
Tamil Nadu	8,881	18.4
Tripura	310	15.1
U.P.	23,453	21.2
West Bengal	12,001	22.0
Andaman Nicobar	NA	NA
Arunachal	3	0.5
Chandigarh	64	14.1
Dadra Nagar Haveli	2	2.0
Delhi	1,122	18.0
Goa, Daman Diu	23	2.3
Lakshadweep	NA	
Mizoram	NA	
Pondicherry	97	16.0

7

Backward Classes and Minorities

BACKWARD CLASSES

Backward Classes, the deprived sections of society, is an omnibus expression embracing the Scheduled Tribes, the Scheduled Castes, the denotified tribes, nomadic tribes and other (economically) Backward Classes (O.B.C.).

Deprived Sections of society have been classified into three categories They are: 1. Scheduled Castes, 2. Scheduled Tribes and 3. Other Backward Classes. The Other Backward Classes (O.B.C.) include denotified Tribes, formerly known as 'Criminal Tribes' and 'Nomadic and semi-Nomadic Tribes.'

The Indian Constitution says:

> "15 (4) Nothing in this Article or in clause (2) of Article 29 shall prevent the State from making any special provision for the advancement of any socially backward classes of citizens or for the Scheduled Castes and Scheduled Tribes."

Thus, a category of Other Backward Classes has been recognised in the Constitution. A provision is also made in Article 340 whereby the President may appoint a commission to investigate the conditions of socially and educationally backward classes.

Such a Commission was appointed by the President under the Chairmanship of Kakasaheb Kalelkar on the 29th January, 1953, and report was submitted on the 30th March, 1955.

The Commission was requested, among other things, to suggest a criterion, if necessary, to treat any other communities (in addition to the Scheduled Castes and Scheduled Tribes specified by notification issued under Articles 341 and 342 of the Constitution) socially and educationally backward. The Commission was also, if necessary, requested to prepare a list of such communities setting out their approximate numbers and their territorial distribution. Further, the Commission was expected to investigate conditions of all such socially and educationally backward classes and the difficulties under which they laboured.

Criteria of Backwardness

The Commission suggested that the following groups be considered backward:

(a) those who have low social position in the traditional caste hierarchy of Hindu society;

(b) those who suffer from stigma of untouchability or near untouchability (these are already classified as Scheduled Castes);

(c) those tribes who are not yet sufficiently assimilated in the general social order (these are already classified as Scheduled Tribes);

(d) those who owing to long neglect have been driven as a community to crime (these were known as Criminal Tribes and now known as ex-Criminal Tribes or Denotified Groups);

(e) those nomads who do not enjoy any social respect and who have no appreciation of a fixed habitation (these may be called Nomadic or semi-Nomadic Tribes).

The Government of India accepted only the last two groups under the head "Other Backward Classes" because the denotified Groups and the Nomadic Tribes in their opinion had some special problems in addition to those which they shared with the other weaker sections of the Indian society.

Backward Classes Movement

During the British regime the socially advanced classes got the advantage of the traditionally inherited skills, education and employment opportunities. The Brahmins and other advanced classes could take advantage of the facilities offered by the British administration for education and employment. They were also fortunate in getting into the Government service in good numbers. Lower sections of the society, among whom were also those who suffered from untouchability, on account of their economic condition and social and cultural backwardness, could not avail of the educational facilities and consequently suffered in relation to employment opportunities. The lot of the "untouchables" became worse. With changes coming over the socio-economic pattern of life, some of them lost their traditional vocations. This, put them further into dire material poverty. Untouchability, association with unclean occupations, material poverty, denial of opportunities for education and employment, all these together were responsible for the socio-economic conditions in which these sections of the Hindu community found themselves at the beginning of the twentieth century. They came to be described as "depressed classes". Subsequently, the tribal people, people of denotified tribes and the depressed classes were lumped together and were, as a group, called "Backward classes".

Special educational facilities were offered to the depressed classes, particularly in the then provinces of Madras and Bombay. This action was partly taken in response to the movements of Justice Party in Madras and Satya Shodhak Samaj in the then-province of Bombay, organised mainly by non-Brahmins.

The tribal people, members of the "depressed classes", members of the denotified tribes and nomadic tribes had many difficulties in common. But the members of "depressed classes" suffered the most from untouchability and association with unclean vocations. This was not the case with other groups. Problems of the "depressed classes", now known as the Scheduled Castes and whose members Gandhiji called Harijans, would only be considered here. The Scheduled Tribes and the Other Backward Classes and matters related to their welfare have been treated separately.

The Epic Fast

The question of Backward Classes particularly that of the "depressed classes", now known as Scheduled Castes, got intensively politicised by about 1930. On behalf of the "depressed classes" there was a demand for special protection in the Indian political set-up through reservations of seats in legislative bodies. Gandhiji who was detained in the Yarvada prison undertook his epic fast saying "I would far rather see that the Hinduism died than that untouchability lived". He resisted political separation of untouchables from the Hindus by staking his life. The Poona Pact was signed by Dr. B.R. Ambedkar. M.C. Raja and Pandit Madan Mohan Malaviya, on the 25th September, 1932. The fast was broken. Gandhiji's life was saved. Struggle for the rights of the members of the "depressed classes" entered a new phase.

Leaving aside the political aspects of the question, it must be said that the fast and the then, utterly miserable prevailing conditions among untouchables, opened the eyes of the Hindus to the need of doing away with untouchability and working for improving socio-economic conditions of the Harijans, the members of the Scheduled Castes. With a view, to bringing about a change in the conditions under which the Harijans lived, the All-India Anti-Untouchability League with a network of Provincial Boards, was set-up. The Nawab of Bhopal, one of the prominent Indian princes, gave a donation of Rs.5,000 to this organisation. Shri Amritlal Thakkar *alias* Thakkar Bapa of the Servants of Indian Society, a true servant and friend of backward communities, was appointed the general secretary of the League. This organisation came to be known afterwards as Harijan Sevak Sangh. After the release of Mahatma Gandhi from jail, a country-wide campaign for the removal of untouchability was carried on under the auspices of the Sangh. Temples were thrown open in the South where there were not only untouchables but in some rare places there were "unseeables" and "unapproachables" backwards. The famous Guru Vayur temple was thrown open to Harijans, by persuasion and agitation. The temple entry movement and other activities of Sangh broke down the hard core of untouchability. Most of the Hindus were persuaded to consider untouchability a blot on Hindu religion. Some of them were sympathetic to the idea of allowing Harijans to draw water from the same public wells as they used. The social climate started changing, though slowly. The places where untouchability was practised were identified. They were: (i) public wells, and tanks, (ii) hotels and hair-cutting saloons, (iii) temples, (iv) schools, and (v) residential quarters. The practice of untouchability had to be eradicated from at least these places, completely.

Religious Conversion

Another question which is historically inextricably interwoven with the welfare of the Scheduled Castes is that of religious conversion. Many thought that with the change of religion most of the problems of the Scheduled Castes would be over.

Under the circumstances, employment of traditional methods and perseverance of the Christian missionaries won many people from among the Scheduled Castes over the Christianity, during the British days. With the passage of time, however, the Scheduled Tribes living in compact, inaccessible, hilly, forest areas succumbed to mass conversion on a large scale. As a result there are more Christians in and from amongst the Scheduled Tribes today than in and from amongst the Scheduled Castes. Conversion to Christianity among Scheduled Castes, it can now be said, has come to a standstill.

Dr. Ambedkar, one of the foremost leader of the Scheduled Castes, was a man of sterling virtue and of very high order of intelligence. He led a mass movement and struggled to better the condition of Scheduled Castes. As a renowned, constitutional lawyer, he worked with other national leaders of India in drafting the Constitution of the Indian Republic. Efforts were then made to provide in the Constitution remedial measures to improve conditions of Backward Classes including the Scheduled Castes. As a Minister in charge of the portfolio of law in the first cabinet of the Government of Independent India, Dr. Ambedkar gave shape to the Hindu Code Bill which aimed at bringing fundamental reform in Hindu society. This was the second stage of the struggle to give a new deal to those who suffered owing to limitations in Hindu society. Finding it difficult to rid Hinduism of untouchability and social inequalities, Dr. Ambedkar advocated the idea of conversion to his followers from the Scheduled Castes. With the object of liberating the members of the Scheduled Castes from the century-old burden of inferiority, subordination and humiliating conditions resulting in social and political disabilities, he preached conversion, and embraced Buddhism. Dr. Ambedkar later decided to start a mass movement, specially among he followers from Scheduled Castes, for conversion to Buddhism. He held a big rally of about three lakh persons of Scheduled Castes at Nagpur on the 14 October, 1956. He was to have addressed a similar rally in Bombay where about 10 lakh of his Scheduled Caste followers were expected to listen to his massage of conversion. But he got ill and expired soon after. Subsequently, this conversion movement started by Dr. Ambedkar did not show signs of much progress.

The Classification

The credit of classification of Backward Class into three categories, *viz.* (i) Depressed Classes, (ii) Aboriginal and Hill Tribes, and (iii) Other Backward

Classes in which were included some of intermediate classes, goes to the former Bombay Province. This classification was based on the recommendations of a committee appointed for the purpose and presided over by Mr. Start. The Committee had Dr. B.R. Ambedkar and Shri A.V. Thakkar as its members.

The Indian Constitution

It was natural that after the attainment of independence in the year 1947, the Constituent Assembly provided salutary safeguards in the Constitution for the backward communities such as Scheduled Castes and Scheduled Tribes by defining them as socially and educationally backward classes of citizens.

The Constitution also lays down in Part IV under the head Directive Principles of the State Policy as follows:

"That the State shall promote with special care the educational and economic interests of the weaker sections of the people and in particular of the Scheduled Castes and Scheduled Tribes and shall protect them from social injustice and all sorts of exploitation." (Article 46) This is followed up by other safeguards for Scheduled Castes and Scheduled Tribes in particular and socially and educationally backward classes in general. Thus, the Constitution of India is unparalleled and unique not only in proclaiming to secure to its citizens 1. Justice, 2. Liberty, 3. Equality, and 4. Fraternity in the broad sense of the terms, but in spelling out provision in so many articles of the Constitution, for the benefit of weaker sections of the people.

Some of the important points on which safeguards for Scheduled Castes have been provided may be briefly enumerated:

(i) Untouchability to be considered a cognisable offence, punishable in accordance with the law;

(ii) reservation of seats in legislatures both at the Centre and in the State is proportion to the Backward Class population;

(iii) reservation in the Government services consistent with the maintenance of efficiency of administration;

(iv) provision of educational facilities;

(v) appointment of a special Officer (Commissioner for Scheduled Castes and Scheduled Tribes) to investigate and report to the President upon the working of the safeguards and presentation of his report to the Parliament, every year;

(vi) notification by the President of India, of castes or groups or part of a caste to be deemed as Scheduled Caste for the purpose of the Constitution, Parliament alone being competent to include or exclude any caste from the list thus specified;

(vii) provision of special funds for welfare schemes for Scheduled Castes, Scheduled Tribes, etc., and

(viii) appointment of a Commission, periodically, to investigate into the conditions of socially and educationally backward communities.

Limitations of the List

The criterion of a caste for being listed under Scheduled Castes Schedule to the Constitution was mainly 'untouchability' observed by others in relation to a particular caste. According to Article 366 of the Constitution (Part XIX), the expression Scheduled Castes means such castes or tribes or part of group within such castes, or tribes as are listed under the Article 341 for the purpose of the Constitution. The list of Scheduled Castes as is available shows a community which is termed as a Scheduled Caste in a State is not termed as such in another State. Even in some parts of the same State the same caste is not always classified as Scheduled Caste. There are some anomalies in the list of Scheduled Castes which need to be removed. The list will have to be revised having regard to the prevalence of untouchability with reference to each of the scheduled communities.

In accordance with the provision under the Constitution, Backward Classes Commission was appointed on the 29th January, 1953. The task entrusted to the Commission was of great complexity, specially with reference to determining the criterion to be used in considering any section of the people in the territory of India in addition to Scheduled Castes and Scheduled Tribes specified by notification under Articles 341 and 343 of the Constitution, to be treated socially and educationally backward. A simple and clear-cut criterion could not be suggested by the Commission. A number of claims were pressed before the Commission which included 2,399 communities out of which 913 alone accounted for an estimated population of 11.51 crore. Scheduled Castes and Scheduled Tribes made up another 7 crore. Thus, the bulk of the country's population, it was felt, had to be counted as suffering from backwardness. This made the task of the Government difficult. The idea of listing other backward classes on the all India basis except the denotified and nomadic tribes which were classified as Other Backward Classes, was given up. The State Governments, however, have their own lists of Backward Classes.

The composite State of Bombay which is now succeeded by Gujarat and Maharashtra, took a bold step by adopting a means test and not the caste basis for assessing backwardness. It stipulated that an annual income of Rs. 1,200 or less would entitle a person for educational and other facilities. This decision brought within the reach of many others some of the facilities which the members of the Backward Classes enjoyed.

Legislation to Abolish Untouchability

Although untouchability stands abolished under Article 17 of the Constitution it still shows itself in some form or the other, more particularly in the rural areas. In order to have an effective check on the practice of untouchability and its resultant disabilities, Parliament enacted the Untouchability (Offences) Act, 1955, which came into force throughout the country on the 1st of June, 1955.

An important point which deserves attention in this context is that the Central Act does not deal with the question of throwing open all temples to all the sections of Hindus, Section 3 of the Untouchability (Offences) Act, 1955 ensures to every person belonging to a religion, the religious denomination or a section of a religion, religious denomination entry, etc., into the place which is open to persons professing that religion or religious denomination as the case may be and to prevent untouchability within the same religion. Thus, the scope of Section 3 of the Act is obviously very limited. It aims at preventing discrimination within the same class on the ground of untouchability. It was suggested by the Commissioner for Scheduled Castes and Scheduled Tribes in his report of the year 1956-57 that the Central Act may be suitably amended so as to facilitate the entry of sections and classes of Hindus to all types of Hindu temples. It was not considered advisable to amend to Central Act on the pattern already adopted by the State of Bombay, U P., and Madras.

Public Opinion

Legislation has its limitations and unless it is backed by public opinion it may not produce the desired result. The Government of India, therefore, encouraged non-official organisations of all-India character to publicise the legislative provisions for the removal of untouchability and educated people in their responsibility in the matter even though it has not been stipulated expressly in the Constitution as the responsibility of the Government as is done with regard to the welfare of Scheduled Tribes in the Article 275 of the Constitution.

The Estimates Committee under the Chairmanship of Shri Balvantrai Mehta submitted its 38th report on the subject of Scheduled Castes and Scheduled Tribes and Other Backward Classes on the 28th March, 1959, wherein it made recommendations for the removal of social disabilities of Scheduled Castes. Among these recommendations the following are worth noting:

"1. The Committee further suggests that a large percentage of expenditure programmes for the removal of untouchability should be incurred to eradicate this evil. The non-official organisations engaged in this type of work should as far as possible consist of both Harijans and non-Harijans and should be non-political in character."

"2. The Committee feel that the Ministry should take a more lively interest in this matter and should impress upon the States, municipalities and local bodies that it is of utmost urgency that the practice of carrying night soil as head-loads be eliminated within the shortest possible time."

The Study Team on Social Welfare and Welfare of Backward Classes appointed by the Committee on Plan Projects under the Chairmanship of Shrimati Renuka Ray submitted its report on the 9th of July, 1959. The report has a separate chapter under the heading "Special Problems of Scheduled Castes" and has made important recommendations.

Five Year Plans

In pursuance of the provision of Articles 46 and 275 of the Constitution, funds were provided in the First, the Second and the Third Five Year Plans for schemes for the welfare of Scheduled Castes with a view to helping them to come to the level of the rest of the citizens.

While the shortfall in expenditure indicated cannot but cause disappointment, the fact remains that considerable progress has been made during the Second and the Third Plans as against the First Plan. In view of the urgent need to banish poverty, ignorance and disease amongst these backward communities, all those who are interested in the welfare of Scheduled Castes and are working for it must insist on the full and efficient utilisation of the funds provided.

A Plus Provision

The development programmers for the welfare of Scheduled Castes for which provisions were made in all three Five Year Plans were intended to supplement and not supplant benefits accruing to them from the general programmes of development in different fields such as 1. Agriculture, 2. Small Industries, 3. Communications, 4. Educations, 5. Health, 6. Housing, 7. Rural Water Supply and Others. The Third Five Year Plan in this behalf clearly lays down:

"One of the principal lessons of the past decade is that for a variety of reasons, in the ordinary course, the weaker sections of the population are not able to secure their fair share of the benefits of provisions made under different heads. To enable them to do so, it is desirable that the normal patterns of assistance should provide, wherever necessary, for an element of special consideration for the weaker sections and in particular, for the Backward Classes. It is observed that in a number of schemes formulated in favour of Backward Classes, the financial resources provided for this section of the population are proposed to be utilised in part to meet the cost of additional subsidy or other assistance to enable the Backward Classes to avail themselves of the general development programmes. This had the effect of reducing the scope of additional development to be undertaken from the special provisions made for the Backward Classes. The problem needs further consideration, since on the one hand it is essential that the general development programmes should be so designed as to cater adequately for the Backward Classes and on the other, the special provisions in the Plan should be used as far as possible for securing additional and more intensified development."

Mandal Commission

On the basis of the provision for appointing a commission to enquire into the socio-educational conditions of Backward classes under Article 340(1) of the Constitution Mandal Commission was appointed about two decades back during the prime ministership of Morarji Desai. This Commission identified Other Backward Classes (O.B.C.) who number 52 per cent of the Indian population. Thus, this Commission increased its preview from 23% to 75% of Indian population. Formerly, it included 66% Harijan and 33% tribals. Now it includes 70% Backward Classes, 20% Harijans and 10% Tribals. On 13th August 1990, the Government took out the Mandal Commission report from cold storage and announced an additional 27% reservation for O.B.C. in addition to the reservation already in vogue. This resulted into more than 50% reservation. It was argued that this will remove more than 1500 years disparity among Backward classes and higher castes. This opened a new controversy since castes like Jat etc., and minorities like Muslims and Christians started demanding reservation. The whole Indian elite and the entire Indian press together with almost the entire student community opposed the application of the recommendation. The Mandal Commission report was submitted to the Government of India in December 1990. It was hurriedly prepared by the Commission and to bring credibility to it some renowned sociologists and anthropologists like professors M.N. Srinivas, Yogendra Singh and B.K. Roy Burman were associated although little concern was shown for their expert advice. They have already shown their discontent with the report. The Commission used the 1931 census data to delineate 3,743 Social and Educationally Backward Castes (SEBC) since caste-based data were not collected in subsequent census operations. According to experts, there are technical and methodological errors in identifying Backward Classes and the report is 'unscientific' and biased.

MINORITIES

Who are Minorities?

We may define a minority as a group of people, who because of their physical or cultural characteristics are singled out from the others in the society in which they live for differential and unequal treatment; and who therefore regard themselves as objects of collective discrimination. "Differential and unequal treatment" does not necessarily mean that one is at the bottom. If two well trained and competent persons compete for a job of high prestige and income and one loses out on the grounds of his group membership alone, this does not indicate a low-class status, but rather a minority group-status. A minority group is a group which, regardless of whether it is on the class ladder, faces barriers to the pursuit of life's values that are larger or greater than the barriers faced by persons otherwise equally qualified. This is a distinction superimposed on the class system. A member of a minority group, then, is not necessarily a member of lower class, but he is lower on the stratification ladder than he would be were it not for his group membership. Wherever, there are minority groups there is, by definition, discrimination. It implies the application of standards which are arbitrary and unfair by dominant standards. The central meaning of 'minority group' of those who are thus, identified is precisely that they are judged by standards which are in violation of major social values.

Distinctive marks of Minorities

The symbols by which minorities are distinguished may be religion, language, national origin, race or some combination of these and other characteristics. All over world the minority majority scale is prevalent in different degrees of discrimination. The Negros are the popular minorities in the U.S.A. even today. In India, the term minorities is often applied to Muslims, Harijans and backward classes on account of their general disabilities accorded by the dominant groups. In India, the caste system with the ritual sanction is responsible for the creation of a minority of people who are given discriminatory treatment by the bulk of the society. The untouchables and other depressed castes, the scheduled tribes etc. have been the oppressed in our society down the ages. The Brahmins who were the dominant castes not only enjoyed a privileged order in society but aimed at an occupational superiority and its retainment as a vested interest so that the untouchables never had sufficient opportunities to rise up the social ladder.

Types of Minorities

Though, social scientists contend that minorities do not imply low-classes in India, the untouchables stand an illustration of that group of people who were the ritual minority to begin with in terms of their racial inferiority in comparison to the Aryan race but who subsequently remained the lowest class also on account of their inability to rise up the socio-economic ladder. The scheduled tribes who form a bulk of our population have also been grouped as a minority because of the lack of opportunities to rise up.

Women down the ages have also been considered a minority in India. Inequality of treatment and lack of adequate opportunities for development suppressed the initiatives of this sex. But the status of women has changed significantly in modern times due to the impact of Western culture on Indian thought. The legal sanctions afforded to this erstwhile minority by way of the Widow Remarriage Act, the Sharda Act, and other legal bills prohibiting female infanticide and raising the age of consent for marriage have improved the lot of women in our country. Voluntary organisations and social reform movements have brought about a change in the status of women in our country and even today the interest of this minority group is of main concern to the Constitutionalists.

The Muslim Minority

Muslims are another minority element in our country. To begin with the history of the Muslims dates back to the period of conquests which the Khilji dynasty had inflicted on our population. The relation between the Hindus and Muslims was on a conqueror-conquered scale and the Britishers played their part in their unification or otherwise. In comparison to the Muslim-majority countries like Arabia, Africa, Pakistan etc., in India they are a minority. In "*The Muslim dilemma in India*" by M.R.A. Baig, he gives a exemplary exposition pf the fix this minority group is in. Is it better for Muslim Indians to assimilate and thereby lose their identity? Or are they bound by Islam to preserve their identity and thereby suffer the mental, physical, social and economic consequences of non-assimilation with the Hindu culture? This, according to the author is the Muslim dilemma. His thesis is that Islam as practised in the Muslim majority countries has to be adopted to conditions in which Muslims are a minority. Theological, historical, sociological, psychological, political reasons have resulted in division of India which culminated in the creation of Pakistan. The dilemma of the Muslim Indians is indeed great since the ability with which one can fit into an entirely opposing social setup of the Hindus in India is not easy-coming. To the Muslim practice of polygamy for example, the Hindus raise their eyebrows. The Indian constitution though purporting secularism has been accused of framing laws which are Hindu-oriented. Polygamy is condemned. Nevertheless, this minority group has not been completely rejected through total abolition of the one-man-many-women ethic. The Muslim Marriage Act pays special regard to the private and personal sanctions of the community and allows polygamy under varying conditions. So, this is the case with other features of their social life which is ill fitting in a Hindu society.

Status of Minorities in India

India being a secular nation, the minority groups whether based on religion like the Muslims, racial and ethnic origins like the untouchables have to be supported. The political recognition of the uniqueness and value of every simple individual in terms of civil liberties has gone a long way in improving the lot of the minorities. The caste drags of the untouchables and other depressed classes have been elevated on the social scale by the passing of the *Caste Disabilities Removal Act.* The Harijans today are the advantaged sections of society. Special privileges are offered to them and reservation of seats in both educational and employment avenues has indeed heralded the growth of this section of the community. Likewise political representation to the minority group in every state in a proportionate basis enable their advancement in political sphere too.

Social progress in general is aimed at the uplift of the minorities as well as equal opportunities to them for advancement. No discriminatory treatment or segregation is possible under the legal order. Discrimination is indeed punishable. But one has to remark in this context laxity of legality on a social set-up.

What India needs today is not laws alone. Social thinking and education should be directed towards a free social intercourse of the majority-minority population without any traditional inhibitions. Safeguards should be taken against any breach of the legal code and a smooth interflow of interaction should be made a national phenomenon rather than a legal force. For, social scientists contend that there is no power less powerful than coercion and no strength stronger than nationality.

QUESTIONS FOR EXERCISE

1. Write an essay on Backward classes in India.
2. What is Untouchability? Discuss its disability and causes.
3. Who are minorities? Discuss the status of minorities in India.

8

The Hindu Family: Joint Family

Though, the Hindu family has passed through several stages of development, since, the times of Vedas, many of its fundamental characteristics have remained the same. The important characteristics are as follows:

1. Joint Family. The most important characteristic of Hindu family is that it is joint. In it the wife and husband, the parents of the husband, his brothers and sisters and also some other relatives live under the same roof. The management of the joint family is in the hands of the head of the family who is not always the earning member but generally the most aged. The members of the family have equal rights in the income and property of the family, however, they may differ in their earning capacity. The food for the family is cooked in the same kitchen.

2. High Status of Women. The women have always been given a very high status in Hindu family. Their presence has been considered to be necessary on religious occasions.

3. Religion and Spirituality. The members of Hindu family are not connected merely by social bond but, they are also bound together by religious and spiritual affinities. There is more emphasis on duties than on rights in Hindus family. Every member of the family follows his duties according to his status in the family. In this respect, the Hindu scriptures have elaborately prescribed rights and duties for every member of the Hindu family.

4. Welcome of the Guest. Another important feature of the Hindu family is that the guest is always welcomed in it. The Hindu house-holder provides for food and rest to the guest in whatever difficult circumstances he may himself live.

Chief Ideals of the Hindu Family

The institution of the Hindu family occupies a unique position in the institution of family in different cultures of the world. Its chief ideals are as follows:

1. Procreation. The chief ideal of Hindu family is procreation. The birth of a son has been considered to be necessary from the worldly as well as the other worldly viewpoint. According to Manu, a man cannot even renounce the world without procreating a son. In different Vedas, Samhitas and Brahmans the birth of a son has been declared to be necessary for paying off the debt to the ancestors. The word 'Putra' signifies one who saves a person from the hell of 'Puta'. Thus, in Hindu social philosophy the birth of a son is absolutely necessary even for religious and spiritual purposes.

2. Fulfilment of Dharma. An important ideal of a Hindu family is the fulfilment of dharma. The world 'Patni' signifies that woman participates with the man in religious ceremonies. No man was permitted to carry out religious celebrations without getting married. Kalidasa has called wife as the source of all religious activities. The Grahastha-Ashram has been called the basis of all other Ashramas and the chief ideal of the Grahastha-Ashram is the fulfilment of dharma.

3. Enjoyment of Sex. According to Hindu scriptures, of the four aims of life Dharma, Artha, Kama and Moksha, the fulfilment of dharma and the enjoyment of sex are the two important ideals of the household life. The Hindu scriptures have been the life from an integral viewpoint. The enjoyment of sex, therefore, has been given an equal status with the fulfilment of dharma. According to Vatsyayan, the man attaining the age of 100 years should gather knowledge in childhood, enjoy sex in youth and attain dharma and liberation in the old age. Thus, the ideals of Hindu family are based on a harmony of enjoyment and renunciation.

Changes in the Ideals of Hindu Family

The influence of Western culture in modern times has led to some changes in the ideals of Hindu family. Formerly, man used to aspire for a good number of sons. But, now, family planning has become necessary due to economic difficulties. Again, no one believes in the ideas of heaven and hell and the necessity of the birth of a son for the other world. With the change in the status of women the desire for son is not appreciably dominant than that for the daughter. The joint family has constantly disintegrated. Fulfilment of dharma is no more the ideal of Hindu family. Thus, the only two aims of a Hindu household at present are Artha and Kama. Of these the latter is more important. Therefore, at present there is more emphasis on biological and psychological satisfaction through the marital relationship. Love is gradually becoming the basis of marriage. Thus, the ideals of Hindu family are gradually coming closer to the family in the West. The biological, psychological and economic advantages of the family life are being emphasised. And yet due to the nature of Hindu marriage as a religious sacrament, the essential core of the Hindu family is still maintained.

JOINT FAMILY

Joint family is a group of kins of several generations, ruled by a head, in which there is joint residence, hearth and property and whose members are bound with each other by mutual obligations. The chief characteristics of joint family are common residence, common kitchen, joint property, common worship, rule of the *pater familia* and consciousness of mutual obligation among family members.

Definitions of Joint Family

1. *J. Karve*: "A joint family is a group of people who generally live under one roof, who eat food cooked at one hearth, who hold property in common and who participate in common worship and are related to each other as some particular type of kindred."[1]

2. *Jolly*: "Not only parents and children, brothers and step-brothers live on the common property, but it may, sometimes, include ascendants, descendants and collaterals upto many generations."[2]

3. *I.P. Desai*: "We call that household a joint family which has greater generation depth (*i.e.*, three or more) than the nuclear family and the members of which are related to one another by property, income and mutual rights and obligations."[3]

Characteristics of Joint Family

The most important characteristic features of the joint family are as follows:

1. Joint Habitation. The most striking feature of the joint family is the living of several families in one house. In this the father, son, son's wife and children all live together. According to Sir Henry Maine Hindu joint family is a group constituted of a known ancestor and adopted sons and relatives related to these sons through marriage.

2. Joint Kitchen. As long as the one kitchen does not serve the entire group, different families cannot be regarded as a joint family even if they live in one house. The food for all members of a joint family, consisting of a father and mother, their sons and their son's children, is cooked in one kitchen. Brahaspati has said that those people who have the same kitchen, their ancestors, gods and Brahmin's are worshipped at the same place. In this way, by having one kitchen in the joint family other activities are also performed by all members together. The moment the kitchen is separated, the joint family ceases to exist.

3. Joint Property. In addition to joint habitation and a combined kitchen a characteristic feature of the joint family is joint property. In a joint family, the ownership, production and consumption of wealth take place on a joint basis. Writing about the joint family, Melly writes in "*Modern India and the West*" that it is a cooperative institution, similar to a joint stock company, in which there is joint property. The head of the joint family is like a trustee who manages the property of the family with a view to deriving material and spiritual benefit for the members of the family. The total earnings of all the family members are pooled. The head of the family makes proper use of it on behalf of everyone.

4. Authority of the Head. Yet another characteristic feature of the joint family is the rule of the head. Maine calls him the absolute authority. But in practice he

1 Karve, J., *Kinship Organisation in India*, p. 10.
2 Jolly, *Hindu Law and Custom*, p. 168.
3 Desai, I.P., *The Joint Family in India*, an article in Sociological Bulletin, Vol. V, No. 2, Sept. 1956, p. 148.

makes more use of persuasion and love than command. He keeps in mind the needs of all members and employs them according to their ability.

NEW SOCIAL LEGISLATION

Joint family has been very much influenced by certain new social legislations in India. These have some direct bearing on the characteristic features of joint family *viz.,* joint habitation, combined kitchen, joint property and the authority of the head. The following are the major ones among these social legislations—

1. Hindu Married Women's Right to Separate Residence and Maintenance Act. This legislation was enacted in 1946. According to it, under specific conditions a wife can demand alimony while living separately from her husband.

2. Hindu Marriage Act. According to para 13 of this Act, any husband and wife, who have been married either before or after the enactment of this legislation can under specific conditions, apply to the court for divorce. This law was enacted in 1955.

3. Hindu Succession Act. This act became law in 1956. According to it, the daughter was given equal rights to the property of the father and the women also got the rights to dispose of mortgage, and use their property in any manner they pleased.

Effect of Present Legislation of Joint Family

The foregoing Acts of legislation have influenced the solidarity of the joint family. As a consequence of the Hindu Marriage Act the number of divorces is increasing. Previously, the women silently suffered many injustices and outrages. The status of women was extremely low in joint families. Sometimes the mother-in-law behaved inhumanly towards them. Their husbands also treated them as they wished and yet the joint family did not disintegrate. Now having got the support of the law, women have initiated a strong revolt against this oppression which is leading to a disorganization of the joint family. With the enactment of laws providing for their separate maintenance and residence, the women no longer need to submit to oppression in the joint family due to financial considerations. Upon being maltreated they can now leave their husbands and live separately and can demand money from them in order to carry on their expenditure. This provision has dealt a severe blow to the joint families. One feature of the joint family is that of joint property. The Hindu Succession Act has influenced it adversely.

Now that women have the right to sell their property and the girls to share equally in the property of their father, it is almost impossible to maintain the family property conjointly. Hence, the result is that the joint families are disintegrating at a rapid rate. Modern legislation has put an end to male ascendency. This too has profoundly influenced the organization of the joint family. The wives in the joint family come from other families. Thus, it is only natural that they should resent having to sacrifice their own pleasure for the well being of the family. Previously, they had to suffer silently the doings of their husbands. Having got equal rights in almost all respects as a result of modern legislation, the women whose husbands earn more can now force their husbands to break off from the joint family and set-up an independent establishment. The parents-in-law also realise their power. The husbands too cannot do what they will with them. They also have the same rights over the children as their husbands. Due to all these causes even the slightest misunderstanding results in a situation where separation from the family is the only course open to the couple as they cannot coexist with their relatives. Actually, the causes of the disorganization of the joint family are not constitutional but mainly social. But there is no doubting the fact that the present legislation has also played a part in its disorganization.

The class of job workers constitutes a major part of adult Indian population today. For the sake of their job most of them have to live at far off places away from their ancestral home. Again, due to unprecedented rise in the cost of living and diminishing of the value of money very few are in a position to carry the burden of a joint family. In villages educated young men are going to cities in search of white collar jobs. In cities small residences, high rents and high prices make it difficult for person to live in joint family. These and many other characteristics of economic life have led to disorganization of Hindu joint family.

Merits of the Joint Family

The chief merits of the joint family are as follows —

1. Economic Advantage. The joint family system has proved to be a very advantageous institution from the economic viewpoint. It prevents property from being divided. Land is protected from extreme sub-division and fragmentation. Land when divided into many small pieces becomes an uneconomic holding. Besides keeping the land intact, the joint family also assists in economic production. In a joint agriculturist family the male members do such work as furrowing, sowing and irrigation. Women assist at the harvest. Children graze the cattle, collect fuel and manure. In this way, the co-operation of all members helps to save money which would otherwise be paid to a labourer. In the rural areas the joint families of such artisans as the blacksmith, carpenter, etc., also function as units in which men, women and children collaborate. Even among the middle and upper classes the family can obtain capital and reliable assistance from the joint family for establishing and expanding a business.

2. Protection of Members. Praising the joint family system Shri Jawaharlal Nehru had said that the system of joint family is an insurance for the family members which has carried a guarantee for those who are mentally and physically weak. In times of crises the joint family can provide assistance to the children, the old, the insane, the widows and the helpless. The joint family is capable of providing much assistance at such times as pregnancy, sickness, etc. If a person dies, his wife and children are looked after properly in the joint family. In the joint family a place is provided for all members to which they can retreat at all times and their honour, wealth and prosperity are protected collectively.

3. Means of Recreation. The joint family is one of the best means of recreation. A stimulating atmosphere is created by the cumulative effect of the stammered talking of the children, love between brother and sister, mother's love, the reproach of the elders and the fun and frolic of the other family members. In this way, the joint family also naturally takes over the role of a club.

4. Development of Personality. The joint family system makes possible the ideal development of the good qualities of man. In the care of elders the undesirable and antisocial tendencies of the young are checked, they are prevented from straying from their path and they learn to exercise self-control. In the joint family young men and women learn the lesson of generosity, patience, service, cooperation and obedience. A sense of sacrifice replaces selfishness in the bosom of each member of the family. All members learn to obey family administration and to respect those older than themselves.

5. Co-operation and Economy. The joint family fosters co-operation and economy to an extent achieved by few, if any, other institution. A sense of cultural unity and an associational feeling exists among the members. There can be much economy in expenditure since a large saving can be made in the payment of rent and in cooking for a large family unit. The joint family has been called "An ideal centre of co-operation and mutual aid".

6. Socialism in Wealth. According to Sir Henry Maine, the joint family is like a corporation the, trustee of which is the father. According to Jathar and Berry, everyone in a joint family earns according to his capability but obtains according to his need and in this way to a large extent achieves the socialistic order from each according to his ability, to each according to his needs.

Defects of Joint Family System

The following are the main disadvantages of the joint family system:

1. Hindrance in the Development of Personality. The most glaring defect of the joint family system is the hindrance in the development of the personalities of its members. In the joint family the head is the absolute ruler or administrator. This head is usually the oldest member of the family who looks upon men and women as children even when they attain adulthood and behaves towards them accordingly. In this way, there is very little opportunity for the fostering of individual autonomy and freedom.

2. Bad Condition of Women. This is also a major defect of the joint family system and is at the same time an important factor in its disintegration. In the joint family, the daughter-in-law do not get an opportunity to develop their personality. They serve the entire family like slaves not getting any time to look after their own children. They hardly ever meet their husbands during the day and when he returns late at night he either falls asleep or gratifies his sexual impulse with her. The invariable presence of other family members ashames the bride and she cannot even tell her husband anything. In this way she does not receive love from any source. There is no limit to the injustice done by the mother-in-law, and the other relatives do everything to add to that suffering. In some cases this oppression becomes so inhuman and intolerable that women become fed up and commit suicide. Any natural love between the husband and wife or between the mother and children is prevented from blossoming by these artificial circumstances.

3. Strife. If the daughter-in-laws oppose this oppression or if their husbands choose to speak in their favour the house becomes strife born and a centre of conflict. When they talk back to their mother-in-law, they are abused and even beaten by their husbands who are provoked by their mother. Hatred and jealousy between the wives of brothers may lead to a conflict between brothers which may assume dangerous proportions. There is continuous strife and fighting over the doings of children. Much of the time of the adult members is consumed in the solution of petty problems.

4. Laziness. Due to common responsibility many people take their minds off their work and become completely lazy. In this state, the condition of those who literally break their backs and those who are very lazy is, more or less the same. Hence, laziness is encouraged. When a person can eat comfortably without exerting himself he is unlikely to indulge in any strenuous activity. And the wives of the hard working people tell them to desist from such toil as they do not benefit from it. Mostly, in the joint family, it happens that some people have to exhaust themselves while others lead a life of utter lethargy. There is no dearth of such people in big and rich joint families whose entire routine in life consists of eating, sleeping and begetting children.

5. More Reproduction. In a joint family, the responsibility for the upbringing and education etc. of children is shared. Thus, no individual considers it necessary to lay stress upon controlling procreation. In the family, no distribution in the status of the members is made on the basis of their respective earnings and the corresponding number of children. The offspring of one member will be treated the same way as that of the other, irrespective of the high level of his earnings and the fewer children. In this way, in a joint family no direct benefit accrues to any individual by family planning or by earning more. Consequently, the enthusiasm of the people in this direction looses much of its fervour and intensity, and they become lazy and procreate more.

6. Poverty. As a consequence of almost daily strife, the bad condition of women, absolute rule, lack of responsibility and blind procreation, the economic condition of the joint family becomes very unenviable. If the conflict is strong enough to bring about division of land and property the condition becomes even worse. The property of the family, being jointly owned, is sometimes allowed to go waste and through constant neglect it is gradually lost. Due to strict administration of the old men the younger people do not gain self-confidence and self-dependence, and they fail to adopt new currents of thought.

Thus, the defects of the joint family far outweigh the advantages which accrue from it and have negatived them. Consequently, the joint family is fast becoming disorganised. It is impossible to save the institution of joint family from disorganization, though its advantages can, with effort be reinstituted in novel form in the nuclear families.

QUESTIONS FOR EXERCISE

1. Describe the structure and functioning of the traditional joint family in India.
2. What are the sociological characteristics of the Hindu Joint Family? Discuss the impact of modern social forces on Hindu Family.
3. Explain the factors which have been responsible in maintaining Joint Family System in India, how are the disintegrating trends taking place in this system?

9

The Hindu Marriage

The institution of Hindu marriage occupies a prominent place in the social institutions of civilized world. Hindu marriage can be defined as a religious sacrament in which a man and woman are bound in permanent relationship for physical, social and spiritual purposes of *dharma,* procreation and sexual pleasure. Thus, Hindu marriage is not merely a social contract but a religious sacrament. It results in a more or less permanent relationship between a man and woman. Its aim is not merely physical pleasure but spiritual advancement. It is not merely an individual function but has social importance. Its ideals are fulfilment of Dharma, procreation and enjoyment of sexual pleasure. It exhibits an integral approach to this social institution. The main aims of Hindu marriage can be summarised as follows:

1. Fulfilment of Dharma or Religious Duties. According to the Hindu scriptures marriage is the basis of all religious activities.[1] In the words of K.M. Kapadia "Marriage being thus primarily for the fulfilment of duties, the basic aim of marriage was *Dharma.*"[2] According to *Mahabharata,* "Wife is the very source of the purusharthas, not only of *dharma, artha* and *kama* but even of *moksha.* Those that have wives can fulfil their due obligations in this world; those that have wives can be happy; and those that have wives can lead a full life."[3]

2. Procreation. In Hindu family the child is given a very important place. According to *Rigveda,* the husband accepts the palm of the wife in order to get a high breed progeny. According to Manu, the chief aim of marriage is procreation. *Mahabharata* has also maintained the same view. The birth of a son is necessary in order to fulfil our debt towards ancestors.[4]

3. Sexual Pleasure. According to Manu, marriage is a social institution for the regulation of proper relations between the sexes.[5] The Hindu scriptures have compared the sexual pleasure with the realization of divine bliss. According to

1 Kalidasa, *Kumarasambhava,* p. 13.

2 Kapadia K.M., *Marriage and Family in India,* p. 168.

3 *Mahabharata,* Adi Parva, 74, 40-41.

4 *Manu,* IX, 106, *Baudhayana,* II, 6, II, 3.

5 *Manu,* IX. 25.

Vatsyayan sexual pleasure is the chief aim of marriage. A maiden who has attained youth should herself get married without waiting for the assistance of elders.[1]

Traditional forms of Hindu Marriage

The Hindu scriptures admit the following forms of marriage.[2]

1. Brahma Marriage. In this form of marriage the girl, decorated with clothes and ornaments, is given in marriage to a learned and gentle bridegroom.[3] This is the prevalent form of marriage in Hindu society today.

2. Prajapatya Marriage. In this form of marriage the daughter is offered to the bride-groom by blessing them with the enjoyment of marital bliss and the fulfilment of Dharma.[4]

3. Aarsh Marriage. In this form of marriage a *rishi* used to accept a girl in marriage after giving a cow or bull and some clothes to the parents of the girl.[5] These articles were not the price of the bride but indicated the resolve of the *rishi* to lead a household life. According to P.K. Acharya the word *aarsh* has been derived from the word *rishi.*

4. Daiva Marriage. In this form of marriage the girl, decorated with ornaments and clothes, was offered to the person who conducted the function of a Purohit in *yajna*."[6]

5. Asura Marriage. In this form of marriage the bride-groom gets the bride in exchange of some money or articles given to the family members of the bride.[7] Such form of marriage was conducted in the case of marriage of Pandu with Madri.

6. Gandharva Marriage. This form of marriage is the result of mutual affection and love of the bride and the bride-groom. An example of this type of marriage is the marriage of the King Dushyanta with Shakuntala. In this form of marriage the ceremonies can be performed after sexual relationship between the bride and the bride-groom.[8] *Kamasutra* has admitted this form of marriage to be of the ideal type. In *Taittariya Samhita* it has been pointed out that this type of marriage has been so named because of its prevalence among the Gandharvas.

7. Rakshas Marriage. This type of marriage was prevalent in the age when women were considered to be the prize of war. In this type of marriage the bride-groom takes away the bride from her house forcibly after killing and injuring her relatives.[9]

8. Paishach Marriage. This type of marriage has been called to be most degenerate. In this type a man enters into sexual relationship with a sleeping,

---

1 *Kamasutra,* III, IV, 36.

2 *Manu,* III, 21.

3 *Ibid.,* III, 27.

4 *Manu,* III, 30.

5 *Ibid.,* III, 29.

6 *Ibid.,* III, 28.

7 *Ibid.,* III, 31.

8 *Ibid.,* III, 32.

9 *Ibid.,* III, 33.

drunk or unconscious woman.[1] Such acts were regularised after the performance of marriage ceremony which took place after physical relationship between the man and woman.

About the present conditions of the above-mentioned traditional forms of Hindu marriage, Dr. D.N. Majumdar has said, "Hindu society now recognizes only two forms, the *Brahma*, and the *Asura*, the higher castes preferring the former, the backward castes the latter, though here and there among the higher castes the *Asura* practice has not died out."[2] This view of Dr. Majumdar rightly describes the present position of the traditional forms of Hindu marriage.

Modern Changes in Hindu Marriage

Due to the influence of Western culture and English education the Hindu marriage system has undergone considerable changes, the important among them being the following:

1. Marriage is not held as Compulsory. In Hindu society formerly marriage was considered to be absolutely compulsory for both male and female. According to Hindu scriptures, a person who does not beget a son through marriage cannot attain heaven. The birth of a son was considered to be necessary for the wellbeing of the ancestors. No man could perform *yajna* without a wife. Marriage, therefore, was necessary even for religious purposes. But, due to the influence of western culture many males and females do not consider marriage to be necessary these days. Due to economic difficulties also some persons do not enter into matrimony. The modern educated Hindu girl is not prepared to accept slavery of male. She marries for love and if it is not forthcoming she refuses to marry. Many girls, specially those who are in a job, do not marry unless they get a suitable match and if such a match is not available they do not marry at all. The educated men and women do not believe in the ancient religious values and therefore do not consider marriage to be necessary.

2. Breaking of the Taboos of Sagotra and Sapravar Marriage. Ancient Hindu tradition forbids the marriage of persons belonging to the same *Gotra* and *Pravar*. This very much restricts the field of choice of mate. Therefore, at the present the educated persons are gradually violating the restriction. It has also been rejected by law.

3. Opposition of Child Marriages. In medieval India the custom of child marriage was very much in vogue. After the passing of *Sarada Act* child marriages have become illegal. Another factor leading to the restriction of child marriage in Hindu society is the tremendous increase of women education. Due to the customs of dowry also poor parents fail to arrange for a bride-groom at an early age. The boys also do not marry early because of late settlement in career.

4. Permission of Inter-caste Marriage. Formerly, inter-caste marriage was considered to be wrong in Hindu society. It has now been legally permitted.

1 *Ibid.*, III, 34.

2 Majumdar, D.N., *Races and Cultures of India*, Asia Publishing House, Bombay, p. 173.

With the increase of co-education, women education and the democratic ideal of equality and liberty, inter-caste marriages are now considered to be signs of forwardness. The bonds of endogamy are, therefore, gradually breaking and the number of inter-caste marriages increasing.

5. Prohibition of Polygamy. Formerly, a man was allowed to marry several women in order to get a son. With the increase of women education the ladies are demanding equal rights in marriage. *The Hindu Marriage Act of 1955* has declared polygamy to be illegal. No one can marry a second time, while the former spouse is alive.

6. Permission of Widow Remarriage. Due to the untiring efforts of social reformers and educated persons widow remarriage is no more considered to be wrong in Hindu society. Consequently, its incidence is now on the increase.

7. Provision for Divorce. *The Hindu Marriage Act of 1955* has introduced a significant change in the institution of Hindu marriage by permitting divorce under certain specific circumstances.

Disorganization of Hindu Marriage

The above-mentioned changes in Hindu marriage are indicative of progress on the one hand and disorganization on the other. The increase in the incidence of divorce, the increase in the age of marriage and rise in the incidence of extra-marital sex relationship are indicative of disorganization in Hindu marriage. Changes such as the prohibition of polygamy, the restriction of child marriages, the permission of widow remarriage and freedom in the choice of mate are healthy signs of progress. Thus, on the whole, it cannot be said that the changes in Hindu marriage in recent times have led to its degeneration. The sanctity of marital bond has however, diminished. It is no more unbreakable. It can be broken if there is no love and harmony between wife and husband. In fact, the Hindu marriage system is passing through a transitional stage. English education, women education, influence of western culture, urbanization and industrialization have changed social values of the Hindu male and female. The institution of family is changing fast. Familial and marital disorganization are inter-dependent. The disorganization of Hindu family has created circumstances leading to disorganization of Hindu marriage. Romantic marriages are increasing. This has led to an increase in the number of divorces. In spite of these fast changes, it can be safely predicted that there is no immediate danger to the institution of Hindu marriage, because of the psychological security which it provides.

SCOPE OF MATE SELECTION

In Hindu community the scope of the selection of mate is limited by the rules of endogamy, exogamy and polygamy etc.

Endogamy

Endogamy is the form of marriage in which one must marry within one's own caste or other group. This rule does not permit marriage of close kin. Endogamous marriage is that which is confined within the group. As a matter of fact, endogamy and exogamy are relative words. That which is endogamous from one viewpoint is exogamous from another viewpoint. In the sub-caste exogamy of Hindus the marriage is contracted outside the sub-caste but the same marriage would be endogamous from the viewpoint of the race or nation.

In India, the following forms of endogamy are to be found:

1. Divisional or Tribal Endogamy. This is the endogamy in which no individual can marry outside his own tribe or division.

2. Caste Endogamy. In this form of endogamy marriage is contracted within the caste.

3. Class Endogamy. Class endogamy is that in which marriage can take place between people of only one class or of a particular status.

4. Sub-Caste Endogamy. This is the type of endogamy in which choice for marriage is restricted to the sub-caste.

5. Race Endogamy. Race endogamy is that in which one can marry in the race. People of the Veddah race never marry outside the race.

Generally speaking, the following can be the causes of endogamy:

1. Policy of Separation. An important cause of endogamy is the policy of separation meaning whereby the will to live in separation from others.

2. To Keep Wealth in the Group. When any woman of a group marries into another group, her children also belong to the other group and in this way the numerical force of the first group suffers.

3. Religious Differences. Generally, marriage between people of dissimilar religions is not considered desirable.

4. Racial or Cultural Difference. Racial exogamy does not take place due to racial and cultural differences.

5. Sense of Superiority or Inferiority. At the root of caste endogamy and racial endogamy is the sense of superiority or inferiority of one group from another.

6. Geographic Separation. People who are separated by long distance naturally do not prefer to marry one another.

Roughly, the following are the main advantages derived from endogamy:

1. It tends to maintain the sense of unity within the group.
2. Women are happier within their own group.
3. Other people do not gain authority over the group's wealth.
4. The business secrets of the group are kept intact.
5. Purity in the group is maintained.

The following are the disadvantages from which endogamy suffers:

1. Endogamy shatters the national unity, because the nation is divided into small endogamous groups.

2. The scope for choice of a life partner is limited[1] due to which malpractices

1 "The multiplicity of groups thus restricts the choice of a mate within the bounds of a few families varying in number from 50 to 300." Kapadia, K.M., *Marriage and Family in India*, Bombay, p. 160.

such as unsuitable marriages, polygamy, dowry system, bride price, etc., are fostered.

3. It generates hatred and jealousy for other groups. This is the main cause at the root of casteism in India.

In this way, at the present time, it has become necessary, both in the national and the international interest, that the endogamous tie be made void. The unfortunate consequences of dowry and other similar institutions are to be seen in the form of suicides committed by marriageable persons. Polygamy, unsuitable marriages and late marriages lead to corruption in society. The one method of avoiding such consequences is to put a stop to endogamous marriages. These ties are being constantly broken by the effect of modern Western education and civilization.

Exogamy

Exogamy is the contrast of endogamy. While in endogamy one can marry only within one's own group, in exogamy marriage in one's group is not permitted and brides are sought from other groups. While endogamy exhibits conservative attitude, exogamy is progressive. Exogamy is approved of from the biological viewpoint. It leads to healthy and intelligent offspring. But, this fact applies only to marriages outside the wider group. This benefit cannot be derived by forbidding *sagotra* and *sapravara* marriages. In the Indian society more harm than benefit has resulted from exogamous marriages. Most people do not intentionally approve of marriages within groups but do so only when the group is considered as limited only to the children of one's parents or to two of their future generations. There can be no benefit in declaring marriage within group unlawful when the group includes a greater number of people. In the *1911 U.P. Census Report*, Blunt calculated that in the higher Hindu castes, some 2121 possible relatives are negated by disallowing marriage in 7 generations on the paternal side and five on the maternal side, whereas among the Christians this number was only 30. In his book *Hindu Exogamy* Karandikar writes that the system of exogamy is so prevalent among the low caste Hindus that in Northern India there are 1359 distinctions of exogamy among the sweepers. In this way the scope for the choice of the bride and the groom becomes very limited which tends to encourage dowry. The daughter cannot be happy even if a loan has been taken for the dowry because the parents of the bridegroom can never be satisfied as the value of the groom is rising. Consequently, the bride has to suffer much in her in-laws home. Other serious consequences of rising bridegroom value are the suicide of many young women and the unsuited marriages of many more. Being unable to provide sufficient dowry, poor parents marry off their daughters to aged husbands. Besides this, due to difficulties present in contracting it, marriage is delayed, and illicit sex relations in society increase. This injustice and corruption is further augmented by the untimely widowhood of many women who have been unsuitably married. As a result of these defects in the system of exogamy, laws of exogamous marriage in Hindu society are breaking down. Even among the *sapinda* relations marriages are being contracted except between very near relatives. It is not impossible that, in the near future, the offspring of only one parentage may be considered *sapinda* for the purpose of exogamy.

Forms of Exogamy

The following forms of exogamy are to be found in India:

1. Gotra Exogamy. Among the Brahmins the prevailing practice is to marry outside the *gotra*. People who many within the *gotra* have to repent and treat the women like a sister or mother. The offspring resulting from her is believed to be heathen. This restriction has been imposed since people of one *gotra* are believed to have similar blood.

2. Pravar Exogamy. Besides forbidding marriage within the *gotra* the Brahmins also forbid marriage between persons belonging to the same *pravar.* People who utter the name of a common saint at religious functions are believed to belong to the same *pravar.* Thus, *pravar* is a kind of religious and spiritual bond. According to Dr. Altekar and Sri Dange, marriages within the *gotra* and *pravar* were not forbidden in ancient India. These have been treated as forbidden from the time of Dharmasutras.

3. Gotra Exogamy among the Kshatriyas and Vaisyas. Among the Kshatriyas and Vaisyas it is the *gotra* of the *purohit* which is taken into consideration for the purpose of exogamy. In these the ancestry is carried on not through the saint but some follower. In the Rajputs the gotras start from victors or the first man of the ancestry . Sometimes the *gotra* takes the name of the village where this first person lived. In this way thousands of gotras have come into being.

4. Village Exogamy. Among many Indian tribes it is the recognised custom to marry outside the village. This restriction is prevalent in the Munda and other tribes of Chhota Nagpur of Madhya Pradesh. Among some tribes of Baroda, marriage is forbidden within the village since residents of the village were regarded as relatives. For example, the Naga tribe of Assam is divided into Khels. Khel is the name given to the residents of the particular place, and people of one Khel cannot marry each other. The Garo tribe is divided into two Katchis or Phratries called Marak and Sangama between which inter-marriage is prohibited. There are five exogamous groups among the Ao and Lhotado Nagas and two among Lonte tribe. Erulla tribe of South India is divided into six sub-groups. Five among them can inter-marry. In this way there are two exogamous groups among these people.

5. Pinda Exogamy. In Hindu society marriage within the *pinda* in prohibited. There is no one opinion as to who can be said to belong to the same *pinda.* According to Brahaspati, offspring from five maternal generations and seven paternal generations are *sapinda* and they cannot inter-marry. The opinion of Brahaspati is not universally accepted. In several parts of India the generation of the mother is not considered to be *sapinda.* At some places the prohibition extends over three maternal and five paternal generations. According to the *Baudhayana*

Dharmasutra marriage with the offspring of the maternal uncle or father's sister is improper. But many examples of such marriages are forthcoming from ancient India. Among the Brahmins in the South, with the exception of Namboodari Brahmins it is considered good to marry the daughter of one's maternal uncle. The Velum caste of Madras does not forbid marriage with one's niece while in the Telugu-Tamil districts and among the lowly Brahmins this union can be contracted with the daughter of one's sister-in-law. In Northern India, generally, *sapinda* marriages do not take place.

Sagotra and Sapravara Marriages

As has been already mentioned, *sagotra* and *sapravara* marriages are forbidden by Hindu Dharmasastras. Vashist, Gautama and Shankh Dharmasutras state that it is not proper to marry a girl whose *pravara* coincides with that of the bridegroom. In the Visnu, Manu and Yajnavalkya Smritis, the prohibition in marriage extends to the girls who are of the same *gotra*. According to Baudhayana in the event of marrying a girl of similar *gotra*, one should resort to a form of repentance called Chandrayan and should treat her as a sister or mother.

It is written in the *Satyashaadh Iliranyakeshi strotasutra* the *gotra* is the name given to the offspring of eight saints. These eight saints are: Vishvamitra, Jamdagni, Bhardwaj, Gautama, Atri, Vashistha, Kashyap and Augustya. The word *gotra* is found used in Vedic literature denoting the enclosure made to protect cows. On this basis Max Muller has conjectured that people who kept their cows at one place were considered to be the children of one ancestral saint who lived there and were accepted as members of one *gotra*. According to Panini, the offspring of the grandson was included in the same *gotra*. But Patanjali accepts only the offspring of eight saints to be of one *gotra*. Medhatithi has clarified it that *gotra* does not mean that they are the offspring of a saint, born at a particular time, but rather that *gotra* is a traditional name of the *vansh* just as some are traditionally accepted as Brahmins. According to Vigyaneshwar that name is called the *gotra* which is famous in the tradition of the ancestry. According to *Mitakshara*, the meaning of *gotra* is proximity of blood. To conclude in the words of Prabhu, "The three terms *gotra*, *pravara* and *pinda* used in connection with the laws of exogamy, have undergone so many changes, additions and modifications in their meaning and implication through the ages since their origin, that it becomes well nigh impossible to find out their original implications."[1]

The *pravaras* are also in the name of ancient saints. According to Vigyaneshwar, only the *gotra* of Brahmins are pravaras. The gotras and pravaras of the Kshtriyas and Vaishyas are dependent upon their purohits. There are no *gotra* and pravaras of the Sudras. Pointing out the difference between *gotra* and *pravara*, P.V. Kane has stated that gotras are the names of those ancient saints who have been traditionally believed to be ancestors or kins of an individual, but pravaras are those very old saints who were very learned and great and were the ancestors of even those who

1 Prabhu, *Hindu Social Organisation*, Popular Book Depot, Bombay, pp. 154-55.

introduced gotras. The word *pravara* comes from the root meaning selection. Hence, producing evidence from Vedic literature, Sri Kane has proved that *pravaras* are the selected names of those saints which were uttered of his own volition by a person while engaged in performing *yagya,* a religious sacrifice. Later on, the number of saints of pravaras was counted and determined. This number is believed to be forty-nine.

Scholars differ in their opinions as to the prohibition of *sagotra* and *sapravara* marriages. According to Karandikar, the Aryans adopted this practice from non-Aryan races who married outside their totem. Most people seem to think that people of the same *gotra* are related by blood. For this reason, *sagotra* and *sapravara* marriages have been forbidden in order to avoid the bad consequences of near relations. But actually, this restriction is baseless because, as has been pointed out by Medhatithi and Vigyaneshwar, *gotra* is that name of an ancestor which has been traditionally handed down. Sri P.V. Kane has written that in ancient times while engaged in the performance of *yagya* the host uttered the name of very old spiritual saints and said that, "The offering I am giving or making to the fire is the same as that made by Aurva, by Bhrigu, by Shuchi or by Angira. May my *yagya* be successful as were theirs."[1] The saints so chosen of one's own free will were called pravaras. It is evident from these opinions that the words *gotra* or *pravara* are not indicative of any blood relationships. Then, actually pravaras and gotras are confined only to the Brahmins. The gotras and pravaras of Kshatriyas are accepted to be as that of their priests. The history of gotras and pravaras is so ancient that people do not remember even the names of their gotras and pravaras and it cannot be determined. And even otherwise it seems meaningless to forbid marriage on the basis of *gotra* and *pravara* when there have been hundreds of generations in the interval.

According to A. S. Altekar, *sagotra* and *sapravara* marriages are not found before 600 BC.[2] The word *gotra* has not been used in this sense in the Vedic literature. According to Sri Paad Dange, social beings tied together by the *yagya* methods of the ancient Aryans could not even dream of marrying outside their own *gotra* or lineage. The practice of not marrying one's own relatives that is prevalent among us today has been developed over a period of many thousand years.

Inter-Caste Marriage

Inter-caste marriage means the union of a man and woman belonging to two different castes. According to sociologists, inter-caste marriage existed in the very ancient India. The strict laws of endogamy came into force only when the varaa-system was transformed into the caste system. This leads to difficulties in finding a bride-groom resulting in such malpractices as dowry, unsuitable marriages, bride price, etc., come into existence. The sole means to putting an end to such

1 Kane, P.V., Gotra and Pravar in Vedic Literature, *JBBRAS,* 1935.

2 Altekar, AS., *The Position of Women in Hindu Civilization,* Motilal Banarasidas, Banaras, 1958.

malpractices is the encouragement of inter-caste marriages. Two forms of inter-caste marriage were accepted — *anuloma* and *pratiloma* marriages.

Anuloma and Pratiloma Marriages

Although Manu looked upon marriage between people of similar *varna* as the best, yet he had considered *anuloma* marriages acceptable. In the *anuloma* marriage system men of higher castes wed women of lower castes. To quote K.M. Kapadia, "According to this rule a Brahmin can marry a woman from his own *varna* as well as from the other three Varnas. A Kshatriya can have his wife from his own Varna and from the two other lower Varnas. A Vaishya can have only two wives and Sudra only from his own Varna."[1] There is ample evidence in Indian epics and other literaturer to show that *Anuloma* marriages were prevalent. In 150 BC King Agnimitra of the Shung family wedded a Kshatriya princess Malavika. Yajnavalkya permitted the Brahmin or Kshatriya to marry a Kshatriya or Vaishya girl though he did not permit them to marry a Sudra girl. But nevertheless Manu and Yajnavalkya have written on the inheritance of sons born to a Brahmin by a Sudra wife. From this, it is evident that such marriages did take place.

Pratiloma marriage is also a form of inter-caste marriage in which men of lower caste marry women of superior castes. Manu has bitterly criticised and decried *pratiloma* marriage. But subsequent commentators have accepted it. A Brahmin King named Kakustha Verma gave his daughters in marriage to Gupta Kings.

Anuloma and *Pratiloma* marriages retained their acceptability till the end of the tenth century because till that time there were not many cultural differences between Brahmins, Kshatriyas and Vaishyas. Gradually, the rituals among them diverged further and further till in the 9th century this divergence became so marked that both these forms of inter-caste marriages rapidly vanished. In 1020 AD, Alberuni writes that the Brahmins of the time considered it improper to encourage the three lower castes and did not hence take girls in marriage from among them. The writers of the 15th and 16th centuries have made mention of the prohibition of inter-caste marriages in Hindu society.

The rejection and prevention of inter-caste marriages is based upon the notions of purity and the cultural differences between various castes. But as a result of the influence of Western culture the cultural differences between the various castes in India are gradually being developed. There is nothing wrong with inter-caste marriages, and, even more, their plurality will help eliminate or remove such malpractices as dowry, bride price, unsuited marriages, etc.

Hypergamy

In old days much importance was given to family nobility in Bengal. Therefore, hypergamy became very popular there. Everyone wanted to marry his daughters into the nobility though the supply of eligible noble bachelors was very low.

1 Kapadia, K.M., *Marriage and Family in India*, p. 202.

Among the noble (*kulin*) Brahmins the contracting of such marriages became their occupation and their livelihood. One noble Brahmin married anywhere from 30 to 100 girls. After marriage these girls continued to live with their parents. The noble Brahmins migrated from their habitat in winter to earn money which would last them the year. In this connection Babu Abhaya Chandra has written that he knew two noble Brahmins of whom one had sixty and the other hundred wives. Each of these two had a notebook in which he wrote the names of the villages in which he had been married and alongside wrote the names of the fathers of his wives. Generally, it happened that father and son, and husband and wife met as strangers. Risley too has mentioned noble Bengalis the number of whose wives exceeded fifty.

PROBLEMS OF HINDU MARRIAGE

The following are the chief problems faced by the institution of Hindu marriage recently:

1. Child Marriage. The problem of child marriage was very serious in Hindu society till the passing of *Sarada Act.* Since, then the age of the marriage of boys and girls has been gradually increasing so much so that in some cases it is thirty for the boy and more than twenty-five in case of girl. In fact, the reasonable age for marriage is eighteen to twenty-two in the case of girls and twenty-five in case of boys. The reasons behind child marriages in Hindu society were religious conservatism, endogamy, van-custom, the custom of dowry and the joint family. *The Hindu Marriage Act of 1955* has fixed the valid age for marriage of the boys and girls at 18 and 15 respectively. These legal steps could not work immediately because of the widespread conservatism among Hindus, incompleteness of Prohibitive Act and the absence of female education. With the removal of these difficulties in the way of restraint of child marriages, this problem has appreciably diminished in Hindu society.

2. Widow Remarriage. About the condition of widow remarriage in ancient India, A.S. Altekar has written, "Side by side with *niyoga,* the widow remarriage also prevailed in Vedic society."[1] The custom of widow remarriage, however, disappeared gradually and it was considered to be wrong as early as 200 AD. The restriction on widow remarriage resulted in the increase of immorality among widows, sexual exploitation of child widows, increase of prostitutes and the lowering of the general status of women in Hindu society. It led to large scale conversion of Hindu widows to Islam and Christianity. Much can be said about the ethical justification of widow remarriage. It gives the fundamental human rights of marriage to the young woman who has ultimately lost her husband. It eliminates the possibilities of the increase of immorality and prostitution. From the social viewpoint it results in the increase of the number of Hindus, saves the society from evils of religious conversion, immorality and prostitution. From legal viewpoint it ends the share of the widow in the property of her late husband, while,

1. Altekar. A.S. *The Position of Women in Hindu Civilization,* p. 150.

on the other hand, it gives her all legal rights of inheritance, adoption of child, etc., in the house of her new husband.

Due to the untiring efforts of Iswarchandra Vidyasagar the *Hindu Widows Remarriage Act* was passed in 1856. This Act declared the legal validity of widow remarriage and laid specific circumstances for its validity. At present, though widow remarriage is not very much admired it is not opposed in Hindu society. In the lower castes it was never seriously opposed. In the higher castes it is now gradually being accepted.

3. Dowry. According to Max Radin, "Ordinarily dowry is the property which a man receives when he marries, either from his wife or her family."[1] The *Websters New International Dictionary* has defined dowry as, "the money, goods or estate, which a woman brings to her husband in marriage."[2] In brief, dowry is that money, property or valuables which the bride party has to give to the bride-groom party in exchange of marriage.[3] Thus, the chief evil of dowry system is that the bride party is compelled to give it in exchange of marriage, otherwise the bride has to suffer the consequences at the hands of her in-laws. It is hence that Altekar has rightly said, "It is now high time for Hindu society to put an end to the evil custom, which has driven many an innocent maiden to commit suicide."[4] Some persons have pointed out to some so-called advantages of dowry system. They have maintained that it helps in the establishment of the new house-hold of the newly married couple. It has been pointed out that the lure of dowry helps in the marriage of ugly and uneducated girls. These so-called advantages do not count even for an iota before the glaring evils of dowry system. Some of the gross evils of this system can be seen in the murder of female children, the suicides of young maidens, the late marriages of girls, unmatched marriages, breaking of the settlement of marriage on the question of dowry, the child marriages to avoid dowry, the criminal activities of the fathers of girls and the lowering of the standard of living, increasing family disharmony, immorality, mental diseases and finally in the hindrance to women education. The evil of dowry is persisting because of increase of the value of money, general poverty, unemployment, delimitation of the field of choice of mate, the competition to get the bridegroom from rich family, etc. The evil can be restricted only by strict legal measures against it. Recently, some sort of legal restriction on dowry was made by an Act passed by the Government. This, however, has not been sufficiently effective. With the increase of women education, the incidence of inter-caste marriages and antidowry propaganda, this evil can be appreciably uprooted from Hindu society.

4. Divorce. Before the passing of *Hindu Marriage Act of 1955*, the Hindu women could not divorce her husband even though he made hell of her life. The *Hindu Marriage Act* has divided Hindu marriage into valid, void and voidable. The age-

1 Max Radin, *Encyclopaedia of Social Sciences*, V, p. 230.

2 *Websters New International Dictionary*; I, p. 668.

3 *Encyclopaedia Britannica*, VII, p. 565.

4 Altekar, A.S., *The Position of Women in Hindu Civilization*, 1965, p. 71.

limit in case of boys and girls has been fixed at 18 to 15 respectively. The Act has prescribed monogamy and declared polygamy to be illegal. It has accepted the mother as the guardian of the children along with the father. But its more important prescription is with regard to divorce. It permits divorce in the cases of adultery, change of religion, suffering from some incurable diseases not contacted from the other spouse, renunciation of the world, not traccable for more than seven years, absence of co-habitation for two years after the decree of judicial separation and not following the decree for the restitution of conjugal rights. The wife can divorce the husband even, if his another wife is alive or if he has been found guilty of rape, sodomy or bestiality. The application for divorce can be filed after three years of marriage. In the meanwhile judicial separation is allowed on the following conditions:

(i) Desertion of the Applicant by another party two years before the date of application.

(ii) Suffering of another party from leprosy or any other infectious disease, for one year before the date of application but the disease should not have been contacted from the applicant.

(iii) Madness of the party for two years before the date of application.

(iv) Co-habitation of either person with some man and woman other than the husband and the wife.

(v) After the court gives permission to divorce the man and woman cannot marry for one year.

THE HINDU CODE

The Indian Parliament have passed the following Acts for reform of Hindu marriage, family and the status of woman in Hindu society: *Hindu Married Women's Right to Separate Residence and Maintenance Act, Hindu Marriage Act, Hindu Succession Act, Hindu Adoption and Maintenance Act*, and *Hindu Minority and Guardianship Act*. These Acts are collectively known as Hindu Code.

1. Hindu Married Women's Rights to Separate Residence and Maintenance Act, 1946. By this Act, the Hindu married women can claim maintenance while residing separate from the husband on the following conditions: 1. If the husband is suffering from some loathsome disease which has not been contacted from the wife. 2. If the husband behaves so cruelly towards the wife that her residing with the husband is undesirable and dangerous. 3. If the husband deserts her without her wish. 4. If the husband marries again. 5. If the husband adopts another religion. 6. If the husband keeps some concubine. 7. Other justifiable causes. But the wife cannot demand maintenance from the husband if she is guilty of adultery or conversion to another religion.

2. Hindu Marriage Act, 1955. This Act applies to all the members of Hindu society. It has made the following important changes in the institution of Hindu marriage.

(i) *Classification of Hindu marriage*: According to this Act, Hindu marriage can be divided into three classes — void, voidable and valid.

(ii) *Determination of the age for marriages*: By the provisions of this Act, the minimum age limit for the boys and girls has been fixed at 18 and 15 years respectively.

(iii) *Provision for monogamy*: According to this Act, a Hindu male or female can enter into matrimony only if no spouse of either is alive at the time of marriage. Thus, the section 5 and clause 1 of this Act provide for monogamy in Hindu society.

(iv) *Provision for the guardianship of the mother*: According to this Act, the mother will be considered the legal guardian of the minor son or daughter after the father.

(v) *Provision for divorce*: As has been already pointed out in the discussion of the problem of divorce in Hindu Society, the Hindu Marriage Act provides for divorce by wife or husband under certain specific circumstances.

3. Hindu Succession Act, 1956. According to this Act, the daughter is also given equal rights of inheritance in the property of the father, along with the son. The women got right of the use, sale and mortgage of the property received through inheritance.

4. Hindu Adoption and Maintenance Act, 1956. According to this Act, the husband has to take the consent of the wife while adopting a son or daughter. The issueless widow also got right of adoption. The following conditions should be satisfied to make adoption legal:

1. After the death of husband every sound-minded adult widow has a right to adopt a son or give her son to another for adoption. 2. Every healthy-minded male will have a right to adopt a son but this will require the consent of his wife. 3. The unmarried adult woman will also have the right of adoption. 4. The adopted person will be less than 15 years in age and normally unmarried unless there is a custom of child marriage in his or her case. 5. The daughter can also be adopted and given for adoption. There may be certain undesirable consequences of the adoption of a girl by widower and boy by a widow. Therefore, it has been specified that the widower or bachelor should be at least 2 years older than the girl. Similarly, the widow or the unmarried woman should be at least 21 years older than the son. Again, the age of the boy or the girl at the time of his or her adoption should be less than 15 years.

The Hindu Adoption and Maintenance Act provides for the maintenance of the adopted son and daughter, the deserted wife and widow, the disabled old man or woman and the helpless persons. In this connection, the following important provisions have been made: 1. The Hindu wife will have the right of maintenance during the life time of her husband. The wife deserted by the husband or living separate from him by her own wish will have the right of maintenance under certain specific circumstances. If the husband keeps a concubine, changes his religion, behaves cruelly, suffers from loathsome disease, the wife will have a right of maintenance though living separate from the husband. 2. The widowed daughter-in-law and the grand daughter-in-law will also have right of maintenance. 3. The widow or unmarried daughter will also have right of maintenance by the father. 4. The minor children, even if they may be illegitimate will have a right to claim maintenance from the parents during the terms of their minority.

5. Hindu Minority and Guardianship Act, 1956. This Act prescribes for the following provisions in connection with guardianship. 1. The child will remain under the guardianship of his mother upto the age of five years. It is only after it that the father will be considered as the legal guardian. After the death of the father the mother will again have the right of guardianship. 2. In the case of unmarried daughter and the illegitimate son the mother will have the right of guardianship and it is only after her death that the father will get this right. The right of the guardianship of the married daughter will vest with her husband. 3. The legal guardian will have a right to do all such things which he considered to be necessary for the good of the minor child. But, he cannot do anything contrary to his other interests. He will not have any right to spend, sell, mortgage or gift any portion of the property of the minor person under his guardianship. For the purposes of this Act, the child below the age of 18 will be considered a minor and under the guardian.

Effect of Hindu Code on the Status of Hindu Women

The above-mentioned Acts under Hindu code have widely influenced the status of women in Hindu society. The following are the important points in this connection:

1. Equal Right to Male and Female. The Hindu code provides for equal rights of the Hindu male and female in almost every field of life. With it the females have secured equal rights with the male concerning inheritance of property, adoption of son and daughter, remarrying after the death of husband, divorcing the husband in certain circumstances and marrying again. Thus, the code has finished the exploitation of women in Hindu society. They have been given all human rights and thus do not depend on males' mercy.

2. End of Male's Domination in Family. The Hindu code have ended the male's domination in Hindu family. Now, the husband cannot adopt a son or daughter without the consent of the wife. In the case of the daughter the mother is the life-long guardian. The husband cannot misbehave with the wife because if he does so she cannot only get divorce from him but also claim for maintenance unless she remarries. The daughters and the widows have rights of inheritance of property. The father and mother have equal rights of guardianship of the children.

3. Abolition of Polygamy. Before the passing of Hindu Marriage Act the evil of polygamy was widely prevalent in Hindu society. The Hindu Marriage Act has put an end to it. Now the husband cannot keep a concubine or marry another woman in the life time of his wife. Thus, the Hindu Marriage Act has established monogamy in Hindu society.

4. Restriction of Child Marriages. The new social legislations have eliminated the evil of the child marriage from Hindu society. The age of legal marriage has been fixed at 18 and 15 for the boys and girls respectively.

5. Increase in the Unstability of Family. With the provision for judicial separation and divorce the Hindu Code has made Hindu family unstable. It has given a blow to the joint family. The number of divorces has increased. The marital relations have, however, improved because the wife and husband both take care to behave properly so that a condition of judicial separation may not arise. This has led to progress in the status of Hindu women.

6. Women's Rights of Inheritance. The Hindu code has given economic equality to Hindu women by providing for their right of inheritance in the property of husband and father.

7. Equal Rights of Guardianship. The Hindu code has provided for equal rights of guardianship of children to both wife and husband. It has thus established equality in this connection.

8. Life Insurance of the Old and Disabled. By providing for the maintenance of the old, disabled, widows and orphans, the Hindu Code has established social security in this respect. It is a life insurance of these persons.

The above discussion of the influences of Hindu Code makes it quite clear that it has improved the status of women in Hindu society. It has met their age-old demands of inheritance, adoption, maintenance, guardianship, separate residence and divorce. It has placed them on equal footing with the males. Though, here and there it may cause the breaking of a family but indirectly it has made marriage and family stronger by placing them on a sound footing.

QUESTIONS FOR EXERCISE

1. Bring out the importance of Marriage in Hindu social system. Why has it been regarded as a sacrament?
2. Explain the concept and types of Hindu Marriage and contrast it with the marriage institution of Muslims.
3. What is marriage? What is the purpose of Marriage according to Hindu thought?
4. Explain the contemporary trends in Hindu marriage.
5. Write a short essay on "Hindu Marriage Today", with particular reference to the selection of a partner and husband-wife relationship.
6. Explain the changing pattern of Hindu marriage in India.

10

The Status of Hindu Women

The status of women in any society is the index of the standards of its social organization. The standard of a society rises and falls in correlation with the rise and fall in the status of women. Society is a web of social relationships of which those between male and female are the most intimate and stable.

Status of Women in Hindu Society

Hindu society has always remained dynamic. The status of women in it has consequently always changed. A study of this change of status will on the one hand show the Hindu women's fights for her rights and, on the other hand, the dynamic nature of Hindu social organization.

Status of Women in Ancient Hindu Society

In ancient India, the women were given an equal status along with men in almost every field of life. They received higher education and participated in the discussion of political and philosophical nature with male scholars. The Vedas, the Upanisads, the *Mahabharata* and the Puranas mentioned the names of the lady scholars, philosophers, poets and politicians in ancient India. In *Mahabharata,* the wife has been called the better half of the husband. In *Aitereya Upanisad,* the wife has been called the companion of the husband. In *Rigveda,* the wife has been blessed to live as a queen in the house of her husband The word '*dampati*' so often used in the Vedas characterises both wife and husband. It is said that *dampati* press the *Soma,* rinse and mix it with milk, and offer adoration to the God.[1] According to Macdonell and Keith this word signifies the high status of women in ancient India. The wife and husband cooperated in different functions of the household. They together performed religious duties, enjoyed and carried out other functions. In *Mahabharata,* the wife has been called the root of *dharma.* prosperity and enjoyment. "The execution of the *dharma* of man depends upon woman; all pleasures and enjoyments also entirely depend upon her Men should

1 *Rigveda,* VIII. 31, 5, X, 186; VIII 27, 7.

therefore serve women and bend their wills before them."[1] No man was allowed to perform religious duties without a wife. Thus, like the status of the women in contemporary western world, the status of Indian women in ancient India was based on liberty, equality and co-operation. What, however, makes them different is the ancient Indian emphasis on spirituality and religion, duty and co-operation in family life.

Status of Women in Medieval India

In the medieval India, the status of women was very much low. The scriptures prescribed rules for child marriages which increased the number of widows. The rules of conduct for the widows were even more rigid. The ancient Indian ideal of the equality of male and female was finished and women were considered to be slaves of men. In Buddhist and Muslim periods, the status of women was lowered even further. In the Muslim time, the custom of veil, the child marriage, and the custom of dying on the funeral pyre of the husband was prevalent.

Status of Women in Modern India

About a century back, the status of women in India was almost the same as it was in the medieval age. Though, it cannot be said that the exploitation of women in India has no parallel in any other country, it can be safely asserted that the women had to face much cruelty and exploitation in modern India. Even, now, the birth of a daughter is not an occasion of happiness for many Hindu families. Ordinarily, the celebrations of the birth of a son are definitely more joyful than those of the birth of a daughter. The daughters are not given equal rights with the son in the matters of food, clothings, education, etc. They are often married even without their consent. In the house of the husband, their status becomes even worse. The husband, the mother-in-law, the father-in-law and other members of the family consider the daughter-in-law as a servant of the family, whose only duty is to obey everyone, to wake up earliest and to sleep late, to eat whatever remains after others have eaten and not to complain anything about it to anyone. If the husband deserts her or remarries or dies untimely, the condition of the woman becomes worst of all, for her family members believe that this calamity has fallen because of her bad luck. The widow gets no share in the property of her husband, nor is anyone prepared to marry her.

The principles of Hindu social organization were formulated by males, who kept the women without equal rights in the social life. For centuries, the Hindu women tolerated all sorts of cruelties at the hands of males. Some male philosophers even called them as the doors of hell as if male was very much pure and great. The male made her a toy for the satisfaction of his desires and put the entire responsibility over her head. The widows were not permitted to marry and males of the household tried to enjoy with her secretly. She was helpless to oppose all this and when some bad consequence followed, the entire responsibility was

---

1 *Mahabharata,* Anushasana Parva, 10.

put over the head of the widow and she was turned out of the house. The helpless, weak and young widow was forced to adopt the job of a prostitute. This is the story of thousands of prostitutes in India. The woman was asked to live as a complete celibate after the death of her husband. She was encouraged to die at the funeral pyre of her husband in an effort to meet him in the heavens. The male could marry several times and the woman had no right to speak against him.

The Demands of Modern Indian Women

With the advent of Women's education in India and the influence of the West, together with the efforts of social reformers of contemporary India, the fore-mentioned account of the low status of women in Indian society has changed. The women rose against the cruelties of the male. They challenged the prescriptions of Hindu scriptures who gave them a lower status in social organization. The educated Indian women re-examined the principles of Hindu social organization. They found that they have been given an equal status in society by God. Hence, they revolted when they were denied this equality. They understood the selfishness behind the principles of Sati, restriction of widow remarriage, child marriage, unmatched marriages, polygamy, denial of equal rights to women in property, etc.

The challenge given by educated women in Hindu social, economic, political, religious and family organization is one of the greatest challenges that Hindu society has faced in modern times. The society was thus compelled to give equal rights to women in every field of life. The Indian women had not to fight a very long battle as it was in the case of western sisters. With the achievement of freedom by India, she was given equal political rights. With the enactment of *Hindu Code*, she was allowed equal rights in matters of inheritance, adoption of the child, divorce and others.

Briefly, the following were the demands of Indian women in the modern times:

1. Restriction of Child Marriage. In the case of child marriage the women had to face the evil consequences in the form of loss of health, early old age, untimely widowhood and others. Therefore, modern women demanded restriction of child marriages.

2. Opposition of Polygamy. The custom of polygamy very much lowered the status of woman in the family. They never enjoyed marital bliss which is only possible in the case of monogamy. They could not fully develop their personality. Therefore, the modern women categorically denied the right of polygamy to the male.

3. Equality in Marital Rights. Along with the restriction on polygamy, the women claimed equality in all marital rights. They wanted to live as true companion of the husband in every walk of life.

4. Right to Divorce. In the medieval times, when woman was not given the right of divorce, she had to face all types of cruelties at the hands of an impotent, a mad, or a cruel husband which made her life impossible. The modern woman sought the right of divorce in such conditions, for she married for love and could not stay with the husband if she was denied of it.

5. Restriction of Dowry. In the present times, the daughters remain a burden on the parents because of the custom of dowry in Hindu society. Their status is very much lower than that of the sons and their parents have to suffer much humiliations at the hands of their in-laws. Many fathers try to earn money through illegal means to get a suitable match for their daughter and to give sufficient dowry. Those who fail to do this, sometimes die with the desire to marry off their daughter. If the dowry is less than expected, the daughter-in-law has to suffer at the hands of her in-laws. The evil of dowry has led to the suicide of many a Hindu maiden and made other's life unbearable. Therefore, the Hindu women have raised a voice against this evil custom. In the present times, however, nothing concrete has been done to meet this demand.

6. Demands Regarding Property. As the women were not given any right in ancestral property, their condition was always of dependence on the male. They depended either on father or on husband or on son. Therefore, in the modern times, they have demanded an equal right of property with males.

Measures to Improve the Condition of Hindu Women

The following measures in modern times have led to the improvement of the status of Hindu women in society;

1. Education. In 1857, when Khurshedji, a Parsi gentleman, sought the permission of the syndicate of Bombay University for her daughter to appear in Matriculation Examination, the Syndicate categorically refused. Similarly, Miss Chandramukhi Bose was not allowed to appear in the B.A. Examination of Calcutta University. In 1877, however, with the efforts of the Vice Chancellor Hobhouse, women were allowed to appear in the examination conducted by Calcutta University. It was only in 1882 that two women for the first time received B.A. Degree of Calcutta University. After this, there was such a strong wave of woman education in India that now it cannot be said that Indian women are in anyway lagging behind men in this respect.

2. Movements of Social Reform. Many movements of social reform in contemporary India did a magnificent work in raising the status of women in society. By the efforts of Raja Rammohun Roy, Pandita Ramabai, Mrs. Ranadey, Keshab Chandra Sen, Swami Dayanand and Mrs. Anibesant, much was done in the direction of restriction on child marriages, permission of widow remarriage and finishing of the customs of Devadasi and Sati. In 1917, the Women's Indian Association was established to carry out reforms in the condition of Indian women. In 1929, the different institutions for the uplift of Indian women jointly constituted All India Women's Conference. Later on, was established Indian Council of Women, which was done important work in the direction of social reform among Indian women.

3. Political Awakening. In 1930, Indian women participated in the Non- co-operation Movement launched by Mahatma Gandhi, in 1932, they were given right to vote in provincial and central elections. In 1936, they were given right to be elected to Provincial and Central Legislatures. Since, then women have increasingly participated in Indian political life, elected to Legislatures and performed duties of a Minister or Governor and even of Prime Minister, in the case of Mrs. Indira Gandhi.

4. Social Legislations. After India became independent, several social legislations were enacted to improve the condition of Indian women. The Hindu Married Women's Rights to Separate Residence Act, 1946 gave her a right to reside separately from the husband under certain circumstances. The Hindu Marriage Act, 1955 classified Hindu marriages, determined the age for marriage, provided for monogamy and guardianship for the mother and permitted divorce under certain circumstances. The Hindu Succession Act of 1956, prescribed for equal rights of the daughter in the property of the father. The Hindu Adoption and Maintenance Act, 1956 permitted Hindu women to adopt a son or daughter and to claim maintenance from the husband under certain circumstances. The Hindu Minority and Guardianship Act, 1956 provided for the guardianship of the mother over the daughter throughout her life and in the case of the son for first five years. These social legislations have considerably improved the status of women in Hindu society and granted most of their demands.

The above-mentioned measures have led to an alround improvement in the status of women in Hindu society. Attempts are being made to abolish the custom of dowry from Hindu society. Women are receiving higher education in large numbers and participation in almost every field of life. In Indian Parliament, there are about a dozen of lady members. In State Legislatures, their number aggregates up to 100. They have reached the high offices of Chief Minister, State Governor and even Prime Minister. Many of them are well-known politicians of all-India level. Others are getting fame in literary fields. In the fields of sports, Indian women, have excelled. They are now entering even the departments of engineering, police and military. The day is not far when they will achieve an absolutely equal status with males in Indian society.

Consequences of Female Education

The above discussion of the rise of the status of Indian women makes it clear that education has played a very important part in women's regeneration. From the sociological point of view, women's education results into the following consequences:

1. Late Marriages. As higher education requires many years the educated woman marries at a late age. At least the custom of child marriages has absolutely disappeared due to women's education.

2. Development of Personality. The purpose of education is an alround development of the personality of the educand. Thus, the spread of education among women in India has given them chances to improve their personality, to think independently, to choose their careers and their companions of life.

3. The Sentiment of Self Regard. Education creates a sentiment of self-regard in the educated person. The educated women, therefore, cannot helplessly tolerate any high-handedness. They, on the other hand, claim equal rights with the male and revolt against all types of atrocities. Thus, women's education has finished the domination of male in Hindu family and given equal rights to the female.

4. Complexity of the Problem of Marriage. The provision of higher education for women, however, leads to the complexity of the problem of her marriage. The educated woman is not prepared to marry a person who does not catch her imagination. Therefore, it is a difficult job for the parents to get a suitable match for her. This, on the one hand, results in very late marriages and, on the other hand, some women prefer to remain unmarried throughout their life.

5. Economic Freedom. The higher education of women creates a tendency to seek economic freedom. They compete with males in all types of jobs and professions. Most of them do not want to be dependent economically on the father or husband. In western countries, women's education has very much improved the number of working women.

6. Increase in Divorce. The educated women do not marry for economic security but for love and marital bliss and if this is not forthcoming they tend to divorce the husband because they have not to think about meeting the economic needs. This tendency has led to an increase in the rate of divorce.

7. Small Families. The educated women do not want to increase the family beyond a certain limit because, on the one hand, this reduces their health and, on the other hand, it restricts the chances of enjoying life. The uneducated women do not know techniques of family planning, nor can they understand its importance. The educated wives can easily understand the techniques of birth control and can convince their husbands in this respect. Education improves the standard of living, while the increase in the size of the family lowers it. Therefore with the spread of education among women, the size of the family has decreased.

The above discussion of the sociological consequences of women's education makes it clear that the rise of the status of women very much depends on their education. Higher education of women definitely creates certain difficulties in some cases but this is the necessary price that we have to pay for any social reform.

QUESTIONS FOR EXERCISE

1. Account for the changing status of women in India.
2. Outline the position of women in the family as visualised by Hindu law givers.
3. Describe the factors that have affected the status of Hindu women.
4. Discuss the impact of various forces that have helped to raise the status of Hindu women.
5. In the light of recent social legislation write an essay on the status of women in India.

11

Muslim Social System and Institutions

The Muslims form an important part of Indian society and therefore the study of their social system and institutions is necessary for an understanding of the modern Indian society and institutions. This is all the more important because their social institutions very much differ from those of the Hindus.

MUSLIM MARRIAGE

The social life of the Muslims is governed by the rules prescribed by their sacred scripture Quran. The laws of Muslim marriage are based on Quran. The marriage among Muslims is a social contract which aims at getting legitimate offspring. Muslim marriage meets all the requirements of a valid contract provided in Indian Contract Act. For the purposes of marriage the bride and bridegroom both must have healthy bodies and healthy minds and should not have any type of illegitimate connections. Boys and girls of less than 15 years of age cannot marry without the sanction of their guardians. The marriages among minors or mad persons are declared void. No religious ceremony or formality is required to make marital contract valid if the above-mentioned rules are adhered. The following are the three essentials of Muslim marriage:

1. Proposal and its Acceptance. Among Muslims the proposal of marriage and its acceptance should be carried out in the same meeting. The proposal of marriage is put in the presence of two males or one male and two females and it should be accepted immediately. If the proposal is made in one meeting and accepted in another, the marriage is not valid. The presence of two persons is for the purpose of witnesses. In the absence of witnesses marriage becomes irregular, but not void. Among Shia Muslims the witnesses are not necessary.

2. Marital Capacity of the Bride and the Bridegroom. In the Muslim Marriage, the bride and the bridegroom should possess ability and capacity to enter into marital contract. Mentally deficient or insane persons cannot legitimately enter into matrimony. The minors are married with the permission of the guardians.

3. Absence of Impediments in Marriage. A legitimate Muslim marriage can be contracted only in the absence of impediments in it. These impediments are of two types, some which make marriage void, and others which make it totally prohibited. The latter do not make a marriage void, but only make it irregular.

In the following circumstances a Muslim marriage is declared as void:

(i) *Polygamy.* The marriage of a woman becomes void if her other husband is alive. The males, however, have a right to marry three women other than the present wife. The marriage with a fifth woman is void.

(ii) *Marriage with near Relatives.* Muslim marriage is declared void if it is contracted with certain very near relatives, for example, ascendants, such as the mother, grandmother, mother-in-law etc., descendants such as daughter, granddaughter etc., among real sisters and brothers, with the niece, granddaughter of the brother, daughter-in-law, wife of the grand-son or the wife of the son or the wife of the son of the daughter.

(iii) *Marriage with idol worshippers.* Muslim religion forbids idol worship. The marriage of a Muslim male or female with an idol worshipper, therefore, is declared to be void.

(iv) *Marriage among insanes and minors.* The marriages among insanes and the marriages of minors without the permission of the guardians are considered to be void among Muslims.

Muslim marriages contracted in the following circumstances are declared to be irregular—

(i) *Marriage with fifth woman.* Islam forbids marriage with a fifth woman while the other four are alive. Such a marriage, however, can be regularised by divorcing one of the former four wives. John Gunther has written that Ibn Saud, the founder of Saudi Arabia, used to divorce one of his four wives before going on a journey, so that he may be entitled to marry any woman he may like during the course of his journey. He thus married legally with at least 120 women.

(ii) *Absence of witnesses.* Among the Sunni Muslims the absence of witnesses in a marital contract makes it irregular. Among the Shia Muslims, however, the presence of witnesses is not considered to be necessary.

(iii) *Marriage with followers of other religions.* According to the Shia rule of marriage the bride and the bridegroom both must be Muslims in order to contract a valid Muslim marriage. But the temporary form of Muslim marriage known as Muta can be contracted even with those who respect the same scriptures such as the Jews, Christians and Parsees.

The Procedure of Muslim Marriage

The proposal of marriage among the Muslims is made only when both the parties have enquired about one another and satisfied themselves. The proposal of marriage should be made and accepted in the same meeting. When both the parties have settled about the economic aspect of marriage, they decide some date to perform the marriage ceremony. On this date the bridegroom offers the settled 'Mehar' to the bride's party. The consent of both the bride and the bridegroom is necessary to make a marital contract valid. From the side of the bride some other person may also disclose her consent. Some adult person must be a witness to the contract of marriage. This witness, who is a relative of the bride's party, goes to the bride and asks her whether she gives him the right to settle her marriage with the man who is offering her 'Mehar'. He also narrates the complete description of the proposed bridegroom. If the bride gives her consent, the bridegroom and the witness are presented before the priest. When the bridegroom gives her sanction the witness tells the priest that he is the representative for the bride. The priest determines from the witness whether the bride has consented to marry the bridegroom after the Mehar has been paid. When both the parties agree to the contract of marriage, the priest recites certain Kalma and the marriage is considered to be performed.

Type of Muslim Marriage

According to Muslim Marriage Rules, the marriages are classified among the following three types —

(1) *Valid Contract.* Such a marriage is contracted by following all prescribed rules and the birth of offspring from it is considered to be ligitimate.

(2) *Void Marriages.* A marriage whose basis is not legal is called a void marriage. It does not create any responsibilities or legitimacy in the marriage contract.

(3) *Irregular Marriages.* A marriage becomes irregular whose basis is sound but in which some formality has been left unfulfilled. If this formality is fulfilled after marriage it becomes regular. For example, the marriage with a fifth woman can be regularised by divorcing one of the former four wives, the marriage among the minors can be regularised by getting the permission of their guardians and the marriage without witness can be regularised by making some one a witness to it even after marriage.

Muta Marriage

The Sunnis among Muslims admit only a permanent form of marriage but Shias accept a temporary marriage known as 'Muta'. This type of marriage is contracted under two conditions. Firstly, the settlement of the period of marriage which may range from one day to several years and secondly, the settlement about the quantity of 'Mehar'. Of the two conditions the former is more important. The Muta marriage is valid if its period has been fixed even if no settlement about Mehar has been made. On the other hand, if Mehar has been settled, while the period of its duration has not been fixed, the marriage remains illegitimate. Both male and female have a right to enter into Muta marriage. The woman cannot marry any non-Muslim while the Muslim male can marry a Christian, a Jew or a Parsee woman. No one, however, has been permitted of contract this temporary sort of marriage with a follower of any other religion. Muta marriage differs from the permanent type of marriage on the following grounds —

(1) *Succession.* The right of succession is secured only in a permanent type of marriage and not in Muta marriage. The sons born through Muta marriage, however, are given a right to inherit the property of both the parents.

(2) *Dissolution of marriage.* A permanent Muslim marriage can be dissolved only through divorce. In Muta marriage the wife has no right to dissolve the marriage before the specified time limit while the husband can dissolve it whenever he wishes to do so. The Sunnis do not accept Muta marriage. In actual practice it is very rare amongst Shias as well.

Option of Puberty

An important principle observed in Muslim marriage is the option of puberty. In India, the age of puberty is considered to be 15 in the case of male and 13 or 14 in the case of female when her menstruation begins. The Privy Council has decided the age of puberty to be 9 years for Shia girl. According to Hidaya, a Muslim scripture, the age of puberty is 12 and 9 in the case of boy and girl respectively. Before the age of puberty the boy and girl are considered to be minors and the sanction of their guardians is considered to be necessary for a valid marriage. But in the case of such marriage the bride and the bridegroom can reject the contract after attaining the age of puberty. This option of rejecting the marital contract performed at the minor age is called the option of puberty in Muslim marriage. According to it if either the male or female refuses to accept the marital contract after attaining the age of puberty, it is considered as if the marriage never took place.

RESPONSIBILITIES AND RIGHT OF MARRIED WOMAN

The Muslim marriage results into the following responsibilities of the woman—

1. To maintain proper marital relationship with the husband.
2. Following the commands of the husband.
3. Providing sexual enjoyment to the husband keeping in view the principles of health and propriety.
4. To feed the child in the absence of anyone else to do so.
5. Following the principle of 'Iddat' according to which the wife is not permitted to remarry for a certain period during which she must remain a celibate. This decides the paternity of the child in case the woman has any conception.

The Muslim marriage gives the following rights to the married woman —

1. The right to receive 'Mehar' from the husband.
2. The right to reside in the house of the husband.
3. The right to receive maintenance from the husband.
4. The right to receive equal love from the husband in case of the presence of other co-wives.
5. The right of bringing up the children.

It is clear from the above-mentioned rights of a married Muslim woman that she has not been given equality with the husband in this respect. While the husband has a right to marry several women at the same time, the wife can marry only one man. While it is very easy for the husband to divorce the wife, it is very difficult for the wife to do so. In the case of adultery the husband can inflict severe punishment on the wife but the wife can only divorce her husband. The married woman has to constantly live under veil in order to avoid others' sight. She is not given equal rights in the property of the husband.

'MEHAR' OR 'DOWRY'

As has already been pointed out, the Muslim married woman has a right to receive 'Mehar' from the husband. According to Muslim law, marriage is a civil contract and 'Mehar' or dower is its necessary consequence. It is received by woman in exchange of her consent to be his wife. It is not bride-price, but shows respect towards the wife. The dower has been classified as follows:

1. Settled or Definite Dower. This is the dower which has been settled prior to marriage or on the occasion of it. It may vary from a few coins to several thousands of rupees. It is settled by the mutual consent of both the parties of the bride and the bridegroom.

2. 'Meharul Misl'. This is the dower which is not decided at the time of marriage, but after it at the instance of the wife.

3. 'Muwajjal Mehar'. This is the 'Mehar' given by the husband to the wife immediately after marriage.

4. Mehar after Dissolution of Marriage. This is the Mehar paid after dissolution of marriage either because of the breaking of the marital contract or by the death of either spouse or in the case of divorce.

MUSLIM LAW OF DIVORCE

Among Muslims the Law of Divorce is very rigid so far as the woman is concerned but it is easier for the male to divorce his wife. The divorce has been classified into oral and written. The written divorce is called the 'Talaquanama'. The oral divorce has been classified into the following types —

1. Talaq-e-Ahsan. In this type of divorce if the husband pronounces the word 'talaq' once, the wife does not resume sexual relationship with him for a certain specified period which is normally of three months. After this period divorce is accepted.

2. Talaq-e-Hasan. In this type of divorce the husband pronounces the word 'talaq' three times during the period of two menstruations and in the period of third menstruation he does not enter into any sexual relationship with the wife. After this period divorce is accepted as valid.

3. Talaq-ul widdat. In this type of divorce the husband pronounces the word 'talaq' three times during the period of one menstruation. This divorce is irregular and it is regularised only after the completion of the time limit.

Formerly, the Muslim woman had no right to divorce her husband. With the enactment of the Dissolution of Muslim Marriage Act, 1939 she has a right to divorce her husband under the following circumstances:

1. If the husband has not been traced any where for the last four years.
2. If the husband has been unable to meet the expenses of the wife for at least two years.
3. If the husband gets the punishment of imprisonment for seven years or more.
4. If the husband is unable to enter into sexual relationship with or without a reasonable cause.
5. If the husband is impotent.
6. If the husband is mad.
7. If the husband behaves cruelly with the wife.
8. If the husband is insance or suffering from leprosy or virulent venereal diseases for the last two years.

The following are the other methods of the dissolution of a Muslim marriage:

1. 'Jihar'. In this the husband compares his wife with some near relative whom he cannot marry. For example, if the husband compares his wife with his mother, he cannot enter into sexual relationship with her unless he repents for this comparison and if he fails to do so the wife can divorce him.

2. Ila. In this the husband, swearing by God, promises not to enter into sexual relationship with the wife for four months or more. Now, if the husband follows his promise for the specified period, the marriage is considered to be dissolved. This type of dissolution of marriage is no more prevalent in Muslim society.

3. Liyan. If a husband imposes a false charge of adultery on the wife, the wife prays to the court that the husband be ordered to take back his charge. And if the husband fails to do so the marriage is dissolved. If the husband and wife both accuse each other of the charge of adultery, their marriage is considered to be dissolved.

4. Khula. In this the wife asks her husband to set her free from the bonds of marriage in exchange of some amount of money from her. If the husband accepts his wife's request, the marriage is dissolved by mutual consent.

5. Mubar-at. This type of dissolution of marriage also occurs by mutual consent, but in it the wife has not to pay any money to the husband.

In spite of the enactment of the Dissolution of Muslim Marriage Act, 1939, there is much inequality in this respect between the Muslim wife and husband. It is only when this inequality is removed that the Muslim woman can attain an equal status with her husband in society.

COMPARISON OF HINDU-MUSLIM MARRIAGE SYSTEMS

The following are the similarities among Hindu and Muslim marriage systems:

1. Permission of Polygamy to Males. The scriptures of both the Hindus and the Muslims allow the male to marry several times, though among the Muslims this concession is more liberal. According to Hindu scriptures, a man can many a second time with the consent of his wife for getting a male progeny. But among the Muslims no particular cause of marriage or consent of wife is required in the case of four marriages at the same time and the fifth marriage can be always regularised by simply divorcing either of the former four wives. The Hindu scriptures do not permit such polygamy without restriction. According to 'Apastamb' Dharmasutra, a male guilty of deserting his wife without any reason should be made to wear the skin of a donkey for six months. But in practice in medieval times there were hardly any restrictions on polygamy among Hindus so much so that some used to marry dozens of women at the same time. In the case of 'Kulin' marriage in Bengal, the Kulin brahmins used to marry sometimes over 100 women, noted their addresses in their diaries and used to visit them at their father's place once or twice in a year. At present the Hindu Marriage Act has finished the custom of polygamy among the Hindus but no such law has been formulated for Indian Muslims.

2. Custom of Child Marriage. The evil of child marriage has been prevalent in India both among Hindu and Muslim communities. The option of puberty among the Muslims provides the adult male and female to reject child marriage and to marry again. The Hindu Marriage Act has specified the minimum age for marriage in the case of boy and girl and thus declared child marriage to be illegal.

The following are the important differences found between Hindu and Muslim marriage systems:

1. Aims of Marriage. The aims of marriage among Hindus have been specified as Dharma, Kama and the birth of a son. Among the Muslims, the marital contract is made for the satisfaction of sexual urges and procreation.

2. Basis of Marriage. While Hindu marriage is a religious sacrament, the Muslim marriage is civil contract. To quote K.M. Kapadia, "Hindu marriage is a sacrament. It is considered sacred because it is said to be complete only on the performance of the sacred rites accompanied by the sacred formula".

3. Field of Exogamy. Among Muslims the law of Exogamy is applicable only to very near relatives which include some nine relations. They have no restriction of Gotra and Pravara. Among Hindus marriages cannot be contracted between the seven generations from the paternal side and five generations from the maternal side. In 1911, Blunt concluded, from the Census Report of U.P. that due to restriction of marriage among Sapinda relatives the scope of getting a match is considerably limited and the number of relatives who cannot be married reaches four figures. Besides, there is a restriction of Sagotra and Sapravar marriages among Hindus. Inter-caste marriage is also forbidden while the number of castes reaches several thousand. Thus, the field of getting a match for matrimonial purposes becomes very much limited in Hindu community as compared with the Muslims.

4. Distinction in Dowry and Mehar. Among Hindus there is the custom of dowry which is very much different from the custom of Mehar found among the Muslims. While dowry is given by the bride's party to the bridegroom and the bride has no right on it, mehar is given by the bridegroom to the bride's party and the bride has the sole right over it. While dowry is given only on the occasion of marriage, mehar can be given even after marriage has been solemnized. And normally, it is only settled on the occasion of marriage. But now-a-days, the demand of dowry and mehar is increasing beyond limits so that both in the Hindu and Muslim communities reformers are trying to eliminate this custom.

5. Provision of Temporary Marriage. While there is no provision of a temporary marriage among Hindus, in Shia Muslims there is a provision for a temporary marriage known as 'Muta'.

6. Rules about Widow Remarriage. Formerly, there was no provision for widow remarriage in Hindu society and even now when it is legally accepted, in practice no one likes to marry a widow. Among the Muslims, on the other hand, widow remarriage is a normal feature. In the case of widow remarriage among Hindus there is no provision like the rule of Iddat as found among the Muslims.

COMPARISON OF THE STATUS OF WOMEN IN HINDU AND MUSLIM SOCIETY

The comparison of the status of women in Hindu and Muslim society requires a study of the rights and duties of the married women in both the communities. The following are the important points in this respect:

1. Custom of Veil. Among Muslims the custom of veil is a religious principle. The Quran commands the women to remain in veil so that they may maintain their purity. This veil has very much lowered the status of Muslim women. Veil is a symbol of man's lack of confidence in them. It severs the connection of the outer world and restricts their freedom. It has an adverse effect on their health and is an impediment in their education. Because of the religious sanction behind it this custom cannot be easily eliminated from the Muslim community. In the medieval times the Hindu women also began to observe veil due to the influence of the Muslims and also to save themselves from the Muslims. But, in the modern times, the Hindu women easily cast off the veil and they had not to struggle for it.

2. Women's Education. Women's education is far more prevalent in Hindu community as compared with the Muslims. Consequently, the status of women in Muslim society is much lower as compared with that in Hindu Community.

3. Polygamy. Though, polygamy was formerly prevalent among Hindu also, the Hindu Marriage Act has declared it to be illegal. There is, however, no such provision for the Muslims. Islam considers four wives to be valid and only marriage with a fifth woman is considered to be irregular. On the other hand, while polyandry is prevalent among some classes of Hindus, it is not found among the Muslims.

4. Dowry or Mehar. While the custom of dowry considerably lowers the status of women in Hindu society, the rule of Mehar enhances the status of Muslim women. At present, however, the form of both dowry and Mehar has been so much distorted that the reformers in both the communities are seeking to eliminate it.

5. Divorce. Before the enactment of Hindu Marriage Act in 1955, the Hindu women had no right to divorce. The Muslim women had already received this right with the Dissolution of the Muslim Marriage Act in 1939. At present, however, both Hindu and Muslim women enjoy a right to divorce but while the conditions of divorce in Hindu community are equal for the wife and husband, among the Muslims it is easier for the husband to divorce the wife. This inequality with regard to the right to divorce has lowered the status of women in Muslim society.

6. Punishment for Adultery. While among the Hindus the husband can leave his wife in case of adultery, among the Muslims in some countries the husband has a right to kill his wife as well as her lover. According to the prescription of Abdullah Ekandi, the property of the deceased woman will be received by her husband. Though, Quran does not provide for a very severe punishment to the wife in the case of adultery, Hazrat Mohammad has prescribed the punishment of one hundred canes for her. On the other hand, if the charge of adultery on the wife is found to be false, the husband will be given a punishment of 80 canes.

7. Sanction to Widow Remarriage. Among Muslims widow remarriage is a normal feature though the widow cannot remarry immediately after the death of her husband and has to wait for at least three months. Formerly, there was no provision for widow remarriage in Hindu society, but now they have been legally permitted to do so.

8. Right of Inheritance. Among Muslims the daughter gets a share in the father's property equal to half of the share of the son. The widow gets one half of the husband's property and one-fourth if she is without any issue. Thus, the Muslim woman has not been given equal rights with male in matters of succession. Formerly, the Hindu women had no right to succession and property but with the enactment of Hindu Succession Act, 1956, the daughter gets an equal right to succession and property along with the son. This provision has improved the status of women in Hindu society as compared to that in Muslim community.

The above discussion regarding the status of women among Hindu and Muslims makes it clear that however backward may be the status of Hindu women formerly, their present condition is far better than that of their Muslim sisters. An important reason of this difference is the religious dogmatism and an opposition to all types of social reforms in Muslim community. The influence of Western culture is, however, gradually awakening Muslim women and they are demanding equal rights with men in different spheres of life. It may be that in future they get equal rights with males as their sisters are enjoying in Hindu community.

QUESTIONS FOR EXERCISE

1. Examine the Muslim law of marriage in relation to the husband-wife relationship.
2. Whereas Hindu marriage is a religious sacrament, Muslim marriage is a contract for legalising sexual intercourse and procreation of children. Analyse the statement.
3. Compare and contrast the status of women in Hinduism with the status of women in Islam.

12

Christian Social System and Institutions

The Christian Community is the largest in number in India next to Hindus and Muslims. Of course, Christianity is the most populous religion of the world. Proselytisation, spreading the Gospel, is the most fundamental tenet of the Christian creed. Accordingly, the followers of Christianity are spread all over the world and their number in most of the countries of the world is fairly sizeable. Christianity is based on the tripartite plank of faith, hope and charity and is strenuously opposed to any distinction between man and man. All men are equal before God. Yet, paradoxically enough, the Christian society is classified and the differences among its classes are sharp and deep. In India, however, the main basis of these differences is wealth, rank and social status. The Western Christians are broadly Catholics and Protestants with so many subclasses. Caste distinctions as noticed in Hindu society are absent in the Christian society; but the evil of casteism has surreptitiously infiltrated into the Indian Christian community. In his *Myth of Caste System* Dr. N. Prasad has distinguished following groups in Kerala Christians. Kerala, incidentally, is the Indian state which has highest concentration of the Christians. In Kerala, the Christians control and dominate the state politics. Following are the groups of Christians in Kerala: (1) Chaldean Syrians; (2) Jacobite Syrians; (3) Latin Catholics; (4) Marthomite Syrians; (5) Syrian Catholics and (6) Protestants. In these groups of Christians we find same type of differences, tensions and competition as in the case of castes among Hindus. Each groups considers itself to be most near the original Gospel and, therefore, higher than others in order and hierarchy. Many Christians look down upon backward Hindu castes and observe a system of untouchability. They do not employ them as domestic helps. Thus, though Christianity is strenuously opposed to casteism and classes among men in theory, in actual practice they observe casteism and practise untouchability. As India's most enlightened Statesman Jawaharlal Nehru observed in his book *Discovery of India*, "Christianity comes here 1800 years ago and settles down and gradually develops its own castes." Such is the climate and social environs of India that all outside groups while passing on something of their own to the Indian society assimilated into them the basic character of Indian culture and could not avoid Indianization.

CHRISTIAN FAMILY

The conception of family in Christianity is quite different from that of other religions. In order of the solemnization of Matrimony in the Anglican Book of Common prayer the following three aims of the family have been given:

1. Propagation of Race. In the fear of God and praising His kindness and Garce to propagate one's kind.

2. Remedy Against Sin. The persons who are unable to control their sexual impulse and lead the life of celibacy marry and procreate.

3. Fellowship, Help and Comfort. In hard times and the time of sickness and disease man and woman may help each other and provide comfort and succour.

Thus, the aim and purpose underlying the Christian institution of family is threefold: procreation, avoidance of sin and mutual aid. The founders of Christianity realized that flesh is weak and man easily descends into the morass of orgy of sex and violence. The free love leads to utter promiscuity and exclusive concentration to the ways of flesh, as a result of which man sinks into bottomless pit of immorality. In order to save man from leading a life of sin and destruction, Christianity advocated the institution of family whereby wild human impulses could be kept in check and continuation of human species could be ensured. The head of the Christian family is the father but the mother has also been given her due share. In practice the mother has come to play a crucial role. The Christians living the villages are usually living as joint family; but in cities the single unit of family is the rule. The customs, traditions, mores, rites and practices followed by Christian families in India are heavily influenced by the Western civilization and culture.

MARRIAGE IN CHRISTIANITY

As may be clear from the foregoing discussion of the Christian family, the institution of marriage is not ineluctable, not an absolute imperative or necessity according to Christianity. The highest ideal of human life is a life of celibacy. Sexual indulgence is sinful. However, since, it is not practically possible for the vast majority of humanity to lead the life of celibacy, sex must be controlled and regulated. Without control and regulation sex is an unpardonable sin. Therefore, according to Christianity the institution of marriage is such a way to regulate and control the sex and ensure healthy procreation and mutual love among men and women. Some Christian fathers are eloquent about the virtue of sex control through marriage and have declared that marriage is an institution sanctioned and blessed by God. The primary aim of the Christian marriage is procreation and healthy development of the personality. The secondary aim of the marriage is the establishment of the family. According to the constitution of the United Church of Northern India, marriage is a sacred institution and it has been blessed by God and it is a natural thing. The marriage is a sacrament in which man and woman are bound for ill or well. They share each other's destiny and ride the course of life together through all its ups and downs. The Christian marriages are solemnized in Churches and require the blessing of the Bishop for completion.

In the choice of life-partners, Christians provide ample freedom to boys and girls. Unlike the arranged marriages in Hindus, the general rule in the Christian marriage is that it is born of free choice of the man and the woman and it is an expression of mutual love and affection. A Christian marriage is preceded usually by a long period of courtship in which the prospective spouses have ample opportunity of understanding each other and knowing the good and bad in each partner.

Besides, the scope of Christian marriage is wide. With the exception of blood-relations, *e.g.*, brother, sister, nephew, niece, Christians are permitted to marry anyone they like. Marriage is regarded as a bond of love by Christians, therefore they attach crucial importance to love. For marriage, the boy and the girl must be member of some church and no marriage is considered solemnized unless there is Church certificate to that effect.

After the desire for marriage is conveyed to the priest by the parents of the bride and the bridegroom, the priest conveys the same to the council of Bishops. Thus, when the consent of the council is obtained, a day is appointed for betrothal. On a fixed day, the members of both the sides gather in the Church and an exchange of finger rings, coconut and money is made as an expression of the acceptance of the marriage bond. The parents of the bridegroom throw feast to the other party. Subsequent to betrothal the boy and the girl are free to meet each other though they are not expected to have sexual congress.

Three weeks prior to marriage, a notice regarding a particular marriage is posted in front of the Church on every Sunday. Anyone can file objection with the Church after submitting the fee for this purpose. If the objection is upheld by the Church, marriage cannot take place, otherwise marriage is solemnized on the fixed day.

DIVORCE

Though, Christianity considers marriage a sacrament and, therefore, marriage is indissoluble, the practice of divorce is quite common among Christians all over the world. The marriage and divorce among Indian Christians were first sought to be regulated in 1872 by *Christian Marriage Act.* The Divorce or Marriage Dissolution Act of 1896 is applicable to Indian Christians, too. This act provides under certain specific circumstances, for judicial separation, protection order and Restitution of Conjugal Rights.

In Christians, re-marriage is allowed and widows and widowers are encouraged to marry. There is, however, no system of child marriages among Christians. Today, the most besetting and baffling problem for Christians is the instability of marriage, growing tendency towards free-love, divorce, wife swapping and the general disregard among Christians about the sanctity of marriage. The Church leaders and other thinkers are disturbed over it. The historians likens the present state of affairs to the declining Roman Empire days.

INDIAN CHRISTIAN MARRIAGE ACT, 1862

This Act determines the categories of Christians who are entitled for marriage. They are given licence for this purpose. The central and provincial governments are authorized to appoint a Registrar for this purpose. The same function can, however, be performed by a Magistrate as well.

According to the rule no. 10 (ten) of the Act, the marriage can be solemnized any time between 7 A.M. and 7 P.M.

The Rule No. 11 (eleven) provides that marriage should be solemnized in Church alone.

The Rule No. 12 (Twelve) provides that either of the spouse shall inform the priest and fill the form given in schedule no. one.

The Rule No. 13 (Thirteen) provides for the publicity of the marriage. It should be notified every Sunday, three weeks before marriage on the Church Notice Board.

The Rule No. 14 (Fourteen) says that if marriage is solemnized at some private place the Registrar will be informed thereof and he shall publicize the marriage.

According to Rule 15 (Fifteen) if any of the spouse is a minor, the fact should be brought to the notice of the Registrar.

According to Rule 16 (Sixteen) in case any spouse is a minor the consent of the parents is essential.

The fourth chapter of the Act deals with the registration of the marriage.

The fifth chapter contains Rules 38 to 59 and these pertain to the system of the marriage.

The sixth chapter contains rules for native Christians. The important among these are—

(1) At the time of marriage the age of the boy should be more than 16 and of the girl more than 13.

(2) At the time of marriage no other spouse, that is, wife or husband should be alive. This is rule forbids bigamy.

(3) There should be two witnesses for a marriage and the parties to marriage should take oath of marriage before the Registrar.

In the seventh chapter of this Act, penalty for any irregularities committed in connection with marriage had been prescribed. For taking false oath or submitting false certificates, the person concerned could be sent to jail under the Section 193 of Indian Penal Code. He could be fined as well. For a person who married without licence, three years' imprisonment was prescribed.

INDIAN DIVORCE ACT

This Act promulgated in 1896 was applicable to all those marriage in which at least one spouse was Christian. Of course, if both were Christians, there could be no doubt about its applicability. This Act was divided into 14 chapters having 62 sections and 14 schedules.

The sections 10 to 17 of the Act dealt with the dissolution of the marriage. According to section 10 wife could ask for divorce on the following grounds:

(1) Forsaking of Christianity by husband and entering into another marriage.

(2) Desertion of wife by husband.

(3) Sexual immorality by husband.

(4) Marriage with another woman and sexual indulgence.

(5) Raping of the wife or forcing her to submit to anal intercourse or sodomy and other bestial acts with wife.

(6) Immoral and sadistic behaviour.

(7) Desertion of wife for two years without reason and sexual indulgence out of marriage.

The husband can seek dissolution of marriage if the wife is sexually corrupt. The section 11 gives exceptions in this matter.

According to the section 17 of the Act after a thorough examination of the charge levelled by either spouse against the other and satisfying itself about their veracity the district court can grant divorce. But this action of the District Court must be endorsed by the High Court. Without an endorsement by the High Court the instrument of dissolution of marriage is not valid.

In accordance with the Section 16 of the Act, either husband or wife can apply for the dissolution of the marriage.

According to Section 19, a marriage can be declared void on the following grounds—

(1) If at the time of marriage or at the time of litigation the husband is impotent or woman is sterile, or unable to bear.

(2) If either of the spouse is a blood relation.

(3) If either of the spouse is mad or an idiot or had previously married and the husband or wife of the previous marriage is alive.

The order nullifying the marriage must be endorsed by the High Court.

According to Section 12 of the Act, judicial separation can be sought on grounds of sexual corruption, desertion or brutality. The judicial separation is a sort of temporary dissolution of the marriage.

If a wife is not covered by the Indian Succession Act, she may seek protection order. Thus, she reserves right to her property.

The Section 32 of this Act accepts the right of Restitution of conjugal rights, *i.e.*, on the expiry of judicial separation the partners may reunite in matrimonial bond.

According to Section 34, the aggrieved husband may demand compensation from a man who has sexual indulgence with his wife.

According to Section 57 of the Act, six months after the dissolution of the marriage the spouses can remarry.

It is clear from the above description that divorce and judicial separation is relatively easy among Christians. Due to this laxity the Christian marriage is threatened by instability and disruption. To improve matters the divorce should be made difficult so that the rate of divorces may be checked and the consequent state of broken home may be checked from deteriorating beyond recovery.

THE STATUS OF CHRISTIAN WOMEN

On the whole, the condition of Christian women, is far better in Indian society in comparison to the condition of Hindu and Muslim women. The Christian women have equal and same opportunities of development and progress as are available to Christian males. The percentage of literacy is relatively high among Christian women. In Kerala, 46% Christian women are educated. Besides being educated, Christian women have earned name and fame in fields of music, fine art, radio and television. They are good singers, dancers, painters and radio-artists. Christian women enjoy equal conjugal rights. They have same rights to marriage and divorce as are enjoyed by their husbands. The Christian women are particularly skilled in nursing, secretaryship, office work, salesmanship etc. They are free to marry or stay unmarried. Marriage is a matter of choice and not compulsion for them. Many Christian women prefer not to marry but there is no social stigma against them as in the case of Hindu and Muslim women. In economic field and social mixing they are equal to men. Men do not play dominant role. Rajkumari Amrit Kaur, Mrs. Violet Alva etc. have enjoyed glorious positions in political field. They have worked as Ministers in the Central cabinet. Compared to their Hindu and Muslim counterpart, Christian women are more fortunate in enjoying good social status. However, freedom of movement and equality of rights have not been wholly beneficial to Christian women. Some of them used their opportunities to lead clandestine immoral life. They are considered by Indian menfolk to be more receptive to their advances and in the process some are lead astray.

QUESTIONS FOR EXERCISE

1. Write an essay on Christian society and rural institution in India.
2. Explain and evaluate the status of Christian woman as compared to Hindu and Muslim woman.

13

Tribal Social System and Social Institutions

According to Dr. Rivers, the tribe is a simple social group, the members of which use a common dialect and work together in war and in carrying out other common projects. In the definition of tribe, Rivers has not held common residence at one location to be an essential characteristic since most tribes are of the nature of wanderers. But, in spite of possessing the habits of wandering, tribes do possess a definite habitation. In this definition Rivers has stressed the unity of tribes in times of war. On the other hand, there are many tribes within which one faction clashes with another. In the same way many tribes have neither any leader nor any central or any other kind of rule of administration. According to Imperial Gazetteer, "A tribe is a collection of families bearing a common name, speaking a common dialect, occupying or professing to occupy a common territory and is not usually endogamous though originally it might have been so." In defining the tribe Dr. D.N. Majumdar has only clarified this description. According to him, "As tribe is a collection of families, bearing a common name, members of which occupy the same territory, speak the same, language and observe certain taboos regarding marriage, profession or occupation and have developed a well assessed system of reciprocity and mutuality of obligation."[1]

This opinion, however, does not hold true for all the tribes. In the beginning the members of the tribe did necessarily marry within their tribe but now the practice to marry outside the tribe is more prevalent among them. From this viewpoint, the definition by Imperial Gazetteer is appropriate.

Characteristics of Tribe

1. The tribe inhabits and remains within a definite and common topography. In the absence of a common topography, the tribe would also lose its other characteristic features as community sentiments, common language, etc. For this reason a common habitat is essential for a tribe.

---

1 Majumdar, D.N., *Races and Cultures of India,* Asia Publishing House, Bombay (1958), p. 355.

2. But any group of people living in a particular geographical area cannot be called a tribe as long as its members do not possess a mutual sense of unity. This mental element is an invariable and essential characteristic of the tribe.

3. The members of a tribe speak a common language. This also helps to evolve a sense of communal unity among them.

4. The members of a tribe generally marry into their own tribe but now due to increased contact with other tribes, the consequence of an increase in the means of transportation, the system of marrying in the tribe is also changing.

5. A major cause of the sense of communal unity in the tribe is the tie of blood relationship between its members. The members of a tribe believe in their having descended from a common, real or mythical ancestor and hence believe in blood relationship with the other members.

6. The members of a tribe always experience the need for protection. Keeping this need in view, the political organisation of the tribe is established and all authority for administration is vested in one person. This leader employs his mental power and skill in protecting the entire tribe. A tribal committee is formed to render assistance in the form of advice to the tribal chief. As a general rule the tribal chief accedes to the wishes of the committee. The tribe is divided into numerous small groups each of which has its own chief. These chiefs solve the problems of their own groups and act according to the directives of the tribe.

7. In this way each tribe has its own political organisation which maintains harmony and avoids notes of discord among its members and protects them.

8. Religion is of great importance in the tribe. The tribal political and social organisation is based on religion, because social and political laws become inviolable once they are granted religious sanctity and recognition. The authority of a common religion is an important characteristic of tribe.

9. The tribe has a common name.

10. A common culture, resulting from a sense of unity, common language, common religion, common political organisation, etc., is found to exist in a tribe.

11. A tribe is constituted of many clans. There exist laws of reciprocity among its members.

TRIBE AND HORDE

A nomadic horde is a group of small number of People. *When the members of the nomadic horde increase to a very sizeable figure it is christened a tribe.* A very strong community feeling exists in both horde and tribe which differ from each other mainly in respect of size. In both, such economic activities as collection of fruits, animal hunting, animal husbandry, fishing etc., are carried on. In both, a similarity of blood relations is to be found. In both, there is a conglomeration of families. The chief is well respected and obeyed in both. In spite of such a great extent of similarity, the horde and the tribe differ from each other in the following respect—

1. In the tribal group as against the horde, the need of protection stands out prominently.

2. The tribe is bigger in size than the nomadic horde.

3. In the tribe, religion is more developed than in the horde because in the latter a greater solidarity and strength of political and social laws is to be expected.

4. Being of a larger and more cumbersome size the tribe possesses a weaker sense of unity than does the horde.

5. The tribe is divided into many smaller groups but the horde has no such sub-divisions.

6. Agricultural occupation is an accepted mode of life in the tribe whereas in the horde agriculture is not indulged into any large extent.

7. The tribe inhabits a definite place. Instead of staying at a definite place the horde wanders over a definite geographical area.

TRIBE AND CASTE

Marriage within the clan is forbidden both in the tribe as well as in the caste. Both generally condemn marriage outside the group. The modern development in the means of transport and communication has induced increased contact between members of various tribes and castes and has weakened the laws of endogamy in both. The two do exhibit considerable similarity, yet they also differ in the following respects:

1. According to Risley, the convention of endogamy is not rigidly enforced in tribe whereas such is the case in a caste. But this view of Risley does not appear to be universally true since the law of endogamy is enforced with extreme rigidity in some tribes.

2. Max Weber writes in *Social Structure* that when an Indian tribe loses its territorial significance it assumes the form of an Indian caste. In this way, the tribe is a local group whereas the caste is a social group.

3. The caste was originated, in ancient Hindu society, with a view to division of labour on the basis of profession and occupations. The tribe came about because of the evolution of community feeling in a group inhabiting a definite geographical area.

4. According to Dr. D.N. Majumdar, the tribe looks upon Hindu ritualism as foreign and extra-religious, even though indulging in it, and in the worship of gods and goddesses whereas in the caste these are necessary parts of religion. The tribes of Madhya Bharat which are called Hindu and Kshatriya tribes are better acquainted with their own 'Bonga' than with the Hindu gods.

5. According to Max Weber the status of all people is similar in the caste, whereas there is much difference of status and rank in the tribe. This view of Max Weber does not apply to all castes. Difference of rank and status can be found in many castes also.

6. There is greater consciousness of differences in status and rank in the caste than in the tribe.

7. The caste is never a political association whereas the tribe is a political association.

8. The names of clans in castes are adopted from some saint or mystical savant such as Vashisht, Vishvamitra, Bharadwaj, Kashyap, etc. In the tribe the clans are based on totem, for example, the clans in the Komti tribe of Mysore are named after all kinds of fruits, vegetables, spices, food grains, etc. The list presented by Thurston in *Castes and Tribes of Southern India,* seems to indicate that hardly any name in the animal and vegetable world remains to be used as the basis for a totem name.

9. In the caste, individuals generally pursue their own definite occupations because functions are divided under the caste system. In the tribe, individuals can indulge their fancies in whatever profession they please because there is no fixed relation between them and the occupations.

Actually, now the tribes are gradually being converted into castes. Risley has mentioned four processes in the transformation. 1. By changing one's lineage. 2. By accepting the principles of any school of Hindu religion. 3. By joining Hindu religion. 4. By entering into relations with Hindus without changing name. According to D.N. Majumdar a tribe can enter Hindu society by adopting the clan and name of a caste. As a result of these changes the difference between tribe and caste is being continually reduced.

THE CLAN

Tribal group is divided into clans. The clan or sib is an important part of the tribal organisation. It is only an extensive form of lineage constituted of blood relations. A clan is constituted by including all the relatives of either her mother's or the father's lineage and all the offsprings of ancestors in such a lineage. In this way, many lineages constitute a clan. The clan emanates from some major biblical or imagined ancestor of the family. Being prominent and respected, this ancestor is accepted as its founder. All the lineal descendants of the family are introduced by his name. A clan is never constituted by combining the lineage of both the mother and father. It is invariably unilateral. Its descendants are of either matrilineal or patrilineal lineage. *Thus, in brief a clan is that collection of unilateral families whose members believe themselves to be the common descendants of a real or mythical ancestor.*

Characteristics of Clan

The following characteristics of the clan are evident from its foregone definition:

1. Exogamous Group. The clan is an exogamous group, since all the members of a clan believe themselves to have descended from one ancestor. Consequently, they do not many any member of their clan. Marriage is contracted only out of one's own clan.

2. Common Ancestor. The organisation of the clan is based on the conception of a common ancestor. This ancestor can be real or mythical.

3. Unilateral. The nature of the clan is unilateral *viz.*, in one clan there is either the collection of all families on the mother's side or of all families on the father's side.

Types of Clan

According to its unilateral nature, clan may be of two types—

1. Matrilineal Clan. In this all the offsprings of one woman are held to be members of one clan. At the same time the sisters and brothers of the woman are also members of this clan. In this way, a matrilineal clan includes the woman, her offsprings, her sisters and their children. But, it does not include the children of the brothers.

2. Patrilineal Clan. In this clan are included the man, his children, his brothers and sisters and the children of the brothers but not of the sisters.

Clans have different names based on various different grounds. The main grounds among them are the following:

1. After the names of saints, for example, Shandilya, Bhardwaj, etc.
2. After the names of the totem such as Kunjam, Naagsori, etc.
3. On the basis of substitute names such as Kamaar, Jagat, etc.
4. On the basis of some topography, for example Mahanadiya, Jaunpuriya, etc.

Functions of Clan

The main functions of the clan are as follows:

1. The members of a clan possess a 'we feeling' because of their belief in descent from a common ancestor. They are prepared not merely to assist one another but even to lay down their lives for each other. When one member of the clan is injured all the members share his pain. Two sayings are prevalent among them (i) "Strike my clan brother and you strike me." and (ii) "The blood of the clan is my blood."

2. Individuals indulging in antisocial acts are extradited from the clan. In this way, the conduct of clan members is controlled. Extradition from the clan proves more effective and disastrous than even a death sentence for the members.

3. It is the universal legal function of the clan to punish miscreants and maintain peace and order in this matter.

4. With the help of the law of exogamy the clan arranges marriages from outside the group. This, on the one hand avoids conflicts within the clan between men for a woman and on the other serves to increase cordiality and friendship with the members of the other clans.

5. The clan performs all the administrative functions for its members. The heads of the various clans meet and form a committee for the tribe which serves to mediate in the conflicts between clan members and takes political decisions in war and peace time.

6. In the villages where agriculture is carried on it is the clan which arranges for agricultural land. The head of the clan distributes the land. When a person is deprived of the membership of the clan he is also deprived of this land. Members can only rent the land.

In addition to the above mentioned functions, the clan also caters to the religious preferences of its members. Generally, the head of the Clan is also its priest. It is he who consummated the religious undertakings of all the members.

Distinction between Clan and Caste

Clan and caste differ from each other in the following respects—

1. Clan is a well organised group based on a mythical ancestor. Caste is a real, actual, organised group.

2. Clan is an exogamous and caste an endogamous group. Members of the clan marry outside the clan. Members of the caste cannot marry outside the caste.

3. In the clan individuals possess the same status. In the caste individuals possess higher and lower social status.

Distinctions between Clan and Tribe

The clan and tribe are different and distinct from each other on the following counts:

1. Clan has no definite topographical area whereas members of a tribe generally live in a definite geographical location.

2. Clan has no definite language, the tribe has a common language.

Clan is an exogamous group. The members of a clan do not wed a member of their own clan. The tribe is commonly an endogamous group although, with increasing contact among neighbouring tribes consequent upon an increase in the means of transportation, the tribe has now lost some of its endogamous character.

TRIBES IN INDIA

1. North-eastern Aboriginals. These tribes are found in Assam, Tripura and Manipur. Their number totals around two millions. They belong to Mongol race and their language resembles the languages of Austric family. The important tribes in this class are the Kukis, the Nagas and the Mikirs etc.

2. Central Aboriginals. These tribes live in Vindhyachal. Satpura, Kekal and Aravali mountains. The important among these are the Gonds of Madhya Pradesh, Bhils of Rajasthan, Santhals of Chhota Nagpur, Ho of Singhbhumi and Manbhumi, Gond and Kharia of Orissa, Sawara of Ganjam and the Mundas. This class of Indian aboriginals includes their biggest number. The number of Santhals alone is more than two million. Most of these aboriginals carry out shifting cultivation. Some are engaged in small scale cottage industries. Some of these live in very dense forests and difficult terrains of mountains. They lead a very primitive type of life away from the civilized world.

Table 8: *Scheduled Tribes in India 1981*

State/ UT	Total Population ('000)	Percentage
India	51,629	7.8
A.P.	3,176	5.9
Assam	N.A	N.A
Bihar	5,811	8.3
Gujarat	4,849	14.2
Haryana	N.A	N.A
HP.	197	4.6
J & K	N.A.	N.A
Karnataka	1,825	4.9
Kerala	261	1.0
M.P.	11,981	23.0
Maharashtra	5,772	9.2
Manipur	388	27.3
Meghalaya	1,076	80.6
Nagaland	651	84.0
Orissa	1,915	22.4
Punjab	N.A	N.A
Rajasthan	4,183	12.2
Sikkim	74	23.3
Tamil Nadu	520	1.1
Tripura	584	28.4
U.P.	223	0.2
West Bengal	3,071	5.6
Andaman Nicobar	22	11.9
Arunachal	441	69.8
Chandigarh	N.A	N.A
Dadra Nagar Haveli	82	78.8
Delhi	—	—
Goa Daman Diu	11	1.0
Lakshadweep	38	39.8
Mizoram	462	93.6
Pondicherry	—	—

3. The Southern Aboriginals. These are the tribes of South India. The most ancient tribes in India are found in Kerala, of which the maximum number is that of Kadar. Other important tribes in this class are the Todas of Nilgiri, Chenchu of Hyderabad and the Kanikar and Kurovan of Travancore-Cochin. In some of these tribes there is a matriarchal type of social organization and matrilineal type of family.

Besides, the above mentioned main classes of Indian aboriginals, tribes are found in Andaman and Nicobar, Northern Himalayas, the districts of Chamba and Mahasu, Dehradun and Darjeeling. Some of the Indian tribes, such as the Nagas, and the Santhals are absolutely isolated from civilization.

MATRILINEAL SOCIETIES AMONG INDIAN TRIBES

In contrast to the patrilineal society found in the civilized world, some tribes have matrilineal society which is recognised by the following characteristics:

1. Succession Through the Mother. While in the patrilineal society the succession follows through the father, in matrilineal society it follows through the mother. Since, the members of the group receive their family name through the mother, the society is known as matrilineal.

2. Succession of Property to Female. Because in the matrilineal society the father resides with the mother, the succession of property is decided from the female side. Normally, the son of the brother or sister of the mother succeeds her property. In the case of kingdom also similar rule is followed in matters of succession.

3. Matrilocal Family. While in the patrilineal society, the bride goes to the house of the bridegroom after marriage and resides there along with her children, in the matrilineal society, the husband lives at the residence of the wife. Thus, the family in the society is matrilocal.

The example of matrilineal societies can be seen among the Garo and Khasi tribes of Assam in India. In Garo, matrilineal society, the succession is decided from the mother's side. It is believed that a female was the original founder of this tribe. In matters of marriage the proposal is made from the woman's side but a man has a right to marry at least three women at the same time. There is no exchange of money at the time of marriage. The women succeed to the property and therefore a widow is not allowed to marry for a certain period after the death of her husband. The purpose of this delay in remarriage is to keep the property within the family and allow the minor sons to become adult. The male resides with the female after his marriage.

Among the Khasi matrilineal society of Assam, the tradition begins from females or princesses. The Creator God in their religion possesses characteristics of a female. The mother has sole rights over the family property and after her the right to property is given to her daughter. The male resides with his in-laws after marriage. The religious functions are in the hands of women, who serve as priests on religious occasions. This, however, does not mean that in these societies, the wife dominates the husband, because the word used for the husband in this society means the master. Divorce is allowed only by mutual consent. And the male is given all the rights of the husband.

THE TRIBAL MARRIAGE

Ways of Acquiring Mate

The institution of marriage among the tribals is different from that in the Hindu society. Marriage among the tribals is not a religious sacrament but a social contract with the purposes of enjoyment of sex, procreation and companionship. The forms of marriage, the ceremonies, the taboos and the laws of dissolution of marriage are different in the tribal world from civilized society.

Forms of Marriage

Normally, the tribal male marries only one woman, because he is not rich enough to maintain more than one wife and the number of males and females in a tribe is usually equal. The following are the important forms of getting a mate in tribal society:

1. Marriage by Purchase. The most prevalent method of securing bride in primitive societies is marriage by purchase. This is equivalent to Asur marriage described in Hindu scriptures. According to Robert Lowie, however, the bride price is not paid as the price for the girl but symbolises her utility for the male and the compensation to the parents for giving away their daughter in marriage. Again, among some Indian tribes there is the custom of dowry, which finishes the value of bride price. This is particularly true about Santhal, Ho, Oraon, Kharia, Gond, Naga, Kuki and Bhils among Indian tribes. Like Hindus, the problem of bride price is becoming complex in tribal society. In the Singh Bhum district the amount of bride price in the Ho tribe is so much that very few persons can pay it with the result that other forms of marriage are preferred.

2. Service Marriage. This is a special type of marriage by purchase. While in marriage by purchase the bridegroom gives some money or gift to his father-in-law, in service marriage he pays off for the marriage in terms of service rendered to his father-in-law. This custom is particularly found among those persons who are too poor to pay any money as bride price. In the Gond tribe the bridegroom, desirous of marrying through service, is known as Lamnai and Lamsena in Vega tribe. In Himachal Pradesh he is known as Kamaoos. In service marriage the youth has to serve his future father-in-law for three to five years. During this period, if the father of the girl is satisfied with the youth, he gives his daughter in marriage to him. If, however, the father is dissatisfied, he dismisses the youth and gives chance to another person. During the course of service the young man can meet the girl but cannot enter into sex relationship with her.

3. Marriage by Capture. An important method of securing a bride in Indian tribes is marriage by capture. This form of marriage is prevalent due to different types of causes. In the Ho tribe its cause is the excessive bride price. Another cause is the misbehaviour of the woman with her sister-in-law so that the sister-in-law is always waiting for someone to carry her by force. Though, the relatives apparently try to revenge for the capture of the girl but in 99% cases the capture is regularised by means of marriage in which the young man has only to apply vermillion on the forehead of the girl. The custom of marriage by capture is found among the Santhal, Munda, Bhumij, Gond, Bhil and the Naga tribes. Among the Bhumij tribes, it is considered to be the best form of marriage, so much so that even after the settlement of marriage the parents of the girl request the bridegroom to run away with the bride. In the Kharia and Birhor tribes of Bihar if a young man forcibly applies vermillion and oil on the forehead of a girl, she is declared his wife. Among the Nagas of Assam, a cause of marriage by capture is the death of women in their own tribe due to the evil custom of killing just born daughters. With the application of Indian Penal Code in Tribal circles, the custom of marriage by capture is gradually disappearing.

4. Marriage by Mutual Consent and Elopement. An interesting form of securing **a** bride prevalent in Indian tribes is marriage by mutual consent and elopement. This was known **as** Gandharva marriage in the ancient Hindu scriptures. Among the Ho tribes of Bihar it is known as 'Rajikhushi' marriage. In this form of marriage the girl elopes with a young man by her own consent and does not return to parents till they give consent for marriage. Naturally, no bride price is demanded in this type of marriage.

5. Marriage by Exchange. In this type of marriage when a man's son is prepared to marry another's daughter, the latter's son accepts the former's daughter in marriage, thus an exchange of boys and girls is made between the two families.

6. Probationary Marriage. This system of marriage is found in the Kuki tribe of Assam. In this system the bridegroom stays in the house of the girl for a certain period. If during this probation period they decide to many, the marriage ceremony is solemnized, otherwise the young man leaves after paying some compensation to the parents of the girl.

7. Anader or Intrusion Marriage. This method of marriage is followed if all other valid sources of marriage have been closed so much so that even the parents of the girl fail to marry her with the desired boy. In this type of marriage the girl forcibly enters the house of her lover and does not leave it in spite of suffering all types of insults and cruelties. If she does not leave the house for a sufficiently long period, she is married with the young man. This custom of marriage is found among the Oraon, Ho and Birhor tribes.

8. Marriage by Test In this type of marriage the young man is allowed to marry the girl of his choice after he successfully passes the test for his bravery. A strange custom of this type of marriage is found among Bhil tribe which is known as Gol Gadhedo. In it a social function is celebrated around a tree or a high pole at the top of which a coconut and some sweets are put. The boys and girls dance around this pole or tree, the girls remaining nearer the tree and the boys forming their circle outside the circle of the girls. Now, a young man suddenly tries to break the circle of the girls and reaches the pole or tree, eats the sweets and breaks the coconut. The girls beat him and try to restrain him. If he comes out successful in his aim he is given a right to select any girl from the gathering as his wife.

Besides the above mentioned methods of securing a bride found among the Indian tribes there are some other methods as well. Of these the following two are worth mentioning:

1. Levirate. In this type of marriage when a person dies, his younger brother marries his wife. The custom is found in the Santhal, Gond and Kharia tribes among others.

2. Sorrorate. In this type of marriage when the wife dies, the husband marries her unmarried sister. This type of marriage is found in Gond and Kharia tribes.

Ceremonies of Marriage

The celebration of marriage in a tribe is a social occasion for much festivity and rejoicings though the marriage ceremonies are quite simple. In some tribes, the mere application of vermillion on the forehead of the girl by the bridegroom is the sole ceremony of marriage. In some other tribes, the blood of the bride and the bridegroom are mixed as a token of their intimate union. In Gond tribe the procession of marriage starts from the bride's place instead of from the bridegroom's house. There are almost no religious *sanskars* observed on the occasion of a tribal marriage, but generally there is provision for community songs and dances and feasts.

TYPES OF MARRIAGE: POLYANDRY

Marriage is normally of two types: monogamy and polygamy. Polygamy again has been classified into polygyny and polyandry. In polygyny a male marries several females. In polyandry on the other hand, a female marries several males at the same time. The custom of polyandry is found among the Khas tribe of district Dehra Dun, the Tiyan, the Kurumb, the Kot of Kerala and the Toda tribe of Nilgiri. Martin has mentioned its prevalence in the Oraon tribe and Maine has mentioned it in the case of the Santhals. This custom is also found among the Nayars of South India. It is also found in Laddakh, Kangra, Chamba, Kulu and Mandi.

The custom of polyandry has been divided into following two types:

1. Adelphic or Fraternal Polyandry. In this type of polyandry a woman marries all the brothers of her husband. Such is the custom found in the Khas tribe of district Dehra Dun, which has been elaborately studied by D.N. Majumdar and R.N. Saxena. In this tribe, while the elder brother marries a woman, she is considered to be the wife of all his brothers. No younger brother is allowed to marry any other woman. If at the time of marriage any younger brother is a minor or he is born after marriage he is considered to be the husband of the woman after he becomes adult. But, if a younger brother marries any other woman after being an adult, the elder brother has an equal right over his wife also.

In the Khasi tribe though the woman is considered to be the wife of all brothers, the eldest brother has special rights over her. She cannot refuse to cohabit with him, failing which she can be divorced. If the eldest brother asks her not to cohabit with any other brother, she has to follow his command. If the other brothers quarrel over this issue only the elder brother has a right to allow for the dissolution of the marriage. If the woman has got any child prior to marriage, the eldest brother has the sole rights over the child.

In Khasi tribe, the paternity is decided by a social ceremony. According to D.N. Majumdar if there are three brothers in a family, the children will call them by the names of Bari Baba, Danger Baba and Bhedi Baba respectively. According to Frazer, the eldest brother is considered to be the father of the eldest son, the youngest brother that of the youngest son and also in the case of other children.

The eldest brother is the head of family. He has sole rights on the house, fields, gardens, cattle and grain etc. He is the highest authority concerning the matters of women and children. In the case of division of property, he is given the biggest share and the wife and children stay with him. The children, however, have a right in the property of all the fathers. In these people if it is desired to marry more than one woman, generally this other woman is the sister of the first wife. This is done to ensure the peace of the family. The Khasi tribe is patriarchal. The system of polyandry in it is consequently known as patriarchal polyandry.

2. Non-Fraternal Polyandry. In this type of polyandry, as is clear by its name, the husbands of a woman need not have fraternal relationship among themselves. Thus, the woman can also choose her husband from the males other than her husband's brothers. She successively lives in the houses of her different husbands, and while she is staying with someone, the other husbands have no right over her. Non-fraternal polyandry is also known as matriarchal polyandry because in it the woman has all the rights of property and otherwise. The example of non-fraternal polyandry in India can be found among the Nayars of Malabar. According to Aiyappan, this custom is also found in Iangu tribe. Among the Nayars the girl stays with her family even after marriage and visits her sometimes. Sometimes the man has no relation with the wife after a certain period and the girl maintains sex relationships with several boys while living with her parents. The husbands have no right over the children or the property of the wife.

The following are the important characteristics of polyandry found in Indian tribes:

1. A woman can marry more than one husband.
2. The several husbands of a woman may be brothers or may not be so.
3. Though, every husband has got right over the woman the eldest brother has the maximum right.
4. If there are more than one woman in the family every brother is free to enter into sexual relationship with any one of them.
5. The eldest brother or the first husband has maximum rights over the property and children.

6. In matrilineal families, the woman herself selects the husbands and lives with them successively. But, while she is living with some one husband, the others have no right over her.

7. Both men and women have equal rights of dissolving the marriage through divorce.

The following are the two important causes of prevalence of polyandry:

1. Poverty. In Laddakh, where the custom of polyandry is found, its cause is poverty. It is seen that when a person gathers sufficient amount of money, he prefers to marry a woman and live separately from his house. According to Summer, in Tibet, where agricultural products are insufficient, several males together keep a woman. According to Lowie among Chinese several males together use a woman and meet her demands. According to R.N. Saxena, the Jaunsari woman is herself anxious to have several husbands because a single person cannot earn sufficient money to meet her demands.

2. Scarcity of Women. According to Westermarck, an important cause of polyandry is the scarcity of women. For example, among the Todas of Nilgiri, the number of women is much less in comparison with that of men and therefore polyandry is the normal custom. Now, with the increase of the number of women due to legal check on murders of daughters, the custom of polyandry is gradually diminishing. This reason advanced by Westermarck may be true in some cases. But, as has been rightly shown by Robert Briffalt, polyandry can be prevalent even where there is no scarcity of women. For example, there is no appreciable difference in the number of males and females in Lahaul, Sikkim, Tibet and Laddakh and yet the custom of polyandry is prevalent there. It can be, however, safely admitted that scarcity of women though not the sole cause of polyandry, is an important cause of it.

The custom of polyandry is very much defective and therefore, it is gradually diminishing. The following are its important disadvantages:

1. It injures the health of women who develop many venereal diseases because of sexual intercourse with several males.

2. According to some thinkers this custom encourages barrenness among women.

3. In the long run polyandry leads to population problems.

4. According to some thinkers, in polyandrous marriage, there is more likelihood of the birth of sons and therefore, the cycle of polyandry never ends.

5. Polyandry increases the number of divorces.

Thus, the custom of polyandary does not fulfil the psychological and spiritual requirements of a marital relationship. It is not even a sufficiently legal contract. It, however, cannot be eliminated without the elimination of poverty.

Polygyny Among Tribals

Polygyny is the custom of one male marrying several females. Due to several causes the custom of polygyny has very much diminished among tribes in modern times, though rich males even now marry several females. The custom of polygyny is found in Naga, Gond, Vaiga, Toda and other tribes of India. Its main causes are as follows:

1. In Hills and plateaus one has to work very hard to earn his livelihood. The custom of polygyny provides free and reliable labourers to the husband. There is another economic cause of polygyny as well. The leaders of the tribes of Assam marry several females because they are capable of meeting their needs.

2. In tribes because of the difficulty of daily chores of life the woman is sometimes herself anxious to have several co-wives to help her. Psychologically, this reason does not appear to be satisfactory.

3. Other important causes of polygyny are desire for children, increase in social prestige because of several wives and excessive lust of the male. Sometimes the scarcity of males is also a cause of polygyny.

The following are the so-called advantages of polygyny mentioned by its supporters:

1. Because only powerful and rich males marry several women, therefore, it improves the new generation.

2. Polygyny restricts adultery, because the males get sufficient sexual variety in their own family. This also helps in bringing up the children.

The above mentioned so called advantages are nothing before the obvious disadvantages of polygyny of which the important are as follows:

1. In the presence of several wives, the importance of each one of them diminishes in the family.

2. Due to the presence of several co-wives, the peace of the family is disturbed because of mutual jealousy and quarrels.

3. It is difficult for a man of ordinary status to meet the needs of several co-wives and therefore, polygyny in such cases creates economic difficulties.

4. The greatest disadvantage of polygyny is that it is against the equality of male and female. Psychologically, it is against the establishment of conjugal love among wife and husband. The woman does not receive psychological satisfaction from such a marital relationship. Therefore, a majority of thinkers are against the custom of polygyny. With the spread of education among tribals, this custom is gradually disappearing.

RESTRICTIONS CONCERNING MARRIAGE

In every tribal society there are certain restrictions connected with the institution of marriage. The important amongst these restrictions are exogamy and endogamy.

Exogamy

According to the rule of exogamy a man can marry only outside a certain group. This group may be his caste, tribe, clan or totem. Generally, the tribals are forbidden to marry within their clan and totem group. The custom of totem exogamy is also universal in Indian tribes. Among Khasi tribe clan exogamy is the custom. In some tribes, one finds village exogamy in which marriage cannot be contracted within the village. An example is the Munda tribe of Chhota Nagpur. In South India the Erula tribe observes class exogamy. Similar is the custom among the Nagas of Assam.

Different scholars have advanced different reasons for the custom of exogamy. According to Risley, the reason behind the custom of exogamy is the desire of novelty. Because of his desire for novelty the male does not want to marry any woman of his acquaintance within his group. Psychologically, novelty is a factor in marital relationship but it cannot be said that novelty cannot be secured in one's own group. According to Westermarck, the main cause of exogamy is the prohibition of incest. This is definitely an important factor in exogamy. According to Audrey Richards, the cause of exogamy is the scarcity of women because of the evil custom of killing daughters. It is because of scarcity of women in the group that most of the males are compelled to find their mate from some other group. This is an important cause of exogamy. But, the most important causes of exogamy are the prohibitions concerning totem and clan. The members of a totem and clan are considered to have blood relationships. The custom of totem and clan exogamy is, therefore, quite understandable.

Endogamy

Thus, in contrast to exogamy, in endogamy a man has to seek his mate within his own group. This group may be his caste, tribe, clan etc. Endogamy is prevalent among the different classes of Bhil and Toda tribes. The following are the important causes of endogamy:

1. The most important cause of endogamy is the primitive man's natural fear of strangers. They think that the stranger may harm them by means of magic and therefore, they prefer to marry within their own group. This is the cause of endogamy in Korawa tribe.

2. The racial and geographical differences create a gulf among different tribes so that they fear each other and do not enter into marital relationships.

3. Different tribes have a natural desire to protect their cultural, linguistic and other specialities. This is possible only in the custom of endogamy.

4. Among other important causes of endogamy are absence of sufficient means of transport and communication, illiteracy and self-sufficient nature of a tribe etc.

DIVORCE AMONG TRIBES

There are no strict rules concerning divorce among tribes. Marriage is nothing more than a social contract and most of the males marry to fulfil the desire for children and the satisfaction of sex. There are different rules of divorce observed in different tribes. Among the Korawa tribe of Mirzapur the procedure is very simple. When a dissatisfied husband asks his wife to leave him and refuses to maintain her, she leaves him and goes to her father. She is now considered to be divorced and can marry again. In this tribe the divorced women are very much respected. The women divorced seven times is the leader in religious and social functions. Among Bhils, the husband desirous of divorcing his wife, calls the Village Panchayat and publicly gives her a piece of cloth from his turban declaring that he is deserting her and henceforward treat her as his sister. The woman hangs this cloth from the roof of his father's house, where it remains hanging for a month. It signifies that her husband has no more rights over her and she can now marry again.

Among Gonds if a woman divorces her husband without his consent his second husband has to pay compensation to the former. Among the Muria tribe, the divorce is never considered to be valid, unless the amount of compensation is paid to the former husband. This amount is decided by the tribal panchayat. In the Lushai tribe of Assam when the husband divorces his wife, he has to pay off the remaining bride price to the bride's party. But, if the woman is guilty of adultery or she herself deserts her husband, she has to return bride price paid by the husband.

The causes of divorce are not similar in different tribes. Among Gonds divorce can be secured in the circumstances of the indifference of wife towards household affairs, her barrenness, her quarrelsome nature, breaking of the marital bond etc. In the Kharia tribe, a woman can be divorced on the grounds of barrenness, adultery, refusal to live with the husband and even laziness. Among tribals both male and female have a right to divorce. The customs concerning divorce, however, are changing because of the influence of Hindu and Christian cultures on tribal people these days.

YOUTH DORMITORY

The most important social institution in the tribal social organization is the youth dormitory. This institution is found in almost every tribe and the social life is centred around it. It is known by different names in different tribes, for example, among the Nagas of Assam, it is called 'Morung' while the female youth organization is called 'Yo', among Angami Nagas, it is called 'Kinchuki.'

In Uttar Pradesh, it is known as Rangbang, while among the Mundas and Ho tribes of Madhya Bharat, it is called Gitiora. The Oraons call it Dhoomkuriya, the Bhuiyan call it Dhangarbassa and the Gonds call it Gotul.

These youth dormitories are centred in big buildings made of straws and thatch. There are separate houses meant for boys and girls. All the youths of the tribe pass their night in the dormitory. The boys and girls sleep separately. In the villages where there is no dormitory for the girls, they sleep in the house of some old woman. Such is the custom in the Munda tribe. In Bastar, the boys and girls of the age of 15 and 16 sleep in the dormitories. The Oraon youth has to pass night in the Dhumkuria situated outside the village. In the Ho tribe, the unmarried boys and girls live in separate dormitories. In the Lhota Nagas of Assam, the boys can get leave from the Morung only in the case of serious illness of their mothers. Among the Miami tribals of Assam both boys and girls sleep in the same dormitory. While the girls sleep on the ground floor, the boys sleep on the first floor. Similar is the custom in the Muria tribe of Bastar. Their dormitories are situated outside the village. The unmarried boys and girls gather here at night, sing and dance and participate in other social activities and finally sleep.

The following are the important characteristics of the tribal youth dormitory:

1. While at some places there are separate dormitories for boys and girls, in other tribes they live in a common dormitory. This is the custom in the Muria tribe. On the other hand, among Konayak Nagas of Assam, the boys live in the Morung and the girls sleep at Yo.

2. Normally, the dormitories are situated outside the village in the forest, but they may also be near the fields as it is in the case of dormitories of the Nagas. In Oraon tribes, the dormitory is situated in the centre of the village.

3. The life in the dormitory is based on certain traditions and customs which are invariably followed by the members.

4. The age of membership of the dormitory differs from tribe to tribe. As a general rule it is four or five years in most of the tribes.

5. The boys and girls live in the dormitory till they are married when their membership is automatically dissolved.

6. If a girl becomes a widow she can again enter the dormitory as its member.

7. In the evening the members of the dormitory gather after taking their meals at their homes. At the dormitory they make a fire, sit around it, tell stories, sing, dance and play and finally sleep.

8. The members of the dormitory are divided into two classes according to age: seniors and juniors. The head of the dormitory is selected from senior group. It is his job to take care of all the members of the dormitory and maintain discipline among them. The juniors follow the commands of the seniors and receive different types of education from them.

9. It is the duty of every member of the dormitory to keep everything secret about it.

10. The members of the dormitory carry out several functions together *e.g.*, construction of a house on the occasion of marriage or helping the village folk in harvesting the crop etc.

THE GOTUL OF MURIA AND GOND

Among the dormitories of Indian tribes, the Gotul of the Muria and Gonds of Madhya Bharat is worth mentioning. It is raised on the bamboo poles and the roofs of straw. There is no door or window in it. The members enter through a small hole sufficient to permit entry. All the unmarried boys and girls gather here in the evening, make a fire, sing and dance, tell traditional legends and sleep at night. The juniors serve the seniors and receive different types of training from them. Among the members of the Gotul, different boys and girls are given diffemt status and the corresponding roles. The head of the dormitory is known as Challan or Silledar.

Under him there are Dewan, Tehsildar, Subedar and Kotwal etc. Similar positions are also given to the girls. According to Majumdar, the purpose of the Gotul is to save the village folk from the attack of wild animals. The youth remain waking for most of night and sleep only in its last lap or in the day. They help their parents on the field or in grazing the cattle in the forest. In the evening, they go to Gotul after taking their meals. Among the Muria tribals, the girls massage the bodies of the boys. Verrier Elvin has described the sexual life in the Gotul in details in his book, *The Muria and their Gotul.* He has pointed out that the senior girls train the junior boys in matters of sex. In *The Gondwana and the Gonds* Inder Jit Singh has denied any type of sexual activity in the Gotul. D.N. Majumdar and Hutton also agree with Singh. In fact, Mr. Elvin has himself admitted and wondered that there is hardly any case of conception among the members of the Gotul. According to Majumdar and Hutton, the Gotuls are the centres of social education. In it are shown the dances imitating agriculture, hunting, gathering of honey and economic activities carried out by the village folk. The conceptions of crime and punishment and good and bad actions are taught through different stories.

Scholars do not agree about the origin of tribal dormitory. According to one view, they are residues of the ancient communal houses when the whole village used to live under one roof and there were no individual homes. According to another view the purpose of the dormitory is to keep boys and girls unaware of the sexual relationship of their parents. According to Majumdar, the purpose of dormitory is to gather the youths of the village at one place to save the village from the attack of wild animals and the village maidens from the attack of males of other tribes. Besides, the origin of the dormitory may be due to want of houses, the bliss of communal life and the development of tribal culture. Whatever may be the origin of dormitory, it is undeniable that it is the centre of tribal culture in a tribe. In it are taught the lessons of the traditions, norms, ideals, religious beliefs, methods of earning livelihood and discipline to the boys and girls of the tribe. According to S.C. Roy, the tribal dormitory carries out the following three functions:

1. Helping in the gathering of edible things and consolidating economic organization.

2. Educating boys and girls in social and other duties and imparting them education in the matters of sex.

3. Following the principle of endogmy and keeping the movement of women limited and controlled.

Weakening of Dormitories

At present unfortunately the institution of dormitory is gradually weakening in the tribes. The two important causes of this development are as follows—

1. Due to the contact with urban people the tribals are gradually forgetting their social ideals and institutions and following urban culture. As the education is

now being provided by the schools, the children do not go to dormitory to receive education.

2. The spread of Christianity among tribals and the presence of the Christian missionaries among them have adversely affected their youth cultural set up. The institution of youth organisation is gradually weakening, which has led to social disorganization among the tribes.

In fact, as has been rightly pointed out by Elwin, the condition of the social organization of a tribal group can be rightly estimated from the condition of its youth dormitory which is the centre of the maintenance and development of tribal culture.

TRIBAL RELIGION IN INDIA

Tribal religion is the most primitive form of religion found in human society. The following are the important characteristics of the Indian tribal religion:

1. Faith in Mana. Defining faith in Mana found in tribal society, Codrington has pointed out that Mana is "A force altogether distinct from physical power, which acts in all kinds of ways for good and evil, and which is of the greatest advantage to possess or control." Thus, Mana is a supernatural power which is useful to man in the control of many natural phenomena beyond his power. According to Majumdar and Madan, "Entire religious life of the primitives is born out of their belief in certain mysterious, impersonal, non-material and unindividualized supernatural power which takes abode in all the objects animate and inanimate, that exist in the world."[1] According to Max Muller, Mana is an attempt to define certain natural phenomena in terms of an impersonal power. The high mountain, the river, the thunder and all other natural phenomena, according to the tribal people, act with the power of Mana. This power acts both for good and for bad. It is connected with the soul, ghost of the departed man and the living being. The Ho and Munda tribes of Chhota Nagpur call it Bonga.

2. The Concept of Bonga. According to these tribes, Bonga is a mysterious and impersonal power at the back of rains, tempests, cold, floods, epidemics and the wild animals. Everywhere activity is due to the power of Bonga. Thus, Bonga is a form of Mana.

3. Animism. Another important characteristic of Indian tribal religion is animism. According to Risley, tribal religion is animism. The tribal people believe in the presence of super-natural powers at the back of high mountains, flooded rivers, big trees and epidemics. They try to please these powers by means of different types of propitiations and worships. Sometimes, they are worshipped even without being given any name. An important type of animism is ancestor worship which is found among the Santhals and Oraons. The Santhals worship deities of family and village deities. Among the Korawa tribe, there is a goddess of crop, one of animal and a deity presiding the rains. The tribal people try to please these gods

1 Majumdar, D.N. and Madan T.N., *Social Anthropology,* Asia Publishing House, Bombay, (1957), p. 157.

and goddesses by offering the sacrifices of different types of animals and birds before them.

The principle of animism is based on the following two beliefs —

1. There are powerful souls besides powerful gods. The souls are connected with men, and feel pleasure and pain through them. They influence the events in this world and also control them.

2. The soul of man survives even after his death. The word 'animism' was used for the first time by E.B. Taylor in antropological literature. Animism, according to Taylor is, "the ground-work of the philosophy of religion from that of savage upto that of civilized man".[1]

4. Animatism. According to animatism there is some impersonal power behind eveiy material object besides the living beings. Thus, in the tribal religion is found faith in the presence of supernatural power in bones and feathers etc. The impersonal power is worshipped to maintain peace and prosperity in the group. It is difficult to distinguish between animatism and animism. The following distinctions, however, have been pointed out between the two. While according to animatism there is some mysterious, unknown, impersonal power at the back of all living beings and things, according to animism there is animal spirit found in all movable and immovable things. An example of animatism is found in the tribes of Bihar. They consider the bones, beads stones and feathers to have living and magical powers. The stones are considered to be the children of mother earth and worshipped. The tribal people worship only those powers which can do some harm to them, but sometimes such powers are also worshipped which cannot do any harm, for example, the Sing Bonga of the Munda tribe. Though, it is difficult to say as to which type of nature worship is found in a particular tribe in India, generally one finds animism as well as animatism in most of the tribes. From the comparative point of view, however, antimatism is more widespread than animism.

5. Naturalism. A universal characteristic of tribal religion is naturalism or nature worship. The Garo tribe of Assam worships sun and moon. The Munda people worship Sun god. Besides, other tribes worship rivers, mountains, stars, trees and other natural objects.

6. Faith in the Immortality of Soul. Among many tribes there is a custom of observing funeral rites two times. This is because of their faith in the immortality of soul. Sometimes the second rite is considered to be more important than the first. The tribals believe that the soul is not destroyed on the death of the body and requires food etc., for a sufficiently long time. Among the Nagas and tribals of the Nicobar island the skull of the dead man is placed on a wooden statue believing that the soul of the dead man will pass from the skull to the statue. Now, the statue is served like a living human being and efforts are made to fulfil all its needs. Sometimes the statue is made of brass. Such is the custom among the Garo tribe of Assam. In south India, in Kerala, the statue of a dead person is worshipped at

1 Taylor, E.B., *Primitive Culture*, John Murry, London (1913), p. 842.

least once a year. The tribals believe that the soul matter can increase the fertility of land and produce life. In the Naga tribe there is a custom of worshipping soul of the ancestors at the time of sowing and in the need of rains.

7. Faith and Rebirth. Most of the Indian tribes believe that after death the soul of a man survives the body and enters into the body of some animal, bird or other living beings. Among the Bhils, efforts are made to find out as to which body will be entered into by a particular soul. Similar beliefs are found among Nagas of Assam, Ahirs of Bengal, Kamar and Gond tribes.

8. Faith in Magic. The most important characteristic of tribal religion is faith in magic. According to M.F. Keesing, "In its technical sense, magic is a term which summarises a variety of methods by which man purports to influence automatically the course of events by that touch of the supernatural. A magic act is a rite carried out to twist Nature in a specific way to satisfy human desire."[1] Different types of magical acts are prevalent in different tribes. The tribals believe in magicians and witches. If a woman is declared a witch by the magician of the village, she is given all types of tortures. A strange type of magical act is found among the Bhils to contradict the effect of epidemic. In the event of the spread of epidemic, some people hang some pitchers and baskets in a bamboo pole and run on the main street crying 'Toraka, Toraka'. Hearing them other people of the village help them in carrying this load out of the village. The load is carried to the nearest river or jungle and by throwing it the people believe that the epidemic has been thrown out of the village in the river or the forest.

9. Totem and Taboo. The custom of totem is an important characteristic of tribal religion. Different Indian tribes believe in different types of totems.

Totem is the object or animal who is supposed to have mystic relationship with the members of a tribe. The members of the tribe very much respect their totem. The animal of totem cannot be killed or eaten except on certain special occasions. Thus, taboos are linked with totems. In the list of totems of different tribes in India one finds the names of almost all animals and vegetables. Defining totem, E.A. Hoebel has written, "Totem is an object, often an animal or a plant, held in special regard by the members of a social group, who feel that there is a peculiar bond of emotional identity between themselves and the totem."[2] Thus, totem is the object, plant or animal with which a particular social group feels supernatural relation and has faith in it which fosters the consciousness of unity among the members of a tribe. The following are the important characteristics of totemism:

1. The totem is considered to be the originator of the tribe and all the members are related to it.

2. It is believed that there is some supernatural and mystic relationship among the members of the same totem.

---

1 Keesing, M.F., *Cultural Anthropology,* (1958), p. 332.

2 Hoebel, E.A., *Man in the Primitive World,* McGraw Hill Book Co., New York (1919), p. 512.

3. It is believed that the totem protects the social group in difficult times, warns the members about the future danger and also predicts about future happenings.

4. The skin of the tottem is considered to be sacred and worn on special occasions. The figure of the totem is tattooed on the body. Mourning is observed on the occasion of the death of animal of totem and funeral is carried out in all its details.

5. As the members of the totem group consider themselves to be having blood relationship, they strictly observe the rule of exogamy.

6. The killing, eating or burning of the object or animal of totem is strictly a taboo.

Totemism is the basis of the religious organisation among tribals. It maintains community consciousness and brotherhood among the members of the group. It keeps their group organised and is a symbol of its unity. A tribe is divided into several sects according to different totems. Different interpretations regarding the origin of totem have been presented by Hopkins, Tylor, Rizley, S.C. Roy and Hutton. Whatever may be the origin of totem, it can be said that it occupies the most important place in tribal religion, not only in India but almost everywhere in the world.

MODERN TRENDS IN TRIBAL CULTURE

Due to contact with Hindu and Western culture, the tribal culture has constantly changed. This cultural change has been affected by the following processes:

1. Simple Adoption. In the process of cultural change a tribe simply adopts the culture of another tribe, for example, the Worli tribe of Bombay state, formerly used to wear only a cloth. Now, they use shirt, turban and dhoti due to the influence of Koli tribe.

2. Acculturation. Where a culture almost engulfs another culture and changes it, the process is known as acculturation. This involves a wider and deeper culture change. For example, the Indian tribal culture is being constantly influenced by Hindu culture, so much so that some tribes are almost Hindu in culture. An example of this type of cultural change can be found in Gond tribe.

3. Assimilation. In this process of cultural change, a culture is not only adopted, but also assimilated and, therefore, becomes an integral part of the adopting culture. This process is seen in the tribes who, leaving their difficult mountain tracks and deep forests, come to plains and stay there. Such tribes in India have been assimilated in Hindu society *e.g.*, the Santhals of Bengal have assimilated Hindu culture in almost every aspect of their social and cultural organization.

According to D.N. Majumdar, the Indian tribes can be classified into two groups on the basis of processes of cultural change. Firstly, there are assimilated tribes whose culture has been completely assimiated by some other culture. Secondly, there are adaptative tribes whose culture is gradually adapting to some new culture.

IMPACT OF HINDU AND CHRISTIAN CULTURES ON TRIBES

The impact of cultural contact with Hindus and Christians has resulted both in evil as well as in favourable consequences. This cultural contact has removed many superstitions and evil customs from the tribes. The Christian missionaries have opened hospitals and schools for the benefit of tribal people. These have decreased the influence of diseases and illiteracy. The Christian missionaries are also running several orphanages in tribal areas. They are giving monetary help to the needy tribals and helping in the improvement of the levels of health and education. These favourable influences, however, are nothing before the evil consequences of the cultural contact. The following are the most important evil consequences in this connection:

1. Degeneration of Collective Life. Due to the influence of western culture many of the tribals have begun to hate their traditions and customs which are gradually disappearing with the result that the collective life is degenerating.

2. Social Disorganisation. This has led to disorganization of family and social institutions. The tribals who have converted into Christian religion, try to imitate European culture and hate their tribal brothers. This has led to social disorganization everywhere.

3. Economic Exploitation. The civilized traders, contractors and religious missionaries have also exploited the tribal people economically. Misusing their ignorance they have caught them in the net of indebtedness and robbed their money and land.

4. Moral Degeneration. The civilized people have spread gross moral degeneration in tribal society. The poor women have been made to prostitute themselves. The evil of drinking and using all sorts of intoxicants has increased in the tribals. Prostitution has led to increase of venereal diseases. The tribes living near the cities are very much morally degenerated.

5. Gradual Disappearance. The above-mentioned evil consequences of tribal contact with other cultures have led to gradual disappearance of some tribes, as it is in the case of Andmani, Korawa, Toda and Chenchu tribes.

TRIBAL PROBLEMS

The Indian tribes at present suffer from mainly two types of problems. Firstly, those which are also found in other people of the country, and secondly, those which are peculiar to tribal people. In this later type of tribal problems the following are the most important—

1. Cultural Problems. Due to contact with other cultures, the tribal culture is undergoing a revolutionary change. Due to the influence of Christian missionaries, the problem of bilingualism has developed which has led to indifference towards tribal language. The tribal people are imitating western culture in different aspects of their social life and leaving their own culture. An important influence of cultural contact is seen in the form of disappearance of youth dormitories. Imitation of the western dress and modes of living has led to the degeneration of tribal life and tribal arts, such as dance, music and different types of crafts.

2. Religious Problems. Due to the conversion of many tribal people to Hindu and Christian religion the tribal groups have been divided into several sects on the basis of religion. This has shattered their collective life and conflicts and dissensions are increasing. The tribal people are gradually forgetting their tribal religion. This has led to social disorganisation.

3. Social Problems. Due to the influence of Hindu community the tribals are facing the problem of increasing bride price. This has encouraged elopment of girls and their forcible lifting by males. Another social problem created by the tribal contact with Hindus is the evil custom of child marriage. The contact with the civilized society has increased the number of premarital and extramarital sexual relationships in tribal society and the number of dissolution of marriages. This has also increased the incidence of prostitution and venereal diseases.

4. Economic Problems. The contact with the civilized world has disintegrated the entire economic system of the tribal people. They have forgotten their ancient crafts. Most of them are working as labourers in plantations, agricultural farms, factories and other jobs. The employers everywhere misuse the ignorance of the tribal people, take maximum work from them and give them minimum money in return.

TRIBAL WELFARE

The Indian Constitution has laid down important provisions for the welfare of tribal people. Posts have been reserved for them in public services, in States and Centre. Seats have been reserved for their representatives in the State Legislatures and in the Indian Parliament. Special provisions have been made regarding their administration. District and regional councils have been established to cany out their welfare. The government have given special attention to their educational and economic development. All this, however, has not appreciably improved the condition of tribal people. The following suggestions can be made in connection with tribal welfare.

1. Economic Reforms. Efforts should be made to encourage tribal people to permanently establish for cultivation because the shifting cultivation practised by them results in much wastage. The cooperative forests utilization societies can help the tribal people in utilization of the forests in which they live. The government should arrange for technical help and education to improve the condition of tribal crafts and provision should be made for the marketing of the goods produced by them. Laws should be strictly imposed in tribal areas to solve the problem of indebtedness and to restrict exploitation. Cooperative credit societies can be organised to provide money for small scale industries. Labour laws should be strictly enforced in tribal areas.

2. Educational Reforms. At the base of the fallen state of tribal society is their widespread illiteracy. Educational expansion, therefore, should be given primary consideration. The tribal education should be given through their own language and in their own cultural background. Colleges should be established to safeguard the tribal fine arts. Provision should be made for technical and commercial education in the tribes. Along with the education the tribal music, dance, plays and recreation should be encouraged. Religious dogmatism and superstitions should be removed through scientific education.

3. Reform in the Level of Health. Efforts should be made to improve the level of health of the tribal people. This will require provision of medicines, pure water, nutritive food, clean and properly ventilated houses and general healthy atmosphere.

4. Social Reforms. Whatever may be the opposition from certain vested interests, efforts to carry out social reforms in tribals must be realized. The evil customs of bride price, magic and ritualism, child marriage, prostitution etc., should be removed. These social reforms can be carried out only after economic reforms.

5. Political Reforms. It is a pity that the Government officials posted in tribal areas misuse the ignorance of tribal people and exploit them for different purposes. They scorn the tribal culture and are completely indifferent to their welfare. The Government should appoint such officials as are conversant with the tribal culture to improve the condition of tribal people.

GOVERNMENTAL EFFORTS FOR TRIBAL WELFARE

In free India, the State and Central Governments have made incessant efforts in the direction of tribal welfare. At the central level a commissioner attached with Home Ministry takes care of tribal welfare. Under him there are several Regional Assistant Commissioners whose number has now increased to 16. In the States, there are special Directorates of Tribal Welfare. In Assam, five District and Regional Councils have been established for tribal welfare.

Tribal Research Institutes for the study of tribal culture and language are working in Bihar, Madhya Pradesh, Orissa and other States. Efforts are being made to expand educational facilities in tribal area. Thousands of scholarships have been granted for special seats for tribal people in medical, engineering and technical colleges. Posts have been reserved for them in public services. Primary and Secondary Schools have been established in tribal areas where there is provision for free education.

In the political field, the tribes send their representatives to State and Central Legislaturer, some of whom have risen to the rank of Deputy Ministers and Ministers. Many tribal youths qualify in All India Services and their number is gradually increasing.

For the economic regeneration of the tribes, the Government has enforced rules regarding land ownership and utilization of land. Crores of rupees have been spent for the development of cottage industries. The Community Projects have been established everywhere. Grain shops have been opened which provide for improved types of seeds. Laws in connection with debt have been enforced. Special multi-purpose tribal blocks have been created. Shifting cultivation is restricted and tribal families have been permanently settled on suitable lands. Efforts have been made to provide housing facilities in some tribal areas. Hospitals have been opened which provide free medicines, check epidemics and cure all types of diseases. Research institutes have been opened for the study of tribal culture and language. New roads have been constructed and old roads improved in the tribal areas. Personnel working for tribal welfare are given special training for this purpose. Institutes for their training have been established in Madhya Pradesh, West Bengal, Assam, Rajasthan, Bombay and other States.

The above brief outline of the Governmental efforts in the direction of tribal welfare shows the extent of work that has been done in different five year plans. This has definitely led to some improvement in some directions. The solution of tribal problems, however, requires a multisided planning. D.N. Majumdar has rightly said, "There is no one solution to tribal problems, there is no common platform to demand it. There are levels of cultural development and there are different patterns of life that the tribes own. In any scheme of rehabilitation of tribal life, the attitudes and configurations of culture must be known to work out plans, and what is true of one culture area may not be so for a second."[1]

QUESTIONS FOR EXERCISE

1. What is a tribe? Distinguish it from horde.
2. What are the various ways of acquiring mate in Indian tribes?
3. Write short note on (i) Divorce in Indian tribes, (ii) Gotul.
4. What are the problems of tribal people in India? Point out governmental efforts to solve these problems.

---

1 Majumdar, D N , *Races and Cultures of India,* Asia Publishing House, Bombay (1958), p. 385.

14

Rural Social System and Social Institutions

History of Rural Community in India

From the pre-historic period, the village has been an important unit of the Indian social and economic organisation. The oldest books in India are the Vedas. And even among them, Rig Veda is considered to be the most ancient. According to Rig Veda, society is divided into many dynamic, heirarchical groups. Of these the smallest unit is the family. Many such families constitute one village. One *vish* is composed of many villages. Many such *vishas* taken together constitute one *Jana* and many *Janas* together make one nation. In this way, according to Rig Veda, the village is the unit of social and political organisation of India. In the ancient literature, the word village was interpreted as a group of families living at one place. The Leader of village was known as *Gramini.*

Literature succeeding Rig Veda is more profuse in its description of the village. Mahabharat whose period is estimated at between 200 B.C. and 200 A.D. has mentioned many types of groups. According to Mahabharat, forts were contructed for the defence of the local groups. The population surrounding the forts was called the village, towns were bigger than villages but smaller than cities. The Mahabharat does not confine its description to the organisation of the village but also includes the description of inter-village organisation. According to Mahabharat, the village is the rudimentary unit of administration. Its leader was called Gramini. The duty of a Gramini was to arrange for the defence of the villages within a radius of two miles. A group of many villages was governed by their leader. As a general rule such a group contained ten villages whose leader was called Dash Gramini. The ten villages in this group had intimate mutual relationship with each other. Over two Dash Graminis, or in other words, over two groups of ten villages each there was one Vinshatik leader. Accordingly, the Vinshatik had twenty villages under his governorship. The group of villages was not limited to so small a number but went on to a hundred or even a thousand villages. The leader of a group of hundred villages was a Shat Gramini while the administrator of a thousand villages was called an Adhipati.

Table 9: *Distribution of Villages in India (1981)*

State/UT	Less than 1,000	1,000 to 1,999	2,000 to 4,999	5,000 to 9,999	10,000 & above	Total
1	2	3	4	5	6	7
A.P.	14,085	6,464	5,609	1,058	163	27,379
Bihar	49,617	10,841	5,842	1,054	192	67,546
Gujarat	9,814	5,108	2,725	418	49	18,114
Haryana	3,275	1,883	1,346	221	20	6,745
HP.	16,348	364	93	3	—	16,807
J & K	5,017	1,046	393	20	1	6,477
Karnataka	18,631	5,239	2,722	401	35	27,028
Kerala	7	13	72	222	905	1,219
M.P.	61,029	8,118	2,046	155	4	71,352
Maharashtra	26,101	8,954	3,604	579	16	39,354
Manipur	1,758	174	90	12	1	2,035
Meghalaya	4,793	85	24	—	—	4,902
Nagaland	921	143	47	1	—	1,112
Orissa	40,710	4,561	1,234	47	1	46,553
Punjab	8,146	2,819	1,256	120	1	12,342
Rajasthan	26,823	5,468	2,335	321	21	34,968
Sikkim	372	60	8	—	—	440
Tamil Nadu	5,698	4,570	4,381	1,000	182	15,831
Tripura	265	253	274	56	8	856
U.P.	83,235	20,380	8,148	751	52	112,566
West Bengal	25,319	7,538	4,383	702	82	38,024
Andaman & Nicobar	460	23	8	—	—	491
Arunachal	3,176	63	16	2	—	3,257
Chandigarh	12	5	7	—	—	24
Dadra Nagar Haveli	33	27	7	3	—	70
Delhi	54	74	71	15	—	214
Goa, Daman Diu	185	102	90	34	1	412
Lakshadweep	1	1	4	1	—	7
Mizoram	629	62	30	—	—	721
Pondicherry	209	48	28	6	—	291
All India	4,06,723	94,486	46,892	7,202	1,834	557,137

Besides Mahabharat, many other books of ancient literature have mentioned the village but none of them has such wealth of detail. Mahabharat was succeeded in its description of village, by Manusmriti. Manu has called the distinction between a village, a town and a city. These were placed in an increasing order of population. According to Manusmriti, the village is the smallest unit of administration. The village had its own official and its individual organization. In Manusmriti, as in Mahabharat, the leader of the village has been the Gramini. A majority of the problems arising in the village were solved by the villagers themselves. For example, things and places of public utility like wells, tanks, lakes, meadows, parks etc. were looked after by the people of the village. Besides this, various problems relating to different aspects of the family, caste and society were taken up and solved by the villagers in their different villages. According to Manusmriti, there was an authoritative person named Sahastresh over one thousand villages. The Sahastresh governed the Shatesh who held charge of a hundred villages. In this descending order the Shatesh was followed by the Vinshi who was incharge of twenty villages. Next came the Dashi who was responsible for ten villages. And finally, there was the leader of each village who was called a Gramini.

In this way, the villages in India have been continually developing over a very long period extending back into thousands of years. Fundamentally, the village is still the unit of the country in spite of the innumerable changes which it has undergone since the days of Mahabharat and Manusmriti.

Today, no less than at that time, there is a leader of the village who is responsible for the entire village in all matters. Even today many villages combine together to form groups in which many different mutual relations are possible. Hundreds of villages combine to constitute one cultural area which lends its individual cultural characteristics to each of these villages. But notwithstanding this fact it has to be remembered that no village in India today is completely self-dependent and independent. From every view point, be it social, economic or political, the village of today is dependent to a large extent upon people not belonging to the village. The villager of today is no longer a member of just a single rural community but a member of a caste, a religion and a nation as well. Hence, religious and political reasons compel him to think in terms of other people who are not members of his community. India is a democracy in which there are many states which, though united under a central government, are independent in many respects. Every state is further subdivided into districts and each district into tehsils. In each tehsil there are a number of villages. In this way, from the administrative view point, the public representatives or the leaders depend upon the officials of the tehsil. Different villages are governed by different men because they belong to different tehsils. But none the less, the general laws of the state have to be obeyed by everyone. Besides this in big villages or in a number of small villages grouped together there is a panchayat which serves to solve many of their social, economic and political problems. It is obvious that the modern Indian government wants to make the villages in the country self-dependent and independent units. The future of the country depends upon the organised villages, the more these villages are prosperous the more will the country be organised and prosperous. All the intelligent people in the country are aware of this fact. This has encouraged the study of the villages and movements have been organised for improvements in the villages and these movements have been helped by government.

STUDY OF RURAL COMMUNITY IN INDIA

The study of sociology in India is not very old but even then there has been quite a detailed study of the different aspects of the rural communities. Since, the country became independent the studies of rural communities were assisted by the government. Similar studies were further encouraged by the point four programme and America's Ford foundation. Under the direction of professor D.N. Majumdar the study of Mohana village in Lucknow district was carried out by the economic assistance given by the Ford Foundation. Later some assistance was forth-coming from the Planning Commission. The results of this study were published in 1958 in a book by D.M. Majumdar entitled '*Caste and Communication in an Indian Village*'. This assistance by the Planning Commission was not a novel enterprise since similar researches have been financed by it even before and after this particular instance. Dr. D.G. Karve, who was at that time the chairman of the Programme Evaluation Organisation of the Planning Commission, invited Oscar Lewis who studied Rampura, a village near Delhi. The results of this study were published in 1958 in a book entitled, *Village Life in Northern India* published by the Illionois University. Before the publication of either of these two books, Dr. A.R. Desai in 1935 in his book, *Introduction to Rural Sociology in India* shed some light on the study of rural community and made an impassioned appeal for research in this direction. In 1955, when this book was no longer available, Dr. Dasai published another book, *Rural Sociology in India* in which the latest studies of rural community in India were assimilated.

Besides D.H. Majumdar and A.R. Desai, the name of Dr. S.C. Dubey deserves mention among other scholars who have studied the rural community in India. The study of Shamirpet village in Hyderabad made by Dr. Dubey, was published in 1955 under the title *Indian Village.* This book occupies an important place in literature relating to rural community in India. In 1958, another book, *India's Changing Village* was published by Dr. Dubey. In 1956, the Journal of Asian studies published a research paper, *Cultural Factors in Rural Community Development* which was written by Dr. Dubey. Besides Dr. Dubey, Mr. M.N. Srinivas also did important work in the field of rural sociology in India. In 1958, he edited a book, *India's Village*, which was a collection of studies of various villages in different states of India. The year 1952 saw the publication of his book, *Religion and Society Among the Coorgs of South India.*

The books mentioned above do not constitute the entire body of literature on this subject, besides these a number of other works have been published on the study of rural community in India. It is neither feasible nor indispensable to make a detailed description of these books and research articles here.

ESSENTIAL CHARACTERISTICS OF THE VILLAGE COMMUNITY

From the view point of sociology, the village and the town differ in respect of their importance. In our society, the major essential features of the village from the sociological point of view are as follows:

1. Bases of Social Organisation. In India, there are more than half a million villages. 28 per cent of the Indian population lives in villages. India is predominantly an agricultural country. Thus, in every respect the future of India depends upon the villages.

2. Intimate Social Relationships. The relations between the primary groups and families in the villages are intimate. The family fulfils the needs of its members in all aspects of their life and exercises control over them. It is through the family that the new members are initially introduced to the customs, conventions and culture of the society. In this way the village people hold family as an institution having revered status, and the result is that individuality does not develop properly in the members of a family. Due to limited contact with the external world, their view point is narrow and they are aggressively opposed to violent change. In the village the relations among the people are direct and intimate so that often the entire village is organized like a family.

3. Preservers of Ancient Culture. From the sociological viewpoint also the villages are important, because they preserve the ancient culture of society. India is an agricultural country. The life of the villages depends considerably upon natural forces due to their occupation, which is agriculture, and thus they worship natural forces like the sun, rain etc. They are sometimes observed resorting to magic in order to gain the assistance of these forces. The villagers in India still exhibit faith in the doctrine of *karma*, a fundamental principle in Indian culture, and lead a simple and natural life dominated by sacrifices, theistic tendency and the importance of religion in every aspect of life.

4. Ideal Democracy. In ancient times, the Indian village was an ideal democracy. Life in each village is self-dependent. Most of the people are agriculturists and, besides agriculture, the farmer is quite capable of handling the work generally done by a carpenter, blacksmith, mason, veterinary surgeon, woodcutter and sometimes even a weaver. In some developed villages these occupations are carried on by different people, but whatever the conditions, all the needs of the villages are generally fulfilled in the village itself. In the village even today the sense of neighbourhood is not ignored and is given considerable importance. The community of ideals and customs and social forbearance is even today an important feature of the village. In its long history, the Indian society retained its strength and organisation as long as the villages were well knit and well organised. From the medieval ages till now the condition of the village has continuously deteriorated. But now, after the country has become independent, the network of social reconstruction is being implemented with the village as the unit and the basis. Thus, from the sociological point of view, the villages are more important than the towns.

In this way the importance attributed to the villages is far greater than the importance which may be attributed to the towns of India. It is for this reason that thinkers like Mahatma Gandhi accorded a central place to rural reconstruction in the over-all plan for the reconstruction of the entire country. The Ram Rajya of Mahatma Gandhi is based on the uplift of the village. The Indian Government has also accepted the importance of the development of rural industries and rural reconstruction. Social and economic reconstruction of India's rural communities is being implemented through the establishment of co-operative societies and community development plans. India is a democracy, hence the future of the country depends upon the village because the major portion of the population lives in the villages and the country cannot hope to achieve any progress without removing the social and economic backwardness of the villages. Social and economic reconstruction of the country can be achieved only by a social and economic reconstruction of the villages.

5. Joint Family. Another characteristic of the life of the village is the joint family system. In the village, the family has strict control over the individual. Generally, the father, is the head and representative of the family and is also invested with the duty of maintaining discipline among the members. His orders are obeyed by all the members of the family. In marriage, festivals, business etc., it is he who manages the affairs of the family occupations, members of the family share the burden of the family occupation. The men plough the field, the women harvest the crops and the children graze the cattle. In this way, working together the villages maintain a sense of co-operation among themselves. Much attention is directed towards the preservation of the family honour and utmost care is taken to observe and maintain the traditions of the family.

6. Simple Living. The villagers have limited means and they do not license ostentation. People who go about in a manner calculated to attract attention are not looked upon with respect. Even in the materialistic age of today the generally accepted ideal in the village is a simple life and high thinking. In the village every individual endeavours to attain and observe the ideals of his family and caste. The villagers are a simple and plain people. They are incapable of making a false pretence of cultured behaviour and gaudiness, nor are they capable of boasting. They have sympathy for man and want to meet each other on a natural and human plane. Their life is tranquil, peaceful and plain. Mental conflicts and complexities are almost absent. They spend natural life in the lap of nature. In their life, there is a determined pattern and method for everything, so that they are spared the agony of continually pondering over them. Certain norms governing marriage and business etc., are irrevocably fixed. Hence, there is not much occasion for mental conflict. Trade in the village is not carried out on a large scale and consequently there is not much specialization of occupations. The small needs of life are fulfilled by the farmers themselves. Class conflict is generally lacking. Rich and poor, small and big, high and low all live in an atmosphere of natural co-operation and accept the discipline of the village. The level of morality is high. Any girl in village is generally treated as a sister or a daughter by most of the male members of the village, by the very virtue of her being a member of the village.

In this way, life in the village is more natural and orderly. There are many occasions for conflict between father and son, master and servant, creditor and debtor, husband and wife, mother-in-law and daughter-in-law etc. In spite of the fact that the income of villagers is very low, their life continues in a vain of satisfaction because of its very simplicity.

CHANGE IN VILLAGE LIFE

But the elements of village life which have been delineated above can be found to exist only in those villages which have remained unaffected by the influence of the towns. Otherwise, as a general rule, these elements are vanishing from the village life. The community consciousness in village life is steadily decreasing. The control of the caste panchayats is almost non-existent. The villagers who work in the towns as labourers acquire such habits as drinking, prostitution, telling lies, ostentation and needless boasting etc. and when these villagers return to their native village they spread extreme immorality. The village youths studying in the town also become addicted to irresponsibility and sedantary habits and when they exhibit the same habits in their villages the other simpleminded adolescents are also corrupted. The village belle living in the town is even more adept at the use of cheap cosmetics and on her return to the village. She also spreads this habit among her sisters in the village. Now-a-days, the villagers are using aids to make body beautiful in larger measure than before and the level of health in the village is fast deteriorating because milk and its byproducts from the villages are sold in the towns and, secondly, the money thus earned is being wasted on useless things. Though, education is spreading the people have turned their back to the old ideal of simple living and high thinking. Even though they may appear plain in their dress and ways of living due to poverty and simple due to insensitivity, they are not the least scrupulous in adulterating commodities, which they sell.

The convention of hospitality is no longer observed. Sex relations are marked by a lack of responsibility. The joint family is fast disintegrating. The number of thefts, abortions, murders, assaults, litigation etc., are steadily increasing. The old customs are being violated. The bonds of caste and society are disregarded. Similarly, family ties are also being discarded. Individualism, materialism and rationalism are increasing. Hence, the only elements which now characterize village life are agriculture which is the major occupation of villagers. The village population suffers lack of transport facilities, lack of scientific comforts, and have to live in mud houses, suffer discomfort of unmetalled roads and polluted environment etc.

In fact, the villages everywhere are at present passing through a transitional period. The old relational bonds and ties have fallen into disfavour and they cannot be reinstated in the original form. Even now the villages can be given an equally simple if not simpler, plainer and higher life by improving the conditions in these villages, through the establishment of panchayats, spread of education, economic reform in agriculture etc. Rural reconstruction through scientific method is very essential for this. In all the agricultural countries in the world, this matter has received considerable attention and much progress has been made in Russia and China. It is a matter of great satisfaction that the Indian Government is not oblivious of this. Crores of rupees are being spent on new plans of rural reconstruction direct towards the improvement of life in villages. As a result of these endeavours the village will once again become as well organised and integrated as before.

Factors of Change

A study of the factors and patterns of change in the rural community will provide an insight into the development of welfare work in the rural sphere because development is nothing more than change in any desired direction. In order to affect social, economic, political and any other kind of development in the villages it is necessary to change them. With respect to the way in which this change can be brought about, it is necessary to know the effect of some particular factors upon the rural community, as well as the direction of and the reason for this change.

Even though it is very difficult to analyse all the direct causes of change in rural community, still it is possible to recognise the major factors which may be placed in the following categories:

1. Natural factors,
2. Technological factors,
3. Social factors,
4. Economic factors,
5. Cultural factors,
6. Political factors.

1. Natural Factors. The natural factors of change in the rural community include all those natural elements which are found in the place in which that specific rural community exists. For example, the villages which have sprung up close to the rivers and the villages prospering in mountains show apparently the effects, respectively, of the rivers and the mountains. The social, economic, cultural and religious life of the rural community settled in the bamboo forest exhibits the effects of the bamboos. In places frequented by seismographic disturbances the houses are constructed of wood. The vegetation and the animals peculiar to any place are most frequently consumed and employed in their native land. In the same way, the cottage industries which develop in any place bear a direct co-relation to the minerals found in that area. In this rivers, floods, storms, rain, hale storms, earthquakes, mountains, vegetation and animals etc. are the natural factors which influence the rural community. Whenever any one of them changes, the life of the rural community also changes at the same time. The geographists have written numerous books on the subject of the effect of the geographical environment upon human life. The natural factors shape the geographic environment. Their effects are universally known. If the Ganges river alters its course miles away from the one which it was previously pursuing then not only the economic life but also other aspects of the rural community situated upon the old banks of the river will be changed.

2. Technological Factors. The natural environment alone does not transform human communities, because man constructs a fair portion of his environment for himself, and this also has widespread effects upon his life. Man creates a novel environment with the assistance of the technical factors and adopts natural environments to himself. These technological factors include all the inventions. Whenever electrical power has been made available to the villages, it has completely transformed the rural community. According to Prof. Ogbum, the invention of the radio alone has resulted in nearly 150 major changes in social life. Machines have not been used as much in the Indian villages as they are in the villages of the West. But even then the work of grinding wheat and refining cotton has lost its flavour for the rural families since machines for such purposes were installed in their villages. This has influenced the life and conditions of the women. With the invention of steam and electrical power all the aspects of human life have undergone some change or the other.

3. Social Factors. The social factors have a comprehensive effect upon the social life of the rural community. For example, the existence or the absence of sati custom, child marriage, negation of widow remarriage have some effect upon the life of the rural community, its effect being particularly evident in the condition of the female population. The major social factors which influence the life of the Indian rural community are caste system, joint family, Jajmani customs, various laws of marriage as well as social and religious customs and traditions etc. Any change in anyone of these factors results in a change in the rural community. For example, when the caste panchayats grow weak or lose power completely the intercaste relations in the villages undergo continuous change. In the same way changes can also be seen in the mutual relations between different castes due to the Jajmani relations having been broken off.

4. Economic Factors. The economic factors include those which are related to agriculture, business and industries. As a result of the pressure upon land having increased in the villages, many people have migrated to the towns in search of employment. Living in the towns the moral life and values of a rural youth undergoes a change which have their influence upon the moral life and values of other people in the village when he returns home. Wherever factories or mines have been established in the villages the relations between men and women have been influenced by their working together. Poverty is an economic factor and its widespread effects upon the life of the community are only too well known.

5. Cultural Factors. Cultural factors include beliefs, assumptions, values etc. Changes in them have repercussions in the entire social life. In India, wherever the Hindu, Muslim and Christian culture have had an opportunity to meet, the cultural life of the rural community evinces clearly the influence of this. As a result of the influence of western culture, the institution of youth dormitory is vanishing from many tribal villages. In rural girls and boys, who are influenced by western culture, tendencies of individualism, materialism and irresponsibility increase and these exert important influence upon rural institutions like family, marriage, caste system etc.

6. Political Factors. The rural communities are also influenced by the political factors. For example, distinct differences may be seen between the rural communities under Hindu, Muslim and British governments. After the country achieved independence much awakening was in evidence in the villages. Besides the government, political partyism also influences the villages. India is a democracy in which the public elects the representatives who run the administrative machinery. This is awakening political consciousness among the villagers.

METHODS OF CHANGE IN THE RURAL COMMUNITY

Along side the study of the foregoing factors which bring about change in the rural community it is also necessary to know factors by means of which social organisations or political parties create change in the rural community. The description of these will also make evident as to which method should be employed in bringing about the desired change in the rural community in developing the rural welfare work. The following are the important among these methods —

1. Reasoning. Some people having confidence in reasoning with the village people in an effort to bring about some change in the rural community. This method does have some benefit but its major defect is that the people who make use of it do not themselves do any thing actively and thus their word does not carry enough weight.

2. Demonstration. Thus more importance is attached to the demonstrative method than to the method of reasoning for it sets examples to the villagers. For example, advocacy about the utility of any agricultural implement cannot be as beneficial as making use of it in some farms. As a result of viewing its functions the farmers will themselves take interest in it and adopt it.

3. Compulsion. As is obvious by its name this method resorts to enforcing the change compulsorily upon the rural population. In other words, the population is obliged to accept the desired change, and it is obvious that only the government can employ this method. Many states in India have forced the villagers to behave gently towards untouchables by proclaiming the practice of untouchability to be a crime. The advantage of this method is that the change are affected quickly but it suffers from the drawback that it cannot create internal changes which can be brought about only by the reasoning and demonstrative methods.

4. Social Pressure. Social groups make most use of the method of social pressure in controlling and transforming the conduct of the individuals. As is obvious by its name, this method obliges the individuals by exerting social pressure upon them. For example, the caste panchayat of the villages obliges the members of the caste to accept their decision by threatening social extermination. This method certainly does prove quite effective due to men's sociability but it too suffers from an inability to achieve internal transformation.

5. Contact. Major changes can be seen in the rural communities which have come into contact with the urban communities. Change in the mode of living, dress, customs and values is seen when the tribal villagers come into contact with Hindu and Christian culture, when the uncivilised people come into contact with the civilised people and when the villagers come into contact with western culture.

6. Education. In India, efforts are being made to introduce change in the villages through basic education and social education etc., and much success is also apparently being achieved. In order to create communal and political consciousness in the villagers it is necessary to impart proper education.

There are limitations to each of the above mentioned methods for creating change in the rural communities and thus any method alone cannot serve the purpose. For this reason need is often felt for using more than one method. In order to achieve the desired changes in the direction of rural development reasoning needs to be supplemented by demonstration. When some people are not prepared to take the trouble of understanding it, is proper to introduce the compulsion and social pressure methods. In every change education complementary to it should be imparted. In this way the desired changes in the rural community can be attained only by understanding all these methods and making use of them according to need and occasion.

Sphere of Change in Rural Community

Having studied the factors of change and the methods of change, attention may now be directed towards the changes taking place in the different aspects of rural community life. This change can be seen in the following spheres —

1. Change in the Caste System. During the British rule the caste system suffered a severe set back in the village. Due to the British economic policy and new laws different castes abandoned their traditional occupations and adopted other professions. Many Brahmins and Kshatriyas started farming. The members of the untouchable castes became agricultural labourers. The control of caste panchayats weakened. The status of an individual in the village was now determined not only by his caste but also by his personality, financial condition and activities as well. Although, the Brahmin is addressed respectfully, the wealthy untouchable is not the recipient of any less respect even though he belongs to a lower caste. And at some places it may even be that he may be respected even more than the poor Brahmin. Being assisted by government laws, the lower castes no longer look upon themselves as inferior and in south India at some places the untouchables consider themselves defiled if they touch a Brahmin. If any Brahmin happens to come into their sector, he is assaulted with brooms and in extreme cases strict measures are taken to purify the place which he has made impure by his touch.

Thus, all castes are engaged in strengthening their individual organisations. Some castes have formed their organisations, by forming associations for the protection of their interests. But even then the power of the caste panchayat, exercised in the form of control over the individual's behaviour, food habits, ways of living etc., has completely died away. Even in such villages where the laws regarding touchability in the caste are observed, freedom is given towards violating them in the towns. Although marriages are still contracted within the same castes even then there is no obstacle to contact, eating, conversing etc., between different castes. But although the caste system thus appears to be growing weak on the one hand it seems to be gaining in strength upon the other. Casteism is increasing due to vested interests. In recent political elections it was observed that most of the people voted for the members of their own caste. Even the political parties issued tickets only to those members whose caste was in majority among electorates. The same had been the case in the previous elections and the elected persons had even tried to gain advantage for their own caste. In this way due to political and other interests, casteism is increasing, some administrative authorities in government and non-government factories, offices, colleges and other works think it desirable to employ only the members of their own caste.

2. Jajmani System. Jajmani system was based on the exploitation of the Kammen by the Jajman. As a result of the declaration equating all the citizens of free India and the efforts of the government to improve the condition of backward classes, the backward classes have now gained a certain degree of self-respect and their Jajmani relations with other castes are in the process of being broken. Secondly, the circulation of money in place of services in the villages has also had a degenerating effect upon the Jajmani system. Thirdly, the Jajmani relations are also dying out because the caste panchayats have lost their power and the occupations are no longer based on caste. Mobility is also increasing in the rural areas due to an increase in the facilities of transport. All these causes have together worked towards the deteriment of the Jajmani system, but this does not mean that it has been completely eliminated from the villages. Signs of its presence are evident in all the recent studies of the rural communities although signs of their growing extinction are also evident in most studies.

3. Family. Although, the joint families are still viewed with respect they are no longer the unit of rural community, having been replaced by nuclear families. Groups based upon similar interests are becoming stronger in place of the groups constituted from ancestry. With the increase of individualism the families are becoming smaller and the control exercised by the family over the individual members is also decreasing. But the ancestral group has not yet lost its power over the family completely. In the villages, as is wont to be in the towns, many of the activities of the family are being taken over by other groups. For example, in the villages where a grinding machine has been installed the wheat is ground in the mill instead of at home. The women are progressively being more educated and being given many social, economic and political rights with the result that they are conscious of their position in the family which is continuously improving.

4. Marriage. The institution of marriage, much the same as the family, is changing. The area of the selection of mate is increasing. There are not many examples of intercaste marriages even today. Generally, marriages are contracted between members of neighbouring villages. Although, the marriages are decided upon by the parents, it is considered quite proper to take the assent of the boy and girl, in particular that of the boy. The number of love marriages and divorces is negligible in most villages in India. The basis of the selection of the other party is also changing. Although, the ancestry is still an important factor in marriage, more importance is now attached to the financial condition and education of the boy and the qualities of the girl. Among Hindus the demand for dowry is increasing and so is that of Mehar among Muslims. At the same time much wasteful expenditure in marriage ceremonies is now being avoided and the party accompanying the bridegroom is now smaller. The customs of marriage are also undergoing change. The system of child marriage is in its last throes and widow remarriage is accepted.

5. Customs and Conventions. The conventions of rural social life are continually changing. The panchas of the caste have also lost some of their respect. Efforts to reduce the expenditure at social and other occasions are evident. The expenditure at various Samskaras of life, death, christening etc., have decreased. The expenditure in marriage has increased due to dowry. It has now become common to educate the boys and even education among girls is increasing. With the spread of education the superstitions are decreasing.

6. Food Habits. The laws governing inter-caste food habits are being relaxed. The use of vegetables, wheat and milk etc., is increasing in the villages even though in the case of the villages near the towns such commodities are transported to the towns and sold. The consumption of vegetable oil is increasing in villages, it cannot be seen in use in the higher classes. The consumption of tea, sugar and tobacco has definitely increased in the villages. In some families in the villages, tea is used throughout the year. The use of vegetable oils is also increasing.

7. Clothing. The clothes worn by the population in the villages are undergoing change. Among the men, Gandhi cap is replacing the turban while the younger girls have started wearing frocks. The boys have taken to shirts. The ladies wear blouses and the conventional skirt is no longer as popular as it used to be. Previously, people used handspun cloth but now-a-days mill-made cloth is used more extensively. The women folk in the villages are now consuming more clothes of artificial silk, artificial jewellery and cheap cosmetics. The heavy silver jewellery has gone out of fashion. The boys have taken to keeping their heads bare while some educated young men use western dress. In spite of the increasing propaganda for khadi the villages are using more of fine cloth than the thick khadi.

8. Housing. Although, the condition of housing in the villages is still very bad, it is certainly improving. The number of cemented houses in the villages is increasing. The houses are more airy and cleaner than they used to be. In the houses more comforts are now provided. In the villages where electricity is avilable radios and electric fans can be seen in the more prosperous families. The tendency towards engraving figures is decreasing because it unnecessarily increases the expenditure. Latrines are not found in many houses and even in these houses where they are provided, only the women make use of them and that too very seldom. Previously, the floors in the houses used to be uncemented whereas today they are made of bricks and cement. Among the more prosperous families the drawing rooms can be seen to contain tables and chairs. Formerly, the houses used to be decorated with pictures of gods and goddnesses but the pictures of such leaders as Gandhi and Nehru can now be seen. Previously, oil used to be burnt for light but now kerosene oil lanterns are used more popularly. Even stoves are now used for making tea in some families.

9. Cleanliness. Although not much attention is paid even now to cleanliness the attention directed towards it is certainly more than it used to be. Sometimes schools, panchayats, development blocks and other public institutions as well as the entire villages are cleaned. Even personal cleanliness is being attended to more than in the past. The use of safety razors is increasing. With the popularisation of the methods of making manure from cowdung, the cowdung which formerly used to lie around in the streets is now profitably consumed. The panchayats have directed their attention towards the cleaning of lanes, wells, public places etc.

10. Health. With the progress of sanitation and an increase in the number of doctors in the village, health has improved in a few villages. On the other hand, although medical facilities have definitely increased this progress has been counteracted by an increase in the number of diseases. Not much enlightenment has spread among the village folk in spite of the spread of family planning and birth control by the government. The state of health of the women will definitely improve when the simple means to control of conception heralded by proper education become available. Due to the food problem existing in the country the poor people of the villages cannot get adequate and nutritious food and thus their health is not very good. As a result of the arrangements made by the government for vaccination and distribution of patent medicines some control over small pox, malaria etc., has been achieved. The health of the female members can be said to have improved with the end of veil system and the improvement in the condition of houses. But, on the other hand, the increasing use of tea, tobacco, vegetable oil etc., is undermining the health of the villagers.

11. Education. Literacy is increasing among the inhabitants of the villages. Basic education and social education are increasing, many of the states are making efforts to provide have. Many of the young men of the villages are going to the towns to receive higher education. In the bigger villages, high schools and even intermediate colleges can be seen. In the rural areas, many institutes, agricultural colleges and degree colleges have been established.

12. Economic Changes. The standard of living is rising in the villages creating a demand for new things, for which shops are being opened in the villages. The educated youngmen from the villages prefer paid white collar jobs. The use of new tools is increasing in agriculture. The production has increased as a result of the new tools, new seeds and modern methods of farming. The condition of minor professions has improved with the opening of co-operative societies. The condition of financial capital has been improved with the opening of co-opertive credit societies, grain banks and co-operative banks, and the indebtedness has decreased. The cottage industries has been encouraged by government aid. The per capita income have increased but so have the prices of the commodities. The condition of the farmers and people engaged in minor occupations has improved with the removal of intermediaries.

13. Political Changes. With the establishment of panchayats in the villages, political consciousness has increased. The villagers have also started criticising the actions of the government through the right of the adult to vote. In some villages even newspapers are available which, along with the radio, help to increase the political knowledge of the villagers. But the political parties have also created disunity and factionalism within the villages. The villagers are not as awed of the government officials as they used to be before independence Even though, there are panchayats, litigation has increased in the villages The community feeling has increased even though national consciousness has been aroused. Selfishness and individualism have increased along with co-operation.

RURAL RELIGION

In all parts of the world, the rural population compares favourably with the people who inhabit the cities in matters of religion, being more inclined in this direction. This disparity arises from a number of factors of which the most prominent is their preoccupation with agriculture, which depends very much upon nature despite stupendous progress that science may have made in any country. This dependence upon nature gives an added importance to the natural forces in the life of man, who consequently indulges in a variety of religious activities, offerings and prayers designed either to pacify' or to please the deified powers which play such an important role in his life In the villages, life is spent in the lap of nature, in sharp contrast to the life in the cities, where the invention of modern scientific implements has reduced materially the influence of the seasons and nature upon the lives of the inhabitants. The life of the people in the villages is almost completely exposed to the vagaries of nature, but at the same time the rustic derives satisfaction from the opportunity of observing at first hand nature at its most beautiful and red in the tooth and claw as well. Thus, rural religion originates in the worship of nature. The same holds true in the context of Indian society also. Science has not made much progress in India, the preponderance of nature and spiritual being evident in every aspect of life. All these causes, taken collectively, have the effect of giving much importance to the rural people in India.

Indian Rural Religion is Practical

Thinkers in all times and at all places have agreed in regarding Indians as a religious-minded people. In the words of Sir Harcourt Butler, "The Indians are essentially religious as Europeans are essentially secular. Religion is still the alpha, and the omega of Indian life." Besides being religious, Indians are also prone to a philosophical propensity. Many people have looked upon Sankara's Mayavada as representative of Indian thought. Most thinkers conceive of Indians as a people who contemplate interminably upon religion and philosophy, the after world, heaven, hell and salvation. Morris Opler has written, "The fact that the highest goal of Hindu is to eliminate earthly concerns, desires and personal existence itself, introduces a large element of asceticism, intecllectualism, detachment and withdrawal into Hindu philosophy. In no other country have so many men renounced the world, and in no other place is there so much fasting and mortification of the flesh. The world is considered transitory and an appearance. Reality is an escape from the world and from the forms which make existence in the world necessary." Thus, Opler conceives Indian religion as impractical and escapist in the extreme. But, on the other hand, Oscar Lewis found Indian religion essentially practical and realistic, in the course of his study of Rampur village. Distinguishing between Indian classical religion and Indian rural religion, S.C. Dubey has written, "Clearly, Hinduism as it is practised in the village, is not the Hinduism of the classical philosophical systems of India for it possesses neither the metaphysical heights nor the abstract content of the latter. It is a religion of fasts and festivals, in which prescribed rituals cover all the major crises of life. Analysis of life histories reveals that spiritualism cannot be said to be the keynote in the life of the community, far from it the religion appears to be a practical one." Although it would not be very efficacious to apply the conclusions derived from the study of one particular village to the rural population of the country as a whole it can nevertheless be confidently asserted that rural religion which does not bear the mark of Sanskritization, is realistic and practical. There are numerous causes which have precipitated this state of affairs, among them is the tremendous effort every villager has to exert in ensuring the livelihood of his family beside himself, which has the effect of limiting his viewpoint to the practical. For another, the villagers of India are not properly acquainted with the traditional Indian philosophy and in the absence of this orientation they do not evince any vivid stamp of philosophical thought. Yet another reason is the poverty and lack of education existing among the villagers. They harbour many superstitious beliefs and they have to labour hard in life. In these circumstances it is almost inconceivable that there should be an element of intellectuality and spirituality in their religion. It is a different matter that it may appear more spiritual and escapist or fatalist in comparison to the rural religion characteristic of other countries.

Rural Gods and Goddesses

In general, the following classes of Gods and Goddesses are worshipped in Indian villages:

1. Gods and Goddesses of Hindus. The rural Hindus everywhere worship the Gods and Goddesses of the Hindu Religion. The most important among them is Shiva, who is worshipped in different forms and under different names. Besides Shiva, the names of Sankara and Bholebaba are also famous for this deity. Hanumana is also worshipped in the villages. His worship is believed to be instrumental in preventing many kinds of catastrophes. Besides, these two the other deities worshipped in the villages of India are Vishnu, Rama, Krishna, Agni, Valmiki, Jagannath and Sun God etc. People offer water to the Sun God, who is believed to ensure a good day ahead for the worshipper. Besides, these Gods, numerious Goddesses are worshipped, among them are Durga, Kali, Laksmi and Sarasvati etc. On the festival of Diwali, Ganesha is worshipped along with Lakshmi. The worship of Ganesha is considered essential on the auspicious occasions. Kali is believed to be capable of getting rid of different diseases. Durga wards off any impending disaster, while Lakshmi is the Goddess of wealth. Saraswati is the goddess of knowledge.

2. Non-Hindu Gods and Goddesses. The Indian villager does not rest satisfied with worshipping this formidable repertoire of Hindu Gods and Goddesses, but extends his respect and reverence to many other deities which cannot be called Hindu by tradition, among them being Shitala Maharani who protects people from smallpox epidemic and who sends troubles in the form of smallpox when displeased, Bhuiyaan Devi who is considered to be very powerful and Sati Maharani, etc. In any village where any Sati has become famous the place in the village is worshipped and sometimes even fairs are organised. Besides them, many saints are also worshipped in some villages. To these acts of worship are attached many stories of local interest.

3. Rural Gods and Goddesses. Besides the above mentioned Gods and Goddesses, every village has its own local God and Goddess. Often the place of worship of such a deity is outside the village, and it is worshipped from time to time. To it, too are attached many interesting and common tales.

4. Worship of Plants, Trees and Animals. In the villages of India many trees, plants and animals are considered divine. The banyan, neem and pipal are treated as divine and worshipped. The worship of Tulsi is particularily considered important everywhere. The cow is considered to be sacred. Cow dung is used to cover any place which is to be purified. At some places even the ox and the snake are objects of worship. In the village where a tribe lives, the animals and plants of totem are considered divine.

Beliefs in Ghosts and Witches

Besides the numerous Gods and Goddesses worshipped in the Indian villages, the rural populace credit the existence of ghosts, instituting different kinds of activities designed to appease them, please them or get rid of them. Whenever a man or a woman in the village comes to an untimely demise, or dies in an accident, or is murdered, or commits suicide, it is believed that his or her soul is dissatisfied and roams the village in some or the other form. The souls of men become ghosts while the souls of the women become witches, both of whom are believed to inhabit trees, graveyards, the banks of rivers, of ponds and sometimes even in the houses. The two kinds show an affinity for their own types and harass the living member of their corresponding sexes. When any man or woman comes under the influence of these ghosts and witches, his or her behaviour becomes manifestly abnormal and unconventional, and all the efforts made by the affected person take on a peculiar hue. The many kinds of mental derangements are not recognised as mental diseases affecting persons but are considered to be the effects of ghosts and witches and are treated accordingly. In order to get rid of the shadows of ghosts which over the demented person, peculiar kinds of treatments are applied. The specialist in these matters is the witch doctor, who may belong to any tribe. He is supposed to do away with the ghosts and witches by the force of his magic. He sometimes makes use of food and sweetmeats in getting rid of the ghosts. In this way, every effort, in the form of violence, threat, entreaty and skill, is made to appease these cruel souls and to get rid of them. In the process the diseased person suffers extreme persecution which often takes the form of extreme physical torture which may sometimes lead even to the death of the person. But sometimes the person is cured and the witch doctor retains his custom. As a protective measure the witch doctor dispenses some charms also, which are tied round the arm or the neck of the person in the belief that it will cope with, and negativate, the effects of the wicked souls.

Belief in Good Souls

The inhabitants of the villages do not confine their credulity to a belief only in wicked souls but they extend to it belief in some good souls as well. These souls do not suffer from any discrimination on account of sex, being either feminine or masculine. They are benevolent and assist people in different ways. If after the passing away of a saint or a great personage the people believe his soul to be dwelling within the village, they take it for granted that it is protecting the entire village. All kinds of gifts are deposited at the supposed dwelling place of this magnanimous being.

Faith in Dreams

Besides belief in these invisible souls, rural religion also includes faith in dreams. The faith in the importance of dreams is almost universal but their explanations in different places do not correspond. Generally, whatever a person dreams after four o'clock in the morning is believed to be prophetic, either for good or bad. Actually, even though the villagers themselves do not perceive any visible and special relation between what they see in dreams and the real worlds, yet they persist in their beliefs about the dreams. The main cause of this notion is their lack of education; due to which many facts are unthinkingly associated with dreams.

Ideas of Auspicious and Inauspicious

Many kinds of superstitions concerning good and evil, are to be found in rural people. For a particular activity some particular days and months are considered auspicious and as having a good potent. In the case of important works and rituals the local pundits make calculations and advise the interested parties in respect of the auspicious day and hour. In this way, any ritual necessitates the determination of a particularly conducive moment. But in a general sort of way, Friday and the month of Chaitra are considered auspicious. Besides these, particular attention is directed towards this aspect by the villagers in respect of travel. For example, it is considered a bad omen, even, down right ominous, to travel towards the north on Thursdays and Fridays. Travel in an easterly direction is not advised on Mondays and Saturdays. Sundays and Fridays are not to be utilised travelling to West while Thursdays are not to be considered fit if one contemplates travelling towards the South. But to acquiesce to this consideration of the auspiciousness of particular days may become a hiderance in the performance of important activities. It is saying something in favour of human inventive genius when we say that the pandits have overcome this difficulty by suggesting that if one leaves the village before the break of day, this day leaves the discretion of travel unmolested or uninfluenced by its auspiciousness or maliciousness.

Religious Considerations in Dietary Habits

Besides travel, another aspect of human life to be influenced by the auspiciousness of the various days in a week is the food taking. The morning meal, to be taken after a bath, consists different ingredients on different days, so it is ordained. For example, it is good to eat betel on Sunday and curd on Tuesday.

Consideration of Good and Bad Omens

Along with the thought of the auspicious, rural religion devotes attention to considerations of good and bad omens. Especially, it is considered very detrimental if some bad omen bodes ill when some new activity is being initiated. These bad omens have taken a variety of forms. It is considered to be a bad omen if one comes across a person blind in one eye during travel. It is not considered good to sneeze at the start of a journey and if one does sneeze, one must wait for a few moments. Similarly, it is a bad omen if a cat crosses one's path while one is proceeding somewhere. If a wolf accompanies a cat on such occasion, it does not do anything to improve matters and the omen stays bad. If one looks into an empty pot, the success of a venture is jeopardized, it being safer to look into it when full, whence it constitutes a good omen. Similarly, a washerman or a dead body are good omens towards the successful completion of work.

Superstitions in Natural Phenomenon

The villagers attach all kinds of superstitions to natural phenomenon. For example, the solar and the lunar eclipses are believed to be the causes of the catastrophies of Rahu and Ketu. An earth tremour is attributed to the undulations of the snake which bears the world on its fange, a hard job by any standards. Absence of rain or drought, too much rain, untimely rain etc., are attributed to displeasure on the part of the God Indra. Superstitions are even more numerous in tribal villages where there is even greater ignorance and ineducation, the fundamental causes of superstition.

Assumptions Concerning the Supernatural

In rural religion where there is superstition, ignorance, unnecessary ritualism, etc., on the one hand, there are also a considerable number of assumptions pertaining to the supernatural on the other. For example, heaven, hell, rebirth, salvation, virtue, sin, etc., are everywhere believed to be real even though people differ from village to village in their explanations and understanding of them. Most of the people believe that heaven and hell are two good and bad places where the souls of good and bad people respectively enjoy in pleasure and suffer after death. On the other hand, some people believe that heaven and hell are attained not after death but in this very life. In the same way people believe that man has to pass through eighty-four lakh forms of life, although some, and probably a large majority of people do not corroborate, or agree with this. Good action is known as virtue and bad as vice but there is no concurrence of opinion with regard to what constitutes good and bad activities.

Moral Beliefs

In this way, many moral beliefs are also conjoined to rural religion. A good person is a soul superior to all and sundry, and yet all people do not agree as to the elements which are characteristic of these superior souls. Nevertheless, a benevolent person of high character who worships God with fervour is commonly recognised as a religious person or superior soul. And yet, there is fair amount of polymic on what exactly benevolence is. Some people look at public service in constructing the concrete wells and tanks as benevolent while others would append benevolence to leading money without charging interest. In spite of a lack of agreement, people generally look upon acts of kindness and assistance, both moral and concrete to the poor and the helpless, as benevolent. In quite the same way, people have not any one recognised opinion regarding sin. Theft is considered sinful in all civilized villages but tribal villages are more tolerant in this respect because they do not call this human shortcoming of making unpermitted use of another's property, sin. In the same way the rural population of India does not tolerate extra marital sexual relations and does everything to prevent their inception, and yet the same strictness of spirit on this subject is not universal. Prevarication, chicanery etc., are everywhere considered sinful. Homicide or murder is almost universally considered sinful and treated as a heinous sin, and yet it may be considered justified by a group of person under certain conditions which are unusual. Most of the people in the villages consider every act of violence or killing as sin, while others differ in their opinions.

Various Influences on Rural Religion

As a matter of fact, people belonging to a variety of religions, beliefs and cultures are found co-existing in the villages of India. The difference in culture is very well marked and evident in a comparison between civilized village society and tribal village society. And there is an adequate difference between Hindu religion and tribal religion. In the same way, some particular religions characterize certain villages when there is preponderance of people of one sect over people of another, while in most village one comes across the most divergent religions. One comes across people belonging to both Hindu and Sikh religions in the villages of India, and Muslims are scattered over the entire country. Besides the influence of the variety of religions, rural religion is influenced also by distance which separates the village and the town. The village further away from the town will generally have a religion which is more dogmatic, superstitious, ignorant and credulous in matters pertaining to the supernatural, in comparison with the religion existing in a village which is more accessible to urban influence. There the influence of the town has the effect of moderating these factors. Another influential factor is the effect of education upon the institution of rural religion because in a village where educated people abound, the religion will not have much faith in superstitions, ghosts and the like. Thinking about such matters becomes common in the absence of education. In much the same way transformation in rural religion as a result of modern scientific tendency is fairly evident because in areas which have progressed scientifically the introduction of the modern means of communication has led to a closer touch with science, the cumulative effect of which has been to dispel the clouds of ignorance and superstition. Again, rural religion is not immune to the effect of economic conditions since, generally speaking, the poorer people as a class are more superstitious.

Dynamic Aspect of Rural Religion

In this way, it is necessary to keep an eye on its dynamic aspect if rural religion, as it is in India is to be understood. In the present age, efforts are made to achieve progress in every sphere. In the villages of India, the efforts at progress are all embracing, encompassing the political, social and economic aspects. Education is spreading in the villages. With the increase in urbanization in the country, the villages are also being continuously transformed. Besides, the increase in the railways, buses and other travel facilities, has led to an increase in the mobility of the villagers, and the rural population is adopting the habit of travelling far and wide. The adventurous and ambitious young man of the villages travel to big cities to try their luck and, upon returning tell their comparatively immobile and senile kinfolk about what they have seen. The radio serves to keep the village folk generally in touch with the major happenings of the world. In the exhibitions which are organised from time to time they see novel things. All these things have their effect upon rural religion. One of the first effects of these influences is that they put an end to the beliefs in ghosts, witches etc., and thoughts of superstitions and omens. Religion is sanskritized and modernised. Secondly, the religiousness itself looses its grip upon the individual, and faith is transferred to science from religion. But this does not lead to the utter annihilation of rural religion. Religiousness is a fundamental element of Indian culture. The villager of today still dines to tradition and is no wit less religious than his ancestor despite the many and varied changes that may have intruded into his religious notions and beliefs.

THE VILLAGE TEMPLE

Importance of the Village Temple

The village temple holds a very important place in the life of the village. It, of course, has its religious importance but in the village it also exerts ostensible influence upon the social sphere as well. As a matter of fact, the temple in a village becomes the centre of public programmes. And even otherwise, the inseparability of rural religion from the life of the villager lends to the village temple an importance in rural life.

Description of Rural Temple

Sometimes some property in one form or another in attached to the village temple, the income from which serves to meet the expences of decoration, communal feeding and the livelihood of the priest or pundit. Some villages have more than one temple. In the villages in India, different temples are constructed for different deities, these temples differing somewhat in structure. Among the Indian gods, the more popular, in the sense of the number of temples dedicated to them, are Mahavira or Hanumana and Mahadeva or Sankara. In a village where people have faith in different groups or schools of thought, the temples are dedicated to them so that in a village where people belong to the group of the disiples of Shakti the temple is also dedicated to Shakti while the same temple would have been dedicated to Shiva had the villagers belonged among his disciples. Besides these, one can see temples dedicated to many other female deities like Kalidevi, Saraswati Devi, Durga Devi, Sati Devi etc., in a number of places. Wherever a woman sacrifices herself on the burning pyre of her husband and some supernatural element is seen in her, a temple is erected in her honour and the other women in the village visit it from time to time to offer prayer. As a general rule, the local God also finds some place in the village but this place is more in the form of a sacred place than a temple.

Public and Private Temples

The rural temples are looked upon as community property and a particular family traditionally looks after it and performs the part of the priest. But some temples are also private, as are the ones constructed by the rich landlords within the precincts of their own gardens. Commonly, the public temples are in no worse condition than those privately maintained, the former being visited by all the villagers. Formerly, members of lower or untouchable castes were not permitted to enter them but since the anti-untouchability campaign and the declaration of the practice of untouchability as illegal the temples in most villages are open to all and sundry. But even then the people who perform menial tasks are generally prohibited from entering the temples. On the other hand, the private temples are utilised by the members of only one family though, as a general rule, no one is barred from worshipping in the temples.

Importance of the Priest in Village Life

The temple is not merely a place of worship. If the priest of the temple is an intelligent and learned person he has an important status and role in the village life. He becomes a respected leader of the village, to whom much importance is attached by the villagers who look upon him as a representative of God. Often his premonitions and forecasts have profound influence upon the thinking and conduct of the villagers. In this way, the temple priest is an astrologer, prophet and doctor, conductor of prayers and story-teller all at the same time. In these circumstances, the temple in the village has a comprehensive influence upon the life of the village, and instead of remaining merely a place of worship, the temple becomes an institution.

Religious Importance of the Temple

First and foremost, the temple has a religious importance. At almost, all the major occasions of religious importance, festivals are held and the entire population of the village congregates to the temple to worship. In the temple an idol of God is placed. A Brahmin priest makes arrangements for the maintenance of the temple. He bathes the idol of God and worships it daily and at these times many of the villagers are present. After the prayers the priest distributes sweet among the predominantly adolescent audience. In addition to this daily routine special congregations are invited and organised for praying, at more or less regular intervals. Group discussions are also help. At the major festivals the idol is decorated, the attendance being more numerous and the distributed sweets being in greater quantity.

Social Importance of the Village Temple

As has been mentioned on a number of previous occasions the temple has importance for the life of the village from the social viewpoint also. The temple becomes a place for congregating in when people from all the castes get together to take part in the occasions being celebrated at the temple. Through the medium of the temple people of different castes get an opportunity to meet each other. In this way, the temple becomes a centre of social meeting. And at times, other than when the prayers are being conducted, old men and women can be seen gossiping, thus transforming the temple into a place for mutual relief of overwhelming thoughts and desires or some such thing. Sometimes even the most important meetings of the village are held in the temple, for it is a sacred and important place besides which it is spacious enough to accommodate many people. Many programmes for social welfare are conducted in the temples. Sometimes, the temple is used as a medium for collecting funds in order to finance different kinds of public work in the village.

Moral Importance of the Temple

Besides, its social and religious importance, the village temple is important from the moral viewpoint as well, because it is a symbol of the village morality and its religious fervour. Often, the priest in the temple is called upon to make judgment of good and bad in the moral problems which beset the villagers. This sort of thing has been carried very far because incidents are not completely lacking where a person considered guilty and worthy of punishment is released on the mere word of the pundit on the ground that the priest is a religious and benevolent person whose words are invaluable.

Cultural Importance of the Temple

The cultural life of the village is also enriched by the temple. In the temple group devotional songs and congregations for this purpose, are held. On such occasions, all sorts of musical instruments are used. Dances are also arranged in temple and performed in front of the idol of God. This kind of practice is particularly in vogue in the temples of South India. The temples which possess a fair amount of property are generally well and lavishly decorated. In this way, the temple has both artistic and cultural value.

There is yet another point of cultural importance of the temple. In the life of the rural people, many kinds of rituals are related to the temple. The marriage performed at temple, be it publicly performed or secretly, is held to be sacred and inviolable. In many villages, the marital rituals are performed in the village itself. On some sacred occasions the husband and wife go together to visit the deity and to receive his blessing. In the temple, the wives and mothers propitiate respectively for their husbands and their children and make presents when their desires are fulfilled.

Educational Importance of the Temple

In ancient India, the temples were educational centres as well and even today schools are held in many temples. Mostly, the priest is the teacher. And this leads to people to believe that the education imparted by the priest to them will make them religious and moral. Besides the children, the priest educates adult men and women also in various things. If the personality of the priest is magnetic and inspiring the villagers take their problems to him and accept the solutions which he suggests.

Recreational Importance of the Temple

The temples do not fall short of material for the recreation of the village people. Often, gymnasia are attached to the village temple, because, for one, the temple is generally situated outside the village in a clean and open place and, for another, it is considered more beneficial to take exercise under the protection and benevolence of Gods like Hanumana than otherwise. Every now and then, competitions in wrestling are organised, the whole affair being characterised by a lot of fanfare and public acclaim. The arrangement for new programmes at regular intervals in the temple serves to relieve monotony and create variety, all of which serve to entertain the people.

The population of the Indian villages looks upon a person invested with the powers of meeting out justice as a representative of a messenger from God. And for this reason, the village priest, in his part of a representative or messenger of God, is sometimes called upon to intervene in complicated cases and to do justice. In addition to doing justice the priest also prescribes the kind of penance which a person should do in order to remove the stains of sin done to him.

Festivals of the Temple

The festival of temple often take place at times when they can influence quite considerably the activity of agriculture. And because the festivals of the village generally coincide with these, the whole process attaches even more importance, for the villager, to the temple and makes it the actual symbol of the religious aspect of rural life, the result is that the temple thus becomes related to the general life of the village.

From the preceding description of the importance of the temple in rural life, it is evident that the temple contributes in an important way to each and every aspect of life which the villager leads. But, with the advent of new thought and the influence of the town, which is making rural life secular the temple is losing its importance. Since, the institution of zamindari has been abolished, the landlords can no longer afford the lavish expenditure they were accustomed to and the temples consequently suffer because of the discontinuation of grants and aids given by the landlords. But nevertheless, the villages that retain their faith in religion still attach the old traditional importance to the village temple. Now, India is a secular state but it would not be advisable to abolish or be careless towards the temple because it is not merely a place for religious practices but a centre of the various activities of village life. The need is for a slight transformation in the programmes organised in the temple.

CULTURAL ASPECT OF RURAL LIFE

The present topic is devoted to only two important aspects of rural cultural life *i.e.*, village festivals and sanskars. Festivals and celebrations have a great importance in Indian rural life and particularly in the Hindu community. It is more unlucky month in which the village people do not celebrate some festival or the other. Studies concerning these festivals have been made in various parts of India. In 1918, Mukherjee made a special study of the festivals of Bengal and Uttar Pradesh. In 1919, Gupta based an exposition concerning Indian festivals on his study of Bombay, Bengal and Madhya Bharat. Stevenson, in 1920, based his description on a study of Kathiyavara and Gujarat. It was Maharashtra which became the object of study in 1921 when Underhill undertook this task. Briggs in 1920 and Fuches in 1951, made a study of individual tribal festivals. In 1951, Oscar Lewis presented a description of the festivals performed by the rural community in Rampura village, which he was studying. In the same year, D.N. Majumdar studied the festivals of community of Mohana village, in the course of a study. In this way, the Indian rural festivals have been studied from various sundry aspects all of which differ from each other in one way or another. The difference in rural festivals corresponds to the variations in caste, community, area of residence, culture, etc. And yet there are some festivals which are celebrated in different months. This is explained in the following table:

Months	Festivals
1. Magh (January-February)	1. Sakat
	2. Makar Sankranti
	3. Basant Panchmi
2. Phalgun (February-March)	1. Holi
	2. Shiv Ratri
3. Chaitra (March-April)	1. Ram Navami
4. Baishakh (April-May)	1. Worship of Jagan Nath
5. Jaith (May-June)	1. Dushehra of Jaith
6. Assar (June-July)	1. Assart
7. Saavan (July-August)	1. Raksha Bandhan
	2. Naag Panchami
	3. Teej
8. Bhaadon (August-September)	1. Janmashtami
9. Kwaar (September-October)	1. Vijaya Dashami
	2. Pitra Paksh
10. Kartika (October-November)	1. Karava Chaoth
	2. Kartika Poomima
	3. Dipaavali
	4. Bhaiya Dooj

All the villages in India do not celebrate these festivals in their entirety, but, nevertheless, most of them are celebrated by the Indian villages. A brief description of these festivals now follows:

1. Sakat. Sakat is a festival celebrated to guard against catastrophies. On this occasion, the mothers of male children pray to Sakat Maharani to defend their children from evil. On the day on which this occasion occurs fried food is prepared. In the evening, the Sakat Maharani is worshipped, following which the females take milk and fruits, but no grains.

2. Makar Sankranti. This particular festival is celebrated every year on the 14th of January. On this particular morning every one rises and bathes early, in a river wherever possible. The food in the morning consists of rice and pulse, the fried food being taken with the evening meal. Presents of rice pudding, ghee, salt, etc., are made to the Brahmin. Among the lower castes, the members of the head's family and his relatives gather together and jointly partake of rice pudding known as *khichari.*

3. Basant Panchami. On panchami in the month or Magh, Basant Panchami is celebrated, it being the fifth or Panchami of Magh. On this day, prayers are addressed to the family God or to Shiva or to one of the other deites. In most villages, there is a convention of donning yellow garb on this day, but this practice can be seen in some villages which are near towns, since, this convention is the result of the influence of the town.

4. Holi. It is the biggest festival of Hindus, falling on the day of the full moon in Phalgun. The day following is called Dhulaindi. Long before the actual day young boys roam about the village and collect firewood which they pile on the place reserved for the lighting of the bonefire on the occasion. The female population make bats corresponding to round objects like sun, moon, etc., a week in advance. In the centre of every bat there is a hole, many of them being threaded together on to thin strings to make garlands. The time for lighting the holi is determined by the village priest. At the same time he discovers some letters, the people whose names begin with these letters being forbidden to take part in the proceedings. The time of lighting the fire is broadcast to the entire village. On this day, the houses in villages are given a proper wash and brush on. They need it. The walls are whitewashed and the floors cowdunged. Most of the persons buy a new outfit of clothes and shoes. At the appointed time, the entire village collects at the place. They take with them plants of barley. When the fire is to be lit, a particular person makes three rounds of the pile and then sets it alight. At the same time the assemblage roars in unison "Holi Hai". The entire congregation then takes five or seven rounds of the fire and at every round people throw grains of barley at the fire of Holi, at the end of which five or seven garlands of bats are added to the blaze. On this occasion, many people sing a folk song called Phag. Those who have been forbidden to take part in the activity or proceedings stand at a distance and look on. At some places after the communal circling of the fire, the younger people touch the feet of their elders and utter "Rama Rama". At other places the same words are intoned whenever someone meets another member of family.

The day following Holi is called Dhulaindi and is a day of even more vigorous enjoyment and pleasure. On this day, the villagers give their animals a bath and make an imprint of their hands on animal's back. After the sun has come out, colour is thrown at each other. At present in most villages this part of the festival is restricted to adolescents, but in other villages age is not considered any disqualification, and everyone takes part heartily. Often, the fun makers fall into a group which tours the village, one of them distinguishing himself by acting the part of a clown. It is not uncommon for these people to be intoxicated. This group visits every place in the village, the people making an infernal din the while. This occasion carries with it a licence, accepted by convention, for all sorts of uncouth remarks, no one taking umbrage when made the butt of joke. Uncouth remarks are passed without any consideration of propriety. Some people dance along with the group, accompanied by others singing phag or other songs. The children use syringes, of a most unclinical size and shape, to project coloured water over a fair distance upon the merry makers. The grown up people keep to drier modes of disfiguration. Some inconsiderate barbarians sling mud and not of the proverbial variety either, besides they use coaltar and such things. But such practice is generally looked down upon and considered bad. It is thought good to let bygones be bygones and to be friendly once again on this occasion. The colour throwing is generally stopped at noon; the people don their new garments in the evening and visit one another at this time to convey their good wishes. Generally, people belonging to the lower castes visit their social superiors, there being some more group singing in the same vein at this time as well. Most of the people visit members of their own caste. Meeting each other, they embrace joyfully. But on meeting a member of a higher caste a verbal greeting is considered adequate. On this day, all activities are restricted to those appropriate for the occasion, no other work being done.

5. Shiva Ratri. The festival of Shiva Ratri is celebrated in Phalgun. As is obvious from its names, this day is reserved for worship of Shiva during which flowers of dhatura and other materials are put on the idol of Shiva. After the prayer sweets are distributed in the Shiva temples. Some people fast on the day of Shiva Ratri, but even upon breaking the fast, they still abstain from grains. The women worship Shiva within the confines of the house. On this day too, some people bathe in the Ganges and collective singing of devotional songs is carried on.

6. Worship of Jagannath. Although, the idol of Jagannath ji is established in the famous Jagannath temple in Puri, yet, the worship of Jagannath is carried on in Chait or Baisakh in most Indian villages. It is believed that the worship of Jagannath may lead to prosperity. People from every comer of the country make devotional journeys to Puri and on returning from this pilgrimage they take back with them pictures of Jagannath. After this pilgrimage the people do not have to make annual offerings to the dead ancestors, since, it is believed that, with the blessings of Jagannath, the desires of the ancestors will be satiated. On this day, too, the house is given a thorough cleaning and scrubbing. Fried food is taken in the morning. The worship of Jagannath consists in the recital of his story and offering of prayers to his picture. As a general rule only the married women worship Jagannath, fast on the particular day and restrict their diet to mere cold drinks. It is believed that the worship of Jagannath is conducive to the welfare of the members of the family.

7. Dushehra of Jaith. As is obvious from the name given to this festival, it falls in the month of Jaith. On this day, some people fast and offer water in the temple of Mahadeva, while the members of lower castes do the same at the supposed residence of the local deity.

8. Asaari. The festival of Asaari falls in the month of Asaar. On this day, the higher castes have their diet from amongst fried food and fruits while the lower or inferior castes eat vegetables and roots etc. It is mainly a women's festival. Hence, the women pray to the Goddess. The newly wed women accompany their husbands when the latter visit the temple. Men and women draw lines of cowdung on the walls of their houses, believing thereby to have gained immunity from an invasion by the snake. The children get their heads shaved while the adult women take this opportunity to visit their parent's residence. It is believed that, as a result of worship, the Goddess fulfils the desires of women concerning their sons and husbands.

9. Raksha Bandhan. The festival is one of major importance among the Hindus. On this day, sisters tie colourful Raakhis on the right wrists of their brothers and give them sweets, and the brothers return the sentiment by giving some present or money to their sisters. The Rakhi is the symbol of the protection which a brother offers to his sister. In the village, it is not only a sister who ties a Raakhi on the wrist of the brother but even members of the lower castes do the same to the people of higher castes. The brahmins of the village also tie Raakhis to the people of other castes, getting money or food in return. If a long distance separates the sister from brother, the Raakhi is sent to him by post or by any other means at hand. The brother also conveys his feelings and concrete token as best as he can. On this day, the girls are seen almost bursting with enthusiasm. They paint their palms and sing traditional songs on the swings.

10. Naag Panchami. On the occasion of Naag Panchami, the sanke God is worshipped. This day falls on the fifth (panchmi) of Saavan. On this day, the people wash themselves, and carrying milk, rice, pudding, etc., make a beeline for whatever place they consider to be a possible snake hole. There they pray, and leaving their rice, etc. they return. After the prayer is over they themselves take food. In fact, it is not the worship of the snake God which is the most important, the pride of place, in this respect, goes to the wrestling competitions which are organised. The wrestling matches are held within the village and sometimes people from other villages are also invited. No distinction of caste is allowed in wrestling. If age and weight agree contestants are allowed to wrestle. Men of all ages, verying from children to senile folk, take part. Any person desirous of wrestling steps into the ring and challenges the congregation. Whoever accepts the challenge walks in the ring and weight and age permitting, the two get on with it. The wrestlers are also given prizes by the spectators. Often, the oldest and most prominent members of the community perform the function of judges. All the time, the wrestling is going on, a menial plays on the drum to the tune of 'pick him up and sling him' or some similar tune. Besides, the wrestling, people make most of the occasion and thrash old dolls after the wrestling is over. On this day, one girl from every family goes to the predetermined spot, taking a doll along with her. All the dolls are collected at one place and are thrashed by boys of every caste. The girls also distribute fried nuts to the boys. The married girls go to their parents on this particular day and if they cannot come, their parents send them money and clothes in the form of presents. On this occasion, the swing is in great demand and so are the songs appropriate to the occasion and its spirit. On this day, most people take fried food. The festival of Naag Panchami is of great importance for village life.

11. Janmashtami. The festival of Janmashtami is celebrated to commemorate the birth of the revered God Sri Krishna. It is a matter of belief that Lord Krishna was born on the day of Ashtami in the month of Bhaadon. On this day, men and women keep a fast lasting till midnight, when they celebrate the birth of Lord Krishna. After offering their prayers and receiving the Lord's blessings and sweets the people break their fast. On this day, some people construct monumental scenes in their homes depicting events related to Lord Krishna's life. But, more often a Ramdol is constructed, in the house of a prominent and influential person of the village, and an idol of the Lord is placed in the Ramdol. People of every caste collect in front of this Ramdol and sing devotional songs. The entire village makes contributions towards the expense incurred in the contruction of the Ramdol and in the sweets distributed. This singing continues till midnight, when the priest prays to God. In exchange for his troubles he is presented with some money. After the prayer sweets are distributed. The Ramdol stays with the important person for three days after which the barber takes it round the village, accompained by the priest. Everyone makes some cash presents. Of the entire amount collected, the priest takes three fourths while the barber gets the remaining one-fourth. In some places, the custom is to deposit the Ramdol at some particular spot, after it has been taken round the village, and to enact scene from Lord Krishna's life.

12. Teej. Teej is primarily a festival for the women folk. Both married and unmarried girls wear colourful clothes, sing what is known as the Kajri, and pray. Worship of Mahadeva on the occasion of Teej is considered to be good for women for married life. Only fried food is taken. The girls take their food after they have prayed.

13. Vijaya Dashami. Vijaya Dashami or Dushehra, no less than Holi and Diwali, is an important festival for the Hindus. It is celebrated in remembrance of the occasion when Rama triumphed over Ravana. Durga is also worshipped on this day. Durga is worshipped with a lot of pomp and splendour in the villages of Bengal. Ten days before the occasion of Vijaya Dashmi, Ram Lila is started in the bigger village, at some places, the whole life of Rama being enacted on the stage in the form of a drama. On the day of Dushehra, big fairs are held at certain places in the big villages, where big effigies of Ravana, his brother Kumbhakaran and son Megh Nada, are prepared in paper and erected at a public place. At a fixed time in the evening, these are set fire to. The festival also occasions universal excitement and enthusiasm in village life.

14. Pitra Paksh. Pitra Paksh is the occasion for a fortnight of worship of one's deceased ancestors. It takes place in the first half of the month of Kwaar in which no sexual pleasure is permitted and besides, water is offered in addition to other sacrifices demanded by religion. In shraadh, the priest and the barber are particularly important. In the shraadh feast the relatives also take part besides the Brahmins. Presents are also given to these people. Almost all the castes among the Hindus observe this occasion.

15. Karava Chaoth. The festival of Karava Chaoth is observed by women as it ensures longevity and overall welfare of their husbands. On this day, they maintain a total fast abstaining even from drinking water. After perceiving the moon and worshiping it, they break their vigil.

16. Kartika Poornima. This festival falls on the day of the full moon in the month of Kartika. On these days, very big fairs are organised along the banks of the Ganges where people proceed in millions by whatever means of transportation they can manage to acquire. On the particular day, people bathe early in the Ganges and worship Mahadeva.

17. Diwali. The festival of Diwali is quite as important, if not more so than the festivals of Holi and Dushehra. In most villages, Diwali is celebrated with a lot of pomp and majesty and it, too, like Holi, is spread over two days. The first day is called small Diwali and the second day the bigger Diwali. It is the festival of lights, small earthen ware pots called 'deep' being filled with oil and lighted through a wick. The day is festive in remembrance of Shri Ram Chandra's return to Ayodha after having spent fourteen years in exile. Some of the 'deeps' are filled with ghee instead of oil, and are placed at the place of worship. Fried food is prepared this day. The children buy toys made of sugar while the older people buy small busts of the various Gods like Ganesha, Lakshmi, etc., for these Gods are to be worshipped. Before the Diwali day dawns, the houses have gone through the ordeal of another thorough wash and brush up. The actual festival falls on the second day. Besides the lights, a good amount of fire crackers are also set off, by the children particularly. The confectioners make toys of sugar, which are eaten with kheel. The festival of Diwali is understood to augment prosperity. Many people gamble throughout the night on this occasion and stay awake till midnight, and even after, because it is a traditional belief that Laxmi, the Goddess of wealth, enters the house at this time and she is apt to turn back if she finds the doors barred. Some people worship Lakshmi while others worship books and pens. In the temples, ghee is burnt to give light. The entire village gets a thorough cleaning.

18. Bhaiya Dooj. The day following Diwali is an occasion for another festival, called Bhaiya Dooj. This is especially a sister's affair since, it is meant and celebrated for the welfare and good health of the brothers. On this day, the sisters make a mark with saffron and stick some rice on their brother's foreheads and give some sweets to eat. The brothers also make presents to their sisters.

Story of Satya Narayan

It is a tradition in the North Indian villages to hear the story of Satya Narayan on all festive occasions, over and above the special programme set aside for the occasion. It is told by a priest, and neighbours and relatives, in addition to the members of the family, take part. The recitation takes fairly long time. In this recitation stories are told about the importance attached to the worship of Satya Narayan, all of which convey the meaning that worship of Satya Narayan and listening to his stories can ward off many catastrophies. After the recital, prayers are offered and people make cash presents which they put in the ceremonial plate. The cash is pocketed by the priest besides which he is given food and some more cash by the host after the prayers are over.

Profanation of a Festival

The Hindu people look upon a day of festival as sacred. If some person dies in the family on a day of festivity, that particular festival is not celebrated any more in the family since, it has been robbed of its sanctity. But if in future, a son is born in the family on the same day its profanation is wiped out and its sanctity redeemed, and it is once again celebrated.

Religious Importance of Festivals

Festivals have a lot of importance in Indian rural life. The greatest importance is attached from the religious point of view. As is obvious from the foregoing description of the festivals, they are as many occasions for prayer and worship as for enjoyment. Different Gods and Goddesses are worshipped. Benevolence and pity also come to the forefront on these festive occasions and people give alms to the poor and feed them. On the day of the festival, the people bathe and keep themselves pure, even preventing bad and base thoughts from entering their minds. On occasions of festivity religious meetings are organised, devotional songs are sung collectively. The spiritual atmosphere seems to pervade everything, and there is a stream of people coming from and going to the temples.

Social Importance of the Festival

But, the social importance of the festivals perhaps surpasses their religious importance. On the occasion of festivals, people of different castes meet each other, and this helps to reduce the tension existing between them. People belonging to same classes visit each other's houses and on the occasion of Holi even embrace each other. This serves to strengthen the organisation of the society. And, on many festivals, even personal grievances are forgotten. On the occasion of Holi, for example, people forget their grievances and embrace each other in a spirit of mutual well being, a practical exposition of the proverb let bygones be bygones, which advocates the disregard of old misunderstandings and living a life of love and co-operation in the future. On the occasion of major festivals like Holi and Dushehra, the ceremonies of the festivals are directed along communal lines. This develops the community consciousness among the people and strengthens the organisation of the village. On many occasions of festivity, girls and boys, besides other near relatives, gather in one house. It increases their regard for one another. The festivals serve as an excuse for the parents to call their wedded daughters home again and these married women also get an excuse for meeting their relatives once in a while. In this way, the festivals accord people whether they are different relatives, members of different castes or belonging to different classes in society, an opportunity for increasing mutual inter-course. On these occasions, the work of organisation and arranging for these festivals in public falls to the lot of the head of the village. It serves to maintain their leadership.

Recreation Through Festivals

Festivals are occasions for merry-making. A lot of excitement and enthusiasm is in the air when festivals like Holi, Diwali and Dushehra are approaching. People wear new clothes on these auspicious days, after a more than normally refreshing bath and roam around. On the major festivals, people take the day off from their work and get a chance to have some rest and introduce a bit of much needed variety into their humdrum life, which refreshes them like water does a withering plant. The festivals are very important from the recreational point of view, as every festival does include some material which has recreational values. On Dushehra, the dramatic societies perform for ten days while on the occasion of Diwali the people put on many lights and explode many crackers. On Naag Punchami, wrestling matches are held and the dolls given a thorough thrashing. In the month of Saavana, people use the swings and sing to heart's content whenever there is some festival afoot. On the occasion of Holi, there could hardly be more recreation than when the colours are flying in the air. People dance with pleasure. From the psychological point of view occasions like Holi have their importance because they are an opportunity for the people to give expression to their various tendencies, all of which make it easier for them to keep their mental balance to cooperate with each other. The different games arranged on the occasion of festivals are meant to allow boys and girls to meet and to express their mental tendencies in various ways. Besides, the people get the opportunity to dress properly because on the normal days their activities are such as to prohibit the use of any gaudy clothes and ornaments. Something more sober and utilitarian is then demanded. In consequence, the people justifiably dress in their best clothes and roam about. A lot of jokes and familiarity are tolerated on these occasions. On many festivals, the men and women get an opportunity to meet each other.

Aesthetic Importance of Festivals

In addition to this, the festivals are important from the cultural view-point. In India, some or the other artistic figures are made on festive occasions and figures are drawn on the floors and the walls. Many kinds of things are made from cowdung. The house is cleaned and the things arrayed in new form. On the Janamashtami festival, the Ramdol is a very artistically prepared object, worthy of praise. And when the Ramlila is dramatised, the actors are the ingenuous villagers themselves. Folk music is almost an inseparable part of festivity on any pretext, many instruments being employed for the music accompaniment to devotional singing collectively. Community singing and community dancing increases the community consciousness of the villagers, in addition to maintaining a high level of cultural activity and cultural environment.

Place of Festivals in Rural Life

From the foregoing description of festivals, it is obvious that they bear a close relation to the seasons and various activities characteristic of agriculture. In this way, the festivals become a normal part of the life in the village. Actually, the festivals are those occasions when the villagers, having seen to their business and agricultural responsibilities, express natural joy and enthusiasm in welcoming a new season, being filled with renewed vigour for the work they are to tackle in this season. The poor people benefit in great measure on these festive occasions. Often, they are enabled to store foodgrains which they can consume over a number of days. And besides, they sometimes receive gifts of money and clothes. The people who benefit most on these occasions are the Brahmins or the priests, who get work to do, as well as lavish presents in food and cash. In this way, the festivals are instrumental in reducing the economic inequality and satisfying many of the needs of the poor.

It is obvious from the preceding delineation of the importance of festivals in rural life that they are valuable not merely from the religious view-point, but also from other view-points like social, recreational, health, sanitary, cultural development etc. The festivals manifest the inner core of villagers and enhance the life force.

RURAL SANSKARAS

Number of Sanskaras

In comparison with urban life, changes in rural life are few and far between. It is for this reason that while an almost negligible quantity of the rudiments of Indian culture are found in the town, they are to be found operative in almost all their splendour and untarnished glory in the rural life. Religious rituals are by far the most important in Indian culture. From the time when he is conceived to the time when death, the mighty leveller, marks a glorious end to his frailty and weakness, his power and glory, his pain and pleasure, the life of man has been tied in a chain of sanskaras. The number of these sanskaras is yet undecided all the scriptures and commentators upon religious texts holding divergent opinions. Some believe them to be twelve in number while others count them at eleven. Manu places the number of sanskaras at thirteen. These are given below:

1. Garbhadhan, 2. Jatkarma, 3. Namkaran, 4. Nishkramana, 5. Annaprashana, 6. Choorakarma, 7. Upanayana, 8. Keshanta, 9. Samavartana, 10. Vivaha, 11. Vanprastha, 12. Sanyasa, 13. Antyeshti.

Ashvalayan has counted another two beside these — Punsavana and Simantonayana. Sushrut has prescribed yet another — Kamavedha, making the total number of Sanskaras sixteen. But in rural life, the Hindus do not observe all these sixteen Sanskaras. According to the census of 1901, twelve of these rituals were prevalent among the Hindus, and these too have slipped into oblivion one after another as the time has passed. The first one to go down the path of oblivion were those which could boast of nothing more than a remote relation which they bore to the natural activities of rural life. Of those prevailing today, the most prominent are those concerning birth, death and marriage. But, some of the others *e.g.*, Simantonayana, Namkaran, Choorakarma and Upanayana, are also still observed. Beside, these Sanskaras the women folk of the village also believe in some 'negtehalas' which do not necessitate the presence of a priest, the women being quite capable of performing prayer and rituals themselves. Various kinds of songs are sung along with these tehalas but they are not devotional songs of the common variety. They are sung only for prosperity.

Sanskaras Related to Birth

Concerning birth, four rituals prevail in the villages —

1. Saadha, 2. Prasava, 3. Chathi, 4. Kooan Pujan and Namkarana. Songs are sung on all these occasions. They are further described below —

1. Saadha. This ritual is performed in the seventh month of pregnancy. In Vedic literature, it has been called Simantonayana. The Simantonayana Sanskara is prescribed for observation in the fourth month, but the saadha ritual is observed in the seventh month. In the village, it is also called saadha paherana. According to this sanskara, once it is known that a woman is pregnant, she has to observe certain rules of conduct which continue till the saadha is donned. Among the restrictions is the one that prevents the pregnant woman from wearing new clothes and new bangles besides some particular cosmetics like vermilion. And five to seven days before the performance of this ritual, she is forbidden any form of decoration and even bathing.

When the priest decides the day for the ritual, the parents of the pregnant woman are informed, who send her new clothes, fruits, dry fruits, sweets, etc. On the particular day, a drawing is made with flour on the floor, and two low benches are placed on it, on which are seated the woman and her husband. The priest recites verses and the women perform rituals and take the pair into another room where the two are given sweets to eat. During the performance, flour cakes numbering seven, nine or eleven are placed in the lap of the pregnant woman. They are called 'aas'. They symbolise the fact that the woman can now hope for a progeny. This tradition of the Indian villages is a good example of what Frazer calls Homeopathic magic.

2. Prasava (delivery). Next after the saadha in the circle of birth, is the prasava time. In this case, too, the gods and goddesses are worshipped, seeking favour for a safe delivery. If it is a male child, his arrival is announced by banging a plate or by firing a gun. The priest is called in and a 'janam lagan' made. On the first day, the child is given aqua ptycatis mixed with crude sugar. He is given milk the next day. On the right and left of the place where delivery has taken place, 'Satiya' made of cowdung are placed with coal. The old women of the village present what is known as 'Chama', which can be spun like an earthen wave pot. On this too, lines of cow-dung and satiya are made. In this the water of 'battisa' is prepared for the woman.

At the same time, certain activities are instituted to protect the woman and her infant child from ghosts and witches. For this reason, the child is never left alone. Fire is kept burning continuously in the delivery room and no one is permitted to enter from the outside. In particular, the cats are prevented from entering the place. A knife is placed beside the child's head. To announce the arrival of the son, a barber takes a cake of gur and one and a quarter of a rupee, and goes to the mother's parents who, in turn, send the appropriate requisites on the occasion of chathi and chochak.

3. Chathi. The ritual of chathi is observed almost everywhere, in the towns in particular where it is the most important ritual after birth. In this ritual both the child and the mother are purified. Both the mother and the child take bath for the first time on the sixth day after the delivery. The threshold to the delivery room is decorated with some foodgrains, gur, etc., and both are brought out together. This particular work of bringing the two out falls to the mother's younger brother-in law. Having made her visit to the outside world, the mother returns to the room and sits near the bed on the side on which the head rests, on the ground and worships something called 'bai' made by the midwife. A silver 'hansali' is placed near the foot of the bed, beside which some grain is placed and oil lamp lit. Near this, four cakes of wheat flour, rice and sugar are placed. After some ritual, these four cakes are given to the midwife. The 'bai' is worshipped by sprinkling it with water mixed with haldi, a spice. After this day the mother is allowed to consume foodgrains. The soot is collected and put in the eyes of the child The child is not allowed to see the light of this Lamp. The entire process on this particular day is meant as a precaution against ghosts and witches which may otherwise possess the child and its mother.

4. Kooanpujan and Naamkaran. On the tenth day after birth, the Kooanpujan and Naamkaran Sanskaras are performed. On this day, the priest is called in early and he does what is known as yajna. The child's mother takes him in her lap and sits on a wooden stool. On her side sits either one of the older male members of the family or her husband. The priest performs the 'yajna' and extracts the child's name. Generally, the child is addressed by a name other than this but sometimes this name is used. After the name has been elicited the richer people give a dinner to all and sundry while the poorer give a dinner to their friends and the priest. The visitors bring presents for the child in cash or in kind. The mother takes a bath on this day and the naayan oils her head. This is her third bath after the delivery. The second bath after chathi is between chathi and jasootan or namakaran. After the delivery during the one and quarter month of purification, she takes five baths. The fourth, after the jasootan, can be taken on any day except Tuesdays, Saturdays and Sundays. The same is true for the fifth bath. Sometimes all these five baths are taken within three weeks. On one day of the fifth bath the mother puts sugar in five places in the names of five Gods like Sitala, Zaahar, Meera, Hanumana etc. The Satiyas are placed in a basket. The place where they had been originally placed is cleaned up and satiyas of haldi are put in their place. The mother wears new clothes and carries to the well a pot full of water in which there is a mango plant. The basket of satiyas is carried by her sisters-in-law. The mother then cleans a small space in the parapet of the well and makes five satiyas of haldi on which she places some rice; these are worshipped by throwing some haldi water on them. These satiyas are then either wetted or sowed near the well. On returning home, the coals on both sides of the main door are cooled by throwing water on them, and thus doubling the difficulties in the way of wicked witches, or so it is believed. A small satiya of haldi is sewed on the mother's bed sheet. The mother goes to the child only after she has shaken her clothes over the fire. Before taking the child from his grandfather's lap where she had left it when going to well for worship, the mother gives 'neg' to the grandfather. During Kooanpujan various songs are recited.

5. Annapraashan Sanskara. This comes after the namkaran sanskara. On this day, the child is made to lick milk and rice pudding from a silver utensil with a silver spoon on any auspicious day. After the ceremony is over the silver spoon and vessel is handed over to the child's aunty along with some more presents. Sometimes some people also invite friends and relatives to dinner. This ritual is also called choorakarma.

6. Mundana Sanskara. This follows the Annapraashan Sanskara. Some people perform it at home, but it is tried that, if possible, it may be done on the banks of the Ganges. As usual, a lot of singing accompanies the performance of the ritual.

7. Kamachedan Sanskara. This Sanskara is next in the chain of rituals. According to Sushrut, the Kamachedan Sanskara should be performed in the sixth or seventh month whereas Saint Katyayan prefers it in the third or fifth year. So the people compromise by doing it when they think fit. On the day of Kamachedan, the child's maternal uncle sends new clothes and gold earrings but the poor people use some alloys instead of gold.

8. Upanayana Sanskara. Upanayana follows the Kamachedan Sanskara, it being now performed, though not always, on marriage. According to Manusmriti, a person is untouchable without it. On this occasion, the youth begs for alms, the first to comply being his mother followed by other relatives. A dot of 'kesar' is applied to the boy's forehead and the alms dropped in his outspread cloth.

The other important rituals are the marriage and antyesthi sanskaras which have been described in the chapter on marriage.

THE VILLAGE PANCHAYAT

The organisation, administration and all kinds of progress of the rural communities in India, is based on village panchayats. The village panchayats are the pillars which support the Indian rural social system.

Village Panchayats of Ancient India

In India, in the Vedic age there were panchayats in every village. According to K.M. Panikkar, this is the sole permanent basis of ancient history on which each dynasty of India has prospered. On this subject, Dr. Altckar has pointed out that these gram panchayats worked for the defence of the village and collected the revenue of the State. They imposed new taxes, arbitrated in the disputes of the villagers and implemented the projects for public welfare. Through public loans these panchayats made arrangements for alleviating the distress caused by famines and other calamities. They also organised and established schools, orphanages and colleges and did much cultural and religious work through the temples. With the exception of declaring war and entering into treaty these panchayats were vested with all the remaining rights and authorities of the State.

According to a 10th century text, Shukra-Neeti Sar, the ancient village panchayat had the following characteristics —

1. The members of village panchayats were elected. 2. The members had the rights of the Executive as well as the Judiciary. 3. The members were held in due respect. 4. The panchayats collected the tax on the land and controlled its distribution. 5. The pastures of the village and other forested land were treated as the property of the panchayat. 6. The panchayats also undertook such activities like maintenance of peace, security, health, education and public constructions. 7. The panchayats also negotiated between warring factions of the villages.

In the villages, in ancient India, the entire population elected the members of the panchayats. Certain manuscripts discovered in South India provide some knowledge of their electoral procedure and functions. The manuscripts found in the village of North Maroor of Chingalpatt district in South India show that the members of the village executive were elected by casting vote. In the North, Maroor village there were thirty wards. In these wards, the names of many people were proposed for the membership of executive. Then, the name of each candidate was written upon a piece of paper and the names of all the candidates in any ward were put in some vessel. Then, some innocent child was asked to pick up any one piece of paper. The piece of paper which the child selected carried the name of the representative of that ward. This kind of election did not give any opportunity for propaganda, party politics or bias.

Village Republic

The name of village republic was given by the English to these ancient panchayats of India. These panchayats had the right to nullify any excessive, improper or new taxes imposed by king. They collected the revenue from the public and thus the king too did not interfere in their working but rather listened to them. Sir Charles Metcalf has written that these panchayats had all the characteristics of a republic. Every village was a small independent country. It was completely free from external control. Those things which have not been defended anywhere also have been protected in the village. The organisation of the panchayats of the villages was such that every village was like a small independent nation. Considering the high standard of their independence, self-dependence and prosperity, we can well understand the importance of the panchayats.

Panchayats under British Rule

Although, the Englishmen had great praise for the panchayats, during British Government the rural panchayats of India started disintegrating for a number of reasons. In the British States, the State Revenue was collected from the individual and not from the village as a whole. The work of collecting revenue was also taken away from the panchayats and handed over to Government officials. The disturbances of the village came under the authority of the police. This served to reduce further the responsibility and the rights of the panchayats. Civil and Criminal cases were not dealt within the official courts. As a result the panchayats were deprived of their judicial rights. As a result of industrialisation and urbanisation the rural community disintegrated, the consequence of this was the disintegration of the panchayat organisation. The influence of western civilisation resulted in the strengthening of the individualistic tendency and the weakening of community feeling. The panchayats were no longer respected.

A long time before India became independent some attention was given to the reconstruction of rural communities. The Royal Commission of Decentralisation of 1909, laid particular emphasis upon the fact that the panchayats should be organised and developed in order to establish local self-government in the villages. In 1915, a bill was passed and instructions were issued to the provincial governments that full efforts should be made to initiate panchayats in the villages, through co-operation. In the Act of 1919, special emphasis was laid on the same policy. Following this Village Panchayat Acts were passed in different provinces, in 1911 in West Bengal, in 1920 in Bombay, Central Province and U.P. After this the Governments of Assam, Orissa, Bihar, Travancore Cochin, Punjab, Mysore, Baroda, and Indore followed suit and passed Village Panchayat Acts.

Panchayat in Free India

But while the British Rule lasted, these Acts did not succeed in reorganising village panchayats. When India became independent the native Government paid special attention to this aspect. Mahatma Gandhi used to say that freedom should start from the root. Every village should be a small republic in whom should be vested every right. Provision has been made in the Indian Constitution that the Government will organise the village panchayats and give them all the rights so that they may be in a position to function as units of Swarajya. After the independence of the country the State Governments have made efforts and established Gram Sabhas, independent village panchayats and panchayati adalats (Courts) in the villages of India.

(A) *Gram Sabha.* A Gram Sabha has been established in those villages whose population exceeds 1000. Where the population of the village falls short of this number several neighbouring villages have been combined to constitute Gram Sabhas. In case of villages more than three miles apart, they have the right to form individual sabhas even though their population may be less than 1000. All individuals who have the capability of being members and who are also the permanent residents of the area of the Gram Sabha will be its members. In older to be eligible for membership both males and females should have attained the age of 18 years. But lepers, insane people, bankrupts, those who have served a sentence and those who are Government officials cannot be members of the village sabha. If the person does not suffer from any of these disabilities and continues to reside within the area of the sabha, he can be its member as long as he lives. The Gram Sabha meets twice in a year, once at the Rabi crop and again at the Kharif crop. From among, the members of sabha one Chairman and one Vice Chairman are elected. Their term of office is three years. The Gram Sabha plans all the programmes for development members of the Gram Sabha can oust the Chairman and the Vice Chairman by a two-thirds majority. The gram panchayat actively weilds the power of the Gram Sabha. It imposes taxes and incurs expenditure only if approved by the Gram Sabha.

(B) *Village Panchayat.* The executive constituted by the Gram Sabha for the management of the village is called the Gram panchayat. The Chairman and Vice Chairman of the Gram Sabha are also the Chairman and Vice Chairman of the Village Panchayat. The election of the members of the village panchayat and the Chairman and Vice Chairman of the Gram Sabha is carried out by the system on the basis of the cumulative vote system. The polling officer appointed by the District Magistrate counts the votes through the hands lifted by the voters.

It will be the duty of every Gram Panchayat to arrange for the following things within the area of its authority as far as its funds allow.

1. Maintenance of Public Roads. Constructing public roads, repairing them, maintaining them in good condition and arranging for their lighting and cleaning.

2. Arrangement for Water. To construct public wells, tanks and wells for providing water for drinking, bathing and washing clothes; to improve and to maintain them in good condition and to keep control over the means of obtaining drinking water. To maintain the water drains and places for drinking water in good condition and to look after them.

3. Medical Treatment and Health. To arrange for the care of pregnant women and their delivery, to provide medical aid and to enforce medical measures to prevent infectious diseases and maintain sanitary conditions.

4. Education. To open schools for the primary education of boys and girls and to maintain them.

5. Statistics. To maintain a register of vital statistics and marriages and to acquire detailed information about such other items as animal census, population census, as are required by law.

6. Progress of Agriculture and Cottage Industries. To assist in the progress of agriculture, business and cottage industries and to determine the place for collecting manure. To look after the Kaisere-Hind forests and class two of the mountain ranges in Kumaun division. To provide public pastures, to maintain them and look after and arrange for them. Without infringing the 1930 U.P. Act for exhibitions to control those exhibitions, markets and fairs which are in their areas, and which do not include the exhibitions, markets and fair, organised by Government.

7. Control of Buildings. To protect, to maintain in good condition and to look after these buildings placed under the protection of Gram panchayat and other such property and the building of the Gram sabha. To lay down rules for the construction of new buildings and transformation or extension of the existing buildings.

8. Sanitation and Security. To maintain security in the villages. To make proper arrangement for the disposal of the dead bodies of human beings, animals as well as other foul smelling things. In the event of fire, to help in putting out the fire and saving the lives and property of the people.

9. Administration. To prevent the placing, constructing or throwing of any improper object on public roads, public places and the property of the Gram Sabha and to arrange for criminal and civil judicial procedure. To elect the Panchas for Panchayati Courts.

10. Other Activities. Besides these activities the panchayat can carry out the following activities for the benefit of the village: planting trees, improving the breed of animals, covering dirty drains, organising volunteer groups, establishing cooperative societies, arranging for public radios, lectures and exhibitions etc.

(C) *Panchayati Adalat (Rural Court).* Commonly there is one Panchayati Adalat for four or five representatives from each Gram Sabha. In every Panchayati Adalat there are five representatives from each Gram Sabha. These representatives are elected by direct vote system. In this way, there are twenty or twenty-five Panchas. One Sarpancha is elected from among these Panchas. His period of office lasts three years. For every case, a committee of five is elected, of which the Sarpancha is the Chairman. Of these five Panchas, one pancha necessarily belongs to that place from which the case comes. The judgment on the case is given by majority. The decisions of the panchayat court are final and no appeal can usually be made against them but in the special cases one can appeal to the Munsif or the Hakim Paragana.

Similarities in Ancient and Modern Panchayats

The following similarities of ancient and modern panchayats become evident from a comparative study of them:

1. Both in ancient and modern panchayats the members are elected.

2. The duties for making arrangements for education, security, health, public construction, peace, protection of pastures, public roads and water etc., are found equally in ancient and modern panchayats.

3. In the same way the ancient and modern panchayats also have parallel rights, *e.g.* right over the pastures of the village and other public land, the right to decide cases of civil and criminal conflict, the right to spend money in the activities of public welfare etc.

4. The objectives of both the modern and the ancient panchayats are similar. Both have been desirous of achieving peace, security, prosperity, happiness and self-dependence in the village.

5. The basis of modern panchayats is community feeling, which was also the basis of ancient panchayats. Both depend upon the cooperation of the villagers.

Difference between Ancient and Modern Panchayats

The following differences become evident in a comparative study of ancient and modern panchayats:

1. The major difference between the ancient and modern panchayats is in regard to the extent of Government intervention. In ancient India, the activities of the village panchayats were free of any Government intervention and instead, it were the panchayats which sometimes contradicted the orders of the Government. At their request the king would make a reduction in the tax and would even completely forego it. In the modern village panchayats, the Government officials do interfere. The panchayat inspector, panchayat officer and panchayat director are ordered to check the activities of the panchayats. Unless the panchayat inspector gives his consent, the budget for the Gram Sabha, panchayati adalat or Gram panchayat cannot be passed or finalised. The Government reserves the right of not only looking into the affairs of the panchayat but also the right to disband them altogether. The panchayat officer can prevent any action which is liable to disrupt peace or to injure the interests of the public. In this way, the village panchayats of ancient India were complete independent whereas the modern panchayats are controlled by the Government.

2. The second difference between the ancient and the modern panchayat is with regard to the collection of State revenue. Whereas the village panchayat of ancient India collected the State revenue and passed it on to the king, the modern panchayat performs no such function.

3. With the progress of time the village panchayats of modern India have been entrusted with some new duties like making arrangements for public radios, meetings, speechs, exhibitions, co-operative societies, self-dependent groups etc.

Role of Panchayats in Rural Reconstruction

The reconstruction of rural life in Indian dependent upon the village panchayats. The economic, social and political reconstruction of the village can be brought about only through the panchayats. Jawaharlal Nehru has rightly said that three factors are necessary for the solidarity of India *viz.*, community development projects, superior village panchayats, and good village cooperative societies. If these three are properly developed the foundation of our country will be so strong and solid that it will face all kinds of political and economic catastrophies, and brave calamities fearlessly.

1. Decentralisation of Administrative authority. The administrative power was decentralised in India by the village panchayats and village people obtained the rights of self-Government. According to U P. Panchayat Raj Act of 1947, 36229 panchayats and 8543 panchayat courts have been established by 15th August, 1949. These panchayats had been given the rights to all kinds of reconstruction in the village. The Government officials were anxious to give them assistance and suggestions.

2. Social Reconstruction. The Gram panchayat cultivated in the village people the habit of working together, owning responsibility for the various activities of the village, understanding things of public interest and living in co-operation and charity. The panchayati court taught them to resolve misunderstanding through mutual negotiations. The panchayats did much towards increasing the communal feeling by decreasing the effects of urbanisation which had been manifested in the village youths in the form of a lack of responsibility, selfishness and impetuity. The tendency to look upon the entire village as a family was born in the village people as a result of the communal contribution of labour in the contribution of roads, lanes, drains, tanks, schools and panchayat houses. In this way, the panchayat has a major role in removing their responsibility which had been the outcome of the disintegration of the joint family and removal of caste panchayats. By arranging for radio sets and lectures etc, the panchayats created awakening in the villages. Thousands of primary schools were opened in the villages to spread education among the village children. In order to educate the older members of the community, adult education centres and night schools were opened. Literacy weeks were celebrated and resolute efforts were made to remove illiteracy from the country.

3. Economic Reconstruction. The economic condition of villages of India was at its lowest ebb. The responsibility for this reconstruction also rests with the panchayats. Before the panchayat courts were instituted much of the hard earned income of the villagers was unnecessarily spent on litigation. Even the most trifling quarrels were taken to the courts and it sometimes took months and even years before any decision was arrived at. The cases were always postponed; while a major part of the villager's earnings found its way into the pockets of the advocates, peons, and agents. In spite of all this, justice was at a premium because it was not particularly difficult to get false witnesses. Some villagers had even adopted bearing false witness as a lucrative profession. During the British rule, the rural cottage industries of India suffered a devastating blow. Some cottage industries breathed their last because they could not compete with cheaper foreign goods on the one hand while on the other they did not get any assistance from the government. The industries of the village came to grief also as a result of urbanisation which resulted in the transportation of most rural commodities into the town and also a lack of demand for rural product. On account of this condition of the rural industries the artisans came to work in the urban factories. The village panchayat provided a cheaper means of getting justice and also encouraged the rural industries. Thirty-three per cent of the cases are settled by mutual negotiation and understanding. Bearing false witness became impossible because the matter now was solved within the precincts of the village. Justice was rendered free and without delay. The village panchayat assisted the cottage industries. It arranged for the sale of the produce by organising exhibitions, markets and fairs. It introduced new methods into the villages through radio and other modern innovations. As a result of the spread of education the people came to know many new facts regarding production, sales etc. in cottage industries. Beside the cottage industries, the village panchayat also encouraged agriculture. India is predominantly an agricultural country. The reconstruction of the villages of the country is dependent upon agriculture. As a result of illiteracy the methods of farming, tools etc., had remained antique and the yield per acre was low. The panchayats arranged for modern agricultural implements and cooperative societies for superior seeds, superior manure and sales etc. It increased the knowledge of the specific aspects of agriculture in the people through radio, exhibitions and speeches and got financial assistance from the government. Besides these activities towards economic reconstruction, the village panchayats participated in the work of economic uplift through many other activities like arranging for pastures for animals, plantation of forests for firewood and wood for architectural purposes and improving the breed of the cattle etc.

4. Political Reconstruction. The panchayat generated a social and national consciousness among the people of the villages in the modern individualistic and egoistic age. In the villages, there are panchayat houses in which the people can congregate and discuss over the progress of the village. In thousands of villages Gandhi squares have been constructed so that the ideal of Gandhiji is always present and the patriotic feeling is always awake. At the same time the sense of self-dependence and co-operation is being developed in the villagers through the influence of the contributory movement. A considerable length of roads, wells, schools etc., have been constructed with the help of contributed labour. The elections of the panchayats and the panchayat courts educate the villagers in the democratic method. As a member of the panchayat their ability of administration increases in arranging for the village. In spreading the democratic qualities of liberty, equality and fraternity the gram panchayats have played a major role.

5. Centres of Rural Reconstruction. Actually, the village panchayats are the centres of all kinds of reconstruction in the village. These provide the villagers with opportunity of meeting at one place, sitting together and thinking as well as working cooperatively. Solving their quarrels mutually, arranging for their own village and making the villages ideal rests almost entirely with the panchayat. It is through their efforts that poverty, illiteracy, narrow mindedness, disunity, frivolity and disorganisation can be removed from the village. Only these can make the villagers, the ideal citizens of free India. Only these can give material shape to dreams of Swarajya and Ram Rajya of Mahatma Gandhi, the father of the Nation.

Suggestions for Improvement of Panchayats

The panchayats are making considerable progress in the direction of rural development but this progress cannot be said to be entirely satisfactory. It is true that the villages of India are in such a backward state that much time must lapse before they can be developed democratically, but nevertheless some suggestions may be given in this respect. The gram panchayat can mould the life of the rural community into the right channels by removing its defects and fulfilling the needs of the modern changing life. For this there is need for some change in the management and rights etc. of the panchayats. In this regard some suggestions follow:

1. Education of Panchas in Administrative Functions. In the village, education is not very wide spread. Many of the panchas elected by the villagers are only nominally literate. Most of them are completely ignorant of administration and justice. More often the revered elders are elected who have not the least idea of modern changes, democratic thinking and scientific researches It is true that the officials of the government can assist them in this respect but then it no longer remains the administration of the panchas but rather becomes the administration of government employees, annihilating in the process the very ideal of panchayat. Thus, there is very need for educating the panchas in respect of administration of doing justice, modern scientific researches and democratic way of thinking etc. After being elected, they should be educated in the training centres and their knowledge increased through the media of national and international exhibitions. They should be brought into contact with the leaders of the nation in order to remove and dispel their dogmatism. It is a matter of satisfaction to know that the state governments are working in this direction. Some time back, many panchas came from Rajasthan to see the international agriculture fair at Delhi and gained inspiration by meeting the Prime Minister. Prior to this a trainload of villagers had travelled around the country. Much work is still needed in this direction.

2. Decrease in the Intervention of the Government. Besides educating the panchas the interference of government officials in the activities of the panchayats should also be decreased in order to attain a state in which the panchayats should be given full rights in matters of the village. The government officials sometimes intervene unnecessarily in the activities of the panchayats. This not only hinders the work of the panchayat but also detracts from the respect of the panchas and deprives them of their enthusiasm for work. It is usually seen that the panchayat officer and panchayat inspector is given the most respected place when he adorns the meeting, while even the sarpanch occupies a position of comparatively lower status. This is very improper. The government official, no matter what is his rank, is always a paid and hired servant of the public. He has the freedom of making use of all rights in serving the public, but he will always be given a position lower than the representative of the people in the government of the people and even more so when this representative is an honorary leader. The government officials should try to increase the respect of the panchas in the eyes of the villagers but this can happen only when there is adequate education spread among them and they understand their rights.

3. Control over Formation of Political Parties. Democracy is the government of the people but there is just that much more opportunity for party politics. As in the state and central elections, elections of the panchayats are also infested with the formation of parties on the basis of caste, class and other vested interests, and even after the election, the activities of the panchayats are interrupted by this party politics. The defect is found not only in respect of panchayats but in all elections in the country. There is need for a strong revolution to root out this evil. Without this revolution, the foundations of democracy cannot be strengthened in India.

4. Increase in the Rights of the Panchayat. The rights of the panchayats should be increased for rural reconstruction.

RURAL PROBLEMS

Agricultural Problems

In India, the condition of agriculture is very bad. The major problems in this respect are:

(i) *Old and unskilled methods.* In India, the progressive methods of farming have not yet been popularized so that the farmer persists with the old methods. Ploughing, sowing, harvesting and other allied activities still follow the old pattern. As a result greater labour yields less.

(ii) *Old kinds of tools.* Besides the methods of arming, Indian agriculture is further handicapped by the use of old and outmoded tools. Modern implements like tractors, sowers, mowers and harrow have not been introduced on the scene for the respective agricultural activities. The reason for this backwardness is that the farms are subdivided into small pieces and the farmers have no adequate knowledge of these tools nor the resources to purchase them.

(iii) *Unimproved varieties of seeds.* Not much has been achieved in India towards the improvement of the varieties of seeds and whatever little has been done does not spread over any considerable area. Most of the villagers use unimproved and degenerate seeds on their farms. As a result, the yield per hectare is extremely low.

(iv) *Small and scattered holdings.* Most of the farms in India are small and scattered. Due to the fact that the succeeding sons have equal right to their deceased father's property, the land is divided among the heirs. In this way as the land is further subdivided in each succeeding generation the resulting pieces of land become uneconomic holdings which means that they do net yield food crops in proportion to the efforts expended upon them.

(v) *Shortage in the means of irrigation.* There is a serious shortage of the means of irrigation in India. The crop is not very good because the plants do not get water at the proper time. Mostly, agriculture depends upon the rains for water, which makes it a gamble based upon the monsoon. If the rains come at the proper time in proper quantity the crop is good, otherwise it is a failure.

(vi) *Shortage of manure.* There is a considerable shortage of the supply of good manures in adequate quantities to the villages of India. Consequently, India cannot have the same number of crops every year as those which are possible in some other countries. Most of the farmers are ignorant of even the way of

(iv) Adequate provision of hospitals and maternity homes should be made in the villages where the poor should be treated free of charge. Measures for the prevention of infectious diseases should be implemented.

(v) It is necessary to remove insanitary conditions from the villages if disease is to be prevented. The drains should be widened and cleanliness should be propagated among the villages. This work can also be done by donated or contributed labour.

(vi) There is need for social propaganda for the eradication of untouchability, factionalism and superstitions etc.

(vii) In order to reduce the extent of litigation the panchayat should be given the right of deciding matters of minor importance.

4. Political Awakening. The problem of rural improvement is not so simple as to be successfully solved by the Government alone and unaided, thus there is a great need for political awakening.

RURAL RECONSTRUCTION

Aim of Rural Reconstruction

The term rural reconstruction means construction of the village in a new way or beginning all over again. The rural problems will be solved in this reconstruction. This will create radical changes in the life of villages and the economic system will be renovated or improved. The importance of rural reconstruction is apparent from the aim of rural reconstruction. The objectives of rural reconstruction are very comprehensive. These objectives include the eradication of poverty, improvement in the economic condition, improvement in the methods of agriculture, the organisation of a co-operative economic system by removing indebtedness, regeneration of cottage industries, welfare of labour, development of communal feeling, spread of education, progress of health, sanitation, arrangement of residential quarters, progress in the means of transportation, establishment of co-operative societies, establishment of local administration, arrangement for recreation, removal of social malpractice like untouchability and caste distinctions and other aspects of an integral progress comprehending the social, economic and political aspects of rural life. The nonviolent swaraj of Mahatma Gandhi was based upon the idea of this rural reconstruction.

Importance of Rural Reconstruction

Rural reconstruction will establish a non-violent Swaraj, which has been described by Mahatma Gandhi in just so many words. In a non-violent Sawaraj nobody will be the enemy of any one else, every one will mind his own business, no one will be illiterate, gradually every one's stock of knowledge will be increased. There will be less diseases among the people, no one will be extremely poor and the laborious or willing person will always get work. There will be no scope whatsoever for gambling, wine, corruption or class struggle. The rich people will use their wealth prudently and will not waste it in increasing their comforts and enjoyments. In swaraj, such a state, in which a handful of wealthy people live in jewelled houses while thousands upon thousands live the life of animals in dark and airless slums should not exist. This constitutes Mahatma Gandhi's description of swarajya, the aim of rural reconstruction. The Government of India are also making continuous efforts towards rural reconstruction. By rural reconstruction a socialistic system will be established in the country, exploitation will be eliminated and the rural population will undergo social and economic development. Thus, the importance of rural reconstruction cannot be over-stressed. Indian culture will be regenerated and will further develop through rural reconstruction. Rural reconstruction will lead to the development of agricultural and cottage industries which will solve the food problem of the country and save millions of rupees in foreign exchange which goes towards the import of foodgrains, and it will also increase the national income. Adequate raw material will he made available to the industries in the country through rural reconstruction. Finally, rural reconstruction will result in the establishment of a true democracy in India, because most of the population lives in the villages.

Importance of Rural Planning

In the words of the Planning Commission, "Planning is essentially a way of organising and utilizing resources to maximum advantages in terms of defined social ends." In this way the plans of rural reconstruction will try to take maximum advantage from the available resources, keeping in view the objectives mentioned above. It is obvious that planned reconstruction is the most superior method. Thus in order to make the best use of rural reconstruction it is necessary to avail of planning. Actually, the importance which has been attributed to rural reconstruction in the preceding paragraph is also the importance of rural planning because these objectives cannot be obtained in the absence of planning. In this way, rural reconstruction and rural planning are of the utmost importance in a predominantly agricultural country like India.

GOVERNMENTAL EFFORTS FOR RURAL RECONSTRUCTION

At present, the Government of India is making strenuous efforts to remove the defects in the rural structure and is attempting rural reconstruction by solving social, economic and agricultural problems of the villages. The specific efforts in this direction are the following:

Land Reforms, 2. The Five Year Plans, 3. Co-operative Movement, 4. Community Development Projects, 5. Reorganisation of Village Panchayats.

Of these, the village panchayats have been described in the preceding chapter. Thus, the present chapter will contain a detailed description of the Five Year Plans and the Cooperative Movement.

Besides these government projects rural reconstruction is also being attempted through the Bhoodan Movement under the direction of Vinoba Bhave.

The amount of efforts made to solve the problems of the villages under the Five Year Plans can be seen or estimated by studying the development which is the result of the seven five year plans completed so far.

In most of the states in India, the zamindari abolition laws have succeeded in eliminating the intermediaries from between the farmer and the government. Agriculture is being improved. New methods and new tools together with the methods of using them are being exhibited on the government farms. Arrangements have been made for growing better kinds of seeds on the government farms, which are distributed to the farmers through the government seed godowns. In the different states, laws have been formulated for preventing the extreme subdivision and fragmentation of farms while efforts have also been made to reorganise the scattered farms. The central and state governments have made many major and minor plans for the development of the means of irrigation. Many tubewells have been bored and numerous canals constructed. Factories have been set up for producing chemical manures in the country. Methods of protecting the crops from insects are also being developed. Arrangements for the distribution of seeds and sales of the products are being made through government societies. Money is now available from the cooperative banks at a low rate of interest. In particular, cottage and small scale industries are being encouraged. The means of transport and communication are also being developed. New roads are being constructed while thousands of miles of roads have been cemented besides which new rail tracks are being laid. Efforts are being made to assist the villagers in buying, selling and increasing their knowledge of agriculture, industry and other subjects through organising exhibitions and fairs. New trees are being planted, this process being given a festive look by making it an occasion for celebration. Laws have also been made relating to the forest wealth. The village panchayats have been invested with great authority in the form of comprehensive rights. The panchayat courts have been given the right of looking into minor civil and criminal matters of the village. Attempts have been made to provide as many villages as possible with panchayat radios. Great effort is being exerted towards the development of primary and adult education. The villagers are being taught the lesson of self-dependence and cleanliness through movement for voluntary labour contribution. By encouraging the Bhoodan movement efforts are being made to provide the landless labourers with land. Through community development projects and development blocks a comprehensive effort is being made in the direction of rural reconstruction. Family planning is being encouraged and made popular among the villagers. The number of hospitals and maternity homes is continuously increasing. People are trying to bring the maximum possible number of improved bulls and buffaloes into the villages.

It is evident from the foregoing description that attention has been paid to the solution of all the serious problems of the villages in the plans which are currently operating but the facilities provided by these plans are not available in all villages and neither has the progress achieved by these plans been satisfactory. The facility of hospitals and maternity homes has been provided in very few villages. Free and compulsory primary education is still a possibility which has yet to materialize. The attempts that have been made towards the solution of the problems of the poor breeds of cattle are inadequate and the condition of agricultural labourers remains unimproved. The measures for the prevention of floods and famines etc., are definitely inadequate. Even today, thousands of villages do not have the means of irrigation. The condition of panchayat is not satisfactory and in some places the panchayat courts have served to increase the quarrels instead of decreasing them. The amount of money spent upon the construction of roads in the villages is out of proportion to the quality of the roads which have resulted. Proportionate benefit does not accrue from the money invested in exhibitions. Not much improvement has been achieved in the sphere of cottage and small scale industries.

Nevertheless, the intensity of the rural problems is continually decreasing. Many projects for cooperative societies, cooperative banks, community development projects, development blocks, zamindari abolition, education, the popularization of radios, etc., have been definitely and really beneficial. Actually, the rural problems of India are so diversified and profound that the common measures to solve them cannot produce the desired results. Only radical efforts by the government and the public can bring about the desired improvement in the condition of the villages.

COMMUNITY DEVELOPMENT PROJECTS

The Planning Commission has defined the community development project in these words: "Community development an attempt to bring about a social and economic transformation of village life through the efforts of the people themselves." In this way, the community development projects indicate or mean those projects for social and economic reconstruction in the villages which are implemented with the co-operation of the public itself. In the words of Sri A.R. Desai, "The community development project is the method through which Five Year Plan seeks to initiate a process of transformation of the social and economic life of the village." In this way, community development project is a process controlled by the community itself. Here community implies rural community. Elucidating the meaning of community development projects it has been laid down in India 1971, published by the Government of India, "It is a programme of aided self-help to be planned and implemented by the villagers themselves, the Government offering only technical guidance and financial assistance. Its objectives are to develop self-reliance in the individual and initiative in the village community. Community thinking and collective action are encouraged through people's institutions like the Panchayats, Cooperative Societies, Vikas Mandals, etc."

Aims of Community Development

Writing in his book *India's Changing Villages* Prof. S.C. Dubey has recognised the following two aims of community development projects:

1. To manage or achieve an adequate increase in the country's agricultural produce and a progress in the means of communication; rural health, cleanliness and rural education.

2. To initiate and to direct a process of integral cultural change aimed at transforming the social and economic life of the village.

The following major aims have been recognised in the Ministry of Community Development of the Government of India publication '*A Guide to Community Development*':

1. To create a change in the mental outlook of the masses.

2. To develop responsible and active leadership in the village.

3. To make the villagers self-dependent and progressive.

4. To modernize agriculture on the one hand and to develop cottage industries on the other in order to raise the economic status of the villagers.

5. To improve the condition of the women and families of the villagers in order to make the suggested improvements practicable.

6. To develop properly the future citizens of the nation.

7. To protect the interests of the rural educators.

8. To raise the standard of health among the rural populace and to protect them against disease.

Short Term objective. The aims of the community development projects have been divided into two parts: short term objectives and long term objectives. The short term objectives are the following —

1. The maximum possible increase in agricultural production.

2. To solve the problem of unemployment in the villages.

3. To develop the means of communication in the villages.

4. To improve the centres of primary education, public health and recreation in the villages.

5. To improve the condition of houses.

6. To encourage cottage industries and indigenous handicrafts.

Long Term objectives. The long term objective of community development projects is the complete planned development of all physical and human resources. In it arrangements will be made to provide all villagers with full employment. The goal of community development project is the development of villages in such a way that the citizens of the country may not lack anything, which is the ideal of a welfare state, and that every one should get adequate food and that everyone should progress socially, morally and financially.

In this way, in brief, the community development projects aim at the integral development of the village through the efforts of the villagers and the assistance of the Government.

Importance of Community Projects

Describing the importance which the community projects have for rural life, the Planning Commission had written in the Second Five Year Plan, "It is a problem, briefly, of changing the outlook of 70 million families living in the countryside, arousing in them enthusiasm for new knowledge and new ways of life and filling them with the ambition and the will to live and work for a better life. Extension services and community organisation are among the principal sources of vitality in democratic planning and rural development projects are the means by which through co-operative self-help and local effort, villages and groups of villages can achieve in increasing measure both social change and economic progress and become partners in the national plan."

Social development projects will involve improvement in all the aspects, social, economic and others of rural life. The main effects which development projects have upon rural life are the following:

1. Agricultural Development. Agriculture is the foundation of rural economic life. The happiness and the prosperity of the village depend upon the progress of agriculture. The main cause of poverty in the Indian villages is the backward condition of agriculture. The main problems of Indian agriculture are old techniques of agriculture, dearth of new tools, absence of manures and fertilizers, excessive subdivision of land, dearth of the means of irrigation, shortage of good seeds, etc. The community development projects have made efforts to solve all these problems which beset Indian agriculture. New techniques of farming are exhibited in the villages and manures, seeds, tools and fertilizers distributed. The community projects also undertake the repairing of old wells, supplementing them by sinking new wells in order that the farmers may have available the necessary facilities for irrigation. Efforts are made to protect the land from soil erosion and other maladies.

2. Economic Progress. The greatest problem of rural life in India is it its poverty. The community development projects have encouraged cottage industries and handicrafts. Unemployed people are provided with work through auxiliary and useful services. Although these efforts are as yet quite inadequate, it is hoped that a continuous increase in them will lead to rural life in India becoming more prosperous in the future.

3. Development in Respect of Animals. Another major problem and obstacle to progress in the Indian villages is the deplorable condition of the animals which are even today employed in ploughing the fields. The ox is used for this purpose. In order to improve the strain of the species the community development projects have made use of good oxen. Improved poultry have also been arranged for the development of poultry farming.

4. Development of Education. Most of the people residing in the villages of India are uneducated and illiterate. At the same time they lack modern knowledge. Without the spread of education in the rural areas of India no progress of any kind whatsoever can possibly be expected. The community development projects have paid the desired and necessary attention to the education of children and adults, men and women. Schools for primary and adult education have been opened. Arrangements have been made for education.

5. Training for Development. In the villages of India social and economic development cannot take place in the existing circumstances. It is necessary to have people trained and skilled in rural development. Under the community projects arrangements have been made to train village workers, both male and female, block development authorities and other people concerned with the programme of rural development.

6. Development of the means of Transport. In the villages of India, there is a dearth of the means of transport, serious enough to prove a great obstacle to industry and business. The community development projects have repaired the old roads and also managed to construct new roads. At various points small culverts have also been provided. These measures will not only improve business but will also serve to maintain the contact of the villagers with the world at large.

7. Cleanliness. Dirtiness reigns supreme in the Indian villages. It is the cause of the spread of many kinds of diseases and it lowers the general standard of living of the masses. Development projects have not forgotten to arrange for the purgation of the villages. A considerable length of drains have been constructed and steps have been taken to purify and keep pure the drinking water of the wells.

8. Protection of Health and the Maintenance of a certain Standard. In the villages of India epidemics and many less widespread diseases carry off many men, women and children every year due to the almost utter absence of medication and facilities for delivery. The condition of health of women and children is extremely unsatisfactory. Arrangements have been made for one health centre in each development block. Mobile dispensaries have also been arranged for, midwives and nurses are also being trained to staff all the new dispensaries.

9. Arrangements for Residences. Most of the houses in village are old fashioned and small. The community development projects have decided to assist the villagers in building houses and also arranged for providing them with modern plans and the building methods of good and cheap houses.

10. Social Welfare. The community development projects have also given due attention to social welfare in the villages making arrangement for games, variety shows etc., for the entertainment of the public. Gramophone, radio and cinema provide the villager with entertainment and also serve to enhance his stock of knowledge.

Criticism of Community Development Projects

Looking at the above statistical details of the progress, both social and economic, achieved by the community development projects in villages, it becomes apparent that these projects have completely ignored many social and economic problems like the problem of the condition of the landless labourers, the problem of the backward condition of village and cottage industries, etc.

Secondly, even those social and economic problems which have received attention in these projects, are not being solved in an appropriate manner. For example, the arrangement of free and compulsory education is as yet a thing of the future. The Programme Evaluation Organisation established by the Planning Commission put forward numerous criticisms of the community development programmes in its reports, of which the major ones are given as follows:

1. Lack of the Solution of Local Problems. There is a lack of the solution of local rural problems in the community development projects. This not only hinders the progress of the development programme but it also decreases the faith of the public in these projects.

2. Dearth of Harmony within the Government Departments. The community development organisation is not in proper harmony with the other governmental departments.

3. Shortage of Necessary Implements. There is an acute shortage of required necessary implements in the development programme and as a result even the work which is started cannot be completed.

4. Shortage of Trained Personnel. Much effort has been made for training the officials in community development projects but even then trained people are not available in required number.

5. Absence of proper Public Co-operation. The community development programmes could not become public movement. At present they are not getting the proper active co-operation of the public.

6. Shortage of Female Village Workers. There is a great need for trained female workers for the emancipation of the rural women but, at present, they exist in very small number.

Suggestions

Actually, there is an urgent need for increasing the awareness of the public towards the plans for the success of the community development projects. Some suggestions, of which a few are given below, have been made in this connection.

1. Greater Emphasis upon Local Problems. The pattern of the community development projects should not be the same everywhere. The projects should lay more stress upon the solution of problems peculiar to the locality.

2. Appointment of Officials Acquainted with Rural Conditions. Another way of arousing the interests of the public towards the community development projects is to appoint officials who are acquainted with the rural culture and its ways and are also sympathetic and respectful towards them, in order that they may be able to mix with the villagers and to make these plans the projects and aspirations of the people.

3. Appointment of Workers, both Male and Female; Selected from the Villages as far as possible. Another way of awakening the sense of ownership in villagers towards the projects is to appoint or select the male and female village workers from among the villagers themselves.

4. Organisation of the Maximum Possible Training Camps in the Villages. If a maximum possible number of training camps are held in the villages, the villager will undoubtedly reciprocate heartily and will take a greater interest in the projects.

5. More work and less Propaganda. The officials detailed for the implementation of the development projects should adopt the principle of "More work and less propaganda." It will result in public showing greater faith in the projects.

6. **Establishing Youth Organisations and Eliciting their Co-operation.** Before starting the programmes of development in the villages youth organisation should be established and the programmes of development should be started with their co-operation when such organisations are well underway. The result of this move will be that the whole village will soon start taking interest in these programmes.

BHOODAN AND GRAMDAN MOVEMENT

The contribution of the Bhoodan Movement towards the development of the Indian villages is very important. Bhoodan Movement, as is obvious from its name, is the movement for donating land to the landless people. Through this movement it has been planned to bring about non-violent revolution in the economic field within the country. In any country it is fundamentally impractical to talk of equality and brotherhood where millions of people are landless while a handful of people possess large tracts of land. In order to put the democratic ideals into practice in the life of the country it is essential to make a proper division so that no person may be in possession of land for the cultivation of which he needs manual help and also no man should possess such a small piece of land upon which he cannot cultivate economically. In a society in which millions of farmers are landless and plough the fields of others, the people of the country do not have complete freedom. A large number of the landless farmers spend a life which is in no way better than the life commonly led by slaves. Thus, there have been revolutions for the proper distribution of land in all the progressive countries of the world. In Russia and other Communist countries violent and bloody revolutions were initiated for the proper distribution of land. The violent revolutions have the advantage of affecting the improvements without delay but the improvements which transform only the external structure and not the psychology of the people should not be termed revolutionary in the real sense of the word. As a matter of fact, the real social revolution takes place in the hearts of the public. It is a question of a change of hearts. As long as the feelings of the different classes do not change and as long as these feelings do not approximate, the changes made in the external structure cannot be permanent. And even as it is wherever changes the social and economic structure have been brought about violently these changes have either proved temporary or making them permanent has necessitated constant efforts over a long period of time.

In the modern age, there is need for an economic revolution, not only a political revolution, in India The country has become independent and continuous economic progress through the Five Year Plans is taking place but as long as the land is not properly and equally divided, the condition of millions of farmers cannot be any better than their condition in pre-independence era. The Zamindari Abolition Act in the various States of India is a solid step in the direction of the proper distribution of land because these laws have given proprietary rights to the farmers over the land which they were cultivating. Compensating the Zamindars in various proportions, their lands were taken from them. As a result of this official step the farmers gained a lot of advantage and the economic structure of the village experienced a revolution at least in its outward form. But as far as the question of a change in heart is concerned economic revolution is a thing of the future. The Zamindars did not happily part with their land so that their hearts were filled with hatred for the farmers and the Government. As a result of the increase in this hatred the mutual relations between the village people deteriorated whereas what was needed is that the people of the village should feel that land of the country was every one's property and that it should be used for the benefit of everyone. The Bhoodan Movement was started in order to spread this ideal among the people.

Describing the aims of the Bhoodan Movement, its founder Acharya Vinoba Bhave had pointed out that every one should have a right upon the land in a just social system based upon equality. Therefore, he did not beg for donations but asked for a portion which, according to justice, belongs to the poor. The main aim of the Bhoodan movement is to spread this idea so that economic and social inequalities may be removed without any major revolution. With this objective Acharya Vinoba Bhave started on a tour of the country and going to places on foot, appealed to the people to donate land. The Bhoodan Movement started on 18th April 1951. Its aim was to acquire fifty million acres of land in order to provide every rural family with some land for agriculture. As the movement progressed the Government and many illustrious leaders actively co-operated.

As time went by movements for many other kinds of donations joined the Bhoodan Movement. People were asked to donate wealth for the poor through the wealth donation movement. Through the intelligence donation movement appeals were made for the use of intellectual capacities for the attainment of the ideals of Bhoodan. Through the life donation movement appeals were made to the people to devote their lives to the attainment of the ideals of Boodan. These kinds of movement include house donations and donation of means.

The Bhoodan moment is now, gradually, taking the form of the Gramdan movement. In Gramdan, as is obvious by the name, people think in terms of donating the entire village so that it may be regarded as a property of the rural community. The level of co-operation for rural development is very high in the villages acquired under the Gramdan movement. In a conference organised by the All India Sarva Seva Sangh at Palwal in Mysore State, emphasis was laid upon the need for close co-operation between community development projects and the Gramdan movement. An executive group of the community development Ministry deliberated upon this question and in May 1958, after the conference of Commissioners certain practical decisions in this respect were taken. Now, more attention was given to the villages given in Gramdan than to other villages while opening community development blocks and while starting other programmes of community development.

In this way, the Bhoodan and Gramdan Movements aim at fulfilling the aim of a non-violent revolution under the direction of such leaders as Acharya Vinoba Bhave and with the efforts of the Central and State Governments. Not only Indians but even many politicians, thinkers and scientists of Europe and America, Africa and Asia have shown interest in the application of the non-violent revolution. The success of this experiment will benefit not only the population of India but will make evident to the entire world the possibilities of non-violent economic revolutions. At this stage it cannot be said as to how far the Bhoodan movement will be able to solve the problems of the Indian agriculturist but it can still be said that the present level of achievement of the Bhoodan and Gramdan movement is not negligible. Even if this experiment does not succeed, it can serve as a source of inspiration for future movements of the same kind. Here, it is necessaiy to remember that the Bhoodan movement has not yet achieved any success which can encourage such enthusiasm. Most of the land donated is not cultivable and the intentions of the doners do not seem to be entirely selfless. Even the land so far received falls far short of the expected quantity. But in spite of these difficulties this movement is worthy of praise and deserves co-operation.

SOCIAL EDUCATION

Inaugurating the village, Adult Education Seminar of UNESCO in 1949, Maulana Abul Kalam Azad, erstwhile Education Minister defined social education by pointing out that it means education for the entire man. It will make him literate so that the knowledge of the world may become available to him. It will tell him exactly how he has to adapt himself to his environment and how he has to derive the maximum benefit from his physical conditions. It will teach him the modern methods of handicrafts and production, so that he may be able to affect his financial improvement. It will teach him about the science of immunity from diseases of individual and community, so that his domestic life may be prosperous and happy. Finally, this educates the citizen so that he may be able to assist his government in the decision for making the country strong and establishing peace after he has acquired some knowledge of the corporal things. Originally, the meaning attached to social education was merely literacy of adults but now it has come to include all kinds of education for the adults. In the words of Biharee, "Social education is the stimulation in each citizen of a greater awareness of the advantage of the pattern of society as conceived in the constitution and a persistent desire for progress towards such a pattern socially, economically and culturally."

Aims of Social Education

In the words of Pt. Jawaharlal Nehru, "To educate the adults in the 3 Rs. and the affairs of world, a network of social education organisation has been set up." In this way while social education aims at removing illiteracy it also endeavours to acquaint the adults with the problems of this world. In the words of K.G. Saiyeden, "The aim of the movement is to create a spirit of friendship between people by bringing together men and women of different nationalities." In this way the aim of social education is both individual as well as social. It seeks to elevate all the various kinds of standards of life, be they physical, mental or intellectual, in order that people may be in a position to make active contributions in all spheres of national progress. It teaches them about the reconstruction of the village.

The programme for social education has been divided into the following five phases:

(1) Spread of literacy.

(2) Acquainting people with the laws of health and sanitation.

(3) Improvement in economic level.

(4) Encouraging the sense of citizenship and imparting awareness of rights and duties.

(5) Healthy recreation concurring to the needs of society and individual.

Characteristics of Social Education

The main characteristics of the above mentioned programme of social education are the following —

1. Spread of Literacy. Social education spreads literacy among the adults.

2. Advancement of Handicrafts and Cottage Industries. Besides spreading literacy, social education makes handicrafts and cottage industries popular.

3. Training in Self-Administration. Social education trains the adults in self administration.

4. Training for Ideal Citizenship. Social education tries to make the adults ideal citizens.

5. Education in Health and Cleanliness. Social education informs the villagers about the laws of health and cleanliness.

6. Knowledge of the Problems of the World. Social education imparts the knowledge of the problems of the world to the adults.

7. Integral Development. Social education directs its efforts at achieving the integral development of the adults.

8. Organisation of Healthy Recreation. Social education besides formal education organises healthy recreation through the medium of radios and cultural programmes.

9. Contribution in Rejuvenation. One of the major characteristics of social education is that, besides education, it contributes to every programme for rejuvenation.

Methods of Social Education

It is on the basis of these characteristics that the methods of social education have been developed. Hence, night schools have been arranged in the village centre for teaching the adults. Social education is not limited only to adult males. This education is imparted even to adult women as well as to young men and adolescent boys and girls and the syllabus laid down for them concurs harmoniously with their peculiar psychology. In order to increase the attraction of the programmes such means as the movies, exhibition vans, posters and charts are employed. The chief characteristic of this method is the broadcasting programme over the radio. Community consciousness and nationality are popularised and communicated to the people through social acting, folk dances and folk songs. The people are also informed about the scientific means of agriculture and handicraft and attempts to develop the qualities of leadership are made. At regular intervals sports competitions and development fairs are organised. Educational excursions are also arranged periodically. Programmes for composing adult literature are made and mobile and permanent reading rooms are also arranged for.

Problems of Social Education

In India, there are many problems which plague social education. The major ones are the following:

1. The rural people are not very spirited in their approach to social education.
2. Often the adults do not show much of an inclination towards social education.
3. The night schools are terminated during the peak season in agriculture.
4. There is a serious absence of proper literature for social education.
5. Being brought up in an urban atmosphere, most of the workers are unable to take proper interest in social education.
6. Other programmes besides literacy are not emphasized properly.
7. Proper and adequate means for social education are not available.

Suggestions Advanced by the Planning Commission

The Planning Commission had made some very important suggestions for the solution of problems which infest social education, the more important of which are:

1. In social education, education of life, health, recreation, domestic and economic education should also be given the necessary attention.
2. After imparting the knowledge of language, efforts should be made to restrengthen this knowledge through films, radio, libraries, reading rooms etc.
3. The programmes for social education should be adopted and modified according to the local needs.
4. Much care should be exercised in the selection and training of the personnel for social education.
5. The Teachers Training Colleges should carry out research about the ways of making people literate.
6. There should be a suitable administrative machinery for maintaining a certain standard in the work of social education. It must have become quite

obvious from this brief description of the different aspects of social education that this plan has some predetermined objectives which are immensely beneficial to the country. There can be no two opinions on the subject that the Indian villages are in a great need of social education and it is the only means to their redemption. As it is made obvious by the survey of the progress of social education in India, there is need for much work in this direction. But there is no doubt that the present progress of social education is not entirely dissatisfactory. The suggestions made by the Planning Commission for the solution of the problems of social education are very useful. In India, social education is still in its infancy. But nevertheless, "If today, the villages of India are humming with greater activities than ever before some credit for this must go to the social education movement."

QUESTIONS FOR EXERCISE

1. Describe essential characteristics of village community and differentiate it from urban community.
2. Account for the present changes in Indian villages. What methods may be adopted to change rural community?
3. Write an essay on — Rural religion.
4. Write short note on — Village temple.
5. Write short note on — (i) Rural recreation.
   (ii) Rural sanskaras.
6. Write an essay on Village Panchayats in India.
7. What is the meaning of rural reconstruction? Explain its importance.
8. What are the problems of Indian villages? What steps may be taken to solve them.
9. Write an essay on Community Development Projects.
10. Write short note on Bhoodan Movement.

15

Urbanization and Urban Communities in India

In almost, all cities of the world there is progressive increase in the population consequent upon industrialization. This is a simple and quite easily understandable phenomenon. Wherever some new industry is put up, a large labour force and a sizeable managerial cadre are required. In order to meet this demand there is influx of population to the city where an industry is being set up. In flourishing cities of the world, every day some or the other new industrial unit is coming. Therefore, there is continuous influx of population to cities. This progress in the population has resulted in the problems of overcrowding. The industrialization and mechanization have given rise to a host of social problems. The main consequences of urbanization for the social life in cities are the following:

1. Decline in Social Sympathy. The first consequence of overcrowding and increasing population is the decline in fellow feeling and sympathy. In villages, we find a lot of sympathy and communal feeling. A villager knows almost every other man in his village; knows about his problems, joys and sorrows. He feels for them. On the other hand, the question of knowing others does not arise in cities. And obviously, we can have little sympathy for those who are unknown to us. In cities, everyone is concerned about himself or his friends and lacks sympathy for others.

2. Lack of Social Control. With the decline in fellow feeling, sympathy and concern for others, there is also decline in the social control in cities. As the population increases in cities there is dealing in control of family and caste on the behaviour of an individual. The infection of no control and arbitrary behaviour in cities is catching even rural population. Now-a-days the control of caste and panchayat has declined considerably in villages.

3. Decline in Family Control. The rise in the urban population has led to decline in family control. The family ties have lost their orthodox value and have become rather lax. In cities, there are a number of families where both husband and wife go to work. In such families, in the nature of things, there can be no control over children. Lakhs of labourers live in cities without their families. Obviously, there is no question of family control over their behaviour. After coming to cities they start indulging in licentious behaviour because there is no one there to check them. They start going to cinemas and also visit houses of ill repute.

Table 10: *Rural Urban Population 1901-1991*

Census Year	Population (Million)		Percentage of Total Population	
	Rural	Urban	Rural	Urban
1	2	3	4	5
1901	213	26	89.2	10.8
1911	226	26	89.7	10.3
1921	223	28	88.8	11.2
1931	246	33	88.0	12.0
1941	275	44	86.1	13.9
1951	299	62	82.7	17.3
1961	360	79	82.0	18.0
1971	439	109	80.1	19.9
1981	524	159	76.7	23.3
1991	629	218	74.3	25.7

4. Decline in the Influence of Religion. In cities, the philosophy of materialism is ascendant. Everybody has become self-centred and is madly pursuing his self-interest without any consideration for others. All this is a direct result of the decline in the influence of religion in the urban life.

5. Change in the Status of Women. There has been considerable change in the status of women in cities. There is great awakening among women. They are on the way to achieving economic independence. They are no longer slaves to their husbands. Commenting on this great change in the status of women in cities, Earnest R. Mowrer writes, "The husband is no longer the head of the household in many families, in spite of the fact that he still provides the family name. The wife, on the other hand, finds herself quite equal of her husband in the family circle, if not superior." However, there is an evil side of this awakening among women. There is rise in the incidence of illicit sex-contacts, divorce, and pre- and extra-marital sex.

6. Changes in the Institution of Marriage. In India, marriages used to be contracted by the parents of bride and bridegroom. But now-a-days there is an increasing tendency to choose one's life partner freely and of one's own accord.

7. Changes in Family Structure. In cities, the institution of joint family is disappearing. Everywhere there is an increasing tendency to have limited families confined to husband, wife and their offspring.

8. Majority of Male ratio in Population. The reasons for the greater number of males in the urban population are quite clear. In cities, lakhs of labourers live single: their families live in their villages. Hence, in cities males outnumber females.

9. Professionalization of Entertainment. In cities, relaxation and entertainment are not natural. One does not participate in it but merely enjoys it passively. Of course, one has to pay through his nose for this entertainment. One can go to a cinema, to a hotel to see a cabaret or even to a brothel to see dance or buy sexual pleasure. In short, entertainment in cities is commercial and one has to pay for the entertainment.

10. Scarcity of Living Accommodation. In cities, there is acute shortage of accommodation. More industrialized a city is less is the living accommodation in it. In cities, like Bombay, Calcutta and Delhi people are compelled to sleep on footpath. Even those who find a roof overhead, live like cattles. Ten to twenty persons may be staying in a single room. Naturally this gives rise to all sorts of evils.

11. Slums. This really follows what has been said above. As a consequence of shortage of living space, there are sprawling slums in big Indian towns. In Kanpur, these slums are called *Ahatas*: in Delhi *Basti:* in Bombay, *Chawl* and in Madras *Cheri.* These slums are a blot on the fair name of India. What is rather distressing is that along with slums we find grand mansions of mill owners.

12. Changes in Moral Values. There is change in the moral attitudes of city dwellers. The industrialization leads to mechanization and as a consequence of mechanization man becomes an automation and loses his independence and moral autonomy. The industrialization has produced a man who functions in the manner of a component of a machine. He feels himself a victim of circumstances and is unwilling to assert his will. The attitude of working girls towards sexual relations has changed considerably. As industrialization has created great demand for working hands, women get work along with men. Due to this they have achieved economic independence and are no longer prepared to play a second fiddle to their husbands. The old moral values have broken down. New gadgets have given household women great deal of time to pursue their interests and hobbies. All this has broungt about great revolution in moral thinking and moral values.

13. Breakdown of Joint Family. In cities, the joint family system has broken down. In cities most families consist of husband, wife and their offsprings.

14. Increase in Evil Professions. In cities many an evil professions flourish. Due to frustrating working conditions in the factory, workers drink, gamble and go to prostitutes.

15. Increase in the Incidence of Crime. As R.K. Mookerjee has very aptly observed in industrial centres manhood is unquestionably brutalized, women dishonoured and childhood poisoned at the every source.

16. Increase in Juvenile Delinquency. In cities, there is a sharp increase in Juvenile delinquency. Due to industrialization, unscrupulous employers engage child labour. This is an important factor in producing juvenile delinquency. Besides, the children of those parents who go to work are not properly attended to by their parents. They are left to their own designs and tend to become juvenile delinquents.

17. Corruption, Conflict and Competition. In cities, we find cut throat competition in economic field. Not only among businessmen but among mill-owners there is furious competition. When this competition becomes fierce, evil practices are resorted to. Black-market is a direct consequence of this fierce competition.

The above mentioned social impact of industrialization is to be found in all countries. Some effects are desirable, while others are undesirable. To control the undesirable effects there is town planning in advanced countries.

HETEROGENEOUS POPULATION

In cities, we find people professing a variety of faith, belonging to various communities, castes, sub-castes and hailing from different regions of a country, even from many foreign lands. They speak different languages, dress and eat differently, follow varying customs and traditions, practice different types of rituals at the time of marriage and death and belong to different political and intellectual strata. In metropolitan towns, diplomats, business people and commercial representatives and agents from all over the world live and maintain their establishments.

The heterogenous population affects social relations in many ways. The chief effects are given below:

1. Lack of the Spirit of Tolerance. Due to heterogenous groups living in a city, there is little spirit of tolerance among them. In a village, the population is homogenous and people living there share many a common bond. They belong to same culture, practise uniform marriage and other rites. They share common memories of joy and sorrow and readily come forward to hold each other. But in the city there are very few common bonds and the differences of religion and culture separating them are far more pronounced than the unifying elements. As a matter of fact people in cities are constantly warring on one or the other account. The religious and communal antagonism erupts into violence of riots from time to time. The different political parties have their headquarters in cities and are busy in instigating conflict and plotting against each other. Sometimes, they incite trouble exploiting the linguistic grievance. Sometimes, they fan religious hatred, sometimes they exploit economic grievances. In short, the political parties, for their personal gains, intensify and accentuate the heterogeneous elements in the cities. The people belonging to different cultures and religions consider their reaction among people of other religions. For example these days we find an influx of hippies in big Indian towns. They have caused many difficulties because of their extremely uninhibited ways of life. They peddle narcotics and live a life which other people consider very dirty and obscene. Most of all extreme differences in rich and poor in cities are a source of unrelieved bitterness and antagonism.

2. Class Struggle. As a consequence of vast disparity between rich and poor there is bitterness and frustration among the poor which is exploited by the vested interests. Therefore, trade unionism, strikes, ghettoes and noisy processions are a permanent feature of the city life.

3. Multiplicity of Professions and Trades. A number of professional associations and trade guilds exist in cities. These associations and guilds are exclusive and have no connection with each other. Each professional association or trade guild is interested in protecting the rights and interests of its members. The union of Class III employees and the union of class I officers each tries to push the interests of its members. This many a time leads to bitter controversy and rivalry among various unions. As the various professions are united among themselves, this at times entails working at cross purposes. This heightens and accentuates the feeling of exclusiveness and the development of critical and unsympathetic attitudes towards others.

4. Lack of Social Security. As in a heterogenous group, people do not have common goals or interests and as their self-interests clash with each other, the incidence of crime is very high. Every city has a class of professional goondas who commit offences against payment. All these things are obviously detrimental to individual's security and accordingly, people in cities do not have adequate sense of social security. They feel insecure.

5. Gross Disparities. Another consequence of heterogenous population is that there are gross disparities, both economic and social, among city dwellers. On the one side we have multimillionare industrialists and capitalists and on the other hand there are extremely poor labour unable to get two square meals a day. The clerks in office, labourers, shopkeepers and industrialists all form separate strata of society.

6. Division of Labour. As a consequence of the heterogeneity of population, there is increase in the division of labour in the cities. In order to cater to the variety of needs and requirements of different groups new industrial units are set up. Many types of shopping complexes, hotels and restaurants are opened. Due to too much division of labour many problems crop up and the balance of relations between different groups and individuals is disturbed.

7. Family Disorganization. As people belonging to different cultures, religions and races reside in one city, they come together. There are many points of contacts between them. As a consequence of the meeting of disparate cultural outlooks, the orthodoxy of any culture gets shaken and affected by new and different ideas and ideologies. This leads to gradual relaxation of the rigidities of the culture. Particularly there is liberalization of views with regard to sex and marriage. The young people begin to mistrust the old ways and question the reasonableness of traditions and customs of their ethnic groups. Due to meeting and exchange of ideas between different groups which hold permissive and non-premissive sex mores respectively, the family ties are loosened and people dare to flout the othodoxy of their groups. The meeting of varying and opposite cultures also leads to impersonalness in social relations.

8. Break down of Cultures. The heterogeneity and diversity of people and cultures is not a cloud without a silver lining. While the heterogeneity of population has many bad effects, it also has good effects on the society. Due to contacts between persons of different cultures, religions, regions and lands people develop understanding of others viewpoints and sympathize with them. This widens and broadens the outlook of people and this promotes the spirit of tolerance. People of diverse faiths and cultures have to work intimately and unitedly in educational institutions, government offices and factories. They have to tolerate each other and understand each other. As a consequence of this meeting between people, we find many young people of different religions falling in love and marrying each other. These things give rise to cosmopolitanism among people. Their thinking and outlook becomes international in vision and scope.

The Effect of Impersonalness of Social Relations

The impersonalness of social relations has many consequences for the society. Due to industrialization of towns and the rapid system of communication, people are busily engaged in their works and usually travel fairly long distances to come to their offices and factories. This leaves them tired and disinclined to mix up with the neighbours. The relationships between neighbours are usually confined to mere exchange of courtesies and sometimes even these are missing. They are hardly concerned with each other's woes and weals. In big cities, it often happens that a dead body lies in the neighbourhood and no body moves himself to lend a helping hand. Due to this impersonalness of social relations it is difficult to find an element of love and intimacy among social relations. What to speak of social relations, even in the family various members bear no love for each other and their relations are bare and formal. Each member of the family has his or her own friends and each may belong to separate clubs. Each pursues his or her individual goal and is not much bothered about its consequences for other members. The home sometimes is treated as a mere hotel where we take out food and spend nights. As an indirect consequence of this impersonalness of relations, husband, wife, sons and daughters consider themselves as separate entities and wish to remain free and unsupervised in their activities. Sometimes, this impersonalness becomes violent hatred and each member may thirst for the blood of the other. Instances of murders in family are not very rare. Directly, nobody bothers about the other but indirectly he is hateful and revengeful with regard to others.

Besides the above-mentioned adverse effects, the impersonalness of relation also has some beneficial and progressive effects. If the close neighbourers do not care about each other, they do not equally plot against each other, do not wish unwell of other. This provides everyone maximum opportunity for personal development. The people belonging to different religions and cultures are tolerated if not indulged in. This promotes a healthy spirit of tolerance. In villages, everyone knows almost everything about everyone. Anything slightly deviant of social norms meets with a chorus of disapproval. But in the towns one may live with wife, mistress, prostitute or cousin, no body bothers. Therefore, everyone has opportunity to live as best as one can think. One may even experiment without any detrimental social influences.

Thus, we find that impersonality of social relations has both good and bad effects upon society. There is development and progress of the personality of the individual. There is also growth of the spirit of tolerance. Whereas due to impersonalness of the social relations there is increase in classism, self-interest and hostility, the impersonalness of relations helps in breaking the cultural barriers. Following are the effects:

1. Large Scale Trade and Commerce. The trade and commerce in the cities is not confined to any particular region but covers in its scope and ambit national and international markets. The trade and commerce in cities include importers and exporters, local and foreign traders and businessmen, industrialists, labourers, bankers, transporters, insurance companies etc. These businessmen engaged in different fields have their own associations to protect and promote their interests.

2. Disparities of Intellectual Proclivities, Ideas and Ideals. In cities, people belonging to different religions and customs reside. There are differences in their intellectual capacities and ideals. They pursue different ideas and ideals. There is wide difference in the outlook of villagers and towns-people. The city dwellers are idealists, individualists, intellectuals, materialists and secular-minded. They are liberal about personal morals and due to competitive life of the city are mostly busy in their own works. Therefore, they are non-interfering.

3. Family as an Association. In villages, family is considered to be an institution and is regarded a sacrament. But in cities, family is more of an association than an institution. It is considered to be like a contract entered into for mutual profit and gain. Usually, each member of the family has his or her own aims and aspirations. Usually, they subscribe to different associations and are members of different clubs. Thus, we find much higher percentage of family disorganisations in the cities than in the villages.

4. Dynamic Life. In comparison to rural life, the life in the cities is much more dynamic and busy. There is competition in fashions, educational attainments, money gathering, collection of luxury items etc. Everyone tries to outclass other in fashion and luxury. Besides, there is intense competition and strife.

The following table would bring out with clarity the structure and problems of cities compared to villages.

	City		*Villages*
1.	Multiplicity of industries	1.	Lack of industries
2.	Big industries	2.	Cottage industries
3.	Diversity of intellectual capacities, aims and outlook	3.	Homogeneity of intellectual outlook aims and outlook
4.	Family, an Association	4.	Family, an Institution
5.	Dynamic Life	5.	Slow moving life
6.	Rapid change	6.	Gradual and slow change
7.	Progressiveness and Rebelion.	7.	Orthodoxy and contentment.

Table 11: *Increase in Urbanisation in India*

		1901	1951	1961	1971	1981	1991
	1	2	3	4	5	6	7
I	1,00,000 and More	6,661	27,507	39,883	61,226	94,504	138,802
		(26.0)	(44.63)	(51.42)	(57.24)	(60.42)	(65.20)
II	50,000 - 99,999	2,892	6,137	8,713	11,680	18,190	23,309
		(11.29)	(9.96)	(11.23)	(10.92)	(11.63)	(10.95)
III	20,000 - 49,999	4,007	9,688	13,139	17,126	22,409	28,079
		(15.64)	(15.72)	(16.94)	(16.01)	(14.33)	(13.19)
IV	10,000 - 19,999	5,335	8,399	9,902	11,706	14,930	16,531
		(20.83)	(13.63)	(12.77)	(10.94)	(9.54)	(7.77)
V	5,000 - 9,999	5,139	7,993	5,329	4,756	5,603	5,532
		(20.14)	(12.97)	(6.87)	(4.45)	(3.58)	(2.60)
VI	Less than 5000	1,562	1,906	0,597	473	784	614
		(6.10)	(3.09)	(0.77)	(0.44)	(0.50)	(0.29)
	All Group	25,616	61,630	77,562	106,967	156,420	212,867
		(100.00)	(100.0)	(100.0)	(100.0)	(100.0)	(100.0)
	Percentage of Urban Population	10.84	17.29	17.97	19.91	23.34	25.72

URBANISATION

According to census of 1991, of the total population of India, only 30% live in towns. Thus, about two-third of Indian population resides in villages. This, however, does not mean that there is no increase in the urban population in the recent past. Indeed, the urban population has been increasing gradually since last fifty years and the proportion of urban population has gone up by about 75% during the last five decades.

Nature of Urban Development

About 38% of urban population of India lives in towns having a population of one lakh or more. About 30.1% of its population lives in town whose population ranges between 20,000 and 1,00,000. About 28.6% of Indian urban population inhabits small townships whose population ranges between 5,000 to 20,000. And the remainder 3.3% population inhabits towns having population of less than 5,000. According to the census of 1991, there are hundreds towns in India which have population of more than a lakh; in 1941, the number of such towns was only 59. Now, the number of towns with population ranging between 50,000 and 1,00,000 is 185; there are 582 towns whose population is between 20 to 50 thousands and the number of towns having population between 10 to 20 thousands is 478. There are 610 small townships whose population ranges between 5,000 to 10,000.

The foregoing statistical analysis of growth and development of towns in India makes it quite clear that both the rate of growth and the nature of growth of Indian towns is unsatisfactory. In modern circumstances, the best criterion of the rate and nature of industrialization in any country is the growth and development of its towns. If we compare the rate of growth of towns of advanced Western countries with that of India, the fact of poor growth of towns in India becomes abundantly explicit.

Causes of Growth of Cities

It is very difficult to say when did the first city form or when did it originate. As Gist and Halbert have very aptly observed, "Like the origin of civilization itself the origin of the city is lost in the obscurity of the past." The growth and development of cities in linked with two factors; on the one hand, it is dependent upon the growth of population, and, on the other, it is linked to the growth and development of industrialization. Industrialization results in increased production and the increased production, in turn, leads to division of labour. The produce has to be transported from one place to the other and put on the market. This requires means of transport, markets, godowns, shops etc. With industrialization there is not only increase in production but also in the growth of population. This is due to the fact that wherever there is industrialization, a big labour force is needed: besides, we need enough supervisory staff. Moreover, inasmuch as industrialization involves new construction, creation of markets, shops and business premises, thousands of men would be absorbed in these works. Naturally, therefore, the population of an industrial centre would grow immensely. In response to various needs of the newly grown population, educational, cultural and other institutions and associations come into being. If the population of a place is large, it is bound to be heterogeneous; and a heterogeneous people require large police contingents and other law enforcing agencies in order to maintain law and order. All these factors are instrumental to the development of cities. If a university, High Court or medical college is established anywhere, there is great influx of population to that area. With the substantial increase in the population of a place, many shops, markets, hotels, restaurants, clubs and cinemas come into existence and thus the foundation of a city is well laid. The towns situated on sea coast easily turn into big cities as a result of industrialization. The industrialization implies increase both in import and export. Most of the goods entering into a country or going out of it are carried by ships. If a coastal town has good harbour facilities, traffic through it is bound to increase with industrialization. The greater the traffic through a harbour greater will be its population and greater would be the turn over and handling of goods. All these things naturally help the rapid development of cities. Similarly, the hill resorts or towns situated on coast are liable to become cities if these common good views and the climate is salubrious. In short, wherever there is industrialization or good climate or government offices or scenic beauty and good educational and cultural institutions, such places are liable to develop into cities.

Table 12: *Growth of Cities in India with more than Million Population*

City	Population 1981 (Thousand)	1951	1981/1951 Increase
Calcutta	9,194	4,670	1.97
Greater Bombay	8,243	2,967	2.78
Delhi	5,729	1,437	3.99
Madras	4,289	1,542	2.78
Bangalore	2,922	786	3.72
Hyderabad	2,546	1,131	2.25
Ahmedabad	2,548	877	2.91
Kanpur	1,639	705	2.32
Pune	1,686	609	2.77
Nagpur	1,302	485	2.68
Lucknow	1,008	497	2.03
Jaipur	1,015	304	3.34

The above discussion makes it plain that there is no single factor or cause which can be held responsible for the development or origin of cities. It is not possible to define and enumerate the causes of the origin and development of cities, every city his its personal history and certain causes for its origin and development are peculiar to it. For example, if and when a certain place is declared to be the capital of some state or country, it is bound to become a city overnight. Broadly, following may be enumerated as the main causes of the development and origin of cities:

1. Industrial Revolution. The cities are business centres. The increase in business stimulates industrial activity. When large industrial complexes come into existence, big markets, housing and shopping complexes are a natural sequel to industrial activity. The places situated in the vicinity of large industries automatically become important business centres, and at a business centre there is a collection of a large number of people and when population of a place is big enough it naturally turns into a city.

2. Business Revolution. Wherever, there is large turnover of trade and business that place must in due course turn into a city. As N.L. Sims observes, "Trade is a necessary cause of the existence of a city as circulation of blood is a necessary cause for the life of an organism." A large business centre must naturally have big markets, marts, shopping complexes, housing colonies, educational and cultural associations, clubs, restaurants and hotels. All these things are *sine qua non* of a city and if some place has these it must be a city.

3. Agricultural Revolution. The revolution in 20th century, science has completely metamorphosed the entire structure and quality of agriculture. Today, we possess highly sophisticated agricultural tools and implements and these help us to get far higher yield of crops than before with the help of very few hands. The revolution in agriculture has released high labour force, who hunt jobs. Being available cheap, the capitalist is induced to invest money into new factories in order to utilize cheap labour. When a large labour force migrates to any place, that place grows and tends to develop into a city. In West, agricultural revolution is an important factor in the development of cities.

4. Increase in the Means of Transportation. In the development of cities, means of transport play a crucial role. Without the facilities of transportation and the easy availability of such means as trains, trucks, buses, taxies, scooters etc. no place can become a business centre. Previously, the chief means of transport available was the bullock cart and this means is extensive as well as time consuming. Today, by means of rail, road or air we can transport goods from one place to the other very quickly and inexpensively. In big towns or metropolises, therefore, goods are brought from great distances by air, rail or road transport and they become business centres for national as well as international goods. One of the reasons for the quick growth of metropolises like Calcutta and Bombay is the easy availability of the various means of transport.

5. Development of Communication. With the development of means of communication like postal, telegraph and a wireless services etc. It has now become possible for the businessmen away from each other by great distances to establish contacts with each other. This in turn stimulates business and trade activity. The facilities of communication have helped greatly the growth and development of cities.

6. Political Factors. Owing to political reasons certain places assume great importance; and consequently, become great cities. In almost, all states the capitals have developed greatly and fast. For example, Chandigarh was an obscure village but when it was decided to make it the capital of Punjab it was metamorphosed and became a modern city. Similarly, the growth of London, Tokyo and Delhi can be traced to the fact that these are capitals of Great Britain, Japan and India respectively. Besides, the reason of being capitals many towns develop fast into metropolises if some strategic importance is attached to these.

7. Education Centres. The places which are centres of higher learning, soon become big cities. This is because students and teachers from far and wide assemble at such places and in order to cater to their needs shops, markets, hotels, restaurants and clubs come into existence. Thus, all the prerequisites of a city materialize and wherever there are big markets, shopping and housing complexes a city is bound to come into existence.

8. Growth of Population. In is an evident fact that whenever and wherever there is increase in the population all prerequisites of cities are bound to come into existence. Subsequent to independence of India and consequent blood bath of communal frenzy and rioting there was great influx of population from Pakistan to India. Many a small town in India grew into cities. This increase in the population is an important factor in the growth of cities.

9. Security. A place which is vulnerable to external attack or which is subject to attack by some marauding tribes cannot grow into a city because no body would like to invest any money at such places. People would invest money and do business only at those places which are safe and secure and where life and property are not constantly threatened.

10. Municipal Facilities and Means of Entertainment. In good cities, there are schools, colleges, universities, music institutes, dance centres, medical colleges and industrial training institutes. People can avail of these facilities and enhance their abilities. In villages, in spite of plenty of money with people, there are no means of enjoyment and entertainment. On the other hand, in cities, there are cinemas, music and dance clubs, theatres, night clubs, hotels and restaurants. In cities, people can buy comfort and enjoyment by spending money. On account of easy availability of means of improving one's abilities and self culture and also easy availability of means of entertainment attract people from villages to cities.

The Importance of Industrialization

As referred to above industrialization is a very important cause and factor in the origin and development of towns. But some sociologists regard industrialization to be the only cause of the development of cities. It will be in fitness of things to critically examine this view. It is a fact that in India most of the big cities have developed due to industrialization. In India, this is also true that population his increased much faster in those areas which are highly industrialized. Therefore, the number of cities is more in those states which are more industrialized than in others. In India, maximum number of cities is in Maharashtra which is the most industrialized state of India.

A comparative statistical analysis of growth of population in various states reveals that relative growth of population in descending order is as follows: Maharashtra, U.P., Mysore, West Bengal, Delhi etc. In these states the number of cities has also increased. Interestingly, the growth in population corresponds to the growth of industrialization. Thus, it can be safely assumed that the rapidity of the growth of population and increase in the population, in turn, leads to the development of towns and cities. Therefore, it is quite true that industrialization is an important, perhaps most important, cause of the development of cities; but it would be an exaggeration to say that industrialization is the sole factor in the development of towns and cities. The singularity of industrialization as the cause of the coming into existence of cities is clearly contradicted by the example of Chandigarh. The coming into existence of Chandigarh is clearly a result of political decision and whatever industry we may find there is the result and not because of the political decision. Similarly, the present growth of Delhi is primarily due to large influx of refugees from Pakistan. Thus, we can sum up by saying that though industrial revolution is an important factor, it is, by no means, the sole factor in the origin and development of cities. All the factors enumerated above are indeed more or less important.

Types of Cities

The geographical conditions, population make-up and differentiation and other features of each city are unique. Thus, whereas Delhi is the central capital, Kanpur is an industrial city, and whereas Bombay is an important harbour, Mussoorie is a summer resort. In spite of the unique character of every city there are also some common features among various cities. For example, Agra, Kanpur, Calcutta, Ahmedabad, Bombay are all industrial cities. Therefore, the feature of industrialization is common to scores of Indian cities. We can thus, classify the cities on the basis of some fundamental features shared by all cities of a class. All the cities mentioned above are industrial cities and therefore production centres. In these cities, a variety of goods is produced and manufactured. However, it must be clearly borne in mind that though many cities share some fundamental features, each city is unique and there are features which are peculiar to it alone. For example, Agra, Kanpur, Calcutta, Ahmedabad, Bombay are all industrial cities. Therefore, the feature of industrialization is common to scores of Indian cities. For example, both Kanpur and Bombay are big industrial cities. Both are the centres of cloth production having numerous textile mills; both are important rail junctions. But Bombay is a major port which Kanpur is not. Whereas Kanpur is a centre of leather technology, Bombay is an important centre of film production. Thus, the cities of one class also have numerous diverse features as well.

On the basis of broad common features of the cities we can classify them into following types:

1. Production centres
2. Centres of Trade and Commerce
3. Capitals
4. Health and Recreation Centres
5. Cultural centres
6. Diversified cities.

As we have mentioned earlier there can be no absolute classification of cities, all classifications are relative. Many cities fit in more than one category mentioned above. For example, Delhi fits in with the first there categories. It is an important production centre, an equally important centre of trade and commerce and is, of course, a capital city. Bombay, on the other hand, satisfies the necessary condition of first five categories listed above. It is an important production centre, an important centre of trade and commerce, capital of Maharashtra, a centre of health and recreation and also a cultural centre. Besides, these Bombay also has many other specialities. Being on the sea coast its climate is temperate, and it is also the most important film-making centre. It is also world's renowned centre of entertainment and amusement. Bombay's importance lies not only in the fact that it is capital of Maharashtra but issue from the fact that it is a famous city. Not without reason it is called Gateway of India. Again the importance of Bombay docs not lie in its being a big centre of culture and entertainment but issues form the fact that it is a port through which import and export worth millions of rupees is made. Though, Bombay is a centre of cloth production, it is more important as a centre of trade and commerce. Therefore, after taking into consideration everything we find that Bombay fits in with the second category most, that is it is a centre of trade and commerce. Thus, while classifying a city we have to see as to which of its feature is most prominent. Therefore, though Delhi is an important production centre as well as the centre of trade and commerce, its most important feature is that it is a capital city.

Types are not Pure

It must be borne in mind that the above classification of types of cities has been done on the basis of the most fundamental or prominent feature of city. If a city is a capital as well as big trade and commercial centre our classification will be determined by the fact whether the fact of being capital or being a commercial centre is more fundamental or prominent. To illustrate, Chandigarh is the capital of Punjab and it is also a commercial centre. But the fact of capital is more fundamental and important than the fact of being the commercial centre. On the contrary of Bombay the fact of being commercial centre is far more important than that of its being the capital of Maharashtra. It is generally observed that once a city is made the capital of a state its importance and stature grows. Owing to official patronage, greater security and availability of easy loans etc., such cities become important production centres or centres of trade and commerce. On the other hand, some cities arc big production centres naturally. In modern times, it is difficult to find examples of pure types of cities. Some exceptions may of course be summer resorts or hill towns. Some of these are purely centres of health and recreation. Below we shall discuss the types of cities in detail:

1. Production Centres. Generally, the more important cities of the world arc industrial towns The main reason for increasing urbanisation in modern times is the industrialisation. Consequent upon industrial revolution the urban population all over the world has increased considerably. In India, the majority of cities having population of one lakh or more are industrial towns. According to the kind of production, the production centres can be classified in two following categories:

(A) *Primary Production Centres.* The primary production centres are those places where any materials for industrial use are produced. For example, mining centres where oil, local wood etc. are produced are primary production centres. The population of such places is usually not very large. Generally, only those persons live at these centres who are directly or indirectly involved in the production of raw materials. By elaborate transport these centres are connected with places at which raw materials are further refined. Among such towns in India are Nellore, Masulipatnam, Ranchi, Gauhati, Mysore, Kolar, Dehradun, Bareilly etc. In Dehradun and Bareilly, the wood obtained from forest is sawed and packed to the secondary production centres. Bareilly is also known for its bamboo production. In Gauhati, we have oil, in Ranchi we have coal mines and in Kolar there are good mines.

(B) *Secondary Production Centres.* Most of the centres of production are included in this category. In Secondary production centres, the raw materials obtained from primary production centres are used for manufacture of a variety of goods. At such places population is large and keeps growing. As the primary centres of production produce one or two items, the secondary production centres usually produce scores of items but are famous for one or two items. For example, Ferozabad is famous for its glass bangles, Kanpur for leather goods, Moradabad for brasswork, Gwalior for earthen wares, Aligarh for locks and scissors, Jamshedpur for steel and iron, Rampur for knives and scissors, Bareilly for furniture, Banaras for saris and brocade work, Bangalore for silk sarees. In these towns a major portion of population is involved in the production of goods specific to it. The industrial activity obviously affects greatly the economic and social life of the industrial town. In some cities, same goods are produced. For example, Meerut and Aligarh both are famous for scissors. In some cities, one types of goods is primarily produced. For example, in Moradabad brass works industry is not only major but virtually the only industry. In some cities, numerous things are produced. In Bombay, not only there is cloth production but there is also production of electrical and engineering goods in a big way. If there are more than one industry in any city the chances of unemployment due to economic recession in one industry are less. This is because if one industry faces recession and there is retrenchment, the retrenched men may find jobs in the other industry. Whereas, if all the labour force of a place is employed in one industry and if there is no other industry, the economic recession in the industry would result in wholesale unemployment and the labour would be compelled to migrate.

2. The Centres of Trade and Commerce. Generally, the cities are production centres and centres of trade and commerce; but in some cities, the trade and commerce is the dominant feature and production is secondary. For example, though, Bombay is a major production centre, it is a far bigger centre of trade and commerce. Therefore, Bombay must be regarded primarily to be a centre of trade and commerce. Generally, the cities situated on the seacoast and those which are ports are centres of trade and commerce. Naturally, through these ports large quantity of goods are sent to and received from foreign lands. More than 95% of trade and commerce transacted with foreign lands is made through sea. The major Indian ports are: Porebandar, Surat, Kandla, Bombay, Marmugao, Mangalore,

Calicut, Cochin, Allepy, Quilon, Tuticorin, Dhanushkodi, Neggapattam, Karikal, Cuddalore, Pondicherry, Madras, Masulipatnam, Kakinad, Visakhapatnam and Calcutta. With the exception of Calcutta, Madras and Bombay all other parts are known exclusively for trade and commerce. Though, Madras is primarily a centre of trade and commerce but it is also the Capital of Tamil Nadu. Bombay and Calcutta, however, are so diverse and vast that these virtually fit in with every category mentioned above. While it is true that ports are usually the centres of trade and commerce, it is by no means the case that these are the only such centres. Indeed, there are many inland towns which satisfy the condition of being centres of trade and commerce. For example, Meerut is a big *mandi* for gur, so is Muzaffar-nagar. Dehradun is a *mandi* for rice. In *mandis* goods from far and wide are collected and therefrom distributed to retailers. New York, London, Calcutta, Delhi, Kanpur, Madras are big *mandis* where goods from great distances are collected.

3. Capital. All cities, world over, which happen to be the capitals of states have grown into bigness and shot into prominence. Their importance and eminence is due not to their industry or *mandis* but due to their being the capitals. Indeed, once a place is made the capital, business and industry are but sequel to the main fact of its being the capital. Prior to industrial revolution, capital cities generally were the most eminent cities of the world. The examples of Rome, Paris, London and Moscow amply bear this out. However, as mentioned before, on account of official policy and patronage the capitals tend to become centres of trade, commerce and production. London, New York, Delhi, Moscow, Berlin and Peking can be cited as examples. However, the chief importance of capitals is political rather than industrial or commercial. In the field of industry and commerce Kanpur is the foremost town of U.P. But the city of pride in U.P. is Lucknow and not Kanpur. This is because Lucknow is the capital of U.P. Some cities' importance lies only in the fact of their being capitals: Shillong, Bhubaneswar, Chandigarh, Jaipur, Hyderabad, Thiruvanthapuram, Patna are few such examples. Bombay, Calcutta, Madras, Bangalore, Ahmedabad and Srinagar are capitals respectively of Maharashtra, Bengal, Tamil Nadu, Mysore, Gujarat and Jammu and Kashmir. But the importance of these cities lies not mainly in the fact of their being capitals but in other facts. Srinagar, for example, is a summer resort and health centre. Ahmedabad is an industrial city. Bangalore is famous for its aeronautic industry. Bombay, Calcutta and Madras are centres of trade and commerce.

4. Health Recreation Centres. Many towns have very salubrious and healthy climate owing to their peculiar geographic location and climatic conditions. Generally, the towns situated on the seacoast have temperate climate throughout the year and, therefore, people go there to escape the extreme heat of summer and extreme cold of winter. Similarly, hill towns are cool in summer and their climate and water are beneficial to health. Therefore, people from plains flock in great numbers to such towns in summer months and also go there to watch snowfall in winter. In order to attract more tourists to such places, municipal and state authorities do everything possible to beautify such places and make available all amenities. Many cultural shows are arranged. Many health clubs are opened. Similarly, a number of amusement centres, dance clubs are opened and beauty shows are arranged. In almost, every state of India there are one or more important hill resorts. In British days, these towns were made the summer capitals of governments. Simla used to be the summer capital of India as well as Punjab. Now, this practice has been discontinued, but much official works, particularly, conferences during summer days are arranged in these hill towns. The important summer resorts in India are: in Uttar Pradesh, Almora, Bhovali, Chakrauta, Lansdown, Mussoorie, Nainital and Ranikhet; in Karnataka, Mysore and Bangalore; in Assam, Cherrapoonji and Shillong; in Tamil Nadu, Conoor, Kodaikanal and Ootacammand; in Himachal Pradesh, Dalhousie, Kulu and Simla; in Bengal, Darjeeling and Kalimpong; in Maharashtra, Mahabaleshwar; in Rajasthan, Mt. Abu; in Madhya Pradesh, Pachmarhi and in Bihar, Ranchi. At these places few people live permanently, but in season, the livelihood of permanent residents of these places depends upon tourist traffic. At these places diverse type of entertainment is available. There are big hotels where wine flows freely and cabarets and western dances are staged for the entertainment of the audience. Most of the tourists coming here hail from the rich affluent class and they spend lavishly. These places get their distinctive colour and personality as a result of the kind of tourists reaching these places. Some hill resorts are patronized by government and officialdom, whereas others are patronized by rich industrialists. There are some resorts where middle class tourists can afford to go. Thus, the personality of a hill resort is determined by the kind of tourists. Some health resorts have sanatoria and health clinics and these are visited mostly by the sick. In Bhovali, there is sanatorium for tuberculosis and Ranchi has a hospital for the mentally sick. In Kasauli, there is a Pasteur Institute.

5. Cultural Centres. In India, where religious sentiment dominates many towns have become famous and developed into big cities on account of their religious value and importance. All the towns situated on river banks have an aura of holiness attached to them. Besides, India is a multi-religious country and each religion has one or two places regarded holy by the followers of each religion. For example, Amritsar has a famous Sikh Gurudwara known as Golden Temple. Ajmer is a place of pilgrimage of the Moslems. Ayodhya, Hardwar, Rameshwaram, Prayag, Puri, Mathura etc. are holy cities of Hindus. Bodh Gaya and Samath are holy places of Buddhists. Pilgrims from far and near come to these places to obtain spiritual solace and earn the religious merit. There are a number of historic cities in India renowned for some monument, mausoleum or some other constructions celebrating some historic event. Agra, for example, is well known world over for its historic monuments, Taj Mahal, in particular. Bijapur is known for its circular tower and Chittorgarh for its Victory tower. Delhi is famous for its Red Fort and Jamma Masjid. Sanchi is famous for its Stupas; Nalanda and Taxila for their ancient universities now in ruins; Fatehpur Sikri for its *Buland Darwaza*. Many cities are famous for being centres of higher learning. Allahabad, Bombay, Calcutta, Delhi,

Lucknow, Meerut, Madras, Nagpur, Roorkee, Kurukshetra, Saugar, Tirupati, Cuttack, Dharwar, Ujjain, Shantiniketan, Jadavapur, Burdwan and many other towns are famous for their universities. Pondicherry is famous world over for its Aurobindo Ashram.

6. Diversified Cities. Besides, the cities which fit into one or the other of the above mentioned category, there are some towns which fit into none of the category. They may be holy, but holiness is not the fundamental reason for their growth; they may have a university but this, too, may be incidental. There are places which may be important equally as cultural centres, production centres and as capitals. Thus, it would be unjustified to put them in any one category. Such towns are accordingly referred to as *diversified* town. For examples, Varanasi is a holy city of Hindus; it has a famous university also in which students and teachers of all nationalities get together. It is also a commercial centre. It is also famous for its gold work on saris. Thus, in Varanasi we find intellectuals, merchants, mendicants, beggars and prostitutes. A man may go to Varanasi for business, pleasure, study or for learning merit or reaping spiritual solace. All these things add colour and charm to the town. It is a most appropriate example of a diversified town.

India is a vast country, the process of urbanization is progressing here continuously. Therefore, a detailed description of its many cities would require many volumes. However, broadly speaking, all Indian cities fit into one or the other category listed above. Indeed, the cities of the whole world can be classified in the above mentioned categories.

Table 13: *Literacy in India — Rural Urban Contrast*

	State/UT	Urban/ Rural	Persons	Males	Females
	1	2	3	4	5
1.	A.P.	Total	44.09	55.13	32.72
		Rural	33.74	47.28	23.92
		Urban	66.35	75.87	56.41
2.	Arunachal	Total	41.59	51.45	29.69
		Rural	37.02	47.00	25.31
		Urban	71.59	77.99	62.23
3.	Assam	Total	52.89	61.87	43.03
		Rural	49.32	58.66	39.19
		Urban	79.39	84.37	73.32
4.	Bihar	Total	38.48	52.49	22.89
		Rural	33.83	48.31	17.95
		Urban	67.89	77.72	55.94

(Contd. on next page)

	1	2	3	4	5
5.	Goa	Total	75.51	83.64	67.09
		Rural	72.31	81.71	62.87
		Urban	80.10	86.33	73.38
6.	Gujarat	Total	61.29	73.13	40 64
		Rural	53.09	66.84	38.65
		Urban	76.54	84.50	67.70
7.	Haryana	Total	55.85	69.10	40.47
		Rural	49.85	64.78	32.51
		Urban	73.66	81.96	64.06
8.	Himachal Pradesh	Total	63.86	75.36	52.13
		Rural	61.86	73.89	49.79
		Urban	84.17	88.97	78.32
9.	Karnataka	Total	56.04	67.26	44.34
		Rural	47.69	60 30	34.76
		Urban	74.20	82.04	65.74
10.	Kerala	Total	89.81	93.62	86.17
		Rural	88.92	92.91	85.12
		Urban	92.25	95.58	89.06
11.	Madhya Pradesh	Total	44.20	58.42	28.85
		Rural	35.87	51.04	19.73
		Urban	70.81	81.32	58.92
12.	Maharashtra	Total	64.87	76.56	52.32
		Rural	55.52	69.74	40.96
		Urban	79.20	86.41	70.87
13.	Manipur	Total	59.89	71.63	47.60
		Rural	55.79	67.64	43.26
		Urban	70.53	82.11	58.67
14.	Meghalaya	Total	49.10	53.12	44.85
		Rural	41.05	44.83	37.12
		Urban	81.74	85.72	77.32
15.	Mizoram	Total	82.27	85.61	78.60
		Rural	72.47	77.36	67.03
		Urban	93.45	95.15	91.61
16.	Nagaland	Total	61.65	67.62	54.75
		Rural	57.23	63 42	50.36
		Urban	83.10	85.94	79.10
17.	Orissa	Total	49.09	63.09	34.68
		Rural	45.46	60.00	30.79
		Urban	71 99	81.21	61.18
18.	Punjab	Total	58.51	65.66	50.41
		Rural	52.77	60.71	43.85
		Urban	72.08	77.26	66.121

	1	2	3	4	5
19.	Rajasthan	Total	38.55	54.99	20.44
		Rural	30.37	47.64	11.59
		Urban	65.33	78.50	50.24
20.	Sikkim	Total	56.94	65.74	46.69
		Rural	54.38	63.49	43.98
		Urban	80.89	85.19	74.94
21.	Tamil Nadu	Total	62.66	73.75	51.33
		Rural	54.59	67.18	41.84
		Urban	77.99	86.06	69.61
22.	Tripura	Total	60.44	70.58	49.65
		Rural	56.08	67.07	44.33
		Urban	83.09	89.00	76.93
23.	Uttar Pradesh	Total	41.60	55.73	25.31
		Rural	36.66	52.05	19.02
		Urban	61.00	69.98	50.38
24.	West Bengal	Total	57.70	67.81	46.56
		Rural	50.50	62.05.	38.12
		Urban	75.27	81.19	68.25
	Union Territories				
1.	Andaman & Nicobar	Total	73.02	78.99	65.46
	Islands	Rural	69.73	75.99	61.99
		Urban	81.69	86.59	75.08
2.	Chandigarh	Total	77.81	82.04	72.34
		Rural	59.12	65.67	47.83
		Urban	79.87	84.09	74.57
3.	Dadra & Nagar Haveli	Total	40.71	53.56	26.98
		Rural	37.00	50.04	23.30
		Urban	78.44	86.35	68.42
4.	Daman and Diu	Total	71.20	82.66	59.40
		Rural	61.55	75.23	46.70
		Urban	81.61	91.14	72.35
5.	Delhi	Total	75.29	82.01	66.99
		Rural	66.90	78.46	52.15
		Urban	76.18	82.39	68.54
6.	Lakshadweep	Total	81.78	90.18	72.89
		Rural	78.89	88.66	68.72
		Urban	83.99	91.31	76.11
7.	Pondicherry	Total	74.74	83.68	65.63
		Rural	65.36	76.44	53.96
		Urban	79.88	87.70	71.98

RURAL-URBAN CONTRAST

Hence, rural urban differences form a basic subject of study of urban sociology. An exhaustive analysis of rural-urban differeces gives us a clear-cut idea of the essential qualities and personality of the urban conglomeration. Rural-urban differences exist in every field of life, size of population, social interaction, stratification, etc. To get a basic idea of rural-urban differentials now let us analyse its character as regards to the three chief factors, population, stratification and social interaction.

1. Population. After the size of a city the immediate striking feature is its population. The study of population includes its size, density, composition, etc. Usually a smaller number of people characterise the rural areas. Since, agriculture is essentially a household occupation the rural areas were built originally as family closets and continue to be so with little variation except through births and deaths. Usually, the population of a typical village varies between 100 and 500. There are controversies regarding the size of a city population. We may call a group town if it has more than 1,000 people. There is a further difference in the size of the population of a town and city or metropolis. The same can be said about the density of the population. The cities are relatively more dense than the village since the composition and spread of a rural population is more or less fixed according to its size at any time. Congestion is one of the basic problems of modern cities. Regarding composition, the urban population is more diversified and less homogeneous in all respects, because as already stated, cities developed out of the flocking of a multitudes through of rural population. The urban people come from different places. Usually, the urban population gets added up through migration of rural folks for education and employment. Hence, there exists a disparity in the population structure. Youths and males are usually larger in number many a time. In villages, one can hardly notice such disparities because of the operation of the balancing up process of Nature. The urban population replaces itself from time to time due to migration to other towns etc. Another specific character of urban population is the existence of a larger number of floating population at all times. Thus, while the rural population is static and homogeneous the urban population is diversified and dynamic.

2. Stratification. Stratification is the main factor in any community through which every society tries to adjust its different capabilities into a system of relative priorities and privileges dependent on its value structure. Hence, one may search for essential difference in this aspect between the village and the city which profess different value systems. Rural societies usually profess a conventional value system which gives priority to entrenched privileges and positions. Urban societies are progressive in outlook, place, personal achievement, as the criteria before their people is to achieve social standing. Hence, people everywhere practice a sort of caste system, with population divided along an entrenched social hierarchy with relatively little mobility between the different strata of society.

The accord of priority depends on the quality valued in that society. For example, in earliest peasant societies, the chieftain was a man of physical power and warriors enjoyed high social status. Indian society practices a caste system in which priests are accorded the higher social status. But usually, in a relatively well settled peasant community the land owning and agricultural classes form the top brass while the craftsmen and petty traders form the middle strata. The lower strata is occupied by agricultural labourers and slaves. A man's social position is fixed by his birth into a family of a particular strata. While the people of higher social strata enjoy all the privileges and advantages in society the lower strata are exploited and live a sub-human existence. In contrast, the urban people practice an open class system. In the urban social milieu these caste categories merge into the class categories. Economic factor is the chief differentiating factor of urban stratification. In it, usually, the upper class consists of the wealthy people, industrial magnates and owners of big business. The middle class consists of executives, professionals, etc. The lower class consists of industrial labourers, clerks and other people of lower income. Technical qualification, personal achievement and acquisition of wealth are the main factors of entry into these classes. Usually, relative mobility and a sort of democracy exists between these classes and urban consumption patterns.

3. Social Interaction. Social interaction is the basic prerequisite of social relationships and it decides the nature, structure and functioning of any society. There must be at least a minimal degree of difference in the mode of social interactions of urbanites and ruralites who are parts of different social milieu. These and other differences arise out of the relative simplicity or complexity of a society, the composition of its population and the number of its functions. Rural society is essentially simple and compact society with a relatively homogeneous population who have minimal number of desires and functions. Further, they are in constant contact with each other and hence develop a sort of companionship. Thus, primary relations and informal social interactions characterise a rural society. Intimacy, warmth and concern characterise rural social interactions. On the other hand, the urban aggregate is a diversified social milieu which consists of people of different socio-cultural levels.

ROLE OF MIGRATION

Urbanization is a process which has taken place at a rapid scale in recent years in different countries due to the influence of a variety of causes of which industrialization is the key factor. Urban area is an outgrowth of the existing rural populace. Hence, migration plays a key role in the growth of cities in any country. It is the chief factor which has helped urban growth in all countries in modern times. In fact, the cities could grow only because of the flocking of a large quantity of unskilled labourers to their centres from the villages. Usually, migration is from rural to urban centres and from centres of lower culture to centres of higher culture. It takes place due to various reasons such as moral unemployment and attractions of the glamours of city life. In India, cities existed throughout recorded history as capitals of the various empires. They were usually centres which attracted the flowers of the age to the royal courts and which enjoyed a flourishing trade.

Cities in the modern sense of the word are only a century old. They developed as industrial and administrative centres rapidly during this century. Migration is the chief factor which contributed to the growth of modern cities in India. Besides, the general factors the specific factors which encouraged migration in India are the break up of the handicraft industry in the light of competition from machine made goods and the consequent surplus pressure of population on land and rural unemployment. However, the relatively less developed transportation system and the clinging to the traditional value structure had prevented migration for some time. This partly explains the relatively slow rate of urbanization in India. The causes of migration are as follows:

1. Unemployment. The increased migration of semi-starved artisans and agricultural labourers provided a huge amount of supply of unskilled labourers to urban factories and thus paved the way for gradual urban growth. After independence the process of urbanization has increased and migration in its various facets is playing an important role in this process. As a result of well developed transportation and constant urban contacts rurality today has given up many of its inhibitions and is ready for acquiring and enjoying the advantages of an urban society. Youths took the lead in this process. They usually revolted against the rigidity and staticity of rural life and migrate to the city where they hope to find a relatively prosperous job in a short time and to enjoy new comforts but end up in doing unskilled jobs. Thus, migration provides the needed youth population for the urban milieu.

2. Education. Another novel feature today is the rural migration for education. This process is helped by the growth of cities near villages. The landed aristocrates who are gradually coming to appreciate the value of urban education and employment are sending their children to cities. This has helped in further urban growth and widening of the urban base. Rural people who migrate to cities usually settle there, if they can find a job. Some people with poor means of livelihood make it a point to migrate permanently to the town or city once they can find a base there.

3. Marriage. Further, rural people today make it a matter of prestige to marry their girls to a city bred and city educated youth. This amounts in large scale women migration.

4. Glamour of City. Today, the rich landlords are being attracted more and more by the glamour of city life. Hence, they establish a house there and some of them have even gone to the extent of totally selling out their property and migrating to towns. This process is further encouraged by the recent land legislation.

Today long-distance migration between cities in search of education and employment has also increased and this adds to growth of a particular city. In fact, much of the people of our urban middle class and clerical occupations have a rural base or come from a rural background.

Broadly, following are the main problems of a city:

1. Absence of Community Feeling. Inasmuch as a village is, as a rule, a homogeneous community, there is a feeling of oneness and fellowship in the village. But, in a city where there live heterogeneous communities there is no feeling of oneness and fellowship among the city dwellers. In short, a city lacks the feeling of communal fellowship which is characteristic of a village.

2. Lack of Family Unity. Not only does a city lack the community-feeling, but there is absence of the feeling of oneness and harmony among family members. The father, the mother, the son and the daughter usually are members of their separate clubs and societies and have more kinship with their club members than among themselves.

3. Moral Laxity. The lack of the community feeling and family unity and kinship coupled with the impact of western civilization have resulted in the fall of moral standards. Due to multitudes of people everywhere it is easy to lead a life of anonymity in the city. Therefore, there is considerable increase in the incidence of pre-marital and extra-marital sexual relations. The easy availability of vulgar entertainment and sex-oriental literature in the cities contribute towards moral laxity.

4. Unstable Personality. The moral laxity, unnatural environment, stimulating entertainment coupled with rising expectations among people are helping to generate neuroses. The people have lost firm grip over life and have become aimless. Their moral indifference to the kind and quality of their lives is an ideal ground for the production of simple schizophrenia.

5. Increase in Crime. In cities, every variety of crime flourishes. The smuggling, defrauding, kidnapping, sexual abuse, abortion, murder, rape etc. are common occurrences in the cities.

6. Social Disorganization. As a consequence of the above mentioned features, social disorganization has started in the cities. There is general discontent and unrest among city dwellers. There is rise in the expectation of people and this leads to a continuous class struggle. All sorts of agitations are taking place. Even communal violence erupts from time to time. The people do not feel secure in spite of the presence of large police force.

7. Marital Problems. In cities, the average age of marriage is quite advanced as compared to rural areas. There is no strict institutional control or restraint on pre-marital and extra-marital sex. Many young men and women prefer to stay single, as in cities the incidence of both love marriage and divorce is more than in villages. In cities, there is commercial sex-oriented entertainment and professional men and women are available to cater specialized sex needs of people. This obviously contributes to and complicates marital problems.

8. Slums and Shortage of Houses. In almost, every city the problem of housing accommodation is acute. Lakhs of people are forced to live in inhuman conditions.

9. Diversity. In every big city there is great variety. People of different faiths, rich and poor, professional and non-professional live in the same city. Thus, in a city we have diversity of religion, culture and people.

10. Artificial and Dependent Existence. The life in cities becomes mechanical and is cut off from natural environment. People drink powdered or bottled milk, eat canned food and have to go to overcrowded parks to find a stimulant of nature. Though, cities produce many variety of goods, they are dependent on villages for the essential foods and vegetables, milk and ghee etc.

11. Urban Social Problems. Urban social problems are peculiar to the urban way of life and are the anomalies of urban society. The main social problems that appear in the urban milieu are that of housing and inadequacy of family and neighbourhood lack of stability in the social structure, lack of intimate social relations, congestion, unemployment, pollution, diseases peculiar to urban way of life and increased social disorganization.

Causes of Urban Problems

The factors responsible for these problems are inherent in the concept of urbanization itself. Since, an urban centre is a conglomeration of a haphazardly flocked heterogeneous mass, housing acquires gigantic proportions because of the necessity for providing additional and decent houses according to the class status of the ever increasing population in the limited confines of a city.

QUESTIONS FOR EXERCISE

1. Discuss the consequences of urbanization. What social problems does it create?
2. How do the heterogeneity of population and impersonality of social relations affect the mutual relations of the communities in a city?
3. Do you agree with the view that the entire development of towns is due to industrialization? Discuss briefly the factors which were responsible for the development of towns in the past.
4. Discuss the types of cities. What kind of classification is possible according to functional point of view?
5. Examine the role of migration in India's urban growth.
6. Describes the internal structure of Bangalore.
7. Describe the chief problems of the city.
8. What is urbanization? How far do you think education can help in economic development?
9. Discuss the pattern of social change in urban India.
10. What social factors have influenced the process of urbanisation in India?
11. Discuss the dangers of rapid urbanization. What social problems does it create?

16

Major Religious Groups in India

THE HINDUS

What is Hinduism?

According to *The Concise Oxford Dictionary,* the term Hindu means adherent of Hinduism or the Indian. This wide definition agrees with the definition of Hindu given by Veer Savarkar that any one who considers this country as his motherland as well as fatherland may be called a Hindu. The country of Hindus has been further defined by Savarker as that which extends from the Himalayas to cape Comorin and from Burma hills to Hindukush in the West. Thus, Hindu has been widely defined as Indian. It goes without saying that any one who considers India as his fatherland and motherland maybe termed a Hindu. This wide definition, however, may not be acceptable to those who distinguish among Indians on the basis of religion. The term Hinduism has been defined by *The Oxford Concise Dictionary* as the religious and social system with adherents specially in India, with belief in reincarnation, worship of several gods and caste as the basis of society. This definition incidentally, clarifies the fundamental characteristics of Hinduism. Though, initially Hinduism was based upon Varna system, today, undoubtedly it has castes as the basis of society.

Table 14: *Religious Groups in India, 1981*

	Religious Groups	Numbers (Millions)	Percentage to Total Population
1.	Hindu	547.8	82.6
2.	Muslim	75.6	11.4
3.	Christian	16.2	2.4
4.	Sikh	13.1	2.0
5.	Buddhism	4.7	0.7
6.	Jainism	3.2	0.5
7.	Others	2.8	0.4

Characteristics of Hindu Religion

A brief survey of the fundamentals of religion as pointed out in the preceding paragraph will exhibit the chief characteristics of Hindu Religion. Obviously, these characteristics will serve to distinguish Hindu religion from other great religions. These characteristics are as follows:

1. Sanatan Dharma. According to Swami Dayananda, Sanatan Dharma is the eternal Dharma which has been followed since ancient times and which will be followed till eternity. It is followed by the truthful, the altruistic, the unprejudiced and scholarly persons. Such a religion, according to Dayananda was propounded by the Vedas. The salient points of Sanatan Dharma according to Swami Dayananda, are as follows:

(i) *Definition of Parameshwara.* Parameshwara is the creator, the sustainer and the destroyer, the omnipresent, omnipotent, omniscient, attributeless, eternal god, who provides fruits to the jivas according to their respective karmas. Thus, Sanatan Dharma believes in a creator, a cosmic moral order and the theory of karma.

(ii) *Testimony of Vedas.* Vedas are self-evident and do not require any other testimony about their validity. However, according to Dayananda, the Brahmanas, the Angas, the Upangas the, Upvedas and other works based upon the four Vedas are subject to scrutiny, since wherever they disagree with the Vedas, they are wrong.

(iii) *Definition of merit and demerit.* Dharma or merit may be defined as the conduct which is unprejudiced, just, truthful, and based upon the dictates of Ishwara and the Vedas. On the other hand, Adharma or the demerit means the conduct which is prejudiced, unjust, based upon falsehood and against the dictates of Ishwara and the Vedas.

(iv) *Creation.* The purpose of creation is the expression of Karma, Svabhava and Gunas. Just as the success in the creation of Nature is God's success, the success of the Jivas is in their enjoyment and proper use. The creation is eternal. It has, however, a creator.

(v) *Nature of Bondage.* Bondage is due to ignorance or avidya. It is due to ignorance that one achieves pains and suffering and transmigration in numberless bodies.

(vi) *Liberation.* Mukti or liberation is the removal of bondage, perfect freedom and realisation of Ishwara. It may be realised by devotion, Yoga, celibacy, learning, simple living and high thinking and fulfilment of the purusharthas.

(vii) *Social order.* The social order is based upon varnashram dharma. Everyone should follow his duties peculiar to his Varna and Ashram.

The above are the most important salient features of Sanatan Dharma as pointed out by Swami Dayananda. According to him, Sanatan Dharma is humanist. It is based upon truth of human nature. It aims at the welfare and progress of entire humanity. It is based upon distinction of truth and falsehood.

It aims at complete and integral evolution and benefit. It is not only confined to national community but encompasses the entire humanity. Thus, Hinduism is not a sect or a particular religion, it is a world religion which includes the fundamentals of all the great religions. Though, Swami Dayanand had condemned idolatry, most of the interpreters of Hinduism have permitted worship of gods and goddesses, according to one's innate urge and tendency.

2. Spirituality. If it is asked as to what is the most important single characteristic of Hinduism, it may be called spirituality. Religions are serviceable only so far as they are spiritual. When spirituality is missing, religion is a mere activity of men, powerful yet never a principle of guidance in his life. And spirituality is the very opposite of limitation, fixation, systematization. It is fulfilled by freedom which means the power to expand and grow towards perfection by the law of one's own nature. True religion, according to Sri Aurobindo, is the following of the spiritual impulse in its fulness, and spirituality is "the attempt to know and live in the highest self, the divine, the all-embracing unity and to raise life in all its parts to the divinest possible value."

In the evolution of religion upon earth, Hinduism, according to Sri Aurobindo, has opened the largest and profoundest spiritual possibilities to man. It is this which makes Hinduism a true religion as distinguished from sectarianism, dogmatism, narrow mindedness, the triune characteristics of religionism. In the words of Sri Aurobindo "True religion is spiritual religion, that which seeks to live in the spirit, in what is beyond the intellect, beyond the aesthetic and ethical and practical being of man, and to inform and govern these members of our being by the higher light and laws of the spirit."

3. Unity in Multiplicity. Another significant characteristic of Hinduism is a faith in unity in multiplicity. This faith originated since the beginning of Hinduism in Rigveda, according to which, "They call it Indra Mitra, Varuna and Agni. And also Heavenly, Beautiful Carutman: The Real is One, though sages name it variously..." Thus, while one finds polytheism and heathenism in Vedas, the most dominant tendency is monism, the realization of one in many. The Hindu philosopher, however, does not insist on unity in this formula, he permits multiplicity. He agrees with William James and Bertrand Russell that every one should worship a God who appeals to him most. The principle of unity in multiplicity in Hinduism can be observed not only in its philosophical works but also in the epics, *The Ramayana* and *The Mahabharata* and the innumerable devotional writings of the medieval saints and the contemporary Neo-vedanta thinkers, including Vivekanand, Ramkrishna, Ramtirtha, Annie Besent, R.N. Tagore, M.K. Gandhi and Sri Aurobindo. In the words of Sri Aurobindo, "A religion which is itself a congeries of religions and which at the same time provides each man with his own turn of inner experience, would be the most in consonance with this purpose of Nature; it would be a rich nursery of spiritual growth and flowering, a vast multiform school of the soul's discipline, endeavour, self-realisation." Unity in diversity is not only the characteristic of Hindu philosophy of religion but also its practical discipline. This is explicit in the general belief that the *summum bonum* may be achieved not by one path alone but by several paths, which may be selected according to one's disposition, tendencies, capacities and urges. Thus, Hinduism gives equal recognition to the path of knowledge, the path of devotion and the path of action for God realisation. The most significant point to be noted here is that all these paths are believed to be essentially one.

4. Diversity in Religious Practices. Thus, unlike other great religions of the world, Christianity, Islam, Buddhism, Zorastrianism etc., Hinduism does not insist upon a single set of religious activities, modes of worship and prayer, religious places, festivals, places of pilgrimage, rituals and beliefs etc. It is a congeries of different religious sub-systems within a wide religious system. Polytheism was characteristic of earliest Hindu religion as expressed through the Vedas. This polytheism, in spite of the philosophical evolution from polytheism through Henothism to monotheism, persists even today. In fact, it is the most significant characteristic of Hindu religion. The Hindu saints allowed the choice of Ista Devata by every individual being from a wide variety of gods and goddesses having widely different forms, characteristics and Nature, with consequent differences in their modes of worship and the fruits of religious Sadhana. Among the most notable gods are Brahma the deity of creation, Shiva the deity of destruction and Vishnu the deity of preservation. Of these, Shiva and Visnu have been widely worshipped in India giving rise to what are known as Shaiva cults and Vaishanava cults. These cults were further divided into several sub-cults, with a wide variety of distinctions in places of worship, forms of idols, modes of worship, beliefs and values, sacred books, places of pilgrimages, monastic orders and religious concepts of prayer, devotion, religious goals and religious practices etc.

All the above-mentioned three chief Gods have dozens of names and different sects have been organised around one single name giving rise to a wide variety of religious practices. Again, Hindus not only worship Shiva and Visnu but also their consorts Shakti and Lakshmi respectively. Worship of Shakti has given rise to the cult of Shakta. Leftist form of this cult worship Durga and Kali. Besides, mother worship in the form of so many goddesses has been an important feature of Hinduism. Of these the most important goddesses are Mahalakshmi, Mahasarasvati, Mahakali and Maheshwari.

5. Theory of Rebirth. A significant feature of Hindu religion is belief in rebirth. An individual or Jiva, according to Hindu philosophy of religion, migrates into innumerable births, assuming innumerable bodies according to the status of his consciousness which finally culminates into moksa when the individual is free from all desires for being embodied. According to Hindu eschatology, while the present birth is the result of past karmas, the future birth will be the result of the present karmas. So long as there are karmas there are bound to be rebirths. Therefore, if a man has to escape this cycle of rebirth he must escape from the cycle of karmas. Various prescriptions have been prescribed for this purpose by the Bhagwad Gita and other religious scriptures. It is believed that the cycle of rebirth can be broken by absolute surrender to Divine, whole hearted devotion, knowledge of Atman and Brahman and detached action in the world. Only liberation may lead to cessation of the cycle of karma and rebirth.

6. Theory of Reincarnation. Closely linked to the Hindu theory of rebirth is the theory of reincarnation. In fact, a characteristic of Hindu religion is the description of the life and activities of gods and goddesses on the pattern of human life and activities. Hindu religious writings are full of descriptions of the lives of various gods and goddesses which do not appear different from those of human being, only they exhibit human values in their highest degree. One significant name of the Divine, given by the Hindus, is Sachchidananda meaning the highest existence, consciousness and bliss. Thus, realisation of the God has been also interpreted as the realisation of the highest degree of human values as God is the reservoir of all human values. Just as man is subject to rebirth God is subject to reincarnation, only this reincarnation is self-built and self-planned. It is the divine promise of helping man in his journey of life by interfering in the world process from time to time to keep it on the right track. This promise has been given in the Bhagwad Gita, the most celebrated Hindu religious scripture. The theory of reincarnation has led to a whole mythology of various types of incarnations in the form of a boar, a fish, a human-lion form and the human forms characteristic of different ages. It is believed that in every age, God is reincarnated in a form most suitable for the uplift and well-being of the people. The theory of reincarnation is the substratum for the faith in Divine grace and help of mankind.

7. The Holy Scriptures. The holy scriptures of Hinduism are not only the works of religion but also the works of philosophy and even include sociology, psychology, economics, in fact most of the physical and social sciences in rudimentary form. The most important holy scriptures of the Hindus are as follows:

(i) *The Vedas or Samhitas.* This collection consists of four Vedas composed sometime between 1500 B.C. and 800 B.C., known as the Rig Veda, the Sama Veda the Yajur Veda and the Atharva-Veda.

(ii) *The Brahmanas.* This a large collection of supplements to the Samhitas, containing directions for the proper ritual use of the hymns and prayers.

(iii) *The Aranyakas.* The sacred writings represent a further collection of the Brahmanas, mainly for those who retire into the forest and are unable to perform ritual sacrifices.

(iv) *The Upanisads.* The Upanisads are a large collection of writings attached to the end of the Aranyakas. They are regarded as the basic philosophic frameworks of Hinduism.

(v) *The Bhagwad Gita.* This small work containing more than 700 couplets contains Hindu philosophy of religion in a most popular and brief form. Gita has been considered the main guide of Hindus not only in matters of religion but also in philosophy and Social life.

(vi) *The Epics.* Besides the above five traditional holy scriptures accepted by all the sects of Hindu religion, there are certain other notable holy scriptures of which the most important are the Epics. Epics are two: *The Mahabharata and The Ramayana.* Both these have been guiding Hindu religious life since their origin to the present date.

(vii) *The Dharmasaslras.* These are the systematic works which describe in great details the religious, social and daily duties of Hindus in different varnas and ashramas. Of these Manusmriti has been the most popular while Yajnavalkyasmriti is the most progressive.

(viii) *The Puranas.* The word purana means "ancient" and refers to a collection of ancient lore, mythological material on the genealogy of gods, sages and kings, and writings on the creation, destruction and recreation of the universe. The Puranas, eighteen of which are generally held to be authoritative, are considered to be the product of theistic developments during the first millenium A.D.

8. The Hindu Temple. The seat of religious activities of the Hindus is the temple. Each temple consists of idols of one or more gods and goddesses. The most famous temples have been built for the idols of the bigger gods and goddesses. Besides, there are great temples of the famous incarnations Rama and Krishna. These temples are found not only in every part of India but also in so many other countries of the world. The only Hindu state in the world is Nepal. However, patronage of political and wealthy persons is generally available to the temples. In villages, there are temples for local deities also. The modes of worship in different temples is sufficiently different. Among the more important temple deities in India are Rama, Krishna, Hanuman, Visnu, Shiva, Surya, Kali, Lakshmi, Sarasvati, Durga etc. In the temples of Kali, there is almost regular sacrifice of animals. This is not the case with any other type of Hindu temple. The temples also celebrate important occasions connected with the life of the leading deity. These are also places of social meeting, recreation, education and religious rituals and sanskaras. The temple holds a very important place in the life of a Hindu village. The expenses for the maintenance of the temple are met by donations as well as the rents of the property attached to them. Some temples in India have annual income running into millions of rupees. Besides the priest, some temples have a whole battalion of temple servants both males and females. In the temples of South India, one finds Deva Dasis meant for the service of the deity. While most of the Hindu temples are centres of religion, some of the big temples with large incomes and huge properties alongwith the institution like that of Deva Dasi abound in corruption.

9. Minor Religious Beliefs. Besides the philosophical beliefs already discussed, some minor beliefs are also connected to Hinduism. Their types are not peculiar to Hinduism as they are also found in other religions. However, their form may be considered peculiar. These include beliefs in ghosts and witches, faith in predicting power of the dreams, belief in good souls and evil souls both masculine and feminine, the ideas of auspicious and inauspicious days, things, activities and signs etc., religious considerations in dietary habits, considerations of good and bad omans, superstitions in natural phenomena and assumptions concerning the supernatural. These beliefs are very much influenced by local and regional conditions. Besides, Hindus believe in the worship of so many plants and animals giving different types of results. Some major rivers and mountains in different parts of the country are also worshipped. Different beliefs are current about different places of pilgrimage. These places of pilgrimage are scattered throughout the country, so that a Hindu making a tour of places of pilgrimage implies the idea of national unity, variety and richness.

10. Dynamism of Hindu Religion. In the end, the most important characteristic of Hindu religion, the secret of its longevity and eternity is its dynamism. Not only its modes of worship and religious practices but even the religious spirit have changed from time to time. The movements of reformation in 20th century in India have led to its reinterpretation according to modern consciousness. Movements like Brahmo Samaj and Arya Samaj tried to remove all sorts of superstitions from Hindu religion. Religious reformers and saints including Vivekananda, Ramkrishna, R.N. Tagore, M.K. Gandhi, Sri Aurobindo, Ramtirtha, Raman Maharishi and a host of others have reinterpreted Hinduism in our time, laying emphasis upon humanism, monism, world unity of all religions etc. They have tried to interpret Hindu religion as the religion of Man, the religion of Humanity, a brotherhood of religions, a vast multifarious vivid and lively, substratum for the meeting of men and women of different temperaments, dispositions and taeses with freedom to each of them to select a deity, a mode of worship and a type of man-God relationship according to his own leanings. This reinterpretation has attracted thousands of men and women from the West to the Hindu religion. Thus, among the world of religions today Hindu religion holds the promise for the creation of an ideal world of realisation of human values.

THE MUSLIMS

During the sixth century, the Arab states suffered a very great religious and social disillusionment that was expressed through the excesses of sex perversity, alcoholism, gambling and other similar activities. People of this country prayed to a variety of gods and goddesses. The men did no have much respect for women. The entire nation was divided into small principalities, the kings and caders of which engaged in unending squabbles. Arabs were prone to murder each other at the smallest provocation, since they did not attach any great value to human life. At such a time, in the year 570 Hazrat Mohammad was born in a trader's family in Mecca, to Abdullah and Amena, his father and mother respectively. His father had passed away before his birth, and when he was six years of age his mother also passed away. He was then looked after and brought up by his uncle Abutalab. When he grew up he took to trade and because of his honesty he came to be known as Amin, meaning one who can be trusted. At the age of twenty-five he married a forty-year old widow called Khadija, the first of a number of wives all of whom took active interest in Islam.

Even at a very early age Mohammed would fall into a trance and meditate upon God, and in the same condition he would preach to all those who collected to listen. Later on these sermons were collected and put together in the Koran. Mohammad launched a severe attack on the practice of idol worship. He insisted upon the equality of all men and the perversity of distinguishing between one another, on any pretext whatsoever. He also insisted that his disciples must perform, the following five activities kalama recitation, namaz, fasting, giving jakata or alms and going on Haj pilgrimage. On the one hand, these ideas were circulated among the people rapidly while on the other they were seriously objected, to by the Arabs as a result of which Mohammad was compelled to quit Mecca on 24 September 622 and proceed to Madina. From this date begins the Mohammadan calendar. In Madina Mohammad was given a lively reception and soon he had gathered around himself a group of devoted followers which he led with vigour as well as rigour. He established some rules the obedience to which was obligatory for his followers — rules such as praying with one's face turned towards Mecca, treating Friday as the holiday, fasting during the month of Ramzan, travelling to Kaba, etc. The practice helped to distinguish between his followers and the Jews and Christians.

Compilation of Koran

All the main tenets of Islamic religion are inscribed in the Koran, the religious text, the original form of which is believed to be inscribed on slates and placed in the seventh heaven. Literally, the term Koran means a lesson. As the legend goes, the Koran was read out to Mohammad by Jabril at the direction of Allah, and it was left to Mohammad to give it the form it has at present. All that Mohammad pronounced in a state of trance or meditation was written on pieces of leather or bark of trees, a process that continued for 32 years. After the death of Mohammad, Khalifa Abubakar collected all the inscriptions and compiled them into the Koran which contained 114 chapters of which 90 are collected at Mecca. The other twenty-four chapters are placed at Madina. Ninety smaller chapters are devoted to descriptions of the uniqueness of Allah, man's duty and the day of judgment or kayamat. Twenty-four main chapters are devoted to social organisation, conduct, thought, etc., in addition to the subjects covered by the smaller chapters.

Chief Tenets of Islam

Islam literally means entering peace, and it is believed that faith in this religion leads to the formation of peaceful relations between man and God. Islam has three main parts — Iman meaning religious faith, Ibadat meaning prayer or worship, and Ihasan meaning moral behaviour.

(a) *Iman.* Iman means the generation of faith, within one's own heart, in Allah, his angels, his agents and in the day of judgement. Mohammad was the prophet of Islamic religion and he is called Nabi and Rasul, the first meaning an agent or messenger of God, the second a religious messenger. For a Muslim it is essential to believe that Mohammad was a messanger of God and religious prophet. The basic tenet of Islamic religion means, when translated, that no one other than god deserves to be deified or prayed to or offered supplication and that

Mohammad is the religious messenger of God. According to Koran, it is kufr or wrong to refuse to believe in Allah and Rasul, and one who does not entertain such belief is called a kafir. According to the Koran, there is one Allah, who is detached and uninterested, yet at the same time he observes, enjoys, becomes angered at, takes pity on his disciples and destroys their enemies. Islam also professes faith in the angels or farishta to whom is delegated the responsibility of communicating the wishes of God to his messengers. Such angels were visible to Mohammad on account of his angelic vision.

(b) *Ibadat.* According to Islam, prayer to Allah does not require the presence of any idol or figure or any priest. Man should always remind himself of the existence of Allah. Ibadat has the following five steps:

1. Shahadat. Devoted repetition of the fundamental tenets of Islam is called Shahadat. This Islamic monistic thought which is called Tauhied, is based on this fundamental saying, which provides the religion with its own basic principles. One of these principles is that there is but one Allah and that Mohammad is his messenger.

2. Namaaz. Islam requires that each of its followers should repeat the prayer five times a day, facing towards Mecca, while on the holy day which is Friday, this prayer should be recited in a communal gathering.

3. Jakat. It is decreed that each Muslim shall contribute one fourtieth of his annual income, amounting to some two and a half per cent to the general fund which is utilized in the care of the unfortunate poor people and in the upkeep of the places of worship.

4. Roza. For a Muslim it is essential to fast during the month of Ramzan, for it believed that the Koran first arrived in the month of Ramzan. During the Roza the religious devotees eat only once a day after the setting of the sun.

5. Haj. It is believe essential for a Muslim to make at least one trip to Mecca Sharif and Madina, without incurring any debts for the journey. In this ritual, the visitor wears a gown and makes seven rounds of the Kaba which is called Tawaf. Besides, he makes seven trips between Alsafa and Marwaha and perform others actions prescribed in the ritual and sacrifice of a horned animal.

In addition to the above five steps which are part of ibadat. Jihad or religious war is also held essential by some sects among the Muslims. Jihad is of two kinds-jihade-asgar in which war is waged against the non-believers, while in jihade-akbar, the bigger war, man fights against his own instincts and drives, and wins over them.

(c) *Ihasan.* Ihasan literally means that man should avoid all bad actions and perform the good ones, as the two are distinguished by the Koran. Islam decrees that the highest action man is capable of is the complete subjugation of self to the will of God through knowledge or ilm and action or amala. This objective has validity for individual as well as social life.

Sufism

Many different meanings are attributed to the term Sufi. From the philosophical standpoint the sufi sect leans towards the mystic tradition, while taken etymologically the word implies anything which is extracted from wool. Sufi was the term applied to those individuals who went through life wearing a woollen gown, spending their life in meditation and prayer. Other scholars are of the opinion that the term Sufi is derived from the root Suffa which is applicable to the platform built by Mohammad in the mosque at Madina. Hence, the term sufi applied to those benevolent and pure but homeless people who spent their time sitting on this platform and meditating upon this life and the hereafter. According to Gazzali, the term sufi implies a man's remaining at peace with the world, in meditation upon God.

The term sufi was first applied in 816 A.D. to Abu Hashim, an individual belonging to Sham. In the ninth century, the sufi sect was famous throughout Iraq with Baghdad as its centre. During the tenth century Abu Yajid Jabaid and Mansoor Alhajaaj propagated monistic ideas. It is believed that Sufi Mansoor came to India and that he studied yoga and advaita Vedanta in this country and was punished for this by being poisoned to death at the hands of his enemies. It was Sheikh Muhiuddin Ibnul Arabi who took up the burden of propagating the sect after the death of Mansoor. Such famous Persian poets as Iraqi and Kirntani gave expression to the beliefs of this sect. In the eleventh century, Alagazzali tried to reconcile Islam and the Sufi philosophy. Sufis believe in a single God who is truth or hak, goodness or khaira and beauty or jamal. The entire universe is believed to be an appearance of the manifestation of God, and it is only on account of his folly and over-weaning arrogance that man considers himself to be distinct from God. Every Sufi aims at the destruction of this blinding arrogance, and the only means to this end is the love of God. Sufis believe that corporeal or physical love is a step in the achievement of a supernatural love for God since physical love acquaints man with the difficulties that beset this path and prepares him for journey along the path of supernatural love. Sufi disciples believed that God was their beloved and spent their entire time and life in waiting for the moment when they would glimpse her.

THE CHRISTIANS

Teachings of Christ

The Sermon on the Mount contains the very essence of all that Christ sought to teach The most important statements of his faith are the following:

Blessed are the poor in spirit for theirs is the kingdom of heaven Blessed are the meek; for they shall inherit the earth.

Blessed are the merciful; for they shall obtain mercy.

Blessed are the peacemakers; for they shall be called the children of God.

Think not that I have come to destroy the law or the prophets, I have not come to destroy but to fulfil.

"Ye have heard that it was said by them of old time, Thou shalt not kill; and whosoever shall kill shall be in danger of the judgment: but I say unto you, that whosoever is angry with his brother without a cause shall be in danger of the judgement.

The teachings of Jesus differed radically from the teachings of such old prophets as Moses, and he himself shed light on this difference. He said, "Ye have heard, it hath been said. An eye for an eye and a tooth for a tooth: But I say unto you, that ye resist not evil: but whosoever shall smite thee on thy right cheek, turn to him the other also." Before the coming of Christ it had always been suggested that one should love one's neighbour and hate one's enemies. But Christ opposed this and said, "But I say unto you, Love your enemies, bless them that curse you, do good to them that hate you and pray for them who respitefully use you and persecute you; that ye may be the children of your Father who is in heaven; for he maketh his sun to rise on the evil and on the good, and sendeth rain on the just and the unjust."

Without going into the deeper ramifications of Christian religion one can understand from the foregoing account of the teachings of Christ that his religious thought emphasises the need for non-violence, truth, love, pity, forgiveness, humility, purity, peace, sympathy, friendship and other divine qualities. In this lies the secret of the success of this appeal and the tremendous response to it.

Impact of Christianity on Indian Society and Religion

In the social sphere the influence of Christianity has comprehended much of the social organization since it has effected the family, marriage, caste system, modes of dress, living, and life in general.

1. Influence on Family. In the main, Christian influence on Indian families is evident in the breakdown of the joint family, growth of progressively smaller families, reduction in male dominance within the family, growth of independence of women and general instability of the family institution as such.

2. Influence upon Marriage. As a result of contact with the Christians, members of Indian society came to look down upon child marriage and to encourage late marriages. The basis of marriage changed from ritual to love, and even the methods of marriage ceremonies underwent considerable modification. On the other hand, the relationship itself took on a temporary nature though at the same time monogamy was encouraged. Caste is no longer regarded as an important factor in marriage. On the other hand, many people feel encouraged to remain bachelors, for such a state is on longer considered abnormal.

3. Awakening in Women. As a result of Christian influence and teaching, a new awakening began to spread among the women of India, and the westernized education that they received made them self-reliant and effective competitors of men in all fields. Apart from this many of our women took over the western mode of dress.

4. Effect on caste System. One of the major advantages of Christian influence has been the reduction in the sense of untouchability, and this was achieved by the untouchable caste, who converted to Christianity so that they could equal the higher castes. This helped to remove the superstition from many Indian eyes and there is no general expression of the feeling of untouchability.

5. Effect on Life in General. Influence of Christianity can be seen in every sphere of Indian life, changes in the dietary habits, use of furniture, improvement in the standard of living, dress, interest in hair styles, use of cosmetics, mode of greeting and a hundred and one other forms. Many of the changes listed above can be seen in Indians who belonged here many hundreds of years ago, but in the present times these changes are the result of Christian influence.

6. Conversion. One immediate effect of Christian religion was that many Hindus changed their religion, but then the more intelligent among the Hindus felt impelled to modify their own religion. Besides, the Christians initiated numerous movements aiming at social and religious reform within the country, the more important groups being the Brahmo Samaj, Prarthana Samaj, Ramakrishna Mission and Theosophical Society. It was left to the Arya Samaj to protect Hindu religion.

THE SIKHS

Teaching of Guru Nanak

During Nanak's period religion was marred by an excess of ritualistic details and discrimination between man and man, and he felt the necessity of opposing both these practices. He advocated that there was one God and that there was no need to discriminate between one man and another. While some elements in his teaching resembled the thought of Kabir and other religious thinkers, much of his thought is apparently unique. He resembles Kabir inasmuch that he too laughed at the external ornament which had become an inseparable part of religious practice. He believed that everything that happened occurred by the will of God, and that those who professed to be the followers of God should not exercise discrimination. Like Kabir he communicated his teaching to the poor and backward sections of society, since he too believed that God resides where the poor, helpless and sick were tended to by those, who are capable of such service. He advocated the giving of alms, not merely in money but also in love. He contradicted Kabir in that he did not object to the eating of meat, provided that the animal to be eaten had been killed by a single stroke. Guru Nanak related cleanliness of mind to the cleanliness and purity of body. Most of his teachings were intended for those engaged in social intercourse, not only for those who had renounced the world. In the main, all his teaching and preaching was conducted through the medium of a simple and unostentatious language, which accounts in part for the large following his system of thought had.

Guru Govind Singh's Contribution

Two hundred years after Guru Nanak, Guru Govind Singh was born in Patna, while in the intervening period the Sikh religion had grown into a military organisation. When Gum Teg Bahadur passed away Govind Singh was only IS years old, and in order to ensure his safety from Mughal aspirations he was sent to Anandpur by his followers. He spent the next twenty years here in a peaceful atmosphere and devoted his time to the study of Hindu religious texts. In his work *Dasven Padshah ka granth* are included the stories of Chandi and numerous stories of Hindu heroes of times gone by. By including these tales Govind Singh succeeded in connecting Sikh religion with its origin in the Hindu religion. His main objective was to protect Hindu religion, and it was this determination which led him to proclaim himself the head of the Hindu nation in 1665 when he came out of his voluntary exile.

It is not easy to find any other individual who has done as much as Govind Singh managed in the short span of 42 years. On the one hand lies his profound scholarship evident from the books composed by him, while on the other is his valuable contribution to the Sikh community in the form of organisation and unity that he created within the Khalsas. It was through his efforts that the Punjab that had been ruled with an iron hand by the Mughals for some 600 years found its feet and its courage once again. A century and a half after his death the final blow was dealt to Mughal hopes in the Punjab. As a politician Gum Govind Singh exhibited exceptional foresight. He declared that after him no human being should assume the title of Gum and that the only Gum of the Sikhs would be the Granth Sahib, the religious text of this community. This text is a compilation of the preaching of all the ten saints of this religion, beginning with Gum Nanak and ending with Gum Govind Singh. Besides, it should be remembered that during his lifetime he led not only the Sikhs but also the entire Hindu nation, and it was one of his desires to serve Hindu religion through the medium of the Khalsa sect. This helped him to revive the almost extinct qualities of the kshatriyas. Undoubtedly, Gum Govind Singh can be credited with spear heading the birth of a Hindu nationalism in Punjab.

THE BUDDHISTS

During a walk outside his palace, Siddhartha Gautam came upon an old person, an ill, a dead and a hermit and was profoundly stirred by the sight whereupon he renounced his kingly pleasures and ventured forth in search of truth. He found the causes of suffering and means of removing them. Obtaining this knowledge he was titled 'Buddha'. This knowledge is comprehended in four Noble Truths.

The four noble truths are — there is suffering, there are causes of suffering, cessation of suffering and path of liberation. These four Noble Truths are the foundation stones of Buddhist philosophy and they also reflect the entire cycle of Gautam's spiritual life originated in consciousness of suffering while the consummation was the discovery of means of escaping suffering. In this way,

Gautam's spiritualism is based on solid realism. It is this unique feature which is the reason for the wide popularity of his thoughts.

Eightfold Path

From the philosophical and moral view, Buddha has adopted middle path There are two limits which the aspirant should never approach. On the one hand, pleasures of sensual objects, interest in passions, a low, uncultured, deplorable and undirected pleasure seeking meant only for the low people and on the other hand, the habit of suppressing the self which is painful, worth discarding and useless. Buddha has discovered a middle path which opens the eyes, and which guides towards peace and insight, supreme wisdom and nirvana. Actually, it is only the noble eightfold path.

1. Right Vision. The first means in Buddha's eightfold path is right vision Ignorance generates a wrong view regarding the relation between the world and self, and man mistakes a transient, painful and unspiritual object for a permanent, blissful and spiritual one. The abandoning of this fallacious view and attending to the real nature of objects is said to be right vision. In this way, unflinching meditation on the four noble truths is proper view. This meditation takes one towards nirvana.

2. Right Resolve. The second means is right resolve. The determination to root out thoughts which entertain ill-will towards others and contemplate their harm and attachment to sensual pleasures, is right resolve. The noble truths can be profitable only if life is led according to them. Proper volition should be with a proper view. Proper volition includes sacrifice, benevolence and sympathy.

3. Right Speech. The third means is right speech. As a first step, man should control his speech by right resolve. Right speech means avoidance of falsity, criticism, unlikable and false speech. Every man should avoid bad and adopt good speech One word calming the mind is better than innumerable meaningless sounds.

4. Right Conduct. The fourth means is proper conduct, which means forbearing from activities like destruction of life, theft, sexuality, falsifying, excessive eating, visiting social recreations, artificial means of beauty, jewellery, use of comfortable beds and gold etc. All these laws apply to hermits But married people need obey only five laws. Ordinary people have a number of other laws. Parents should protect their children from evil quality and cultivate good qualities in them, and marry them after their education is over. The offsprings should make themselves noble by serving their aged parents. The students should study, respect their teachers, obey them and fulfil their needs The teachers should behave lovingly towards them and perfect them in the arts and sciences by cultivating good habits in them. The husband should respect his wife, be faithful to her and look after her welfare. The wife should behave lovingly towards her husband, manage the home efficiently, be hospitable to all guests and exemplify marital fidelity. Continuing in the same vein, Buddha has made a detailed description of laws regulating the mutual behaviour between various people related socially. He has preached the lesson of sacrifice, benevolence and sympathy to the multitude in its entirety. His laws aim at making both society and the individual happy. Considering these laws no one can declare Buddha to be an escapist.

5. Right Livelihood. Right livelihood means earning one's bread and butter by right means. Without it right activity cannot be fully practiced. According to Buddha, one should not trade in weapons, animals, meat, wine, etc. It is never good for any person to earn his money, by unfair and bad means like pressure, fraud, bribe, extortion, chicanery, dacoity etc.

6. Right Effort. Along with the obedience of law regarding view, volition, speech, action and livelihood, it is also necessary to stop bad impressions and avoid bad feelings. Endeavouring to this end is called right effort. It includes self-control, negation of sensibility, stopping bad thoughts, awakening good thoughts and concentrating the mind upon universal welfare. Four modes of restricting bad thoughts have been advocated:

(i) Meditate upon some good thought.

(ii) Study the results of acting upon bad thoughts.

(iii) Analyse the causes of bad thoughts and stop its results.

(iv) Control the mind by physical effort. Obedience of dharma depends upon the mind, upon the obedience of dharma is dependent on the attainment of liberation. In this way, even a person who has made some progress along the spiritual path, needs proper exercise in order to eliminate the risk of a lapse in future.

7. Right Mindfulness. Right mindfulness means the retention of the body, conscience and mental states in their real form. Bad thoughts occupy the mind only by forgetting their real form and when action takes place according to them, pain must be suffered and the tendencies become stronger. Right mindfulness includes the remembering of impurities of the body, pleasure, nature of suffering, nature of pain, hatred, and doubtful mind, five skandhas, senses, object of senses, means of liberation and the four noble truths. Right mindfulness destroys attachment and releases one from pains.

Gautama Buddha described right mindfulness meticulously. He preached that body should be treated as constituted of earth, water, fire and air, is filled, it must be remembered, with deplorable things like bones, skin, intestines, spleen, urine etc. One should see the burning of the body in a crematorium, its destruction, conversion to food for vultures and dogs and becoming dust. Remembering these truths makes one forget or lose love and attachment for one's own or another's body. Due to this, the attachment for other bad tendencies is also destroyed. It results in complete lack of passions and elimination of pains. In this way, man avoids worldly attachment due to the effect of right mindfulness.

8. Right Concentration. By pursuing the seven laws propounded above, man's tendencies of the chitta or mind are pacified and he becomes capable of entering right concentration. Before nirvana is attained, right concentration has four stages:

(i) In the first stage, the four noble truths are mediated upon with a calm mind. Pure and detached thought creates unique happiness.

(ii) In the second stage, efforts like meditation are suppressed and reasoning becomes unnecessary, doubts are removed and faith in noble truths increases. Here intuition replaces thought. Profound contemplation results in peace and permanence in the mind. At the same time, bliss and peace are sensed.

(iii) The third stage is one of indifference. Here the endeavour is to remove happiness and introduce indifference in the mind. In this the mind is in equilibrium, but one becomes indifferent to the happiness of concentration.

(iv) The stage of absolute peace is the fourth stage in which pleasure and pain are destroyed. In it the tendencies of the mind are negated. It is a state of perfect peace, perfect indifference and perfect negation. In it, pains are completely destroyed and nirvana obtained.

Buddhist Contribution to Indian Culture

In view of the fact that Buddhist religion continued to grow and propagate for eleven hundred years in India, it cannot occasion surprise that this religion thus, left a deep and indelible impression on the social, cultural, political, and literary and chiefly the religious aspect of life in India Its contribution can be summed up under the following heads:

1. Influence upon Hindu Religion. Hindu religion has been considerably influenced by Buddhist ethics and religious thinkings, although, the latter did not in any degree overwhelm Hindu religion. The chief stress in Buddhist thought was on the practice of ahimsa or non-violence and on the necessity of maintaining an attitude of love and sympathy towards all living beings. Later on, when the Brahmanic religion stressed the need for non-violence it was a derivation from Buddhist thought. The Bhagavat school, which is particularly responsible for this humanitarian attitude in Hindu thought, owes much to Buddhist influence

2. Intellectual Freedom. Perhaps the most important contribution of Buddhist thought lies in its direction to the individual to think for himself and in its assertion that independent intellectual activity assists man's development Brahmanic religion had managed to blunt man's intellectual perceptivity through its excessive rituals and the stress on the repetition of dogma which could be handled only by its priests Man's function at that time was to follow the Vedic laws faithfully, to do and die, but not to question why It was Buddhist religion which provided an antidote to this poison, compelled man to cogitate on the value of his own thoughts and actions, appealed to his reason and aroused in him a respect for its innate simplicity and greatness Buddhism led the revolt against Vedic religion and all that this stood for The religious and philosophical notions of the Buddhists are the result of independent and ambitious thinking on the part of Gautama and the more gifted of his disciples. The fact that Buddhist thought is rooted in dependent thinking which revolted against the religious and social contribution of Vedic religion adds to its value both in the fields of religion as well as of philosophy.

3. Equality and Benevolence. Buddha propagated the values of equality among all individuals found in society, irrespective of caste, colour, creed, social position and eminence. Every individual could seek sanctuary and be given it in his monastries which welcomed everyone who came there. Differences of age, sex and caste were discarded. Its appeal to the human imagination consists in its rejection of caste differences and the lesson of benevolence which it sought to inculcate Many were the princes and kings who were influenced by the Buddhist love of benevolence, non-violence, pity, piety and love.

4. Greatness of its Ethical Theory. Buddha directed his disciples to live in simplicity, following a commonly accepted moral code of social behaviour His eightfold path has great ethical implications that make it an invaluable contribution to ethical thought. It lays stress not only on moral laws concerning pity, self-renunciation, truthfulness, temperate conduct, but also on love, pity, benevolence, equality, non-violence and forgiveness. This does not imply that before Buddha these qualities had been unknown but simply that they had not been able to make a place for themselves in the general scheme of things in society. The greatness of Buddhist religion consists in its success in propagating these ideas among the common people and in conveying its message from door to door It was among the first schools of thoughts which opposed the deterministic trend of Vedic religion by trying to convince the people that man is the architect of his own destiny and that no one, not even God, can interfere in the working out of man's destiny. Buddhism compelled man to initiate a fresh self examination and self-analysis and to a realization of the importance of the greatness of man's action in the whole that constituted his life. In these terms it is possible to conceive of Buddhism as an independent religion.

5. The Simplicity, Naturalness and Intellectual Bias of Buddhism. Buddha advocated the formation of a religion which was not marred by any complex system of ritualistic performances or any intellectual abstraction that took it far away from normal reality. It was a religion which the average individual could understand without any undue strain to his rather limited resources of the mind. Above all, it was not a religion confined to an erudite few. Its success in capturing the hearts of simple folk can be explained by its striking naturalness, integrity of sentiment, use of the vernacular, philosophical simplicity and candour, the use of parables to explain involved religious concepts.

6. Contribution to the Literature in Vernacular. Buddhism achieved immediate success because its propagators had the intelligence to use the language which was spoken by the people to whom they were trying to communicate their message. This led to an unprecedented growth in the prakrat language which prevailed at the time in those regions, all the more so since Buddha himself preached through the medium of this language. Besides, it achieved the very desirable effect of communicating the lesson to every individual since they were delivered practically at every door-step.

7. Buddhist Contribution to Art. Another contribution of Buddhist religion to Indian culture is in the field of architecture and sculpture. Immediately, before the advent of Buddhism the Vedic period had been one of static rather than dynamic cultural activity, and it was left to Buddhist religion to inspire the creative arts. Today, there is a single archaeological museum which does not contain some specimen of Buddhist art, for it was during the period of Buddhist religion that painting, sculpture and architecture developed all over the country. There was an outburst of architectural creation which took the form of temples, pillars, cave sculptures and gardens containing statues. In these creations the entire life cycle of Gautama is eternally recreated on stone on which it will continue to exist till eternity. These pieces of art depict remarkable beauty, expressive of the creativity of the age and of its people. Some of these pieces are reckoned to be among the finest examples of sculpture in the world. The pillar at Sanchi, the Ashoka pillar at Amaravati and the figurines found in Kanehari, Karle and Nasik are among the finest examples. Beauty which is expressed in the sculpture at Ajanta has caused universal respect for Buddhist art.

8. Effect of Buddhism on Indian History. The influence of Buddhism on Indian history in its political aspects will remain for ever, since it was Buddhism which generated a sense of horror at bloodshed and war among the princes of India. The teachings of Buddha have had continuous repercussions in the course of subsequent history, apparent more particularly in the case of Ashoka who dramatically renounced the path of bloody conquering and turned to peaceful propagation of his ideals. Thus, it was Buddhism which was responsible for the respect in which Ashoka is held not only in India but also abroad.

9. Spread of Indian Culture Abroad. Buddhist religion helped to spread the elements of Indian culture in foreign countries, wherever Buddhist religion found its feet. Indian culture as reflected in Buddhist thought did much to render other peoples cultured, and this was made possible by the flexibility which characterised Buddhist religion because it helped it to adapt to conditions completely dissimilar from the ones it had found in India. This was India's greatest contribution to international development in that period. From 3 B.C. to the seventh century after Christ, intellectuals and saints propagated Indian culture through the medium of this religion and managed to modify other cultures by leaving a deep imprint of their own culture. Even today, one can find relics of Indian culture in countries in which Buddhist religion continues to be venerated and followed.

THE JAINS

Life History of Mahavira

Mahavira was the son of Katak's sister, Katak being the king of Vaishali, Katak's daughter had been married to Bimbasara, and therefore, Mahavira was related to the kings of Magadh and Vaishali. He was born in 599 B.C. in a small village named Kund which was near Vaishali, the capital of the defunct royal house of

Vajji. Vaishali is located in the Muzaffarpur district of Northern Bihar. Mahavira was born into the family of Siddhartha who was a kshatriya chief. He was named Vardhman during his infancy and he spent his early life comfortably. He was then married to a princess named Yashoda and a daughter named Priyadarshana was born to them. This girl was then married to Jamali, Mahavira's nephew who later on became one of Mahavira's disciples. When Mahavira was 28 his father passed away. Mahavira himself had shown a tendency to meditate right from the beginning of his life, and now after the death of his father he gave up his domestic life with the permission of his elder brother and went into the forest. After twelve years of deep meditation and concentration he received illumination, and thereupon he returned to the world to spend the rest of his life in the service of mankind and in religious preaching. This latter part of his life was spent in Magadh and the neighbouring areas. The fact that he belonged to the royal family helped him considerably in his preaching and men tended to be less obstinate to his preaching then they would otherwise be. One reason of his success in capturing the imagination of the public was that, like Buddha, he insisted on talking to the people in their own tongue. He also established a union in which me of every caste could find admittance. In 527 B.C., he finally resigned his physical body at the age of 72 in Pawa, the capital of Malla kingdom. Many were the names by which he was addressed, among them Jin, Kevalin, Mahavira. He was called Jin because he had managed to control and to subdue the sense organs; since he was extremely powerful and endowed with superlative qualities he was also called Mahavira.

History of Jaina Religion

The tradition of Jaina religion is traced back to the Vedic times on the basis of the evidence of Rishabhadeva and Arishtanemi. At the time of the Mahabharata war the group was headed by Neminatha who is considered to be one of the Teerthankaras. The twenty-third teerthankara Parshavanatha, was born in 8 B.C. and was responsible for organising the shramana sect of Jaina religion. He was opposed to the shraman vedic ritual. During the time of Mahavira and Buddha some of these shramanas turned Jaina and some turned Buddhist.

Mahavira was the last teerthankara of Jaina religion, and he managed to put the religion on very strong footing before his death. He was among the first to put the principle of non-violence on a firm footing. One consequence of this was that his sect remained organised and well knit even after he had passed away.

At the time of Alexander's invasion of India some Jaina monks were settled along the banks of the river Indus, whether Chandragupta Maurya accepted the Jaina religion or not cannot be determined with any degree of certainty but Ashok's writings prove that Jaina religion was fairly popular at the time. At about this time the Jaina monks living in monastries splitted into two groups over the question of whether the statues of the teerthankaras should be clothed before being exhibited or they should be exhibited in the nude. This also raised the allied problem whether the monks and saints between the two distinct groups to such an extent that by the first century after Christ two distinct groups had been formed, the digambers and the shvetambars. The former remained naked while the latter wore white clothes, as is evident by their respect titles.

In the Maurya period, one group of shramans left for the South under the leadership of Bhadrabahu while another group remained in Mysore to propagate their religion. Kharvel, the king of Kalinga during the first century, accepted Jaina religion. In the earlier centuries after Christ Mathura in the north and Mysore in the South were important centres of Jaina religion. Between the fifth and the twelfth century the Jaina religion found its supporters among the kings of the Gang, Kadamb, Chalukya and Rashtrakuta dynasties of the South. Many Jaina poets also lived at the court of these kings. King Siddharaj and his son Kumarpal, both belonging to the Chalukya dynasty, adopted Jainism as the religion of their state and helped to spread it extensively in Gujarat. Hemchand a Jain scholar lived at the court of Kumarpal. At one time even the Rajputs contributed their mite to spread this religion. Since, the Jainas were quite peaceable they escaped much of the pain and suffering inflicted by the Muslims on followers of other religions. This gain was not merely negative, for Akbar not only saved them from suffering but helped the religious sect in a more positive manner. But slowly the Jaina monastries fell on evil days and disintegrated so that by the end of the Moghal reign over India they had completely lost their influence. At the present time, the followers of Jaina religion do not number more than three millions and the majority of them are traders.

Digambar and Shvetambar Sects

According to the Jaina texts and mythology, two hundred years after the death of Mahavira, the kingdom of Magadh faced famine during the reign of Chandragupta Maurya. The famous Jaina monk Bhadrabahu departed from Magadh along with some of his followers on account of the famine and settled in Kamatak. In his absence the Jainas of Magadh studied and edited their religion. After the famine came to an end the Jainas who had deserted Magadh had undergone much change, noticeably in respect of dress as these people had taken to white dress. But, the people of Kamatak had continued to live according to the old traditions of living in the nude. For this reason, the Jaina belonging to the two towns came to be called shvetambar and digambar respectively. One outcome of this controversy was that the religious texts authenticated by the shvetambars were not accepted as authentic by the digambars. One evidence of this disagreement lies in the fact that the latter do not accept many parts of the religious texts as authentic. These two sects had been separated somewhere between 79 and 82 A.D. In the fourth century before Christ a meeting of the Jainas had gathered to give a scholarly rendering of the Jaina texts, but these works got their final form only in 445 A.D. at Ballabhi. Jaina religion has forty-eight religious texts, though they are accepted as authentic only by the shvetambar group. There is no difference or disagreement or principle between the two sects since their differences are limited to the sphere of moral thinking and religious behaviour.

CONTRIBUTION OF JAIN RELIGION TO INDIAN CULTURE

1. Folk Literature and the Rise of Folk Languages. In spite of the fact that it is a small group Jaina religion has made important contributions to the development of a folk literature and language. Brahmanic literature was written in Sanskrit while that of the Buddhists was in Pali but it was Jaina religion which turned to the local vernacular in every part of the country to which they penetrated and in which they wanted to spread their religion. A sizeable part of their literature is written in Pali. In this way, Jaina religion helped in the development and growth of Prakrat language, and more than that, it was the first to encourage many of the folk languages to turn into literature. Mahavira himself delivered his sermons in Ardh Magadhi in order to make them comprehensible to those who understood Magadhi or Saurseni languages. His sermons which have been compiled into a single book called *Shrutanga*, which contains twelve chapters, are in Ardh Magadhi. Recently, a considerable store of Jaina literature was discovered, written in a language which is the predecessor of such modern Indian languages as Hindi, Gujarati and Marathi. This literature is written in Apbhransha. This Language is a kind of link between the vedic languages such as Sanskrit and Apbhransha on the one hand, and the modern Indian languages that are spoken in various parts of India, on the other. For this reason, this language is of great importance for the linguist and his disciples. It is possible that the literature of the South may hold a key to the motivating force behind Jaina thought. Even, the ancient literature of Kannada is not unaffected by Jainism. The Jainas have written some of their religious texts in Sanskrit, and it would be no exaggeration to state that they have created a great philosophical and creative literature in that language. Jains have even exercised their mind on such technical topics as Mathematics, Grammar, Philology etc.

2. Development of Architecture. Jain religion was at its highest *point* of achievement and influence during the eleventh and twelfeth centuries. Like the Buddhists the Jainas also built stupas to honour their saints. The stupas found in Mathura are the oldest of this kind of architecture. One can find figurines of the eleventh and twelfth centuries in Bundelkhand. At Bejola and Karkal, two places in Mysore, one can see large statues of Gomteswhar, Examples of Jaina sculpture can be found in the rock around Gwalior, dating back to the fifteenth century. Jainas had also built temples by hollowing out vaces during the second century. Examples of this can be found in the Hathi Gumpha cave in Orissa. Jaina temples are to be found in Parshavanath, Pavapuri and Rajgiri in Bihar, as well as at Girnar and 'Palitana' in Kathiara. Statues that are found in these temples represent Jain art at its best. The Jaina temple at Mount Abu in Rajasthan is a living example of the intellectuality and aesthetic sense of the followers of this religion.

Buddhist religion has practically vanished from this country but Jaina religion continues to exist even to the present day, a fact which can be explained in the light of two facts — the first, that the majority of the Jainas belong to the trading class, the second, that with the passage of time the gulf between Jaina religion and

Brahman religion tended to reduce. Another direct cause of the survival of Jaina religion is its explicit faith in non-violence and peace. It is this principle which is primarily responsible for the happy position in which Jaina religion is to be found. Yet, in spite of all this achievement, Jaina religion could not extend the sphere of this influence beyond certain well defined limits. Even within the bounds of the country it did not spread very far. It failed to achieve wide popularity on account of the following reasons — inflexibility of dogmas, steady progress and growth of Brahmanic religion, lack of intellectual independence to some extent, failure to enlist the aid of enthusiastic religious preachers, having to function without the protection and moral support of any major king, theoretical objection to caste discrimination but prejudicial behaviour towards individuals of the higher castes.

QUESTIONS FOR EXERCISE

1. What is Hinduism? Discuss its characteristics.
2. Discuss the birth and main tenets of Islam.
3. Write short note on Sufism.
4. What are the teachings of Christ? Discuss the impact of Christianity on Indian society and religion.
5. What are the teachings of Guru Nanak? What is the contribution of Govind Singh to Sikhism?
6. Outline the main teachings of Buddha.
7. Discuss Buddhist contribution to Indian culture.
8. Discuss the contribution of Jain religion to Indian culture.

17

Contemporary Social Change

The feature of unity in diversity in Indian culture presented in an earlier chapter, is but one aspect of the contemporary social scene. The second aspect would be the description of the nature, directions and factors of social change in India. In this chapter, a brief description of this aspect would be given.

1. Change in Social Philosophy. Nothing is static in this universe. No human society remains the same for all times. The social change is natural to all societies and the Indian Society is no exception to this rule. Therefore, a historical survey of any period would reveal that alongwith economic, political and ideological changes, social changes are also taking place. In our country, the process of integration and disintegration of states has always been going on. At times, small states came together to become an empire and, at other times, big empires split into small units. This dual process has had its varying impact on the social structure. The formation of big states cemented the unity among people and their disintegration encouraged diversity. The viewpoints in social philosophy in India have always been in a melting pot. It is, of course, a fact that in comparison with Western countries, social change has been much less rapid in India and this truth can be more clearly brought out in the discussion on 'Tradition and Modernity'. However, this should not give us the impression that there is no tangible social change in India. Whenever, any particular viewpoint in social philosophy became ascendant, its rival viewpoint appeared on the scene. For example, atheistic ideologies of Charvaka, Buddhism and Jainism appeared on the scene in reaction against the Vedic ritualism. They opposed orthodoxy and traditionalism. This reaction gave birth to many social changes. Historically, these changes were harmful to the country. For example, the spread of Buddhism eroded into the defense potential and protective capability of the country. In order to revitalize the society, the ideology of Vedanta came to the fore. Adi Shankaracharya refurbished in a powerful form the ancient Indian philosophy and its powerful impact virtually drove Buddhism away from its land of birth. In the modern times, there was a social reaction against the long period of slavery to the British influence. In the contemporary India, the thinkers like Aurobindo, Mahatma Gandhi, Rabindra

Nath Tagore, Radhakrishanan, Vivekananda, Rama Krishna and Dayananda presented the ancient philosophy of Vedanta in the modern garb. In this reaction two varying ideologies are clearly to be seen. On the one hand, thinkers like Dayananda revived the ancient Vedic philosophy and the thinkers like Aurobindo and Radhakrishnan tried to harmonize it with the Western thought. On the other hand, contemporary thinkers like M.N. Roy presented a new rationalist outlook under the impact of materialist and naturalist philosophies. This brief analysis clearly shows that the slow change in the ideological structure of social philosophy has been taking place in India and that it has never been so rapid or sharp as to sever the link with the tradition. From this point of view, it can be maintained that the social change in India has been by and large tradition bound.

2. Change in Social Institutions. In the Indian Society, we can perceive a constant change in the traditions and social practices. In the spheres of family, marriage, caste system, social, economic and political institutions there have taken place significant changes. The joint families are now shrinking and are now gradually turning into nuclear families. There is also significant change in the system of marriage. The child marriage in now illegal and has become a rare phenomenon. The re-marriage of widow is now taking place. The women have been granted the share in the property of their parents and husbands. Now, they are also free to adopt a child. The spread of education among women has made them enlightened and they are now participating in every walk of life. In urban areas, they have become much more mobile. As women are now stirring out of their homes in order to earn their livelihood, a considerable change in the structure of the Indian society is taking place.

3. Changes in Caste System. In modern India, caste system is an outcome of a long period of Varna system which is mentioned in Vedas over the period of its development, it has been undergoing changes. Many castes sprung up in the process of this change and the castes have competed with each other to gain a higher status in the society. In this struggle for supremacy, many castes did succeed in improving their social status. Thus, in the social hierarchy, the status of some castes has gone up, but, on the whole, there is little change in the caste system. The role of castes in panchayats which used to exercise great influence on its members has got diluted somewhat. Gradually, the number of these panchayats has also dwindled. In contemporary India, due to political factors, the castes are gaining in importance and influence, but, on the other hand, the spread of education, industrialization, urbanization and democratic forces militate against the strength and influence of castes. The future form of caste system in India is rather uncertain. But, however, this much is certain that this system has never been constant and same in the course of its history and that it is bound to undergo change in the future.

4. Jajmani System. In India, the economic structure of the society was never divorced from the social structure. Generally, the two have been closely inter-linked. For example, the relations between the members of various castes in the rural India are governed by the Jajmani system. Jajmani system determines both the economic and social relations. Under the Jajmani system certain castes are Jajmans of other castes. The relationship of Jajmani is governed by traditions and Jajmaniship is transferable also. In contemporary India, on account of changes in the caste system and particularly due to political awakening in the lower castes the Jajmam system is picking up. Now, the relations among the members of various castes are governed not by Jajmani system but by economic and political considerations.

5. Industrial Change. The social changes in India have been considerably affected by the industrial and technological changes. In comparison to other countries there is a gap between the social and technical changes in this country. However, as a consequence of contact with Western countries rapid adoption of new techniques of production, communication, distribution and management is taking place. The metropolitan towns of India compare favourably with western metropolises in respect of technical advancement. But, on the other hand, the social relations in India and West are quite different. Though, social changes have taken place everywhere, but in India, the social change is very slow compared to the Western countries. In the Asian countries, a rapid industrial and social change has taken place in Japan but such a change has not occurred in India. An important causal factor for the disparity between the industrial and social change in our country is political. In the struggle for independence our political leaders also gave call for Indianization. The Britishers wanted to encourage industrialization and westernization in India. The Swadeshi movement proved to be a hinderance in this process and an attempt was made to revive old values in all walks of life. The thinkers like Aurobindo showed the superiority of the ancient Indian values and by his powerful arguments silenced the critics. From the political viewpoint, the Swadeshi movement was a progressive phenomenon but in the social sphere it baulked the social change and mobility. In the contemporary India, there is a clear trend towards democratization in social change. In the economic, social and political spheres, the values of freedom and equality are getting encouragement. The social control is loosening and individuals are now more and more exercising their discretion and reason to decide what to do. The control of family has also become lax and love marriages are now not uncommon.

6. Importance of Elite. In order to appreciate the structure of social change in India one should have an idea about the role of the elite. The elite is under the influence of urban and industrial civilization. The scientific outlook of West has particular impact upon it. Thus, the elite is on the whole working for rapid social transformation on the western lines, but in certain respects it is bound by traditions. Therefore, among the urban society one finds prevalent a number of superstitious beliefs and ritualist practices. Even the inauguration of many scientific councils is marked by performance of Yojna and pooja. Thus, we see in the elite a coexistence of tradition and modernity. An important reason for this type of state of affairs is the broad based nature of Hindu religion in which many contradictory influences coexist.

CAUSAL FACTORS OF SOCIAL CHANGE

In social change, a number of factors operate. Among these are cultural, technical, biological, economic, geographical, psychological and ideological. A survey of social change in India would reveal the presence of all these factors. Again, these factors are themselves inter-related and inter-connected. If we analyze any particular case of social change we find at bottom a scheme or web of numerous interlinked factors. These factors together produce a specific social change and it is not always easy to determine the relative strength and influence of factors. Briefly, we can see the following main factors in the social change in India.

THE CULTURAL FACTORS OF SOCIAL CHANGE

Culture is a field of values, styles, emotional attachments and intellectual trends. These values, styles and ideas affect social change. By value we understand the goal which any individual or institution tries to accomplish. For example, the goal of a Hindu marriage is performance of Dharma and sexual intercourse of procreation. In modern times, the impact of Dharma has declined quite a bit and the necessity of a limited family have tended to make pleasure the chief goal of marriage. Due to this change in values, the institution of marriage has become rather unstable. This has encouraged disintegration of family. In past, the father used to enjoy a privileged status, every member of the family considered it his sacred duty to follow his command. In contemporary Indian society, a generation gap is quite visible.

Among the cultural causal factors operating in the Indian society the following are the main:

1. Sanskritization. The structure of Indian Society is based upon caste system. There is hierarchy of the castes and certain castes are considered upper and certain others the lower. According to Varna system, Brahmins were on the top wrung of the society because they were the preserver of the culture. After them Kshatriya, Vaishya and Sudra occupied the second, third and the fourth wrungs. The Varna system was based upon the cultural values. The higher castes were considered to be culturally higher also. In the caste system, the social hierarchy is not strictly based upon the Varna hierarchy. At some places Brahmins were considered at the top but at other places, on account of political and economic factors, Kshatriyas occupied better status. The higher castes control and govern the behaviour of the lower castes and the lower castes try to carry out the dictates of the higher castes. According to M.N. Srinivas, by Sanskritization we do not mean only the adoption of new habits and traditions but also the expression of new ideas and values. In the phenomenon of Sanskritization, the dominant caste finds a place of pride in the social hierarchy but the lower castes follow it with great care and caution because blind following leads to harmful effects. According to Dr. Majumdar in India, the processes of sanskritization and non-sanskritization are going on side by side.

2. Westernization. In the modern times, a widespread influence of the Western culture has led to many important social change. Therefore, Westernization is a vital factor in social change. The Westernization has produced profound changes in the structure of family and marriage, personal relations, female education, social mobility etc. It has also affected in important ways the ideological and value system, the means of social control have also undergone change. Among with Westernization, the materialist and scientific outlook of the West has also produced profound changes in the thinking of Indians. The philosophies of utilitarianism, pragmatism and individualism have also affected the Indian society. Still, the culture fall-out from the industrialization and urbanization due to west is less than what it could be.

3. Secularisation. The ancient Indian civilization was dominated by religion, but under the influence of Westernization it is becoming increasingly secular these days. Under the influence of secularisation the influence of religion over social institutions, traditions, practices and usages is declining and in its place utilitarianism and personal predilections govern human behaviour. After independence the Indian government has adopted the ideal of secularism. This has given impetus to the process of secularisation.

4. Democratization. In modern times, democracy is generally regarded to be the best form of government in the West. The main reason for this is that the democratic values of freedom, equality and fraternity are in tune with modern consciousness and thinking. After independence, a democratic government was established in our country. Though, democracy in social relationship is a distant goal, there is sufficient progress in this regard in other fields. The decentralization of power and the recognition of democratic values is leading to decline in the obscurantist forces and the differences based upon caste, religion, sex and region are becoming less marked. The untouchability has been declared illegal. All individuals are equal before law. Every individual has full freedom of undertaking any profession, he is also free to marry any where, receive education from any place, associate himself with any body, institution or organization. Many important steps have been undertaken for the upliftment of women and backward classes.

5. Politicisation. After independence, the Indian Constitution conferred voting rights upon every adult. This means that every worker, every peasant and whosoever is above 18 and not insane is entitled to vote. This has indeed taken politics to every comer of India and all Indian villages are today agog with political activity. Almost the entire length and breadth of India is now covered by radio network and millions of people are now able to see the television. This has kindled deep interest in politics everywhere. Around the election time this interest is all the more intense. In election, every party and each candidate try their level best to wrest power. With the abolition of feudal lords, the power is now concentrated in the hands of politicians. Therefore, the political factors have become dominant levers of social change. Due to political factors mainly, people support and oppose untouchability. Due to political factors alone the disintegrating tendencies like casteism, parochialism and communalism are raising their forehead. The Linguistic chauvinism is encouraged on account of politics. Today, there is so much politicisation in India that the social changes in both rural and urban India are governed by politics.

Economic Factors of Social Change

In the contemporary society, economic factors are the most crucial determinants of social change. Not only in India, but all over the world, the economic factors play the crucial role in the social change. Briefly, following are the main economic factors:

1. Industrialization. Industrialization is the most important factor of social change in the world. Industrialization is the basis of modernity and no country can afford to ignore it. This is so because man wants to conquer nature and this is possible only through industrialization. The Industrialization is the indicator of cultural progress and no country can make any headway without industrialization. The only way to grapple successfully with the bursting population growth is industrialization. Indeed, the progress of any country is directly proportionate to the progress of industrialization in it. Industrialization has led to urbanization in India. This has encouraged trade and improved the means of communication.

2. Urbanization. Though, urbanization has taken place due to causes other than the economic, these have been the primary. Among economic causes, industrialization has been the chief factor in urbanization. All over the world the number of big towns and their development is on the increase. And India is no exception to this rule. In India, also a distinct urban civilization has sprung. As a consequence of urbanization, the characteristics like materialism, individualism, social rapidity, impersonality and mobility have increased. Besides, there is change in the inter-sexual relations and the family is disintegrating. The nuclear family is coming to replace the joint family. There is also increase in the pre-marital and extra-marital relations.

3. Technological Changes. The technological factors have made considerable contribution to the social change. The Introduction of power-driven machines and vehicles and adoption of sophisticated means of communication has brought about considerable change in the society and this has profoundly affected marriage and family. The direct impact of industrial advance can be seen in the organization of labour, the division of labour, specialization, fast and mass production. Its indirect impact can be perceived in urbanization and unemployment, crime, juvenile delinquency and class-war consequent upon it. The use of machines in industry has led to fast urbanization, new classes have come into being and new ideological movements have been born. The status of women has undergone sea-change. The values have undergone drastic transformation. Materialism, individualism, specialization etc. are the result of technological changes. In the urban life, the technological advance has produced decline in the community feeling, over-valuation of time, decline in social control, decline in moral standards, increase in crimes and the rise of tendencies conducive to disintegration of the individual and the society. The social change consequent upon technological change can be explained by a simple example. Previously, when cars had to be started by the use of handle, women did not drive cars, but now with the introduction of self-starting mechanism in the cars, many well to-do women can be seen driving cars. This has also led to changes in dress, mobility and thinking. There is change of value outlook.

Biological Factors of Social Change

In the biological factors is chiefly included the geometrical rise in the population. The excess or lack of adequate population, its distribution led to widespread social changes. For example, the influx of labour force in millions to big industrial towns in India has led to upsetting man-woman ratio. This has given rise to many problems: (1) prostitution, (2) mental diseases, (3) juvenile delinquency etc. The excess of population in a country leads to decline in health standards and increase in poverty. This fact is ubiquitous in India. The excess in population has also led to vast changes in social values. In India, there is a problem of slums and overcrowding. This leads to steep deterioration in the morals of slum dwellers. This is why the Government is so keen on family planning. There is a wide publicity of techniques of birth control. This has led to change in sexual morality. Now, there can be seen the beginning of sexual permissiveness. In order to meet the food and shelter requirement of the increasing populace new techniques are being used. The basic flaw in the demographic structure in India is the greater proportion of rural populace and the high incidence of birth and death.

QUESTIONS FOR EXERCISE

1. Analyse the main trends of social change in contemporary India.
2. Discuss causal factors of social change in contemporary India.

18

Industrialization and Labour Problems in India

Though, industrialization in India is making rapid strides, it is still far behind the industrial growth in Western countries. After India became independent in 1947, the government of India paid particular attention to industrial growth. It helped the local industry to grow rapidly. In order to put India on industrial map fast, the government decided to enter the field of heavy industry which demanded huge investments. The government set up many heavy industrial complexes all over India in order to promote a balanced growth and also to help the ancillary industry to expand fast.

As a result of fast industrialization, the process of urbanization too, is growing fast and this is having deep impact upon society. The industrialization is not only pushing up the urban population but is also affecting the social conditions in nearby villages.

SOCIAL IMPACT OF INDUSTRIALIZATION

The important social consequences of industrialization in India are as follows:

1. Urbanization. As a consequence of industrialization the population in the cities has gone up.

2. Impact of Urbanization. The process of industrialization increases the urban population. It is on account of industrialization that there is progressive rise in the population of cities in India. Whatever, social impact is due to the urbanization is indirectly due to industrialization. Therefore, the impact of industrialization and the impact of urbanization are in fact the facets of the same underlying process, namely, industrialization. Following are some of the important social influences of urbanization:

(i) *Decline in the Community Feeling.* The first and foremost impact of urbanization in India is the increase in the population of the cities, and this, in turn, has resulted in the progressive decline in the feeling of community. In villages, the feeling of community is stronger than in the cities. Therefore, the loss of village population and increase of city population results in the decline of feeling of community.

In cities, the activities of almost everyone are self-centred and governed by the calculus of self-interest and personal gain. Therefore, no one really bothers about other people except insofar as their association is helpful in promoting self-interest. Thus, people in cities prove to be calculating and display little altruism.

(ii) *Decline in Social Control.* With the decline in the feeling of community there is consequent decline in Social control. Due to lack of community feeling and the fear of social disapproval people are bound to become increasingly individualistic and even arbitrary in their conduct. Thus, we find in town today a glaring neglect of tradition and contempt for social approval. Everybody wants to do whatever pleases him.

(iii) *Decline in Family Control.* As the population of cities has grown the cities have expanded. This has resulted in great distances between the places of work and places of residence, between educational institutions and homes. This has meant that people stay away from home environments for the best part of the day. Small wonder, then, that under these circumstances, there is progressive decline in the control of family over its members. The modern education, the excitement of cinema, fashion, clubs and voluntary societies have contributed greatly to this trend.

(iv) *Decline in the Influence of Religion.* The increase in the population of the cities leads not only to the decline of social and family control but also leads to decline in the influence of religion. In metropolitan towns, the life is highly materialistic and individualistic. This in turn promotes atheism. This means that people in cities are not guided by tradition and are indifferent to religious belief. Their conduct is governed by rational or personal considerations. Thus, the life in cities is relatively devoid of the influence of religion.

(v) *Change in the Institution of Marriage.* The increase in urban population has resulted in certain change in the institution of marriage. Generally, care is taken to take into confidence the spouses before marriage. Whereas, in villages, marriage is an affair between families rather than individuals, in cities today no marriage can be solemnized if any of the spouse is opposed to it. Even, the incidence of love marriages is growing.

(vi) *Change in the Institution of Family.* Another impact of urbanization is the gradual extinction of the joint family system and its replacement by nuclear family. Now-a-days, most families consist of husband, wife and their progeny.

(vii) *Change in the Condition of Women.* With the changes in the institution of family, there is also change in the pattern of family. Women are becoming increasingly independent and the education among them is also spreading. They are becoming increasingly conscious of their rights and privileges but along with it there is also a tendency to arbitrary and wilful conduct. The incidence of illicit sexual relations, divorce etc. are also on increase. The ostentation and intense fashion have also become the order of the day.

(viii) *Increase of Male-ratio.* A significant impact of urbanization on the population is that the ratio of male population is increasing. The main reason for this phenomenon is that due to shortage of housing, millions of people are forced to live single in cities. The evil of this phenomenon is that this gives rise to sexual corruption.

(ix) *Commercialized Entertainment.* On account of industrialization there has been widespread growth of commercialized entertainment. The cinemas are tremendously popular, prostitutes do roaring business. Indeed, there is a charge on eveiy kind of entertainment in the cities.

(x) *Housing Shortage.* The growth in population in cities is so fast that it is not possible to provide people with adequate residential accommodation. Indeed, pressure on space in cities is so tremendous that most people are forced to live on roads or in shabby accommodation in cities like Bombay. The shortage of residential accommodation compels people to stay without families. The persons coming from villages are unable to bring their families with them. This phenomenon, as observed earlier, leads to inevitable sexual corruption.

(xi) *Growth of Slums.* Industrialization has resulted in shortage of accommodation and this, in turn, has given rise to slums, overcrowded shabby living quarters. These slums are populated by workers and other indigent people. The persons living in these slums are constantly exposed to all kinds of diseases, are liable to become social deviates and criminals: the loss of morals is an inevitable consequence of living in slums. The *Ahatas* of Kanpur, *Bastis* of Delhi, *Chawls* of Bombay and *Cheris* of Madras are stigmas on the face of India. These shabby quarters are worse than stables of horses and pans of cattles. There is no ventilation, no drainage, no drinking water. A besmirched ragged piece of jute hanging in front of home is an eloquent testimony of their pitiable condition. The glaring contrasts in the palatial lives of industrialists and the dirt-laden existence of workers testify to the hollowness of our socialism and democratic life. Pandit Nehru was so moved emotionally on seeing slums that he wanted them to be burnt down and the persons responsible for them to be hanged. They symbolize extreme moral and physical decline, the nadir of all that is bad in life. According to Dr. Radhakamal Mukherjee, "In the thousand slums of India's industrial centres manhood is, unquestionably brutalized, women dishonoured and childhood is poisoned at its very source."

Economic Consequences of Industrialization

The following are the important consequences of industrialization in the economic field in India:

1. Growth of Capitalism. As a result of industrialization there is tremendous concentration of wealth in few hands. Due to industrialization one man can control a business of crores of rupees and go on amassing wealth unabated. Thus, like other countries industrialization in India has also given tremendous fillip to the growth of capitalism.

2. Mass Production. As a result of industrialization there is production on large scale. In India, steel, cement, sugar, jute, fertilizers, electrical equipment, rail material are being produced on mass scale. India with its vast population is now self-sufficient in these commodities, may, it exports many of these.

3. Growth of Trade, On account of mass production there is unparalleled growth in trade and commerce. The development of fast means of communication has contributed a lot towards this end. The foreign trade has also shown tremendous rise.

4. Division of Labour and Specialization. An economic impact of industrialization is the division of labour and specialization. Gradually, the number of technocrats and highly skilled personnel is growing.

5. Rise in the Standard of Living. As a result of industrialization there is a certain rise in the living standard. Today, electric fans, gas, radio and iron are common household goods.

6. Economic Crisis and Unemployment But, whereas means of comfort and luxury are now easily available there is, on the other hand, grave economic crisis. The mechanization of all production has thrown millions of people out of work. Due to industrialization there is glut of many commodities. This leads to grave economic crisis.

7. Industrial Disputes and Accidents. The industrial disputes and accidents are inevitable accompaniment of industrialization. Wherever there is industry, there are thousands of workers. It is a natural tendency of workers to expect more and more for their work: on the other hand, the industrialists want more production for less wages. Under these circumstances there are bound to be clashes of interest resulting in industrial disputes. The working conditions in Indian industry are not of high standard and accidents are very likely.

8. Problems of Workers. Besides strikes and lock-outs, workers have some other problems. An important problem in this connection is that of rest and relaxation. Firstly, they have to work for long hours so that they get little rest. Secondly, whatever rest they get there are not adequate sources of healthy entertainment available.

9. Spread of Socialism and Individualism. The industrialization has promoted both socialism and individualism. As a result of it capitalism grew and with it spread the ideas of individualism and *laissez faire*. On the other hand, the ideology of Socialism also spread as a result of industrialization. The industrial workers organized themselves into trade unions and political parties in order to gain their support to professed socialism.

10. Class Conflict. Like other countries industrialization in India has given rise to class conflicts and class war. There is continuous tension among the poor and rich. However, the class-war in India is as yet not very intense.

11. Decline of Rural Industry. As a result of industrialization the goods of daily use were produced on mass scale. The quality of machine-made goods is standard and they are cheap. This resulted in large inflow of goods into villages and this ruined the cottage industry of the village.

Social Disorganization

Industrialization gives rise to many such progresses which lead to social disorganization. The industrialization produces many problems at family, individual and community level. Industrialization induces individual and family disorganization. Industrialization gives rise to such factors as are responsible for social disorganization. Following are such factors;

1. Individual Disorganization. The industrialization gives rise to factors which cause disorganization in the individual. Millions of workers migrate from villages to towns for jobs. As there is acute shortage of accommodation in towns and the life is otherwise costly also, they are unable to bring their families to cities. Therefore, after a day's hard work, they can get neither any healthy entertainment nor the peace of home. Lacking all suitable alternative they take to drinking, prostitution etc. This leads to their moral degeneration. The gaudy and exciting urban environment and materialistic outlook of life also contribute to moral degeneration. This produces disorganization not only among workers but in other persons too.

2. Unemployment. While industrialization has created employment opportunities for millions, it has also led to unemployment. The mechanization of production greatly reduces the need for workers. Whenever, a new sophisticated machine is installed in any factory hundreds of workers are thrown out of job. Many rural women come to cities in search for job but unable to find any they are forced into prostitution. The unemployment in turn leads to social disorganization.

3. Crime and Immorality. The process of industrialization has also led to rise in the incidence of crime and immorality. As referred to earlier, thousands of workers in the town are unable to find suitable accommodation or are unable to cope with high expenses of urban life. They are forced to lead secluded existence. Being not highly morally trained they succumb to the twin lure of wine and woman; they drink country liquor and visit lowly prostitutes. The industrialization has also given rise to factionalism, materialism and mechanical character of life. All these things have encouraged crime. As a result of industrialization small boys and girls take to work and they are easily spoilt.

4. Factionalism and Heterogeneity. The industrialization has contributed to factionalism and given rise to economic disparities. This is proving highly subversive of social cohesion and unity. The difference between rich and poor keeps growing and both classes tend to develop anti-social tendencies. Whereas industrialists live in fully air-conditioned palatial mansions, the poor are constrained to sleep on footpath and whereas the former live a luxurious life the latter are unable to make their both ends meet. The economic disparity is productive of social disorganization.

5. Cultural Lag. The process of industrialization results in cultural lag. This is due to the fact that industrialization leads to fast progress in materialistic things. The manner and mode of life outwardly changes very rapidly but there is progress of inward culture. Thus, inward change does not keep pace with outward changes and this contradiction results in cultural lag.

6. Change in Values. Industrialization has resulted in change in values. On account of industrialization jobs are now available to women and children. Women are no longer chattel pieces of men. They enjoy now relative economic independence and their outlook on life has changed. The relations between various people are no longer based on tradition but are guided by the calculus of self-interest.

7. Family Disorganization. Industrialization has resulted in disorganization of family life also. The husband and wife go to their respective places of work and there is no one back home to care and look after children. Where children also do jobs there can be no proper provision of education. Due to changes in values and consequent change in the attitudes the cohesion of family life is severely disturbed. If husband and wife both stay out of home chances of disharmony among them increase. If women and girls go out of home for job the chances of illicit sexual relations increase. On account of all these factors family disorganization results.

8. Urbanization. An inevitable consequence of industrialization is the increase in urbanization. Due to urbanization big cities spring up with populations far in excess of their capacity. As a result a large number of persons have to live in one or two room quarters. In this situation, there is disaffection among married couples and unmarried persons get frequent opportunities to peep upon sexual activities of married persons. This has evil effect on impressionable young persons and they indulge in premature sex. Many a time queer sexual intimacy among family members is the outcome of this hopeless situation. The relations among individuals in cities are of impersonal character. The urbanization results in loosening of social control. The community life is disrupted. The gaudy and exciting life of cities produces imbalance in social and personal relations. The freedom of contact between sexes also disturbs family life. The life in clubs and society is a life of rebellion against social traditions and restrictions. The slums, the epidemics, immoral outlook have all combined to knock the bottom out of harmonious and peaceful life in cities.

STEPS TO CHECK EFFECTS OF INDUSTRIALIZATION

From the above discussion of social and economic effects of industrialization, it is quite clear that industrialization has given rise to a number of evil effects. These include housing shortage, labour problems, unnatural life, increase in crime and exploitation, ruin of rural industry etc.

Following measures should be taken to counteract the evil influences of industrialization:

1. Town Planning. The industries should be at a reasonable distance from the residential colonies and the main centres of the city. The slums should be cleared and replaced by good hygienic houses.

2. Planning of Factories. The factories should be well-planned. They must be well-ventilated and have all amenities. They should be so structured and equipped that the chances of accidents are minimal.

3. Enactment of Labour Laws. There must be well laid down rules for the workers. Their wages, bonus, working hours, gratuity, pension, leaves etc. should be governed by laws enacted by the government and these should be strictly enforced.

4. Promotion of Rural Industries. The government should encourage rural industries. It must give liberal loans for their development.

5. Decentralization. Many an evil effects of industrialization are due to the fact that there is usually concentration of industry at one place. This should be avoided and there should be diversification of industries.

6. Development of Cottage Industry. A number of evil effects of industrialization are due to mechanization and specialization. This lopsided development can be greatly averted by promotion and encouragement of cottage industries.

7. Housing. As a result of industrialization there is acute housing shortage in industrial towns. Numerous evil effects flow from the shortage of housing. These can be avoided by giving building of houses top priority.

8. Healthy Entertainment. The increase in the incidence of crime, juvenile delinquency and prostitution in industrial towns is due to lack of healthy entertainment. If we know the cause of a phenomenon it is easy to control it. Thus, by providing healthy entertainment we can counteract the above-mentioned evils.

All the above-mentioned suggestions for the improvement of urban areas and for counteracting the ills of industrialization have been attended to by Government of India. Fortunately, industrialization in India is still not so intense and concentrated as to produce alarming problems. If some advance steps can be taken at this stage, it is possible to mitigate the more severe types of ills consequent upon industrialization. The acute problems of industrialization are in India confined to few metropolises like Calcutta, Bombay, Kanpur etc. Of course, the efforts being made at these centres to mitigate the evil effect of industrialization leave much to be desired. The existence of slums is a glaring fact of all industrial centres. It is an indelible blot on our society. The working conditions of labour are neither healthy nor hygienic. There is no provision of wholesome entertainment. The government needs pay special attention to this aspect. The closing down of red-light areas is no solution of the problem. The government alone does not have resources to solve the monumental problems posed by industrialization. It needs the co-operation of local self-government and also the efforts of the industrialists.

PROBLEMS OF INDIAN LABOUR

It is a regrettable fact that there have not been sufficient reforms and improvement in the conditions of Indian labour. The Indian labour is not properly organized and does not have its own leadership but depends upon outside guidance. The non-labour leaders are politically motivated and are not really interested in the labour welfare. As a matter of fact, they more often than not use the labour unrest as a means to grind their own axes instead of helping the labour genuinely. The government has not paid enough attention to the real problems and needs of labour and though there is much labour legislations intended to help the labour but in actual practice there is little improvement in the condition of labour. Following are the chief problems of Indian labour:

1. The Problem of Migration. One of the main problems of Indian labour is the problem of migration. The increasing pressure on land due to population explosion, the evergrowing army of landless tillers, the social stigma on Harijans, increase in indebtedness, breakdown of joint families, fast means of communication, ravaging of cottage industries and city oriented education are some of the causes responsible for the exodus of villagers and their influx into industrial town. While by joining the army of industrial labour, there is some improvement in the economic conditions and relenting of pressure on land, the family and social life of these new recruits gets upset. This creates problems of social adjustment, decreases efficiency and comes in the way of the development of healthy employer employee relationship.

2. The Problem of Recruitment. The second main problem of the Indian labour is that of recruitment. As yet there is little direct recruitment. Most of it is done through intermediaries. The services of Employment Exchanges are available to very few. As most of the workers are dependent upon intermediaries and as intermediaries have special type of relationship with the workers, they receive cut-backs and have also to be propitiated by other gifts.

3. The Problem of Absenteeism. The labour force hailing from villages is usually unable to cope with the alien environment of the city. The fresh food, air and light is unavailable in cities. Besides, slums in which the workers live are extremely unhygienic and great breeders of disease. Accordingly the workers are usually unwell. They consume liquor and visit prostitutes. All these factors combined result in large absenteeism from factories.

The chief of absenteeism in India are illness, night shifts; alcoholism; migrating instinct; industrial accidents; prostitution; laziness; frequency of festivals and litigation. The absenteeism produces adverse economic effects on industrial production and earnings of labour. Besides it causes rift and tension between employer and employee. The various measures presently taken to meet this problem are grossly inadequate. A committee set up by the Bombay Textile Mills to investigate the causes of absenteeism and make suitable recommendations for remedying the problem came to the following conclusion: "Proper condition for work in the factory, adequate wages, protection from accidents and sickness and facilities for obtaining leave, rest and recuperation constitute the most effective means of reducing absenteeism."

4. Problems of Trade Unions. In India, the trade union movement is not yet well organized and developed. The lack of education, susceptibility to religious influence, generally fatalistic outlook, deep indebtedness and opposition by employers and intermediaries are some of the factors responsible for slow and uneven growth of trade union movement. The labour politicians have furtherance of their own interests rather than labour welfare at heart.

5. The Problems of Industrial Dispute. The capitalist economic and social structure, the policy of creating dissension among workers by intermediaries, retrenchment of workers to circumvent labour legislation and paying of compensation are the problems which lead to frequent strikes, lockouts, gheraoes and sit-in by workers. At times, these disputes turn violent and labourers suffer heavily.

6. Problem of Wages. The chief problem of workers is that they are poorly paid. In some cases these are below subsistance level. Due to lack of adequate wages, the labour is unable to give proper education to this children. He cannot maintain his health. This leads to decline in his efficiency and in the ultimate analysis the production falls.

7. The Problem of Indebtedness. On account of low wages, bribes to intermediaries, drinking and prostitution, most of the workers are permanently and deeply under debt. It has been estimated that more than 2/3 workers of big industrial towns are under debt and the average amount of debt exceeds their 3 months' salary. Due to heavy indebtedness the worker cannot think progressively and considers whole of his life unrelieved drudgery. The cause of indebtedness are many. Usually, the worker is born in debt and due to drudgery becomes desensitized; therefore, he takes to drastic and powerful excesses like liquor and woman. This further complicates his problem and drives him to die a pauper in debt.

8. The Problem of Living Standard. Due to low wages and rising spiral of prices, the living standard of Indian workers has been dropping constantly. A comparison of wages in India with other countries will bring into relief the pathetic plight of the Indian labourer. The workers in India are underfed and more than 39% suffer from serious malnutrition. In U.S.A., 75 yards cloth is used per head whereas in India it is only 16 yards. There are many causes of low living standard. The main among them are: (1) Low wages; (2) Illiteracy; (3) Population explosion; (4) Intoxication; (5) Lack of skill; and (6) Fatalism.

9. The Problems of Health. Due to low wages and low standards the workers are unable to eat wholesome balanced diet. What is worse, most of them are addicted to smoking, tobacco chewing, drinking and visiting cinemas and bawdy houses. All these reasons coupled with unhygienic living conditions, inadequate clothing, inclement weather, heavily dispose workers to disease and infection. According to Professor B.P. Adarkar a worker loose 146 days, a year due to ill health.

10. The Problem of Efficiency. According to the report of Tariff Board, a worker in India can handle 180 spindles whereas his counterparts in Japan, England and America can handle 240, 450 to 600 and 1220 spindles respectively. As a rule the efficiency of Indian workers is 1/2 or even 1/3 of the workers in progressive countries. Ill-health, lack of education, lack of will to learn and progress, addiction to bad habits are some of the factors responsible for the low efficiency of the Indian workers.

11. The Problem of Working Conditions. The conditions of work of the majority of labourers are extremely bad and deplorable and leave much to be desired. Most of the factories are ill-ventilated and the illumination is improper. The living and working conditions are making workers prone to accident. At many places even facilities for drinking water, toilet etc. do not exist. In extreme weather there is no provision to minimize its effects. Due to lack of amenities and hazardous working conditions the efficiency of workers drops and they are exposed to accidents and infections.

12. The Problems of Child Labour. Though, it is illegal to employ workers under certain age, these provisions are frequently flouted and circumvented. The problems of child labour in India are the following:

(i) More work and less wages.
(ii) Loss of education of children.
(iii) Lack of proper rest and play essential for proper growth.
(iv) The unhygienic and rigorous working conditions.
(v) Low and below-standard productivity.

13. Problems of Women Workers. Following are the main problems faced by women workers:

(i) Unsatisfactory conditions.
(ii) Lack of amenities and facilities for maternity leave, child welfare etc.
(iii) Rigorous labour unsuited to the delicate constitution of women.
(iv) Mal-treatment and enforced immoral life.

It is a matter of gratification that the Government of India, Trade Unions Progressive and enlightened capitalists and industrialists, state government and many non-governmental organisations who are alive to the above-mentioned problems are doing everything under their power to remedy them and relieve the conditions of workers.

LABOUR WELFARE

By the term labour welfare, we mean those acts or activities which in any way contribute to the well-being and happiness of the workers, or which help to relieve or minimize their hardships and privations. But this general and common meaning is not of much use or value to a sociologist. The concept of labour welfare has been variously interpreted in sociology. The meaning and scope of the concept is changeable and keeps undergoing modifications with a change in the circumstances. According to the report of the Royal Commission on Labour, "The term welfare, as applied to the industrial worker, is one which must necessarily be elastic; bearing a somewhat different interpretation in one country from another, according to different social customs, the degree of industrialization and educational development of workers." Thus, the meaning and scope of the concept of labour welfare in any country will depend upon the conditions, educational attainments, social customs, practices and usages of the workers.

For example most of the workers in this country are illiterate or very poorly educated. Accordingly, imparting of elementary education will be an essential and significant part of labour welfare in India. According to the Encyclopaedia of Social Sciences, "Labour welfare implies the voluntary efforts of the employers to establish within the existing industrial system, working and sometimes living conditions of the employees beyond what is required by law, the custom of the industry and the conditions of the market. " Thus, in the labour welfare those acts or amenities of workers are not included which are essential and prescribed by the labour laws, customs of the place and required by the virtue of market conditions. The labour welfare acts are the voluntary efforts, that is, over and above essential under law, for the industrialists to improve or ameliorate the conditions of the workers. A report of the International Labour Organization, a United Nations agency to watch, supervise and help the working conditions of workers all over the world, had defined labour welfare thus, "Workers welfare should be understood as meaning such service facilities and amenities which may be established in, or in vicinity of, an undertaking to enable the persons employed there to perform their work in healthy congenial surroundings and provided with amenities conducive to good health and high morale." Thus, the labour welfare schemes aim at the maintenance and betterment of workers' health and raising of their moral standard and efficiency. A report of Labour Investigation Committee set up by the Government of India has observed, "We prefer to include under Welfare activities anything done for the intellectual, physical, moral and economic betterment of the workers, whether by employees, by Government agencies or by other agenicies over and above what is laid down by law or what is normally expected as part of the contractual benefits for which the workers may have bargained. Thus, under this definition we may include, medical and educational facilities, nutrition (including provision of canteens) facilities for recreation, cooperative societies, day nurseries and creches, provision of sanitary accommodation, holidays with pay, social insurance measures, undertaken voluntarily by employers alone or jointly with workers, sickness and maturity benefits schemes, provident funds, gratuities, bonuses and pensions etc." Thus, all above-mentioned definitions of social welfare agree on this point: it includes all voluntary acts by employers aimed at improvement and betterment of worker's social, moral, economic and intellectual conditions. Those acts which the employer is compelled, on pain of legal actions, to undertake, however beneficial these may be for the workers, are not included in the province of labour welfare. By welfare scheme the industrialists give evidence of their moral and social enlightenment and help all-round development of workers. This, in turn, helps them in the long run, because, as it has been well observed, a well-paid and satisfied worker is an asset and the low-paid unsatisfied worker is a liability.

Responsibility of Labour Welfare

Having discussed the problem of Labour Welfare, the question that is likely to come up in anyone's mind is: who is responsible for Labour Welfare? Whose moral obligation is it to promote labour welfare? The most popular view in this regard is that it is the duty of the employer to look after the social welfare of the workers employed by him. This seems to be the most responsible and well considered view because though the industrialist has to make big investment in the labour welfare schemes, it is by no means a dead investment. A well-fed, well-clad and satisfied worker is an asset. He makes no loss of man hours by absenteeism, strikes, slow tactics etc. Besides he feels a sense of allegiance to the organization in which he works. Therefore, though a costly investment, it pays very rich dividends in the long run. It is a moral duty of every mill owner or industrialist to provide fully for the food and other amenities for the families of the workers who suffer grievous injury in accidents met during working hours. He must also provide medical benefits, pensions, bonuses, incentives etc. However, the industrialist alone is not responsible for labour welfare. It is also the duty of welfare state to look after zealously the interest of the workers and initiate schemes for improvement in their working conditions, raising their morale etc. The Government should also prevent any instance of exploitation of women workers and an abuse of children. In all progressive countries, the workers have their Trade Unions which look after and safeguard and promote the interests of workers. They can compel government and employers to agree to improved benefits for the country. An example of this is the recent announcement of Government of India to allow for 8.33% bonus to all industrial workers. All there, that is, the employer, the Government and the Trade Unions are jointly responsible for labour welfare.

TRADE UNIONISM IN INDIA

Trade Union Act of 1926 conferred a legal and corporate status on registered union and granted them certain immunities in regard to trade disputes. The Act makes provisions for three matters: (1) conditions governing the registration of trade unions, (2) the obligation to which a trade union is subjected after registration, and (3) the rights and privileges accorded to registered unions to be spent for the conduct of trade disputes and for the provisions of benefits to its members.

The amended Act of 1947, contains a provision for compulsory recognition of representative unions by employers. The redeeming feature of the Act is that Labour Courts are to be appointed to hear and decide disputes arising from the refusal of employers to recognise any particular union. The Act specifies certain other acts as unfair on the part of employees. It also declares as unfair practice for any executive of a union to instigate a strike and unfair for a majority of members to take part in an irregular strike.

There are at present 5 central all-India trade union organisations in India: Indian National Trade Union Congress, All-India Trade Union Congress, Hind Mazdoor Sangh, United Trade Union Congress and Centre of Indian Trade Unions. AITUC having become manifestly Communist since December 1929, the Indian National Congress leaders organised their own trade union — the INTUC.

The Praja Socialist Party organised the HMS, CPI (M) made a separate union, the CITU in 1970.

Though, the five national organisations dominate the Indian trade union movement, not all trade unions in India belong to them or follow their leadership. A very large number of small unions stand aloof from their leadership. The sticking examples of these are Ahmedabad Textile Labour Association and National Federation of Indian *Railwaymen. The United Trade Union Congress* have no open political affiliations.

QUESTIONS FOR EXERCISE

1. Write short note on Industrialization.
2. Discuss the impact of technology on caste in India.
3. Discuss the social consequences of Industrialization in India.
4. Distinguish between Industrialization and Urbanization.
5. What do you understand by Industrialization? Classify its influence on joint family and caste system.
6. Discuss briefly the chief problems of Indian Labour.
7. Write a short note on Labour Welfare.
8. Write short note on Trade Unionism in India.

19

Secularization

If we observe the lives of labourers in the factory, the clerks in offices, shop-keepers, medicos, lawyers etc. in modern India, we shall find that though India is considered to be a religion-dominated land, there is little religion in the day-to-day activities of an average Indian. The lives of most of the educated Indians are governed not by any religious consideration but by scientific facts and utilitarianism. Even their adherence to some old traditions is due not to religion but to some practical utility, which they are able to find in it. They would justify their adherence to tradition not by religious authority, but by its being useful to the society. Not only the educated but even the unlettered now show less respect for religion. Though, the secularization of life is more in evidence in the urban areas and among the educationally more advanced persons, the winds of secularism are now blowing all over freely and the religious bigotry is on the retreat everywhere.

In India, secularization is more in evidence among Hindus than among the persons of other religions. There is much less secularization among Jains, Sikhs and Muslims. They follow the religious traditions more strictly than the Hindus.

DEFINITION OF SECULARISM

Defining secularism, Dr. M.N. Srinivas writes, "The term 'secularization' implies that what was previously regarded as religious is now ceasing to be such, and it also implies a process of differentiation which results in the various aspects of society, economic, political, legal and moral, becoming increasingly discrete in relation to each other."[1] Thus, the process of secularization is anti-religious. In other words as secularization increases, religion loses hold. As we have mentioned earlier, in India, secularization is fast progressing, particularly among Hindus, better educated and urban classes. Briefly, following are its characteristics:

1. Decline of Religion. More secularization, less religion, this is universal social law. Wherever the forces of secularism are strong, the forces of religion lose hold

1 M. N. Sriniwas, *Social Change in Modern India*, p. 119.

and become weakened. Among Hindus, in various walks of life, the importance of religion is nominal; and the course of things is decided by reason and pragmatism.

2. Process of Differentiation. The increase of secularism leads to an increase in the differentiation of various aspects of society. Thus, in modern times, an educated Hindu considers the economic, the political, the legal and moral issues separate and does not allow their mixing up as this unnecessarily confuses the issues. The matters pertaining to law cannot be decided on moral basis and the economic issues cannot be resolved politically. Therefore, with secularization clubbing of diverse issues together ceases as is the case with the religious interpretation.

3. Reasonableness. An outstanding feature of secularization is the rule of reason and discarding of superstition. A secular man considers every issue on the bar of reason and is not swayed by the authority of religious scriptures. The personal life of a secular man is guided by reason and intelligence. He is critical of accepting anything on faith and therefore analytically examines each and every issue.

4. Scientific Attitude. The adoption of scientific attitude towards life is an important characteristic of secularism. According to Freud as the influence of science grows on man, the influence of religion declines. The expansion of modern education also re-inforces the values of secularism and militates against religion.

CHANGES DUE TO SECULARIZATION

The above discussion makes clear the nature of secularism. The process of secularization started with the advent of British rule but it got accelerated with industrialization and urbanization. Before going into causes of secularization it will be worth while to examine how it has affected the various aspects of life. The areas most affected by secularization are caste system family and rural community. A brief study to these influences in these areas will be made below:

1. The Impact of Secularization on Caste System: The Distinction of Pure and Impure. In Indian society, the influence of Hindu religion is to be seen in the distinction of pure and impure. From the religious point of view many actions are regarded as impure, in particular if a high caste person does actions reserved for the low castes he will get tainted by impurity. For example, the activities reserved for the sudras, if done by the high caste person, he will become impure. The sentiment of untouchability is linked with this feeling of impurity. The high caste individual was not supposed to have any truck with the low caste or an untouchable, even the shadow of an untouchable was sufficient to soil him. A food touched by the low caste is not eaten by the high caste, because it is considered to have become impure and unfit for consumption by the high caste. The removal of night soil, scavenging etc., are considered to be impure actions. On a number of occasions woman was considered impure. For example, woman is considered impure while menstruating and the food cooked by her was considered impure.

Under the impact of industrialization there is great change in Hindu society regarding purity and impurity. In the past, the high caste person would rather starve than take to the profession of low caste, but now even Brahmins sell shoes.

Now-a-days, a menstruating woman freely moves everywhere and does all house hold duties. She is no longer considered impure, requiring quarantine. Now-a-days, the feeling of untouchability is declining. A Brahmin and Chamar in leather trade share not only business but also eat together. The English educated youngmen are averse to considering any thing pure or impure merely because of religious sanction. Now, on account of enlightenment, the criterion of pure and impure is not religious scripture but the rules of hygiene. A number of traditional actions are still considered valid and adhered to, but this adherence is not on account of religion but the principles of good health and hygiene. Thus, now the distinction between pure and impure is no longer based on religion, its basis had become secular.

2. Change in Samskaras. Samskara is a chief characteristics of Hindu society. For different castes, different types of samskaras are essential on different occasions. For example, without the Upanayan Samskara no Brahmin could be considered twice-born. In ancient times, Upanayan Samskara was ceremonised sometime after the child went to the school. For Hindus, there are numerous samskaras for all life, the chief among these are Garbhadhan (conception), Punsawan, Jatkarma, Namkaran (Baptization), Upnayan, Samavartan, marriage and funeral. For, all of these, there are prescribed elaborate rituals. Now, under the impact of secularization there is great change in the performance of these samskaras. For example, the samskaras like Garbhadhan, Punsawan, Jatkarama are now almost extinct. Now, no educated Hindu performs them. Now, the first Samskara still prevalent is Namakaran and this too has lost its religious significance and has now become an occasion of social get together in which people collect for feasting and expressing happiness over the birth of the child. Even, now, there is a priest to ceremonize the samskaras but now people pay less attention to him than to plates filled with dainties. The Upanayan Samskara is now linked with marriage. Majority of persons prefer to don the sacred thread few days before the marriage. Maximum change of rituals has taken place in the case of marriage. Now, only going round the fire and Kanyadan are held as necessary. Even, these are done perfunctorily and little attention is paid to the recitation of the priest. Thus, secularization has taken the religious sting out of samskaras.

3. Secularization in Family. Family and marriage are the primary institutions, the impact of secularization on marriage has already been discussed. The provision of divorce and civil contract have greatly secularized the institution of marriage. In family, also the impact of secularization is to be felt most in the day to day activities of the persons. In Hinduism, the day to day life of various castes is fixed. For Brahmins worship, scriptural reading and yajna etc. are the must. But consequent upon secularization very few Brahmin families today stick to this routine. The secularization has revolutionised the kitchen and the distinction of pure and impure is now virtually non-existent. In matters of food also there is little religion now. The festivals are still celebrated but now they have become more a social affair than religious. Now, people celebrated but now they have become more a social affair than religious. Now, people celebrate Holi, Diwali etc., not so much for their religious significance, as for their entertainment value. Some festivals are now celebrated on larger scale but this is not due to any realization of their religious significance. Rather, there are psychological causes for it. Now, more people are going to places of pilgrimage but the main reason is not earning of merit as sightseeing and whiling away time. Now, people going to religious places on high altitude and to places not easily accessible are not strictly motivated by the religious spirit. There is more a sense of adventure and a curiosity to know our country which again is the result of education. Now, the respect for Sadhus and mendicants among householders is much less. In urban areas, the place of religion in family is now becoming extinct.

4. Secularization in Rural India. In the urban areas, the impact of secularization is quite obvious, but the rural India also is not immune to this influence. In villages, the effectiveness of panchayats is declining, and wherever, there are panchayats, these are now organized on political rather than religious basis. In the rural India also, now a person is not respected so much for his religion as for his money. That is why in the rural India a moneylender is more respected than a Brahmin. If a member of a low caste has more money he is more respected than a poor high caste. The influence of religion in the family system in the villages is also declining. The changes parallel to those in the urban families have occurred in the rural families also. Even, then, the secularization in rural India is on a lesser scale than in the cities. Though, inter-caste marriages are rare in the village some stray cases can be seen. In Panchayats, now, the problems are discussed from the socio-political angle rather than religious. The festivals have turned into social occasions. In villages, the persons of all castes can be seen to be engaged in the profession of agriculture and cattle-breeding.

CAUSES OF SECULARIZATION

Following are some of the important reasons of secularization:

1. Modern Education. The most important reason of secularization is the modern education which came to India with the British. With the knowledge of English, science and modern socio-political thinking the thinking of people inclined towards secularism. The educated intelligentsia abandoned all the superstitions and false beliefs and put the entire tradition to critical analysis and accepted those parts of the tradition which can stand the test of reason. With the co-education the tendency to inter-caste marriage received a fillip. The educated person is more pragmatic and utilitarian in this thinking and ideas and this encourages secularism. The members of different castes met in the educational institutions and this helped to discourage untouchability and caste feelings.

2. Development of Means of Transport & Communication. The development of the means of transport and communication has helped a lot the process of secularization. The train, bus and taxi have helped people to come together easily and frequently. This has encouraged catholicity of outlook. This gave a blow to caste system and helped to reduce the feeling of untouchability. The development of means of transport and communication helped the villages to come to towns and take the message of liberalism back to their homes.

3. Social & Religious Reform Movement During the British rule, Raja Ram Mohun Roy, Sir Syed Ahmed Khan, Keshab Chander Sen, Mahadev Govind Ranade, M.K. Gandhi, Swami Dayananda etc. led a number of social and religious reform movements which greatly encouraged rational and critical thinking. Naturally, this helped the movement of secularism.

4. Legal Reforms. In modern times, Hindu Code Bill greatly modernized and secularized the Hindu society. The various laws enable women to seek divorce and receive alimony. Property succession provisions, adoption provisions etc. have helped to liberate and emancipate women. This made the marriage and family a non-permanent affair. The 1955 Untouchability Eradication Act gave blow to untouchability and the distinction of pure and impure. In modern times, all adults are equal before law. Besides, the constitutional provision of equality before law, Indian Constitution declares India to be a secular democratic republic. All this has of course encouraged secular forces in India.

5. Contribution of Political Organization. Some political organization like D.M.K. have directly attacked the Hindu society and thus, encouraged secularism. On the other hand, Hindu organizations like R.S.S. and Hindu Mahashabha also helped secularization by calling for reform in the Hindu society.

6. Urbanization. In cities, the separateness of caste is impossible. This indirectly encouraged secularism.

7. Lack of Hindu Organization. From the religious view-point, the Christian, the Muslim, the Jaina and Sikh are more organized than the Hindus. In Hinduism, there are more sects than in any other religion. Though, these sects are nominally Hindu there is little common among them. Therefore, the sectarian organizations are not helpful to Hinduism as a whole. There are many Hindus who are so only in name and believe almost nothing of Hinduism. Hinduism is indeed so catholic a religion that any body, believing in any God and having any life style, may be considered Hindu. On account of this loose organization, the influence of Hinduism today is waning. Because of its loose character and organization, Hindus are not strict about their religious duties and performances. Because of this Hinduism is more vulnerable to secularization than any other religion.

8. Secularization of Indian Culture. Though, the Indian culture is known as being religion-dominated, it is becoming progressively secularized. In this process of secularization, modern education, cinema, radio, newspaper etc. are important factors. In modern times, the foundation of many cultural beliefs is found in secular matters rather than religious. In this way in the spheres of literature, art, music etc. the influence of religion is declining and the influence of democratic, rational and scientific thinking is increasing. India, being a secular country, its publicity department tries to spread the message of secularism.

9. Secularization of Professions. In ancient India, the choice of profession was made on the basis of religion. The religious scriptures had fixed the professions of different castes. Now, the members of modern generation do not consider it obligatory to choose their professions on the basis of religion but are guided by practical and pragmatic considerations in this respect.

10. Lack of Political Support In ancient times, Hindu kings used to support the Hindu religion and this helped it to maintain itself. In the British times also the states like Travancore-Cochin, Mysore, Baroda, Jaipur, Jammu and Kashmir, where Hindu Rajas were ruling were citadels of Hindu Dharma because these kings were supporting the Hindu Dharma. After the independence when the states got merged into federal India the support to Hindu Dharma came to an end. Now-a-days, Nepal is the only country where Hinduism is receiving royal patronage. Of course, the overwhelming majority of Hindus live in India. The withdrawal of government support has dealt a blow to spread and maintenance of Hinduism. As the Hindu institutions are denied the financial help from the government they have become weak and unviable. Even the property of Mathas is coming under state control. On account of decline in the prestige, power and influence of mathas, the heads of these mathas have begun taking interest in politics. All this has given fillip to the process of secularization.

The above discussion of the process of secularization makes it clear that in the near future there is no possibility of this process slowing down. In the recent past, an organization entitled 'Vishwa Hindu Parishad' is trying to consolidate the Hindu interests at an international level. The efforts of this organization may help Hindus to organize politically; but it is not expected that this will halt the process of secularization. Indeed, the spread of secularization is due to the reason that, in order to be a Hindu, it is not obligatory to perform any rituals and carry out any religious observances. For example, a Hindu may or may not go to a temple or observe fast on a particular day etc. A Hindu is left to his own discretion to chalk out his way of life. This liberalism overtakes Hinduism and under its influence a certain minimum code of conduct becomes obligatory for every Hindu, the process of secularization may slow down but it cannot be altogether halted. Indeed, except Hindus the followers of all other religions are under obligation to follow certain rules of conduct and perform certain religious observances. For example, a Mohamrpaden must have innate faith in the prophethood of Mohammad and the unity of God and besides perform 'namaz' five times a day. That is why, the process of secularization is slow among Muslims. If Hinduism wants to maintain its separate entity it must make it obligatory upon its adherents to compulsorily perform certain actions. This would, on the one hand, encourage a sense of unity among Hindus and, on the other, distinguish it from other religions.

QUESTIONS FOR EXERCISE

1. What do you understand by secularism? Give a sociological analysis of the trend of secularism in India.
2. Discuss the impact of secularization on Indian culture.
3. "India is a secular state." Evaluate.
4. "Indian Constitution has established a secular state." Evaluate.
5. "Indian Constitution has established a secular state." Evaluate. What do you understand by secularism? Give a sociological analysis of the trend of secularism in India.

20

Socio-Religious Movements in India

After the British empire had been established in India it appeared that they had got a firm foothold in the country. The British analyzed the social life of the Indians as it then existed and came to the obvious conclusion that the Hindus were lagging behind all others in the religious, social, political and economic fields. They encouraged them in the attempt to impose their own culture and civilization upon the local population, believing that under the circumstances the people of India would be more receptive than otherwise. By this time, most of the social malpractices that had been introduced in Indian society from time to time, such hideous rituals as the hypocrisy of pundits, child marriage, performance of sati, bigamy, caste discrimination, purdah, had all matured and come to their full growth. It was in this milieu that the Christian missionaries started preaching their own religion through the medium of Hindi, a task which was supplemented by the government, which tried to convert Indians to a western culture through the use of English language. That the British succeeded in their design is evident from the rapidity with which the local population accepted this foreign culture and language. One immediate effect of this religious brain-washing was that the more rigid and fanatic Hindus exerted their energies to oppose any reform in their own religion while another section of Hindus immediately took to the English culture and were by heart and soul in favour of adopting it without delay. The latter group of people was attracted primarily by the scientific developments taking place in the West. At the same time another group of people separated itself from either of the two fanatic and extremist thinkers and advocated a synthesis between Indian culture and the new British culture, particularly the latter's work in the field of science. Particular group of thinkers opposed any kind of dogmatic inflexibility where religion is concerned, but also objected to being made slaves of science. It was their declared aim to find some kind of synthesis between the two. And most of the movements for social or religious reform that occurred in the nineteenth century were the result of the energetic working of this group.

Intellectual Awakening

Renaissance is essentially an intellectual awakening. The most important sign of an intellectual awakening is criticism, a critical analysis and questioning of all the dogmas held hitherto in different fields of knowledge such as metaphysical, social, economic and political, etc. The Renaissance thinkers questioned all old concepts and principles in this field. This was party due to the intellectual influence of the West exerted through Western education. It is noteworthy that most of the Renaissance thinkers were educated in the West. This gave them an opportunity to compare their own thought and social institutions with the thought and social institutions of the West. As a result of this comparison they could on the one hand realise their low status and on the other hand understand its reasons. Therefore, naturally, they felt an urgent need of social reform. Examples of this class of thinkers can be found in Raja Ram Mohun Roy, Keshab Chandra Sen, Vivekananda and Ramkrishna among others. These were undoubtedly the first people to question the medieval thinking and practices in India.

Revivalist

In spite of an intellectual scrutiny and questioning of the ideas prevalent in different fields of Indian life, the Renaissance thinkers were basically revivalist. This revivalist goes back to the age of Vedas and the Upanisads. Almost all these thinkers read Vedas and Upanisads and were impressed by their spirit. They found their teachings even more profound than the ideas prevalent in the West. They felt that India need not imitate the West in any field of life, it should rather go back to its own ancient treasurers of thought in philosophy, social thought and political thinking. They realised that the ancient Indian social and political institutions could be the sound basis for a future awakened India. This revivalism can be found in almost all the social reform movements of the Renaissance period including Brahmo Samaj, Arya Samaj, Prarthana Samaj, Ramkrishna Mission and Theosophical Society. The philosophical basis of all these reform movements was supplied by the Vedas, the Upanisads, and the Bhagwadgita. Their religious thinking and cosmopolitanism and a synthetic approach to religion was a direct result of the monism and monotheism taught by the Upanisads. Their emphasis on social service and their humanism was a derivative from the Bhagwadgita. This is true not only about Raja Ram Mohun Roy, Swami Dayanand, Keshab Chandra Sen, Ramkrishna and Vivekananda, but also about our contemporary Indian social philosophers including Sri Aurobindo, Rabindranath Tagore, M.K. Gandhi and others. Thus, the contemporary Indian social philosophy is not so much impressed by the Western thought as it is influenced by the ancient Indian philosophy. In fact, it is a home-coming in philosophy after a degeneration and a downward curve in the medieval ages. It is the revival of the spirit of Swadeshi. This birth of nationalism is not only characteristic of nineteenth century India but the whole of Asia. It could be seen in almost all the Asian and African countries. This awakening was very much influenced by the intellectual awakening in Europe but everywhere it was embedded in the indigenous soil.

CAUSATIVE SOCIO-POLITICAL FACTORS

The factors responsible for reform movement and the new awakening and reconstruction of Indian social thought were intellectual as well as social and political. Social thought, while on the one hand bound with the philosophical traditions of the country, is very much influenced by the contemporary sociopolitical circumstances. In fact, social thought must change with the time. This change does not eliminate continuity. Both continuity and change are equally signs of wisdom. This is particularly in the case of social thought which does not search after eternal truth but attempts to give an integral vision about the social ideal, partly in continuity with the ancient tradition and partly as a result of contemporary circumstances. Indian thinkers were very much encouraged by the remarks of the western Indologists about the worth of Indian philosophical treatises. As the English translations of the Indian works were available in the West, and as great men like Vivekananda introduced Indian thought to the West, a great number of Western thinkers became interested in the study of Indian philosophy. To their amazement, they found that the Indian thought was no less in depth and width than any thought propounded in the West, and they expressed this amazement in so many words. This encouraged the intelligentsia in India to read the ancient scriptures and find out solution of socio-political problems in them. Not only, Raja Ram Mohun Roy and Vivekananda sought the answers to social and political problems in Gita and Upanisads, but Tagore and Gandhi were equally inspired by them. Besides, the intellectual awakening and the urge for revival among Indian intelligentsia the following socio-political factors were responsible for reform movement in Indian society:

1. Western Education. Almost all the important Renaissance thinkers including Bhandarkar, Ranade, Chiploonkar, Tilak, Agarkar, Gokhale, the name only a few, had high academic degrees in Western education. Though, Macaulay aimed at creating a class of civil servants by introducing English education in India, the same education created revolutionary thinkers like Raja Ram Mohun Roy, Keshab Chandra Sen, Mahadev Govind Ranade and Vivekananda. The most important characteristics of western education were: intellectual bias, reactionism, individualism, critical attitude to scripture, synthetic approach to religion, secularism, cosmopolitanism and humanism. All these characteristics were imbibed by the intelligentsia through the growth of Western education in India. Thus, the spread of education by the Britishers in India was undoubtedly the most important social factor responsible for the new awakening and reconstruction of Indian thought.

2. Establishment of New Associations and Societies. Western education and a more intimate contact with the Western society led to an intense urge for social and political reforms in India. This led to the establishment of dozens of associations and societies. Phule established Satya Shodhak Samaj — with the purpose of reform in Maharashtra. Prarthana Samaj was another important institution of social reforms in Maharashtra. In Bengal, Brahmo Samaj was established by Raja Ram Mohun Roy mainly for intellectual awakening but also for social and political reforms. Another important association was Ramkrishna Mission founded by Vivekananda in the name of his master Ramkrishna. Swami Dayananda established Arya Samaj which rapidly spread throughout the northern India and carried out reforms in almost all the directions. Besides, Theosophical Society established by Annie Besant was an important society for religious reforms in India. All these new associations and societies encouraged new thinking and reconstruction of social institutions on the pattern of ancient Indian examples.

3. Indian Approach to the Economic Problems. An important part of the revivalist tendency of the Renaissance period was an Indian approach to the economic problems. Eminent economic thinkers pointed out that Indian cannot solve its economic problems by an uncritical application of doctrines of Smith, Ricardo and Mill. They, on the other hand, pointed out that solutions can be found in the procedures adopted by ancient Indian village republics. M.G. Ranade, in his essays on Indian economics, pleaded for an Indian approach to economic problems. This emphasis is the background of the economic programmes of reconstruction found in the thought of Rabindranath Tagore and M.K. Gandhi in 20th Century.

4. Rise of Nationalism. The Renaissance period witnessed a rise of nationalism in almost all the slave countries of the world including India. Illustrious poets and thinkers wrote works expressing intense sentiments of patriotism. Bankim Chandra Chatterjee found the *Banga Darshan* in 1872 and published his famous patriotic novel *Anandmath.* This novel was highly acclaimed by Sri Aurobindo who was another great patriotic writer that India produced. Swami Dayananda also strongly advocated nationalism in most of his writings. The most important leader of the rise of nationalism in India, however, was B.G. Tilak, who through his two famous weeklies, *The Kesari* and *The Mahratta* took a leading part in spreading patriotic sentiments in the country. Vishnushastri Chiploonkar was another great patriotic writer of Maharashtra. Other poets and writers praised national heroes in their writings and aroused national sentiments in the nation. Ram Das and Shivaji, Maharana Pratap and Guru Govind Singh were praised by these poets and writers. All this created a wave of nationalism and patriotism, very much explicitly in the writings of contemporary Indian social philosophers including Sri Aurobindo, Vivekananda, Tagore and Gandhi.

5. The Growth of Hindi Literature. An important social factor in the new awakening and reconstruction of Indian thought was the growth of Hindi language and literature. This is so since the rise of a nation is very much dependent on the growth of a national language. Hindi was propagated as the national language of India and as a popular vehicle for the communication of national and patriotic sentiments. Among the noteworthy writings of this period were *Premsagar* of Lallulal, *Nasiketopakhyana* of Sadal Misra and *Bharat Durdasha* of Bharatendu Harishchandra. Swami Dayananda Saraswati wrote his famous *Satvartha Prakash* in Hindi. Most of the prose and poetry works of this period expressed patriotic and nationalistic sentiments.

6. Establishment of Western Political Institutions. The most important political factor responsible for new awakening and reconstruction of Indian thought was the introduction in India of Western political institutions such as execrative council, the law member, the law commission and the supreme court etc. These political institutions aroused nationality in Indian political thought and Indian nationalists started demanding more and more political rights and equality before law. There was a growing demand for the introduction of British type representative political bodies in the country by Raja Ram Mohun Roy, Dadabhai Naoroji, Surendranath Benerji, Gopal Krishna Gokhale and other Indian political leaders.

7. Establishment of Indian National Congress. The most momentous event in the history of Indian nationalism was the establishment of Indian National Congress by A.O. Hume in 1885. Though, Hume established Congress with the purpose of creating a class of thinkers, who could advise the British to introduce necessary reforms in India, gradually, Indian National Congress became a platform for the demand of complete freedom from the British rule. The most important contribution in this direction was given by B.G. Tilak, Lala Lajpatrai and Bipin Chandra Pal. After the extremists were separated from the main organisation they carried on their activities separately. In 1920, the same Indian National Congress which was a beginning of political activity in Renaissance period became the herald of Indian Nationalism under the leadership of M.K. Gandhi who demanded *Purna Swarajya.* Along with presenting political demands before the Britishers, leaders of Indian National Congress were active in social and political reform activities. Each one of them intensely thought over the social and political problems of the country and tried to find out solutions on the basis of suggestions from the West and inspirations from the ancient Indian literature.

8. Rise of New Economic Class. No country can progress in thought or in practice without the indigenous economic support. The British rule in India gradually encouraged Indian people to carry on trade and commerce on capitalistic basis. This led to the rise of a new economic class which gradually became the economic base of social and nationalistic movements. It was this class which contributed generously to the funds of Brahmo Samaj, the Arya Samaj and the Indian National Congress. It can be said without exaggeration that without the economic support of this class modern Renaissance could not get a momentum in the country.

9. Western Political Literature. Besides the introduction of Western political institutions, the Britishers introduced western political literature in India. While some of the literature was imported from the West such as the works of Karl Marx, Lenin, Mussolini, Hitler, Spencer, Mill, Tolstoy and Ruskin etc., literature was produced by Indian writers also introducing the life and works of the leaders of Western society to the Indian people. The important among these writers were Surendranath Benerji, Lala Lajpatrai and V.D. Savarkar. Among the later writers were Iqbal and Sri Aurobindo and the celebrated Nobel prize winner Rabindranath Tagore.

10. Social Legislation. All the above factors led to an increase in intellectual awakening and a demand for social legislation in different fields. Almost all the Renaissance thinkers were pained at the condition of women and low-caste people in India. Raja Ram Mohun Roy, Keshab Chandra Sen, Swami Dayananda, Ishwar Chandra Vidyasagar, M.G. Ranade and Telang demanded social legislation in every field of social life. They demanded the abolition of Sati custom, the emancipation of women and elimination of all the drawbacks of the down-trodden elements in the society. Before this demand the Britishers were almost cool to social reform in India. But the demands raised by these eminent leaders gradually resulted in social legislation in different fields leading to social and political emancipation of the backward classes.

The above socio-political factors created a new awakening in the country. This awakening resulted in several social and political reform movements. Of these, the most representative movements of the period were: Adi Brahmo Samaj of Ram Mohun Roy, Brahmo Samaj of Keshab Chandra Sen, Ramkrishna Mission of Vivekananda, Theosophical Society of Madame Blavatsky and Colonel Olcott and last though not the least the Arya Samaj of Swami Dayananda.

BRAHMO SAMAJ

Raja Ram Mohun Roy

The first chief religious reformer of the nineteenth century was Raja Ram Mohun Roy, whose efforts in his chosen field left a deep impression upon contemporary social, political and religious thinking. Ram Mohun Roy was born in a small village named Radhanagar in Bengal in the year 1772. He belonged to a family of Brahmins. He was a linguist who had mastered Sanskrit, English, Hindi, Persian, Hebrew, Greek and Latin. He made use of his knowledge to study the religious books in each of these languages and thereby he became quite knowledgeable on the subject of religion. He realized that if Hindu religion was to retain its life and strength it must undergo some modification, and it was with this end in view that the Brahmo Samaj was established in 1822. The principles of this society avoided all rigidity, stressing the importance of universal brotherhood and equality and the existence of a single God. In the social sphere Ram Mohun Roy opposed all iniquity, child marriage, sati, bigamy, caste discrimination and the rest of the problems that beset Hindu society. In the field of religion he could not and did not support the practice of priestly hypocrisy, worship of stone idols, the elaborate rituals, human and other sacrifices made as part of yagya, etc. He pointed out the need for widow remarriage and the education of women. He did not oppose the western style of education since he was aware that the gulf of scientific learning that existed in Indian society could be filled only by this form of education. He exerted himself for the improvement and advancement of Indian literature and culture. He wanted the people to restrict themselves to constitutional methods in fighting for their freedom. Brahmo Samaj achieved wide popularity among the Bengalis, and after

Ram Mohun Roy it was further propagated by such great figures as Devendranath Tagore and Keshab Chandra Sen. After some time the Samaj broke up into two groups on account of differences on basic principles, resulting in the formation of the Adi Brahmo Samaj led by D.N. Tagore and the Brahmo Samaj headed by Keshab Chandra Sen. Later on the latter became prominent and progressive when such eminent persons as Jagdish Chandra Bose, Bipin Chandra Pal, C.R. Das and Aurobindo Ghose joined it.

Teaching of Brahmo Samaj

The main teachings of the Brahmo Samaj can be summed up as enunciated by Devendranath Tagore as follows:

1. In the beginning there was naught. The one Supreme alone existed. He created the whole universe.

2. He alone is the God of Truth, Infinite Wisdom, Goodness and Power Eternal and Allpervading, the One without a second *(Ekamevadvitiyam),*

3. In His worship lies our salvation in this world and in the next.

4. Loving Him and doing that which He loveth constitute His worship.

The social thought of Brahmo Samaj can be summed up in the following words of Devendranath, "He who desireth the good of mankind must look on others as he looks on himself. It behoves thee to love thy neighbour, since it causes thee pain to be hated by another. Thus, in all things shalt thou deal with others by comparing them with thyself; for as pleasure and pain effect thee, so do they affect all creatures. Such conduct alone is the means of attaining wellbeing. He who adores God and loves man, is a saint. Such a man never rejoices in finding fault with men, for man is beloved of him. He is pained by the sight of a fault in others and lovingly does he labour for its correction. He loves man as man; and owing to that love, is pleased by the sight of good, and grieved by the sight of evil in man. Therefore, he is unable to proclaim the faults of others with rejoicing. The satisfaction of the inner spirit, or, in other words, a good conscience, is the unfailing fruit of the practice of righteousness. In this approval of conscience in self is the approval of God. If the inner spirit is satisfied, all sufferings cease. Without the practice of righteousness, the inner spirit is never satisfied. The mind may find enjoyment in the pleasures of the world, but if the conscience is diseased, then even the height of worldly bliss becomes valueless. Therefore, by the practice of righteousness, ye shall preserve a clear conscience, and ye shall abandon all things whereby the satisfaction of the spirit may be marred."

The Renaissance thinkers advocated a synthetic approach to religion which was followed by contemporary Indian social thinkers. This tendency was most eloquent in the sayings of Ramkrishana. It was circulated by his able disciple Vivekananda. The same tendency was again expressed in M.K. Gandhi's evening prayer where he used to recite Quran and Bible alongwith Gita. Among the Renaissance thinkers Ram Mohun Roy was almost the first to start this syntheitcs approach to religion. He was equally impressed by Bible, Quran, Upanisads and

Gita. He believed in monotheism and monism though he failed to distinguish between the two. He was bitterly against sectarianism, superstition and idolatry but he did not repudiate Vedic religion. Like Spinoza he accepted substance as the ultimate reality, but unlike him he considered attributes as much necessary as the substance. Here he was more impressed by Ramanuj and Vaishnava Saints.

Keshab Chandra Sen and his Brahmo Samaj

Keshab Chandra Sen, though inspired by Ram Mohun Roy differed in some of his views and therefore founded the Brahmo Samaj of India on November 11, 1866, separate from the Adi Brahmo Samaj. Like Roy he had wide reading in religion and was impressed by Bible, the Zend Avesta and the Kuran along with the Upanisads and the Bhagwadgita. Thus, we find an electric and syntheitic approach in the philosophy and religion of Keshab Chandra Sen. He considered God as a creative force and used the word God force. According to him, the design and harmony witnessed in Nature is a sufficient proof for the reality of the creator of the world.

ARYA SAMAJ

Both the Brahmo Samaj and the Prarthana Samaj showed clear influence of Western thinking on their principles, since both admittedly wanted to arrive at some synthesis between the East and the West. It was Dayanand Saraswati, who was born in Gujarat, who tried to revive the Indian traditional philosophy and to modify it to suit the contemporary situation. He was in favour of improving present day society in the light of accepted ideals of old, since, he accepted the Vedas as the basis of all social and religious change that he advocated. It was his desire to revive the Vedic religion, since as he pointed out with perfect truth, there is nothing in the Vedas to support such disliked institutions as restrictions on widows remarriage, child marriage, sati, caste discrimination, etc. He agreed that all such malpractices should be eliminated from Indian society at the earliest, and pointed out that to do so would be in no way inconsistent with Indian cultural tradition. He established his Arya Samaj in 1877 with the intention of reviving the ancient Vedic religion and culture. Under his guidance the samaj started a social revolution against all the evils that could be found in contemporary society. Its main achievement lay in the possibilities that society had opened up to those people who had abandoned Hindu religion and gone on to Christianity and Islam to return to Hindu religion.

THEOSOPHICAL SOCIETY

Among the representative movements of Renaissance period Theosophical Society occupied an important place. It is so since it re-oriented ancient Indian Philosophy of the Upanisads and the Bhagwadgita in modern language. Theosophical Society was established by Madame Blavatsky and Colonel Olcott. Annie Besant became the president of this society in 1907. Under her presidentship, theosophical society became a real force not only in the field of philosophy and religion but also in the fields of social and political reforms in India. Annie Besant was so much influenced by Hinduism that she believed that she was Hindu in past life. She came to India in 1893 at the age of forty-six and devoted herself to social, religious, educational and some times political activities. Her political views were not very mature but she did make a mark in the field of religion and social thought. Her philosophical views were almost the same as found in Hinduism. She was particularly fascinated by Hindu pantheism and considered Advaita Vedanta as the intellectual view between Hinduism and Islam. Her views in the field of religion were similar to those of Ramkrishna, Vivekananda and Dayanand. She believed in all the dictums of Hinduism. She was very much impressed by the Bhagwadgita and wrote a famous commentary on it. Annie Besant believed that so far five main races and their subdivisions have evolved in the world. She thought that in future two more root races will evolve thus bringing the total to seven. She considered Aryan race as the best and thought that central Asia is its place of origin. The following are the important socio-political ideas of Annie Besant:

1. Liberty. Like Roy and Keshab Sen, Annie Besant demanded home rule for India. She wrote, "I demand for every man, whatever be his opinions, that he shall be able to speak out with honest frankness the result of honest thought without forfeiting his rights as citizen, without destroying his social position, and without troubling his domestic peace...Liberty is immortal and internal and her triumph is sure, however it may be delayed...and hers is also the triumph of tomorrow if only we who adore her, only we can be true to ourselves and each other. But they who love her must work for her, as well as worship her, for labour is the only prayer to Liberty, and devotion the only praise. " Explaining her idea of liberty and the free men and women in a free nation she said, "You can only have a free nation when you have free men to build it out of free men and women both; but no man is free and no woman is free who is under the dominance of appetite, or vice, or drunkenness, or any form of evil which he is unable to control. Self-control is the foundation on which alone freedom can be built. Without that you have anarchy, not freedom, and every increase of the present anarchy is paid for by the price of happiness, which is given in exchange."

2. Aristocratic Socialism. Annie Besant was against representative democracy. Like Plato she wanted to entrust the function of Government to a selected class of people. Criticising representative democracy as Majoritarianism she said, "... our ideal of Brotherhood applied to Government claims power for the wise and not for the ignorant; places law-making in the hands of those who understand the complex problems of industry, and not in the hands of those who only know the needs of the household, or perhaps the needs of the town. The people have a right to happiness, but they can never get it for themselves by physical force, by legal violence and by competition, they must be guided to it by knowledge by those who understand." She wanted a socialism based on common agreement leading to the realisation of mutually beneficial and enjoyable adjustment of capacities and functions. Condemning mass socialism she said, "A democratic socialism, controlled by votes, guided by numbers, can never succeed; a truly aristocratic socialism, controlled by duty, guided by wisdom, is the next step upward in civilization."

3. Spiritual Nationalism. Annie Besant started the Gospel of spiritual nationalism which was later on expressed in the writings of Sri Aurobindo, Rabindranath Tagore and M.K. Gandhi. In her presidential speech at the Calcutta session of Indian National Congress she said, "For what is a Nation? It is part of the Divine Fire, a fragment of the Divine life, outbreathed into the world, and gathering round itself a mass of individuals, its powers, in a world, its type, depend on the fragment of the Divine Life embodied in it...The magic of Nationality is the feeling of oneness, and the use of nationality is to serve the world in the particular way for which its type fits it." Thus, each nation is a unique expression of the Divine. Each nation has an individuality and character and its sole *Swadharma* is to express its own character. In the words of Annie Besant, "A Nation is distinctly an Individual with a character, and that character depends on the nature of the spirit at its core and its gradual unfolding to play its part in humanity as a whole...If India still survives all who were her contemporaries five thousand years ago, it is because the same spirit lives in her national body as lived in it then." In the constitution of a Nation she considered national religion as the most important element. She was all praise for India and thought very high about her role in the future world. She adored Hinduism and considered it as the most important world religion.

Annie Besant's writings about the mission of India can be equated with the writings of Vivekananda and Aurobindo on this issue. Pointing out the importance of maintaining national individuality she wrote, "No two individuals are alike, and similarly, no two Nations are alike. It is the totality of all Nations that builds up Humanity the human reflection of Ishvara Himself. Each has its own individuality. That which makes the richness of the national life of India is its marvellous literature, its history, its religion, its science and all these are so highly evolved because the Nation is so ancient a Nation. During the early life of a Nation, religion is an essential for the binding together of the individuals who make the Nation. India was born, as it were, in the womb of Hinduism, and her body was far long shaped by that religion. Religion is a binding force, and India has had a longer binding together by religion than any other Nation in the world, as she is the oldest of the living Nations."

Applauding the role of India in the history of the world Annie Besant, in her presidential speech to Indian National Congress at Calcutta, said, "Is there any other land which evokes such love for her spirituality, such admiration for her literature, such homage for valour, as this glorious Mother of Nations, from whose womb these went forth? And has any land suffered as our India has suffered, since her sword was broken on Kurukshetra, and the peoples of Europe and of Asia swept across her borders, laid waste her cities and discrowded her Kings? They came to conquer, but they remained to be absorbed. At last, out of those mingled peoples, the Divine Artificer has welded a Nation, compact not only of her own virtue, but also of those her foes had brought to her and gradually eliminating the vices which they had also brought."

The essence of spiritual nationalism according to Annie Besant is religion. Religion is a revivifying force. It teaches solidarity. Pleading for the religious basis of spiritual nationalism, Annie Besant said, "I feel strongly that only on the basis of religion can a true Nationality be built up. Religion itself which gives the sense of human dignity joined to the sense of human duty, and the self-respect of India could never have arisen as it has risen today, had not the philosophies and the relations of past-won their empire over the Indian heart; and the virtues that the great religions typify, all of which we find in this sacred land, are virtues that we need for the building of our Nations."

Commonwealth of Nations

Annie Besant, Mazzini, Gandhi and Sri Aurobindo had a vision of a commonwealth of Nations substituting the world empire. After the solidarity of each nations she considered it necessary to integrate all the nations in a world federation so that the ideal of world peace may be achieved. In her concept of universalism the individual, the society, the nation and finally the humanity form ever widening circles, each including the smaller one and each giving place to a wider circle. Explaining her idea of the next stage in human evolution after the realisation of spiritual nationalism, Annie Besant pointed out, "The next stage of the Plan is the building up of a free Commonwealth of Nations in which India plays her equal part. This is why the English came here and others had to go away; and the one Nation that is free in her institutions in her own island, if not free in her practice outside her own island, is the English Nation, chosen to come here and blend with the Indian Nation in the building up now of the World Empire, to be really a World Commonwealth, not a World Empire which was to rule by force but a World Federation which was to govern by love and in peace."

Opposition of Non-Cooperation

Like Ram Mohun Roy, and Keshab Chandra Sen, Annie Besant considered British rule in India as a blessing. Therefore, she developed differences with B.G. Tilak and even with the moderate M.K. Gandhi. She was against Gandhian programme of non-cooperation for achieving Swarajya. She levelled three main charges against Gandhian non-cooperation movement. Firstly, she considered it revolutionary. Secondly, she feared that it will create hatred between the Indian and the British. Thirdly, she thought that non-cooperation may disrupt Indian social structure. Expressing her strong feelings in this connection she said, "Non-cooperation strikes at the foundation of society which is based on cooperation and can only exist through continued cooperation. It means reversion to anarchy, a violent breaking of all the mutual ties which bind men together. It will inevitably lead to rioting and bloodshed, which can only have once result-repression and the putting off of all improvement in our civil conditions."

The above discussion about the social and political ideas of Annie Besant make it amply clear that she was one of those spiritual savants of the country who not only thought out solutions for the present problems but also looked to the future where in an integrated humanity India may fulfil a very important role. Her moderate opposition of the British and her praise for them aroused opposition of the moderates and the extremists but no one can deny that the essentials of contemporary Indian social philosophy such as spiritual nationalism, India's unique mission, and a world brotherhood had their beginnings in her thought.

RAMKRISHNA PARAMHANSA AND VIVE KAN AN DA

Teachings of Ramkrishna Paramhansa

Ramkrishna Paramhansa, born on 18th February 1835, influenced almost all the great men of 19th century in India. He was not at all an academic philosopher, still less a social reformer or a politician, but his great religious status and powers of consciousness force influenced national leaders far and wide. In the tradition of ancient Indian philosophy and religion he preached monism. According to him, reality is one though it manifests in different ways at different places. Through, the help of small stories he explained to his audience that ultimately the essence of every thing is the same. The ancient Indian *Mahavakyas of Aham Brahmasmi* and *Tatwamasi* were the main bases of his religious teachings. He, however, synthesized Advaita Vedanta with Vaishnava cult of Bhakti. On the other hand, he had equal respect for other great religions of the world including Islam, Christianity and Buddhism. He preached that the essentials of all these religions are the same and there is hardly any occasion to fight on this issue. God realisation is the aim of life and Ramkrishna could realise God not only in inner consciousness but sometimes even in his physical body. His contact so much impressed Vivekananda that the latter immediately became his disciple and toured the entire world to preach the teachings of Ramkrishna. As Socrate's ideas are known through the dialogues of Plato similarly the teachings of Ramkrishna are better known through the speeches of Vivekananda.

The chief aim of sadhana according to Ramkrishna is the realization of God. He preached discarding of desire for material prosperity and lust for women and gold. This, however, does not require escape from the worldly life, but a constant meditation upon God. Ramkrishna believed that materialism and attachment to worldly can be eliminated by their redirection towards God. He explained by several parables such as:

"As an unchaste woman, busily engaged in household affairs, is all the while thinking of her secret lover, even so, O thou man of the world, do the round of worldly duties: but fix thy heart always on the Lord."

"As a wet nurse in a rich family brings up the child of her master, loving the baby as if it were her own, but knows well that she has no claim upon it; so think ye also that you are but trustees and guardians of your children whose real father is the Lord God in Heaven."

The life of Ramkrishna was a laboratory for the synthesis of great, religions. He believed that all religions of the world were true and anyone may lead to salvation. He experienced that the spiritual practices in any religion were equally effective. Every religion leads to the path of salvation. He was asked how God could be both immanent and transcendent, to which he said, "Exactly as water can exist in a liquid, solid and invisible form." Again, "As water is called by different names in different languages, so different religions call God by different names like Hari, Siva, Allah, Christ, etc., but all denote the same God."

He was further asked that, "If the God of every religion is the same, why is it then that the God is painted differently by different religionists?" He answered: "God is one but his aspects are different; as one master of the house is father to one, brother to another, and husband to a third, and is called by different persons, so one God is described and called in various ways according to the particular aspect in which he appears to his particular worshippers." This spirit of catholicity and tolerance is the essence of the teachings of Ramkrishna and therefore of Vivekananda. Admitting his debt to Ramkrishna, Vivekananda, while delivering an address at the Shakespeare club of Pasedona, California, on January 27, 1900 said: "Now all the ideas that I preach are only an attempt to echo his ideas. Nothing is mine originally except the wicked ones. But every word that I have ever uttered which is true and good, is simply an attempt to echo his voice."

Alms and Ideals of Ramkrishna Mission

On May 5, 1897 a meeting of the disciples of Ramkrishna under the leadership of Swami Vivekananda unanimously adopted the following aims and ideals of Ramakrishna mission:

1. The Association (Sangha) shall be known as the Ramkrishna Mission.

2. (a) This new Mission is to preach the truths which Sri Ramkrishna has, for the good of humanity preached and demonstrated by practical application in his own life, and to help others to put these truths into practice in their lives for their temporal, mental and spiritual advancement.

(b) To conduct the activities of the movement for the establishment of fellowship among the followers of different religions, knowing them all to be so many forms only of one underlying eternal Religion.

3. Its methods of action are:

(a) to train men so as to make them competent to teach such knowledge of sciences as are conducive to the material and spiritual welfare of the masses.

(b) to promote and encourage arts and industries, and

(c) to introduce and spread among the people in general Vedantic and other religious ideas in the way in which they are elucidated in the life of Sri Ramkrishna.

4. It should have two branches of action:

(a) Indian Work Department and

(b) Foreign Department.

(a) The activities of the Indian Department should be directed to the establishment of Maths and Ashrams in different parts of India for the training of Sannyasins and such of the householders as may be willing to devote their lives to the teaching of others.

(b) Whereas its work in the Foreign Department should be to send trained members of the order to countries outside India to start centres there for the preaching of Vedanta in order to bring about a close relation and better understanding between India and foreign countries.

5. The aims and the objects of the Mission being purely spiritual and humanitarian, it shall have no connection with politics.

6. Anyone who believes in the Mission of Sri Ramkrishna, or who sympathizes or is willing to cooperate with the above mentioned aims and objects of the Association, is eligible for the membership."

Under the able presidentship of Vivekananda, Ramkrishna mission did very important work in the field of social and religious reform. Its branches were spread throughout the country and even outside India. After Vivekananda the illustrious followers of the mission such as Swami Yogananda and Swami Brahmananda carried out the work of the mission.

The foregoing account does not exhaust the list of reform societies that sprang up during this period. It was a very fertile period for reform work. In 1861, Shivdayal, a businessman belonging to Agra, established the Radhaswami Satsang. This group makes no distinction of caste or creed, and treats the guru as an incarnation of God. This group continues its existence in Dayalbagh in Agra. In 1808, the Dev Samaj was started by Shivnarain Agnihotri who had originally been one of the staunch followers of Brahmo Samaj. In 1873, Sanatan Dharma Rakshini Sabha was born in Calcutta, its avowed aim being to propagate the Sanatan Hindu religion.

QUESTIONS FOR EXERCISE

1. Write an essay on Socio-religious movements in India.
2. Write short note on Brahmo Samaj.
3. Write short note on — (i) Arya Samaj (ii) Theosophical Society.
4. Write short note on the teachings of Ram Krishna Paramhansa and Vivekananda.

21

Tradition and Modernity

In India, today we can see social change in the various walks of life. The goals of this change have been variously described. The social change in India is taking place through the instrumentality of factors like urbanization, industrialization, westernization, secularization, democratization and Sanskritization. In the perspective of cotradictory goals being pursued through social change in India the social scientists have pointed towards the interaction of tradition and modernity. Whereas certain trends of social changes are trying to preserve and revive the traditional values, other trends are working towards modernization on pattern of advanced Western countries. Whether the wave, nay, the storm of modernity sweeping through the country will root out lock stock and barrel every vestige of tradition or some permanent traditional values would stay the social scientists are divided in their opinion on this matter. Here, we would first of all define the concepts of modernity and tradition and then evaluate the relative role of both factors in social change in India.

In June 1960, the tenth Congress for Cultural Freedom took place in Berlin. This congress came into being ten years early. In this conference a review was made of the progress in last decade in solving the problems faced by modern society. In this survey it was tried to evaluate as to how much progress was made towards the ideal of freedom in the political, social and cultural spheres. It cannot be overemphasized that the ideal of freedom is the basic plank of modernity. This conference set up four committees. The first committee went into the conditions of social progress the second committee studied the question of culture and the third and the fourth committees went into the questions of counter-culture and tradition. This conference worked in six stages under the Chairmanship of Prof. Edward Shils of Chicago University. One committee discussed the question of modernity and tradition in the developing societies of Asia and Africa. In this discussion a number of important points were raised. The role of modernity and tradition in social change in the developing countries was very relevant to the Current Indian scene. However, this topic was not discussed in detail because it was not the main theme of discussion. The main theme of discussion was 'Social Progress'. The harmonization of tradition and modernity in the Asian and African Societies had not been discussed intensively. In this conference also it failed to get the full attention.

In November 1961, Indian Committee for Cultural Freedom in co-operation with the office for Asian Affairs arranged a seminar in New Delhi on *'Modernity and Tradition in India'*. Under the Chairmanship of Dr. C.D. Deshmukh about twenty intellectuals participated in the discussion. The committee published the proceedings of the seminar in the book *'Tradition and Modernity in India'* which was edited by Dr. A.B. Shah and Dr. C.R.M. Rao. Many useful points emerged regarding Modernity and Tradition in this book. Though, there was no unanimity on any issue, the seminar nevertheless offered many useful hints for future planning.

The main themes which came up for discussion in this seminar were: 'the meaning of tradition and modernity', 'the problem of interaction between Tradition and Modernity', 'how far Hindu tradition is harmonizable with Modernity', 'what may be accepted from tradition and what must be rejected?' etc. As referred to earlier, there was no unanimity on any of these points in the conference.

WHAT IS TRADITION?

In the above seminar no definite meaning was given to the term tradition though it was explained in a broad sense. Both the terms tradition and modernity are a system of ideas, a system of values and system of institutions. The system of ideas, values and institutions are different in tradition and modernity. Therefore, the worlds of tradition and modernity are different though there is no society which is purely traditional. Dr. Yogendra Singh who contributed a paper in the above mentioned seminar has tried to define the term tradition in the following words: "Tradition is a cumulative heritage of a society which permeates through all levels of social organization, for example, the value system, the social structure and the structure of personality."[1] Thus, tradition is a social heritage. In this social heritage there are three levels — a system of values, a social structure and as a consequence of which is personality structure. This is the sociological interpretation of tradition. There can be other interpretations as well, for example, the metaphysical and historical interpretations. The sociological interpretation of tradition is functional. The metaphysical interpretation pertains to those truths which are the expression of ancient wisdom and which are undying. In these truths is to be found metaphysical unity. From the historical viewpoint there is rise and fall of every tradition. Tradition is based upon spiritual forces which are beyond the human comprehension and therefore divinely inspired. All traditions do not form a self harmonious system but are born, flourish and drop out according to their own destiny. The historical interpretation of tradition is based upon the philosophical meaning of the term.

1 Yogendra Singh, A.B. Shah and C.R.M. Rao (Ed.), *Tradition and Modernity in India,* Manaktalas, Bombay (1965), p. 52.

Both historical and metaphysical interpretations of the term tradition are not relevant to social sciences. In social science we go by the functional meaning of term. The functional meaning of the term tradition is rather a new phenomenon. Though, there is always some development taking place in every society there are certain elements like value system, social structure and the structure of personality which remain more or less permanent. These elements may be called tradition.

CONCEPT OF MODERNITY

In order to understand the problem of tradition and modernity in India, it is most desirable to be clear about the concept of modernity. The concept of modernity is based upon the social structure prevailing in highly advanced countries like U.S.A. and Great Britain. Dr. Lemer in his book '*The Passing of Traditional Society — Modernizing of Middle East*' has recounted five characteristics of modernity based upon the social structure of Western Society. The first characteristic is rapid urbanization; the second is growing literacy, the third is meaningful concourse of idea among people by means of new media, radio, television and books etc., the fourth is increase in proficiency and skill which builds up man power to support the economic progress of the country; the fifth is the growth of political consciousness.

Modernity is a consequence of industrialization. The revolution wrought by industrialization laid the germs of modernity. Inasmuch as industrial revolution took place first in the West the Social Structure of the West is understood to be the model of modernity.

The concept of modernity is wider than that of modernization. By modernization we understand a high level of literacy, culture and urbanization. Due to it, geographic mobility increases and mechanization invades most of the walks of life. On the other hand, modernity is a different indicator of culture whose characteristics are discernment, broad-mindedness, diversity, secularism and the respect for the individual. Thus, modernity implies a respect for the opinion of others and a freedom to follow one's own ideas.

An important aspect of modernity is pluralism, particularly the cultural and value pluralism. As a society moves from traditionalism to modernity, the new knowledge, novel experiences and new realm of values come into being. The traditional European society was dominated by religious orthodoxy and the modern European society is based upon science and technology. Thus, in modernity there is compartmentalization of knowledge and experiences open out.

Modernity is a resultant of the development and advance of practical sciences. With the development of practical sciences, there is development of industrialism, individualism, democracy, freedom and the ideologies and social philosophies opposed to metaphysics and theology. This has brought forth new habits in social behaviour. Modernity is opposed to every type of orthodoxy. Nothing is believed upon relied upon because, it has been prevalent for a long time. Everything is tested on the scale of reason and science. Modernity aims at power, youth, efficiency and intelligence. These are the cornerstones of modernity.

RELATIVITY OF MODERNITY AND TRADITION

Modernity is the cultural result or fallout of industrialization. With the progress in industrialization there is progress of modernity. As industrialization has advanced to maximum in the West, the western society presents the ideal of modernity but it does not follow that the Indian society must be Westernized in order to become modern. Of course, the Japanese society has become Western. But, in India in order to modernize society it is neither advisable nor necessary to ignore and supersede the tradition altogether. In our tradition we can find a number of elements which are compatible with the modern outlook. For a healthy development of any society it is necessary to maintain a continuing link with the past and not to make any abrupt breach with it. Only on the foundations of the past can we build the future. Moreover, the institutions which have stood the test of time need not be abandoned on account of industrialization. Only these need be modified so as to suit the contemporary conditions.

The above is all the more true because the tradition and modernity are relative concepts. As we have referred to earlier, no contemporary society can be considered to be wholly traditional or wholly modern, A society can be more modern or more traditional than another society. In comparison to U.S.A., the Indian Society is more traditional while American society is more modern compared to the Indian Society. It cannot be maintained that the Indian society is absolutely traditional and the American society absolutely modern. According to Prof, Shils, "No useful purpose is served by demonstrating that there is some unbridgeable gap between any two societies. A traditional society is never wholly traditional and totally bereft of the elements of modernity nor is any modern society totally bereft of the traditional elements. It is possible that the traditions of one society may go back to few centuries whereas the traditions of some other society may go back to thousands of years. In one society traditions may be in a rapid process of change, whereas in another society this process may be slow. In other words the transition from tradition to modernity is a constant and regular process though its pace and speed may vary from society to society. In contemporary society, the transition from tradition to modernity is rapid on account of the fast pace of industrialization. The importance of tradition is that it is time tested and is based upon long practical experience. For example, marriages everywhere are based upon traditional rites but nowadays these are undergoing some modifications.

TRADITIONAL CULTURE STANDARDS IN INDIA

In accordance with the definition of 'tradition' given above we can discuss the following aspects of cultural tradition in India:

1. Characteristics of Social Organization. The salient features of Indian social organization are caste system, joint family, rural panchayats and other democratic rural organizations. This has been already discussed. In the traditional social organization in India a powerful structure was erected for the determination of social relations, functions and situations. This helped the establishment of a permanent social organization in India. The social rewards and values were determined in accordance with the basic values of the society. From the rural panchayats to state governments a balance was struck between the demands of centralization and decentralization. The caste system is the basis of social stratification of Indian Society. In the caste system, the social status of a person is determined by the basic values of Hindu Society. The professions are also determined by the castes and this further cements the social organization. In the rural India, the relations between various castes are governed by the Jajmani system. The division of labour among the various castes is also determined by Jajmani system. The social status and functions are also determined by the Jajmani system. The caste system and the consequent social stratification has saved Indian Society from the courage of class war. The political struggle in India has been confined to upper castes so far and the lower castes have remained out of its orbit. Even change of kingly dynasties did not affect much the rural India. In the western countries, the principles of social and economic stratifications are different and this induces flexibility and mobility in the social organization. In India, the principles of social and economic stratification have remained identical.

2. Machine & Cottage Industry. The traditional economic system is based upon machine and cottage industry. Money has little value in this system; most of exchange is done through barter system. There are no big industries and therefore the processes of social charge are slow. Modernization is a consequence of industrialization. As in the traditional Indian Society there is little industrialization, there is a fillip to modernization as well. As the traditional cottage industry based upon economic system undergoes changes and turns into an industrialized economic system, the processes of modernization would quicken. The industrial civilization is widely different from the traditional civilization. In industrial civilization the science and technology advance and as a consequence of this social changes take place rapidly. Under it the thinking and actions of the individuals are controlled from outside. Democracy is a result of this civilization. Not only from the economic point of view but from the point of view of morality and organization the modernity is very different from the tradition. In India, there is tussle between the traditional social philosophy and modern ideas to get an upper hand. With the establishment of modern civilization in India we find the emergence of nationalism, democracy, vertical mobility and universal education. The class struggle is inevitably due to it. It takes the society towards individualism. The social relations become personalized and there is loosening of social control. The industrial civilization robs men of their conscience and faith. The behaviour of the individual is determined not by traditional modes or conscience of the individual but by the behaviour of others. The processes of socialization and personality formation are quite different in the two. This difference is evident not only if we compare the Indian and the American civilizations but also in companions of the old and new social conditions in India. This is so because the modern Indian Society is gradually changing into an industrialized society. The modern Indian Society is flexible and synthetic. Indian civilization is a synthesis of many tendencies. The synthetic approach is favourable to industrialization. As Indian culture in the past has been absorbing and assimilating the new elements, it is possible that it may adjust to industrial change without conflict. The Indian culture is passing through a period of transition and in the transitional period there is a conflict between old and new values. The new social structure and new values are coming into being. There is much progress towards this after independence. In this transitional period there is a need for an intellectual class which can formulate appropriate values and disseminate them in the public. This change is also taking place though there is as yet paucity of this class. In the Five Year Plans we find a blue print of change from the old to new society.

3. Importance of Traditional Values in the Life of an Individual. In the traditional Indian culture, there are guidelines for all sorts of activities of the individual. For example, the idea of Purushartha provides the traditional goals of life to an Indian. The ideas of Dharma (duty), Artha (livelihood), Kama (sex) and Moksha (liberation) inspire Indians to lead the life of Brahmacharya (celibacy), Grahastha (household), Vanprastha (pilgrimage) and Samnyas (Renunciation). In Dharmashastras in India, there are long lists of duties, both categorical and conditional. The duty and rites obligatory upon the individuals at the various stages of life are fully enumerated. These obligations are more or less the same for all classes. If the behaviour of a man is inspired and determined by these considerations it will be said to be traditional. For example, if at the time of marriage, starting business etc. the consideration is given as to what the tradition dictates or one consults the astrologers and priests for this purpose then the behaviour is traditional. A man of orthodox views goes by tradition in whatever he does, and follows the tradition religiously. He is not at all critical and is averse to applying his reason or discrimination. Inasmuch as there is a uniform set of traditions in any society there is little variety in the behaviour in a tradition bound society. For example, in India at the time of marriage, elders are consulted for every minute detail. No ceremony is formalized without their prior approval. On the other hand, a man of modern outlook does everything according to the light of his own reason.

4. Hierarchical. According to Indian culture, caste distinctions are based upon the fundamental differences in human nature and the personalities of different individuals. The Brahmins, Kshatriyas, Vaishyas and Sudras are different in their temperament and aptitudes. In other words, the distinctions among castes were made upon the basis of human nature and temperament though the distinction was not grounded on scientific facts. While it is true that in certain Gurukuls, the Guru used to determine the castes after taking into account the individual temperaments; but there was nothing scientific about it.

5. Influence of Sacrosanct Values. In India, the system of values is based upon a religious and spiritual outlook which cares little for the practical and utilitarian. In the Purusharatha system of values, Moksha gets the highest priority. Though, the possibility of liberation during life is not denied yet by and large it is a transcendental and extra-terrestrial goal. In ancient India, the atheistic systems while not acknowledging the authority of Vedas have nevertheless adopted transcendental Moksha as the ultimate goal of life; only Charvaka philosophy is an exception. According to Charvaka, moksha is impossible; only pleasure is the sole aim of human life. Material goods are a means of attaining pleasure. No wise man would sacrifice the mundane pleasures in the false hope of some heavenly gains or bliss. A bird in hand is better than two in the bush according to this philosophy. Charvaka does not believe in God, soul, heaven etc. They have ridiculed the orthodox philosophies — there is no heaven, there is no final liberation, nor is there anything transcendental and the duties prescribed by scriptures are of little avail. *Agnihotra,* three vedas, the travails, the *tapas* and besmearing one's body with ashes are the source of livelihood for persons lacking both in knowledge and action. If an animal offered in sacrifice goes to heaven one may better sacrifice his parents to ensure their place in heaven. If the food offered in Shradha can satiate the hunger of the dead, one needlessly carries food while going on travel. As long as there is breath in one's body one should enjoy the life; one should live with joy even if he has to go under debts because the life once ended can never be revived.

As referred to earlier, the philosophy of Charvaka is an exception in Indian thought and the generally accepted values of Indian life. Synthesis of philosophy and religion, spiritual out-look, belief in Moksha and transmigration of soul and theory of Karma etc. — are quite different from those of Charvaka. In orthodox Indian philosophy, the ideas of Samkara are considered to be the highest culmination of the Indian thought.

According to Samkara, Absolute, the Brahman, alone is real, the world is an illusion and there is no duality between Brahman and Atman. Thus, Samkara believed in the theory of Maya. The theory of Maya is a fundamental plank of Indian social philosophy. As a consequence of this, the material goods are very low in the scale of Indian values and the life of spirit is highly regarded.

Indian culture is religion-dominated. This is an important characteristic of Indian culture. In other words, the values of traditional Indian culture are determined by religion. Though, there is no inherent opposition between religion and science, as has been acknowledged by Western scholars, nonetheless there is tension and opposition between orthodoxy and science. If we remove orthodoxy from religion we are left with a set of philosophical beliefs and a personal relation with the Divine. Such a religion cannot be the basis of a social set up as it would be like a melting pot having no fixed or definite contours. Without a set of well determined principles no social organization is possible. If a man is totally free and is under no obligations there can be no social relationship. If the Indian culture is religious only in the sense of being spiritual having a belief in the divine power it would not in any way obstruct the process of modernization: but this is not in fact so. The concept of liberal Hindu religion may very well be the sincere belief and conviction of a number of intellectuals but for a common man it is nothing but a set of orthodox principles and practices. In society, the beliefs of few are of little consequence. What is really important is the beliefs and practices prevalent in the masses because it is by these that the social values and organization are determined. The people free from orthodox beliefs and ideas are rapidly becoming secular. On the other hand, the people who are influenced by orthodoxy and tradition are proving to be a stumbling block in the march towards modernization.

In India, most of the philosophers have disclaimed all originality for their views and have put forward their views as mere comments or elaboration of Vedas, Upanisads and Bhagwadgita. This is a classic example of intense respect for tradition. A highly enlightened contemporary thinker like Sri Aurobindo has regarded his philosophy to be an elaboration of the philosophy of Upanisads. The main reason for this state of affairs is the fact that according to Indian philosophers Truth is eternal and unaffected by the vagaries of Space and Time. This truth has been revealed in the ancient scriptures. It call be interpreted but not altered. Therefore, Indian philosophy has not given adequate attention to the fundamental changes in social, political and economic aspects of modern life wrought by science and technology. While it is true that the thinkers like Aurobindo, Radhakrishnan, Gandhi and Bhagwandas have clearly recognized the value of science and attempted to integrate with the ancient values, but the general outlook is by and large tradition-bound and it is for the future social scientists to evaluate how far there can be synthesis of tradition and science. As a number of sociologists have pointed out the Indian philosopher of today is working under the contrary pulls of tradition and modernity and it is yet to be seen how he reconciles the two. In Indian philosophy, the respect for tradition is so ingrained that even when something utterly hostile to modern outlook is found in the scripture forcing its rejection, the position and status of the scriptural authority is salvaged by pointing out that the fault lies with the interpretation and not with the original doctrine. As far as Vedas, Upanisads and Gita are concerned these are above criticism and cannot possibly contain anything wrong. It is also claimed that what is not in the epic Mahabharata is nowhere. This tendency has led many Indian thinkers to dig in ancient scriptures to show that each and every new idea is already contained in them. This attitude is of course antithetical to modernity. It is of course a moot point how far modernity is desirable. But, this much is certain that too much faith and reliance in the ancient books and scriptures is a symptom of orthodoxy.

In Indian philosophy, the theory of Karma has had widespread influence on the Indian society. While it is true that the theory of Karma did not originally profess fatalism and only sustained the Varna system in its pristine form, by and by it encouraged immobilisation, reaction and retrogressive tendencies in the Indian society. The theory that man is free to act but not so in the choice of fruits of his actions because the fruition of an act depends upon factors not within his control is quite obvious and therefore unexceptional; but disregard of consequences while performing one's duties is nothing but a prop for tradition and orthodoxy. Thus, the Indian social philosophy is orthodox and tradition bound and it has not changed its values and concepts with the changes in economic and social life. Therefore, it can be justifiably maintained that the Indian social philosophy is orthodox and tradition bound and that a contemporary social philosophy in India is still to emerge. Few intellectuals who have acquired a contemporary outlook under the influence of Western thought have little influence over Indian thinking. The basic outlook of an average Indian is still fundamentally orthodox.

It is usually said that the Indian philosophy relegates morality to a secondary place whereas in the West it occupies the position of primacy. Many contemporary Indian philosophers have tried to refute and rebut this criticism. Dr. Radhakrishnan has tried to show the validity and importance of morality even in the Advaita philosophy of Samkara and nihilism (Sunyatavad) of Nagarjuna. He has stressed emphatically that though in India morality has not been accorded a place of primacy, it has nonetheless been given adequate importance and due place in the scheme of things. But, if the morality is regarded as transitory and the ultimate end is devoid of morality, it is small wonder that such an attitude would not provide adequate inspiration for fruitful action in society. A man who considers himself beyond good and evil and is stead fact in his aim and duty in the face of adversity may be a good person and help the social well-being; but being devoid of strong motivation of some tangible gain he would not be as effective as the person who is inspired by the irresistible lure of some mundane gain and profit. The values of Dharama, Artha, Kama and Moksha espoused by Indian philosophy have provided a multi-sided social philosophy which fulfils all the needs of man, but here again the priority is given to the values of Dharma and Moksha and Moksha is considered to be the summum bonum of life. Thus, other values get a subsidiary place and are only instrumental in character. On account of this conceptual framework, is it any wonder, that Indian thinkers have by and large neglected the social well-being. That is why some thinkers are of the view that the spiritual philosophy of India should be replaced by scientific outlook if there is to be progress towards modernization. The scientific outlook is quite the reverse of the point of view represented by the spiritual philosophy of India. It is quite a different issue that we may consider the spiritual outlook more valid and real than that of science, because the scientific outlook encourages materialism and this may be considered to be a hindrance in the way of spiritual progress. The foregoing review of the Indian social philosophy is made with the view to show that if there is to be progress towards modernity the traditional outlook on life must be revised and the values of scientific culture should be imbibed. Inasmuch as the modern Indian philosophers are proving themselves to be unequal to this challenge, the interest in philosophy in our country has considerably declined. But without a sound philosophical background there can be no positive social action.

SYNTHESIS OF TRADITION AND MODERNITY

In the Western countries the trend towards modernity is due to industrialization. The progress toward modernity has been directly proportionate to the progress in industrialization. In India, the thinkers like M.K. Gandhi believed that the social and economic progress can be achieved without industrialization, and, therefore, they adhered to tradition; but after independence, lip service to Gandhian ideals notwithstanding, India has made rapid strides in industrialization. Now, it is quite clear that there will have to be more and rapid industrialization if the socio-economic problems of India are to be satisfactorily solved. But, as long as we are not prepared to move from tradition to modernity we would not be able to adjust properly with the problems raised by industrialization. In U. S. A. alongwith industrialization there has been progress towards modernization. The same process must happen in India. We cannot avoid modernization because industrialization has come to stay in India. It is therefore advisable that we plan this transition and profit by the experience of other countries so as to avoid the pitfalls faced by them. If the change does not take place in a planned manner it will take place via communism or some other means.

From the view point of history, Indian culture has always been absorbing and assimilating diverse trends. On coming in contact with the Western culture some Indians wanted to go whole hog for Westernization but the dominant trend was for a synthesis of the two cultures. The industrialization in India was started by the English people and this disrupted the traditional set-up of the Indian society. As a matter of fact this was a clash of industrialized and developing societies. This gave rise to conflicting viewpoints in society. For sometime Gandhism and Sarvodaya were the dominant philosophies but now their influence is declining. Now, there is a rapid move towards Westernization. The Westernization is not confined to dress and mannerism but has penetrated to thought structure as well.

Contemporaneity of the Non-contemporaneous

A tradition-bound society is not necessarily a backward society, because there are elements in the tradition which are of universal importance. Therefore, an attempt has been made to reconcile many an element of tradition with the modern elements. The conflict between tradition and modernity is not confined to India. Indeed, it is to be found in all those societies which have won freedom recently and are trying to march towards modernity. In the newly independent countries of Asia and Africa there is conflict and tension between the forces of tradition and modernity. The problem before India is how to modernize the Indian society without violence and disintegration. It is necessary to avoid sudden break and maintain the continuity of social development. Everything cannot be abandoned and started afresh. In many ways, the tradition plays a crucial role. The movement from tradition to modernity is a continuous process and there is always a period of transition. In his book '*Traditional Values in Indian Life*' Dr. Sudhakar Chattopadhyaya has tried to demonstrate that the traditional values of Indian Society are not antagonistic to the Western and American values and that these can be retained without sacrificing progress. Dr. Sudhakar has discussed these values in seven chapters. These are Socioeconomic life, Religion and Philosophy, Politics, Law, Arts, Science and International Relations.

1. Caste and Joint Family. In modern times, the caste and joint family system have influenced the contemporary society most, certain social values have come to light. First of all everybody, no matter to which caste he belongs, is considered equal and secondly the defects of caste system have come to light. In America, in the social sphere everybody has been accorded a place of dignity in Society: he is free and at full liberty to participate in social activity. In America, voluntary service is highly regarded; the place of family in society is recognized; the value of physical and mental health is recognized. Above all the dignity and value of labour for good life are recognized. These modern values are in conflict with traditional values of joint family system of India. In the recent past, there has been disintegration of joint family and caste system and this has given a fillip to modernity; but of late there is once again a revival of casteism in India. The intensification of casteism will definitely prove to be a hindrance in the path of modernity. The same fact applies to the joint family system. Due to the influence of modernity there is disintegration of joint family system. Wherever we find the joint family, it is being maintained not so much on account of its merit but due to the fact that there is no social security in India. There are no veteran homes here.

2. Religion and Philosophy. In India, there are certain traditional concepts about religion and philosophy. Every person here is free to pursue his religion. According to Indian Constitution, nobody can be divested of his political privileges and rights due to profession of a faith. India is a secular country. The Indian religion preaches mutual tolerance and is free from orthodoxy.

All modern social reformers have recognized the basic unity of all religions. M.K. Gandhi, Rabindranath Tagore, Ramkrishna Paramahansa, Swami Vivekananda and others have recognized and acknowledged the basic unity of all faiths. Wherever, there is communal tension and conflict in India, the state intervenes to restore peace and harmony. In spiritual life morality occupies an important place. The new values of Indian society are quite like the values prevalent in America. In America, the Church is separate from the state and everybody is free to go or not to go to Church. Usually, people buttress morality by religion. The religious organizations do commendable social service. Thus, even in West religion and science co-exist in peace and harmony. Therefore, in order to be modern it is not necessary to be an atheist or anti-religion. What is required for the modern outlook is the spirit of tolerance and accommodation and above all innate respect for the viewpoints of others. Many eminent 'scientists like Einstein, Eddington, James Jeans have supported the religious values.

3. Science. In the sphere of science Indians have always believed that in order to improve the living conditions of men it is imperative to control nature. Science should not be used for destructive ends. The science and technology have always received encouragement in India. All these traditional values are in tune with and favourable to modernization. America under the influence of scientific outlook has accomplished rational and sane outlook. The philosophy of humanism which has emerged under the influence of science aims at the total transformation of the world. Generally, people are of the view that science should not be employed for destructive ends. For the nourishment and development of science freedom of the individual is most necessary. A scientist must be objective in his outlook and should not shirk from the conclusions which follow his research. Thus, the traditional Indian outlook on science is not contrary to American viewpoint and the two can be easily reconciled. However, India has not as yet fully incorporated the scientific outlook. Among the intelligentsia both the viewpoints are discernible. On the one hand, the scientific progress is regarded desirable and on the other hand there is a yearning to preserve unchanged many ancient elements. But sooner we incorporate fully the scientific outlook and give up insistence on traditional values contrary to the scientific spirit the better would it be.

4. Politics and Law. In the sphere of politics, the ideals of rule of law and equality before law are prevalent. The Indian Constitution has upheld the ideals of liberty, equality and fraternity. Though, in modern times, these ideals are best cherished in America, but almost all objective scholars concede that the democratic tradition has flourished in India since ancient times. From times immemorial we had *Panchayats* in rural India. In ancient scriptures, the democracy has been described in great details. Now-a-days, however, we are facing the failure of democratic experiment. The reason for this failure is not the lack of proper tradition but illiteracy. In order to suit the democracy to Indian milieu, there have been a number of amendments in our Constitution. With the removal of backwardness and illiteracy the democracy is bound to flourish in India.

Three Viewpoints

The foregoing discussion of tradition and modernity makes it clear that there are a number of elements in our tradition which are favourable to modernization. This fact is known as contemporaneity of the non-contemporaneous. Therefore, India can make progress towards modernization without much conflict. Regarding the relationship between modernity and tradition there are three viewpoints in India.

1. Optimistic outlook. Those thinkers who subscribe to the vertical social progress point of view are of the opinion that the transition from tradition to modernity is smooth and automatic. Therefore, they support fast westernization in India.

2. Obscurantism. Those thinkers who are the votaries of tradition and orthodoxy are obscurantist. Such persons do not wish to abandon tradition at any cost whatsoever. They believe that the old values are eternal and they need not be abandoned. This is a fatalist outlook.

3. Progressivism. Regarding the relation between tradition and modernity this is the most appropriate point of view. This strikes a balance between the views number 1 and 2. This is neofunctionalism. According to this point of view we must progress towards modernity but without sacrificing what is best in the tradition. In the matter of ideology, India is very much advanced though in socio-economic sphere it is quite backward. Today India needs an elite which can remove the obstacles in the way of socio-economic progress. The future shape of India cannot be described in detail, because this will be something undemocratic. In a democracy everyone is free to make progress in the way and manner in which he likes, and no fixed pattern can be imposed. Pluralism is fundamental to modernity. The other characteristics of modernity are scientific progress, industrialization, urbanization, individualism, secularism and positivist philosophy. These characteristics can be seen in India in one form or the other, though we have not fully incorporated in our life this outlook. We are at times very unscientific in our thinking and outlook. In order to remove this discrepancy we must make a planned march towards modernity.

PLANNED PROGRESS

All contemporary sociologists are agreed upon this point that in order to be most productive and fruitful the socio-economic changes in society should be brought about in a well planned and organized manner. Though, change is a continuous process, unless it is well directed there cannot be maximum utilization of energy. Progress means well planned change. This functional approach to modernity has been accepted in most of the advanced countries. It is a controversial point as to what are the elements of Indian tradition which ought to be retained but all are agreed that there should be a synthesis of modernity and tradition.

Characteristics of Modernity in India

There can be different measurements to assess the progress of modernity in any country. For example, various surveys are made to determine how far people are receptive to new ideas. Both in social and economic fields new ideas and inventions are being fast adopted. Agriculture is being mechanized rapidly and new means of raising the farm output are being put into practice. The fast urbanization is breaking various social barriers and different groups of people are coming into contact with each other. In towns the practice of untouchability and casteism is declining though some political groups with vested interests are fomenting and encouraging the evil of casteism. The child marriage, practice of Sati, taboo on widow re-marriage are the things of past and now there is much freedom for women. The spread of education among females is leading to rapid modernization. After independence the backward classes have been guaranteed special privileges under constitution and this is leading to mixing up all classes of society. Many welfare projects are under way to help the backward and down-trodden sections of the society. Now, due to economic exigencies the professions are no longer based on classes. Now, everybody is free to adopt and pursue a profession of his choice.

The Concept of World Unity

An important characteristic of modernity is the ideal of one world or the concept of world unity. This is why modernity is valued as a liberating ideology for mankind. The idea of modernity is founded upon the belief in the basic, unity of mankind. The ancient Indian traditions are not opposed to the ideal of unity of mankind; indeed they are conducive and congenial to this ideal. Therefore, progress towards worlds unity can be made while maintaining the basic tenets of ancient Indian philosophy. The model of modernity inherited by India is that of Great Britain; therefore, the Russian model has little impact upon India. The communist ideologues in India want that India should follow the soviet model; but, however, their number is not very great. Indeed, a true progress towards modernity can be made only by reconciling the old and new values of life. What is old is not necessarily bad or backward; nor what is modern is necessarily good and progressive.

Importance of Education

For a transition to modernity, education is the best instrument or means of such a change. The ideal of universal education has been recognized by our constitution. As long as there is illiteracy in the country the democratic ideals cannot take firm roots in the Indian soil. Therefore, it is imperative to achieve the end of universal education soon. In order to appreciate what is desirable and what is undesirable in the ancient tradition we need sound education. For this knowledge of Sanskrit language and literature is very essential. Modern educationists are unanimous in their view that the Sanskrit language should be given a place of honour in the curriculum of our education. However all, educationists are critical of the current western style of education and want fundamental reforms in it. Lastly, what is needed is not the outward aping of modernity by donning mod dresses or going to clubs etc. but the incorporation of democratic and scientific outlook which means respect for the point of view of others and no desire to impose or thrust one's views and opinions upon others.

QUESTIONS FOR EXERCISE

1. Elucidate the role of traditions in family life in contemporary Indian situation.
2. Are old Hindu values consistent with the values of modernisation? Support your answer with arguments.
3. Write short note on Tradition.
4. Distinguish between Tradition and Modernity. Bring out their indices.
5. Show the points of contrast between Tradition and Modernity in contemporary Hindu social life.
6. Discuss the main problem of bringing about modernity in Indian Society.

22

Sanskritization

In his book *'Social Change in Modern India'* M.N. Srinivas has defined the process of Sanskritization thus —"Sanskritization is the process by which a 'low' Hindu caste, or tribal or other group, changes its customs, rituals, ideology and way of life in the direction of a high, and frequently 'twice born' caste".[1] In this definition the following points have been stressed:

(1) By Sanskritization a caste or a tribal community ventures to gain higher status in society.

(2) In Sanskritization a low caste takes to the conduct, customs and rituals of the higher caste.

(3) The process of sanskritization is found not only in castes but also in tribal communities.

(4) In Sanskritization Brahmins alone are not the object of imitation. Kshatriyas and Vaishyas are also taken as models. But in all instances the lower caste moves towards the higher and therefore follows or imitates the higher caste.

(5) By Sanskritization a caste or a group adopts and follows customs and rituals which would qualify it for being treated as twice-born.

Ideal of Sanskritization

In the process of Sanskritization a claim is made for higher status in the social structure and it is therefore a vertical movement. But in Sanskritization only there is improvement of status, there are no structural changes. In India, besides castes, the process of sanskritization is to be found in tribal communities like Bhils of Rajasthan, Gonds of Madhya Pradesh and other hilly tribes. By the process of Sanskritization a tribal community tries to prove itself to be a part of Hindu Society. In his book on Coorgs, Srinivas had laid undue emphasis upon the ideal of Brahminism. But in his book *'Social Change in Modern India'* he admits that the ideal of Sanskritization can also be Kshatriya; Vaishya and even Sudra.

1 Srinivas, M.N , *Social Change in Modern India,* University of California Press (1966), p. 6.

Vertical and Horizontal Integration

In the Varna system, the three upper castes, namely, Brahmin, Kshatriya and Vaishya are considered to be twice-born, because only members of these castes have the right of wearing the sacred thread during Upanayan ceremony. In Brahmins also there are a number of caste distinctions. As different castes are to be found in the same region, they speak the same language, celebrate the same festivals and take to worship of local deities. M.N. Srinivas has called this process as vertical integration and this is quite different from horizontal integration. Horizontal integration occurs within a single Varna. On the whole, Brahmins have tried to keep aloof from the local influences and these are found mainly among Kshatriyas, Vaishyas and Sudras. The Kshatriyas and Vaishyas in different parts of the country are separated by deep differences. The maximum sanskritization has taken place in certain Sudra castes.

The Dominant Caste

In the rural life of India, there is an agricultural caste, which has the ownership of land. This is the dominant or *prabhu* caste. For a dominant caste the following are the essential characteristics:

(1) The major portion of agricultural land is under its ownership.

(2) Adequate membership of the caste.

(3) In the local social hierarchy it must occupy the highest status.

In the presence of above features of lordship a caste will be called Prabhu or dominant.

In certain villages, more than one caste enjoys the lordship of land, and in the course of time the domination of one caste over the other gets reversed. In the last century various factors have influenced the lordship — Western education, government service, urban sources of income etc. After independence, on account of universal adult franchise, Harijans now feel their importance, power and dignity. Now, the reins of power have gone in the hands of rural rich and with the exception of those villages where Harijans out number others, the seat of power is unlikely to change for sometime in the rural India. A caste enjoying lordship in one village has to observe deference and respect to the caste which enjoys lordship in the whole region. Thus, a local dominant caste is less powerful than the regional dominant caste. In the establishment of lordship the ownership of land plays a crucial role. The ownership of land gives not only power but prestige also. The power and prestige of feudal lords affect their relationships with other castes — for example, in Punjab feudal lords treat Brahmins as their servants and the Thakurs of Madhopur in Eastern U.P. did not accept the food prepared by Brahmins except their preceptors and priests. Though, in secular matters, members of dominant caste are privileged, but in matters of rituals the situation is very different. In India, the sacred matters occupy more importance than the secular affairs. A millionaire Gujarati Bania dare not step into the kitchen of a Brahmin because this would pollute Brahmin's food. If the dominant caste is Brahmin and if it is Rajput or Bania its ideal would be Kshatriya or Vaishya.

Two Tendencies of Caste System

Following two tendencies are to be clearly seen in India:

(1) Besides local religions and moral values, the existence of other cultures is recognized.

(2) The ways and manners of higher castes are followed. However, it needs be remembered that the local rural organization is not entirely independent of the all India organization. The rules of moral conduct, sanctity of the places of pilgrimage, moral dramas and other sacred traditions are derived from various sources. In villages, the elders of dominant caste are the guardians of a pluralist value-system. The dominant caste maintains the structural distance between the caste under its influence. The lower castes also try to follow the customs and manners of dominant caste. The imitation of the life style of upper castes is done in a round about manner because direct invitation of the upper castes will be frowned upon and may invite punishment.

Sanskritization in Punjab

Dr. D.R. Chanana[1] has mentioned about sanskritization in regions where prior to independence in 1947 and consequent upon partition of the state the influence of Islam and west Asian countries was dominant. Sikh religion enjoyed subsidiary lordship. In the matter of religion, Hindus were deeply impressed by Islam, particularly its sufi cult. In pre-partition Punjab and North Western Frontier Provinces, Muslims enjoyed lordship and in certain areas Sikhs enjoyed the subsidiary lordship. Brahmins among Hindus had neither resources nor knowledge and the commercial classes were more important. Arya Samaj and its rival Sanatan Dharma did much to spread education. This encouraged sanskritization of Hindus.

Sanskritization in Tribals

The process of sanskritization is to be found among tribals. On the other hand, Shri S.L. Kalia[2] has tried to show that a process of tribalization is evident among the areas of Jaunsar Bawar of U. P. and Bastar of M.P. The elders of dominant caste administer punishment to those who violate its rules. But, at times the twice-born upholders of great traditions yield to little traditions. It is of course not always true that maximum sanskritization occurs in Brahmins.[3]

Examples of Dominant Caste

It is possible to draw a map of rural India in which the name of dominant caste in each and every village can be given, but this will be a very cumbersome task.

1 D.R. Chanana, Sanskritization, Westernisation and India's North West, *Economic Weekly,* Vol. XIII, No. 9, March 4, 1961, pp. 409-14.

2 S.L. Kalia, Sanskritization and Tribalization, *Bulletin of the Tribal Research Institute,* Chindwara (M.P.), Vol. 2, No. 4, April 1959, pp. 43-53.

3 M. Marriott, Little Communities in an Indigenous Civilisations, *Village India,* p. 211.

Yet, the names of dominant castes can be enumerated. In Northern India, the rural folk nickname the dominant castes *Ajgar* which are indicative of dominant castes among the down-trodden castes. *Ajgar* is formed by the first letter of the names of Ahir, Jat, Gujar and Rajput. In some parts of West Bengal, Sagdip; Patidar and Rajput in Gujarat, Maratha in Maharashtra, Kamma and Reddy in Andhra, Vokilag and Lingayats in Mysore, Wellas, Gandar, Parchayi and Kallar in Madras and Nayar, Syrians, Ijwan etc. in Kerala are the dominant castes. The dominant castes project ideals for the majority in the villagers.

Kshatriyas and Brahmins maintained their lordship for long. The places of pilgrimage and religious mathas are the sources of sanskritization. The spread of sanskritization among the non-dominant castes living in the vicinity of places of pilgrimages and mathas used to be vertical and horizontal in other regions.

Conflict of Varna Ideals

As we have mentioned earlier, there has been no single ideal of Sanskritization. There were three or four such models. There has been conflict among these ideals. For example, in Vedic scriptures we find references to conflict between Kshatriyas and Brahmins. Later on, there was conflict between Buddhism and Jainism. In Buddhism and Jainism, we find mostly trading communities who were resentful of the over-domination of Brahmins. Buddhism and Jainism pointed a way out to get rid of disqualifications imposed by caste system.

In the original Varna system, the place and status of each Varna was fixed. But during the Vedic period there were important changes in the life style of Brahmins. These changes are crucial because other Varnas used to follow the ideals of Brahmins. In Vedic age, the Brahmins began to be treated as sannyasins. In post-Vedic age Brahmins were influenced by Buddhism and Jainism. The spread of Bhakti movement gave an opportunity to the lower caste persons to become religious leaders. Many Harijans and women also attained the status of sainthood. Bhakti movement helped to spread the message of ancient scriptures which were in Sanskrit in the regional languages.

Political Elements in Sanskritization

Before the British rule the instability of political system in India was a powerful source of social mobility. In the 18th century, there were four stages of political organization — Imperial, Intermediary, Regional and Local. At the imperial level there were Mughal emperors. At the intermediary level there used to be Nawabs. At the regional level the Jagirdars or feudal lords dominated. The Jagirdars used to rule through local Aamils. Thus, at the top there was a king under whom used to be Nawabs and under Nawabs there were Rajas who used to control the populace through local chieftains. The officer at the lower wrung was under obligation to provide soldiers to his immediate boss. The 18th century' political conditions obtaining in Gujarat and Banaras were favourable for castes like Bhoomihar, Brahmin, Rajput, Patidar and Kol. In order to give instances of social mobility before the British, M.N. Srinivas has cited examples from U.P., Gujarat and Kerala. In all these areas there was a lot of political mobility. Due to political instability there was social mobility. A Raja had the power to raise or lower the status of castes residing in his region. This was so because in the pre-British India, Rajas were considered to occupy the topmost position under the caste system. Rajas used to offer appointments to various posts in the castes. A person excommunicated from some caste for misdemeanour could approach Raja who could grant him re-entry to the caste. The disputes regarding appointments in the castes were also adjudicated by the Rajas. The king had the authority to punish; he used to consult wisemen before giving his judgement.

Economic Factors in Sanskritization

During the pre-British period the social mobility of the caste was not only due to political factors; there were economic considerations, too. There was no dignity of labour and higher the status less the labour. The feudal lords were not supposed to do any work with their own hands. The manual labour was reserved for low castes. The ownership of land and the economic status were responsible for entitlement to high castes. During the middle ages the social mobility was linked with residential mobility. By change of residence new castes were born and they served their links with their origins.

All the changes which have occurred in the castes are intracaste changes and these have in no way affected the fundamentals of caste system. For this process of change, M.N. Srinivas has used the concept of Sanskritization. The rationality and validity of this concept has been critically examined by Dr. D.N. Majumdar and other contemporary sociologists. The discussion of this evaluation would show the significance and limitations of this concept.

LACUNA IN THE CONCEPT OF SANSKRITIZATION

Sanskritization is not a new concept in the sociological literature; but M.N. Srinivas has used this concept in a peculiar way. In his words, "Sanskritization means not only the adoption of new customs and habits but also exposure of new ideas and values which have found frequent expression in the vast body of Sanskrit literature, sacred as well as secular. Karma, dharma, papa, punya, maya, samsara and moksha are examples of some of the most common Sanskritic theological ideals, and when a people become sanskritized these words occur frequently in their talk. These ideas reach the common people through sanskritic myths and stories." Thus, sanskritization means the adoption of the values of a cultured society.

However, M.N. Srinivas considers this concept to be only useful but not very clear. According to him this concept helped him in analyzing the religious life of Coorgs. He believes that the anthropologists would profit by the use of this concept, though he himself concedes that "Sanskritization is no doubt an awkward term, but it was preferred to Brahmanisation for several reasons".

Process of Sanskritization

In explaining the meaning of Sanskritization, M.N. Srinivas points out that Sanskritization was not always due to Brahmins. Generally, Sanskritization qualifies a caste for a higher status. In the dynastic system, Sanskritization emphasizes the status of dynasty. In Sanskritization sons were considered obligatory as a matter of religious duty and thus sons had a higher social status. Thus, the status and value of daughters was downgraded. According to Srinivas, Sanskritization spread during the British rule. With the development of means of communication, the impact of Sanskritization was felt in the remote comers of the country. With the spread of education and literacy it percolated to the lowest castes. The Western technology, radio, press, rail etc. greatly facilitated the process of Sanskritization. The Britishers introduced the system of parliamentary democracy in the country. This also helped Sanskritization. According to M.N. Srinivas, the economic status of the caste is not an essential factor in the process of Sanskritization though the better economic status did help. Besides, the attainment of political authority, spread of education and the desire for better status also helped the process of Sanskritization. Srinivas has recognized that mere Sanskritization does not help a caste to attain a higher status. According to Srinivas an untouchable caste, no matter how Sanskritized it becomes, will not be able to cross the barrier of untouchability. But a thoroughgoing Sanskritization taking place among the castes may ultimately overhaul the Hindu caste system A question arises if Sanskritization in a one way process. Srinivas believes it to be a two-way process.

Sanskritization is not Universal

Thus, according to Srinivas, Sanskritization is a process whereby a lower caste incorporates in itself the culture and values of higher caste and it does bring it nearer to it. But, it must be borne in mind and under the caste system there is taboo on the lower castes against adopting the norms and values of the higher caste. According to M.N. Srinivas, "In short, it took over, as far as possible, the customs, rites and beliefs of the Brahmins, and have been frequent, though theoretically forbidden." But here we encounter a difficulty. Srinivas accepts that in Hinduism the lower castes are taking to the norms and values of the higher castes. This fact may be true with reference to a particular community or region but it is not universal. As Dr. D.N. Majumdar has shown in his study of Mohana village, in U.P., there is no tendency among the lower castes to adopt the customs and manners of the higher caste nor does it help in elevating the status of any caste. There are quite a few instances where the members of low caste seem to adopt the life style of the high caste but this does not qualify them to be considered the members of the high caste. If a Chamar pastes a 'Tilaka' on his forehead he would not be considered a Brahmin. Dr. D.N. Majumdar asks, "If it (Sanskritization) is a process, where does the process stop and why?" In his study of the Mohana village Dr. D.N. Majumdar has shown that in the social stratification the movement among the castes is not vertical but horizontal. That is even the members of the same caste begin to regard some of them low. For example, all Brahmins are considered highest among the castes. But among Brahmins there are subcastes, like Gaur, Kanyakubja, Sarawswat etc. who consider themselves to be lower or higher than the others. This is horizontal expansion of Brahmins. Similarly, there are many sub-castes among Sudras. Not only among the Sudras, but even within the sub-castes of Sudras there are to be found further sub-castes. For a non- Chamar, all Chamars are at the same level but for a Chamar, another Chamar may be lower or higher to him. From the above examples it should be clear that by the change in the life style in castes there come into being further sub-castes and this change is not a vertical progress but a horizontal expansion.

Sanskritization v/s De-Sanskritization

Dr. D.N. Majumdar is not only critical of the concept of Sanskritization but doubts if it is really taking place. According to him, there are more signs of the reverse process, namely, de-Sanskritization in evidence all over the country. In de-Sanskritization, the members of the higher castes abandon their dress and rituals. For example, many among the Kashmiri Pandits have abandoned their traditional mode of life. Another symptom of de-Sanskritization is taking to professions traditionally reserved for the lower castes. According to D.N. Majumdar, the shrinkage of distances between castes is not due to Sanskritization but its reverse. The lower castes are not moving towards the higher but the higher castes are abandoning their life style.

Impact of Western Culture

The Western culture has greatly facilitated the process of de-Sanskritization. Under the impact of Western culture the various castes are abandoning their traditions. The educated members of all castes are adopting the Western life style and hence coming together. D.N. Majumdar admits that the process of de-Sanskritization is slow in some places but it is going on everywhere. The social mobility among castes is horizontal rather than vertical. Therefore, D.N. Majumdar does not consider that the concept of Sanskritization is scientific. According to him, "Sanskritization connotes a group of concepts and at best is a loose one, devoid of any special merit". He is against the use of the term Sanskritization in reference to cultural change. In particular, it should not be used in reference to horizontal and vertical progress. But in the absence of a more refined concept, it may be of a limited value. As long as a better concept is not formulated to explain the cultural change, the use of the terms Sanskritization and de-Sanskritization is indispensable. From the above examples, it is evident that the changes in the life style result in the formation of new subcastes which move horizontally. Dr. Majumdar is of the view that the process of de-Sanskritization is more evident than that of Sanskritization in Indian Society.

Conclusion

As a matter of fact, adequate study of the cultural changes in India has not been made to enable us to draw any safe and sure conclusions. But we will have to recognize that both the processes of Sanskritization and de-Sanskritization can be seen to operate in our society, at some places the former can be more dominant and at other places the latter. But in the absence of sufficient scientific data, it is difficult to determine conclusively which of the two is more dominant and at other places the latter. But as far as probability goes the view of Dr. Majumdar seems more probable; though it cannot by strictly said to be true. In order to arrive at a more dependable conclusion more extensive research into this matter is called for.

QUESTIONS FOR EXERCISE

1. Discuss the process of 'Sanskritization' and 'Westernization' with reference to social change in modern India.
2. Distinguish between Sanskritization and Westernization. How far are they responsible for social change in India?
3. Discuss the role of Sanskritization in Social Change.
4. What do you understand by Sanskritization? Does it explain caste mobility?
5. Write a short note on Sanskritization.

23

Westernization

In the modern times, Westernization has played a crucial role in bringing about social change in India. Westernization means incorporation of the norms, values and cultures of the West in one's own culture. India came under the influence of Westernization during the British rule. Therefore, M.N. Srinivas defines Westernization thus: "I have used else where the term 'Westernization' to characterize the changes brought about in Indian society and culture as a result of over 150 years of British rule, and the term subsumes changes occurring at different levels — technology, institutions, ideology, values."[1]

Westernization and Urbanization

The impact of Westernization is seen mostly in urban areas; but, on account of this fact, it cannot concluded that Westernization and urbanization are synonymous. In many parts of rural India more Westernization is in evidence than even in the urban areas. Though, on the whole more urban areas have come under the impact of Westernization, nonetheless there are quite a few village in India that are more Westernized than urban areas. Therefore, it will be wrong to think that the Westernization is a result of urbanization. These are two independent entities or processes; that is why these have been treated separately in this book.

Westernization and Modernization

Many people are under the wrong impression that Westernization is modernization because the two are thought to be the same; but in fact the two must be differentiated. Lemer believes that Westernization is a more limited concept than the modernization. All countries have not become modern due to the influence of West. For example, some countries have become modern under the influence of Japan. In modernization, all these elements are included which come about by a revolution in the means of communication, more urbanization, more literacy, increase in the per capita income, adult franchise etc.

1 M.N. Srinivas, *Social Change in Modern India*, University of California Press (1966), p. 47.

CHARACTERISTICS OF WESTERNIZATION

Inasmuch as modernization in India has come about due to Westernization, therefore the above-mentioned changes of modernization can be taken to be the result of Westernization. The following are the characteristics of Westernization:

1. Morally Neutral. Modernization is generally considered to be good, but this is not always so with Westernization. Westernization has been for good as well as evil. In fact, Westernization is morally neutral.

2. Limits of Westernization. A distinction has to be drawn between Westernization and Western culture. All the elements of the Western culture did not originate in the West. For example, Christianity originated in Asia. The decimal system originated in India and via Arabia reached West. Gun powder, printing press and paper were invented in China. All these constitute the important elements of Western culture though these did not originate in the West. The manner in which Westernization operates in India is mainly the result of British influence. The culture of Germany, France and Russia etc., is quite different from the British culture.

3. Wide, Complex and multi-level Concept. The concept of Westernization is quite wide. It subsumes all changes which are consequent upon Western technology and modern science. Secondly, it has had varying impact upon the different aspects of the culture; hence it is a complex concept. Thirdly, Westernization has affected society on different levels. For example, in olden days people used to eat in thalis or banana leaves in squatting position but now they use dining table with all its accessories. While Westernization has had very wide impact, there has been resistance to it in some quarters. Thus, Westernization has had variable impact on the Indian society.

4. Conscious Unconscious Process. Westernization has not been incorporated willingly everywhere in India. At places the copying of British manners and customs was deliberate, at other places it was a subconscious process.

CONSEQUENCES OF WESTERNIZATION

The following are the consequences of westernization:

1. Impact on Institutions. Westernization has influenced caste system, joint family system etc. It gave birth to new institutions like press, electoral system, Christian missionaries etc.

2. Transvaluation. Westernization has encouraged modern values like humanism, egalitarianism and secularism. British civil and criminal law affected Hindu and Muslim laws. The system of slavery was ended and members of all castes were free to get education. Gradually, there was spread of education among women. Theoretically all were accorded equal economic opportunity. Many discriminative religious practices were ended. Among such practices, the practice of untouchability is foremost.

3. Governmental Reform. Under the impact of westernization, the states undertook a number of reforms. The steps were taken to prevent epidemics and famines. An effort to spread education was also made.

4. Re-Definition of Hinduism. Under the impact of westernization, many religious reform movements came into existence and they attempted to redefine the various aspects of Hinduism in the light of modern science and knowledge. In re-defining, Hinduism Maharishi Dayanand, Ramkrishna Paramahansa, Vivekananda, Rabindranath Tagore, Sri Aurobindo, Raja Ram Mohun Roy did commendable job. They indicated to various aspects of Hinduism which required urgent reforms. By their laudable efforts Sati system was ended where a wife was burnt alive on the funeral pyre of her husband. The curse of child marriage was put to an end and widow-remarriage was sanctioned. An effort to eradicate the evil of untouchability was also made.

5. Many Political and Cultural Movements. Besides, the religious reform movements which came into existence under the impact of westernization, many political and cultural movements were also started. Besides, nationalist movement many parochial movements based upon caste, creed, language and religion came into existence.

6. Spread of Education. The most significant impact of westernization is to be seen in the form of modern education taking root. During the British period, many schools, colleges and universities were opened to discriminate the modern education. Press came into existence and many newspapers and periodicals were published which offered a number of view points. An educated class came into existence which became the vanguard of freedom movement.

CARRIERS OF WESTERNIZATION

The British and Indians both helped to begin and accelerate the process of westernization. Therefore, both can be considered as carriers of westernization. Among Britishers three groups can be distinguished. Firstly, there were soldiers and civilians occupying high ranks. Secondly, there were traders and the owners of orchards. Thirdly, there were missionaries. All of these three groups helped to spread westernization. On the other hand, many Indians also helped the process of westernization. Among them the following are included:

1. Indians Who Came in Direct Contact with Englishmen. The Indians who came in direct contact with the Englishmen were influenced by their life style. Among them were the persons who were in the household employment of the Englishmen and also those Hindus who abandoned Hinduism and espoused Christianity.

2. Indirectly Influenced. The primary contribution towards westernization was made not by those who came directly in contact with the Englishmen but by those who were indirectly influenced. Among these are included the persons who received new education, entered into trades or served as petty bureaucrats under the British. All were not middle class persons. For example, Raja Ram Mohun Rai and Rabindra Nath Tagore belonged to aristocratic families. These English educated gentlemen brought forth great change in society by launching various movements. Among the Muslims, Sir Saiyad Ahmed Khan belonged to this category. Among the backward class, Dr. B.R. Ambedkar did great job of modernization. Besides the contribution made by the above mentioned luminaries certain castes among Hindus were especially westernized. These include Vaids of Bengal and Parasi and Bania of Western India.

The impact of westernization was also felt through the patients who were treated in the British hospitals, the persons who had to go to law courts and through the medium of newspapers and books. The port cities near the sea coasts were particularly vulnerable to the westernization. For example, Calcutta, Bombay and Madras were the first cities to receive the impact of Westernization.

In India, Westernization did not take place on a wholesale-basis, rather it was selective. The Westernization in India was the result of the traditional tolerant, catholic and receptive attitude of the Indians. India always has had the tradition of catholicity, tolerance and self-criticism. The luminaries like Vivekananda, Ranade, Gokhale, Tilak, Tagore, Aurobindo, Gandhi, Patel, Nehru and Radhakrishanan who came under the influence of Westernization tried to re-evaluate and re-define the ancient Indian values in terms of modern enlightenment.

INFLUENCE OF WEST ON INDIAN SOCIETY

Regarding the impact of West on the Indian life, Humayun Kabir has observed that the incisive intellect of the West closely examined every belief and idea. This, on the one hand, led to change in the beliefs regarding physical life and, on the other hand, destroyed the very structures, beliefs and traditions. The impact of the West was felt upon caste system, education, social awakening, political awakening, joint family system, economic structure, institution of marriage, untouchability and other rituals.

The impact of West can be studied under the following heads:

1. Western Influence upon Caste System — (a) *Industrialization.* In the industrial factories members of all castes work together. They share their problems and aims. In order to work together they come close to each other. This helps to break down the distinction of high and low caste.

(b) *Urbanization.* As a result of industrial expansion new townships came into existence and people from the villages flocked to these townships in order to earn livelihood. In towns, members of different castes came together and the sense of separateness could not be sustained in the new environment. Thus, urbanization leads to a relaxation in the caste system.

(c) *Means of Transport.* Without the improvement in the means of transport the caste distinctions remained stable and fixed, but with the improvement in the means of transport on account of Western influence the people came together and this lead to watering down of caste distinctions.

(d) *English Education.* The spread of education disseminated modern value of Equality, Fraternity and Liberty. This gave a sharp blow to the caste system. Many went to England for higher studies and they came back fully westernized and critical of narrow and bigoted caste distinctions.

(e) *Influence of Western Culture.* The influence of western culture helped to relax the ties of caste system. Under the impact of Western culture the dress and food habits of members of different castes tended to be similar. Due to dress etc., the visible distinction between people was not that of caste but one of class. When the first medical college was set up in Calcutta the disection of a cadaver for even educational purposes was considered to be an irreligious act, but gradually it came to be accepted as morally permissible if the purpose was education. The supply of water through pipes and eating in restaurant also helped to diminish the feeling of untouchability. Dr. Bhagwandas writes that when water pipe were fitted in Kashi, the project was opposed on the ground that members of low castes may operate the water works but now everyone makes use of them. When Britishers introduced the crops of tomatoes and potatoes in India, people were reluctant to eat them, but now almost everyone eats biscuits, cakes and pastries without bothering about ingredients.

2. Western Influence on Untouchability. Besides undermining the caste system, the spell of westernization also helped to eradicate the evil of untouchability. The rapid development of means of communication urbanization and industrialization helped in the eradication of untouchability because one cannot choose his companions while travelling in buses or trains. The Western education encouraged the sentiment of equality and there was also social and political awakening in the country.

3. Impact of West on Women. There was a profound impact of Western culture on women. Indian women re-examined their status. With the coming of British in India there was a fillip to their status in the light of western ideas. On account of western education they felt that they were in no way inferior to menfolk. The psychological researches have proved that there are no innate or fundamental distinctions among men and women with regard to ability and capacity and that these are all due to environmental factors. Thus, women demanded an equal place with men in a walks of life. There was no moral sanction for higher education among women in India. The recitation of religious scriptures was considered enough for them. The social reformers had to struggle hard to win the right of higher education for women. First of all, Calcutta University opened its gates to women. Gradually, all Indian universities allowed women to enroll themselves as students. The two significant upshots of the spread of education among women are: (1) Discarding Purdah and (2) Demand for Equality.

4. Impact of West on Social Structure. The Indian social structure has been deeply influenced by West. The Indian social structure is based upon caste system. These castes are endogamous groups and are fixed by birth. Under the impact of West the caste system has become weak and is getting replaced by the class distinction prevalent in the West. There is also disintegration of the rural structure of our society. The industrialization and urbanization have thrown the rural social structure out of gear. The society has become more dynamic and traditions are breaking down. In Urban set up the caste distinctions cannot be sustained. In railways, bazars and factories the caste distinctions are not possible. Under the impact of west money has come to be greatly valued. Now in place of caste status, money status is the criterion of man's worth. The western education is secular, therefore the rituals are losing importance.

5. Westernization of the Institution of Marriage. Among social institutions, the institution of marriage has received maximum impact of West. Following are the crucial changes in this respect:

(i) *Change of Basis.* Now, the marriage in India is not merely a sacrament but mutual love and married bliss constitute its basis.

(ii) *Ritualist Change.* Along with the change in the basis there are in evidence changes in rituals attendant on marriage. The civil marriage, though not common, is receiving gradual social acceptance.

(iii) *Freedom to Choose Partners.* In the past, the wishes of bride and bridegroom had no place in the scheme of marriage. It was an exclusive affair between parents but now boy and girl at least meet each other before marriage.

(iv) *Eradication of Child Marriage.* On account of the influence of the West there is a spread of education among girls and now there is a general realization that child marriage is deterimental to health. Due to these reasons there is almost eradication of child marriage from Hindu society.

(v) *Marriage in Mature Age.* Along with the eradication of child marriage there is a natural consequence of marriage occurring in mature age.

(vi) *Admissibility of Divorce.* According to Hindu tradition marriage is a sacrament which can come to an end only by the death of partner. It could not be ended by divorce. Now, under the influence of West divorce is available to Hindus.

(vii) *Admissibility of Divorce.* According to Hindu tradition marriage is a sacrament which can come to an end only by the death of partner. It could not be ended by divorce. Now under the influence of West divorce is available to Hindus.

(viii) *Inter-Caste Marriage.* Under the influence of Western culture intercaste and inter-religion marriages are now possible. In the past such an act would have been visited by the punishment of excommunication.

(ix) *Monogamy.* Under the influence of West monogamy has come to be accepted as the only natural state of marriage. According to Hindu Marriage Act, 1955, no Hindu could enter into a marriage if his/her partner is alive.

(x) *Free Enjoyment.* Under the influence of West there is a tendency among some educated and rich persons to avoid the complication of marriage and lead a life of free sex. The number of men and women who do not wish to marry is growing. This is possible because sex outside marriage is available.

6. Distintegration of Joint Family. Alongwith the institution of marriage, the western culture has influenced the family relations and ideals as well. In this connection the following points are worth noting:

(i) *Distintegration of Joint Family.* Due to Western influence the joint family is on the way to extinction. The individualism of West is breaking down the joint family. Today, young persons do not want to sacrifice their privacy and pleasure at the alter of joint family.

(ii) *Small Family.* The Western influence has not only influenced the disintegration of the family, it has also impelled people to limit their children. Now, all educated persons want small family.

(iii) *Impermanency of Family.* Under the influence of West women are now highly educated and are unable to merge their personalities in the family. As they usually seek employment they are economically also independent. Their affection for child is no longer deep and abiding. Therefore, they may seek divorce. On account of these factors the basis of family is no longer permanent.

7. Influence of Western Culture on Indian Culture. The influence of Western culture can be seen on language, literature, music, art, religion and morality as follows:

(i) *Language.* West has deeply influenced the Indian languages. The English language words used in Indian languages out-number the words of all other foreign languages. Indeed, without the fund of English words the vocabulary of Indian languages is incomplete. All mechanical devices and instruments used in daily life in India are the gift of the West. Most of them have English names, without the use of which we cannot communicate easily.

(ii) *Literature.* The Indian literature has been deeply influenced by the Western literature. The romanticism, existentialism and psycho-analysis have so much influenced the Indian literature that most of the Indian stories and dramas are written under their impact. The free verse of West is now to be found in India. Under the Western influence, short story and one-act dramas have become common in Indian literature. Besides, we can see the influence of ideologies of atheism, secularism, communism, self-indulgence, personal freedom and humanism in Indian writings.

(iii) *Art.* Like language and literature, art has also come under the impact of Western Culture. In Indian Cinema, the use of the Western dance and music is quite common. Musical instruments like violin have influenced Indian music. Modern art is very much a foreign import.

(iv) *Religion.* Indian religion has also been influenced by the Western culture. Due to intellectualism of West, the religious faith of many an Indian has been shaken. They have cast off many superstitions. The ritualism is losing its hold and sancity. Religion is becoming philosophical, mechanical or commercial. Many educated persons have lost touch with the religious scriptures and believed them to be ante-dated on account of their secular training. They are not prepared to take them seriously.

The influence of West on the Indian society and culture is rapidly increasing. Many persons are so dazzled by the Western culture that they are mockful about their own culture and traditions. The leadership of independent India rightly wants to encourage the Indian culture. This is a laudable step. But as we should not be blind worshippers of the West, we should not at the same time worship Indian culture blindly. There should be a synthesis of the two.

DIFFERENCE OF EAST & WEST

Rudyard Kipling's rhyme that East is East and West is West and never the twain will meet is nothing but an expression of an Englishman's pride in the glory of his culture. No doubt, West is very advanced and East is backward, but as Japan has shown, there is nothing inherent or inevitable about it. Moreover, the world today is shrinking so fast, no doubt due to Western Science and Technology, that it will be difficult to treat East and West as two cultures in not too distant future. But, however, there are following differences in the two cultures:

(1) Whereas West is materialist, East is spiritually inclined.

(2) Whereas West is progressive and forward-looking, fatalism is still embedded in the thinking of the East.

(3) West is much more advanced technologically than the East.

(4) Whereas the parliamentary institutions are part and parcel of the West, these institutions are still weak in the East.

The foregoing statements may lead one to believe that there are fundamental differences in the East and West and that there is no meeting ground between two. But both oriental and occidental scholars have dismissed any fundamental incompatibility in the two cultures. Though, traditionally East is considered spiritualist and West materialist it is difficult to come by proofs in the favour of this argument. From the scientific viewpoint East is definitely backward but in the medieval ages the East was more advanced.

Democracy in East

Dr. Kashi Pd. Jaiswal and other scholars have established after their historical researches that till 4th B.C. there were democratic states in India. In Buddhist literature are mentioned ten democratic states in the East Bihar. Till the invasion of Alexander, there were a number of democratic polities in Punjab. At that time a vote was known as *Chhand* and the returning Officer was known as *Shalaka Grahak*. The decisions were made democratically. In order to settle disputes there were Select Committees.

Progressivism of East

Though, the progress may be slow in the East, nonetheless East is progressive. How progressive East can be is clear from the example of Japan. Till 1870, Japan was a backward country, but within the short span of 35 years, it went ahead of Russia. In comparison with Japan the world industry became backward. Japan was ahead of many Western countries. Even today, Japan is ahead of the whole world in certain respects. India also cannot be regarded non-progressive. After independence India has made much head-way in science, technology and industry.

Synthesis of Western Materialism and Indian Spirituality

The difference between East and West is gradually diminishing; but there are certain basic differences between East and West and these would not be bridged in the near future. The West has said good-bye to spiritual values in its zeal for materialism. Dr. Radhakrishnan writes in his *Spirit of Man* that the world we are inhabiting today is the world of self-centred people who are going through a barbaric civilization, a product of intense craze for material comforts. The famous historian Oswald Spengler forecast doom of West. The same view is echoed by Toynbee. Bertrand Russell & P.A. Sorokin are also critical of Western culture and advocate the values of altruism, a fact deeply realized in East since ages.

India is a religious country in which the spiritual values dominate. Liberation from this world is considered to be the goal and summum bonum of human life. The rishis of Upanishads spent their lives in the search of self-knowledge. Vedic seers saw divine powers behind every phenomenon. According to Gita, the realisation of God is the highest aim of human life. According to Lord Buddha, life is sorrow and misery and to get rid of this sorrow and misery is the aim of life. According to Samkara Brahman alone is real and the world is a myth. The mayavada of Samkara has permeated the every nook and corner of Indian life. With the exception of Charvakas, all systems of Indian philosophy are wedded to spirituality and disregard this world. An Indian is interested in immortality, not living the life.

Indian Neglect of Materialism

The Indian spiritualism has become one-sided on account of its neglect of material values. This encouraged escapism. Buddhism gave birth to philosophy of sorrow and misery and this did incalculable harm to Indian life. The bliss of union with God was considered the only worthy goal of humans and enjoyment of the worldly pleasures was considered to be animalistic. No attempt was made to ameliorate the miseries of this world. The philosophy of Charvakas was always a butt of mockery and joke. The neglect of women, child marriage, untouchability and other evils were the results of neglect of society by Indian thinkers. After observing the self-smugness of Indian wallowing in social rottenness, Vivekananda declared that India needs to say good-bye to Vedanta. A youngman will be better occupied playing football than reading Gita.

Gift of Western Materialism

No doubt western materialism suffers from certain defects. There is atheism, self-indulgence, race for power and an unending struggle for self-aggrandisement. According to Rabindranath Tagore, Europe has speed but no direction. It is rich in means but poor in ends. The true goal of life can be had only in Indian spirituality, there may be ecstasy of activity but no peace anywhere else. But, the gift of western materialism is equally precious. The heaven dreamt of by religion is technically possible upon this earth.

Need of Synthesis

As we have seen above neither pure materialism nor pure spiritualism are satisfactory. What we need is a synthesis? Today, all the institutions of the East including language, literature, marriage, family and life style in general have come under the impact of western culture. There is need to be on our guard in the matter. If we allow ourselves to be fully westernized we will inherit dangerous defects of the western culture. It is necessary that each culture must maintain its individuality and uniqueness. We must adopt an integral approach to life. According to integral view of life there is no inherent contradiction between materialism and spiritualism. Indeed, both are complementary to each other. One is not complete without the other.

QUESTIONS FOR EXERCISE

1. Evaluate the concept of Westernization in so far as it describes the changes in Indian Society.
2. Explain the impact of Western culture on Hindu social life.
3. Distinguish between East and West and show her they may be synthesised.

24

Modernization

Before undertaking the discussion of modernization in India, it is advisable to define the term modernization first. According to S.N. Eisenstadt, "Historically, modernization is the process of change towards those types of social, economic and political systems that have developed in Western Europe and North America from the seventeenth to the nineteenth century and spread to other European countries and nineteenth and twentieth centuries to the south American, Asian and African continents."[1] Modernization is the characteristic feature of modern society. As Marrion J. Levy puts it, "My definition of modernisation hinges on the use of inanimate sources of power and the use of tools to multiply the effect I conceive each of these two elements as the basis of continuum."[2]

CHARACTERISTICS OF MODERNIZATION

The process of modernization becomes evident from its characteristics. Following are its characteristics:

1. Social Mobilization. The social mobilization is that process by which the old social, economic and psychological elements are transformed and new social values of human conduct are set-up. The social mobilization is a peculiarity of modernization.

2. Social Differentiation. Another feature of modernization is social differentiation. In this process, there is increase in the complexity in social, political and economic activities and there is progress in the activities of individuals in various fields. Industrialization is a result of modernization. In politics, the administrative complexity in the centre and local bodies is a characteristic of modernization. The political power gets dispersed among adults. Thus, modernization is a way to democratization. As a result of modernization new trends in philosophy, religion, science and literature become visible. Briefly, an increase in modernization leads to an increase in social, economic, political and cultural fields there is more differentiation in these.

1 Eisenstadt, *Modernization, Protest and Change.*

2 Marrion J. Levy, *Contrasting Factors in the Modernization of China and Japan*, 1955.

3. Structural Differentiation and Change. Another characteristic of modernization is structural differentiation and continuous change. In the social and economic fields old organizations break up yielding place to new. In politics new political parties emerge. The collage industries are replaced by big industry. The new means of production develop. Many new professions develop. The production becomes more complex.

4. Change in Organizational and Status System. A feature of modern society is the emergence of a number of specialized organization. Secondly, there is greater division of labour. Thirdly, the organizations based on close kinship lose importance. With the acceleration in the speed of change the status of individuals and families undergoes change. New classes emerge in Society. From the cultural and economic viewpoint there come into being three classes, namely, upper, middle and lower.

5. Urbanization. The phenomenon of urbanization and modernization are inter-linked; one leads to the other.

6. Social & Political Movements. An important feature of modernization is the emergence of new social and political movements which aim at the transformation of society. This transformation becomes imperative in order to make man adjust to fast changing conditions. These movements also aim at casting off orthodoxy and paving the ground for change to modernity. In order to attain the new aims, a change of outlook becomes imperative.

7. Comprehensive and Multi-sided Education. An important aim of modernization is the spread of education. In modern society, it is seen that all should be educated. Besides academic education, under modernization, the need for technical and professional education becomes deep; therefore many technical and professional institutes spring up to meet this demand.

8. Development of International Co-operation. Lastly, the development of international co-operation is the aim of modernization. The national movements gave birth to many nations. For the development of mutual relations among nations. League of Nations and later U.N.O. came into existence.

MODERNIZATION IN INDIA

After discussing the characteristics of modernization in India, the impact of modernization will now be discussed —

1. Industrialization. In modern India, the industrialization is going on at fast pace. The Western model is being followed in this regard. The Western countries, in particular U.S.A., have helped India in industrialization. This has helped to bring India close to the western style of industrialization. In order to meet the demands of fast growing population, every country must perforce to become industrialized. Therefore, India is fully resolved to bring about fast industrialization.

2. Urbanization. The fast growth of population of this country in the last 50 years has lead to fast urbanization in India. The fast industrialization and consequent urbanization has led to many ticklish problems like slums, crimes etc. In order to solve these problems town-planning is imperative.

3. Secularization. Secularization is a consequence of urbanization. The people of India have adopted the ideal of secularism according to which every body is free to follow the religion of his choice. The modern society is pluralist. The compassion and tolerance are the chief characteristics of modernization.

4. Rise of New Social Classes. The traditional social classification in India is based upon caste system. The caste system is incompatible with the egalitarian social values. Under it the status of a person is determined by his birth. Whatever may have been the merit and use of caste system in the past, there is little doubt that in the modern society it is an obstructive force; it is retrograde; it is against the democratic values. Due to current politicization the importance of caste system is growing; but from all other viewpoints its value and importance is declining. Today, both in the towns and villages, the people are divided into classes based upon economic and political considerations rather than caste considerations. The distinction between lower, middle and upper classes is exclusively economic. The classes based on economic consideration are non-hereditary. A low class person by the dint of his labour and application may graduate to upper class tomorrow. The importance of money and possessions in modern society is paramount. With increasing politicisation there is now clear-cut demarcation between those in power and those out of it. Mostly, economically better off persons are politically also better off; but this is not essential. The political class in India is different from the economically rich, but the economically rich support politicians with money and manipulate them to grow in riches. The industrialization is giving rise to an organized labour class and the communist thinking is creeping in Indian society. With the organization of labour class, the capitalist class is also getting organized and they have formed many associations to protect their interests. While there are All India labour organizations, there are also All India level associations of the capitalists.

5. Social Change. Modernization accelerates the pace of change; it is quickened. The change is both the characteristic and goal of social change. Change is a cultural goal towards which every society advances. The change must be towards the achievement of greater human dignity and greater social equality. It is a progress towards democratic values. The social change can be seen in diverse fields. On the one hand, social movements have greatly changed our ideas and concepts about various social matters, and on, the other, youth movement has brought about revolutionary change in the thinking and aspirations of youth. The youth movement can be seen all over the world, this is an important characteristic of modernization and the pace of modernization gets accelerated by these movements. The youth movement is a rebellion against the traditional values and is a harbinger of new shape of things to come. Today, a particular attention is being paid to encourage youth movements at the University level. From time to time youth functions and festivals are held in the Universities in which young persons from all over the country participate. This encourages the national integration and also forms the basis for the building up of the future. In India, the youth movements can be seen in the form of student movements. The youth is demanding a right to participate in the administrative affairs of the Universities. The modern youth is busy evaluating the educational curricula and also the efficacy and utility of examinations. These matters become bone of contention among the students and University authorities.

6. Westernization. The trend towards modernization in India can be seen in the form of a movement towards westernization of the society. The trend towards westernization can he seen in all fields. In social, economic, political, cultural, religious and educational spheres India is following the example of West. Even those who are in favour of retaining the traditional values also want to utilize the good points of the western system. They want a synthesis of western and Indian values. The westernization leads to modernization because the model of modern society is provided by the West. In the social sphere we are following West in matters like dress, life style and town planning etc. The latest fashions of the West are quickly followed by the Indian elite. There is more of westernization in the technical and scientific spheres than in the social spheres. This has given rise to cultural lag. In the social fields we are still sticking to the obscurantist values of casteism, communalism and parochialism.

7. Democratization. In the field of politics, the most characteristic feature of modernization is the process of democratization. India is becoming progressively democratized. There is in India universal adult franchise. Everybody above a certain age is entitled to elect his representative. Everybody is equal before law and enjoys equal rights and privileges. In the economic sphere, an attempt is being made to reduce economic disparities. The compulsory primary education is aiming at universal literacy. All political parties are wedded to the true values of Equality, Liberty and Freedom. There may be differing viewpoints regarding the means to attain these values, but there is no dispute about their validity and acceptance as the ultimate goals of political endeavour. Though, it is undeniable that there was a tradition of democracy in the ancient India, but the modern democratic traditions in India are the gift of West. In this respect also India is following the West. In the promotion of democracy in West, U.S.A., in particular, has helped a great deal.

PROBLEMS OF MODERNIZATION

Modernization, obviously, entails social change. As a consequence of this change, the new organizations are replacing the old, new groups and new trends are emerging. While this leads to progress in various fields, it also gives rise to many problems. The social change promotes social disintegration. There is class war and counter-revolutionary movements come into being. In India, as a consequence of modernization, there is individual and family disintegration. The joint family system is breaking down and it is being replaced by nuclear families. Due to modern tendencies the basis of marriage has ceased to be religious; it is now a social and psychological bond. The incidence of divorce is increasing. The ideas about propriety in sexual relations are also undergoing change. As the opportunities of get together between sexes are increasing there are many instances of violation of traditional ethical values. The unemployment problem is also a result of modernization. While on the one hand, there come into existence new industries, the traditional trades become obsolete. This throws many persons out of employment There is also the problem of adequate use of leisure. In the field of politics warring political factions have come into being. There are rightists and leftists. Both have very dissimilar attitude towards problems. This renders co-operation among people difficult.

In order to resolve the problems arising out of modernization a change in social policy is needed. Modernization requires transformation. This transformation is towards progressive democratic, social and scientific ideals. In order to effect this transformation we require not only structural changes but also functional changes. The most important requirement is to promote the ideals of mutual tolerance, respect and equality, only then there will be all round progress. The modernization and social transformation should be so effected that the ancient values and contemporary needs should be properly integrated. The new values should fit into proper historical perspective. If the conflict of tradition and modernity is not intelligently resolved there can be no progress. In line with this general outlook the contemporary problems should be deeply studied and resolved. The proper leadership is required for the successful tackling of the problems but the choice of proper leadership is in the hands of every citizen.

QUESTIONS FOR EXERCISE

1. Elucidate the concept of modernization.
2. Are old Hindu values consistent with the values of modernization? Support your answer with arguments.

25

Politicization

Tendency towards Politicization

By politicization, we mean the preponderance of politics in the different spheres of life. After independence and the establishment of democracy in India there is concentration of power in the political hands. The politicians nowadays freely interfere in administration and are able to influence it to the benefit of themselves and their friends and relatives. This has naturally made political power very alluring. In modern India, the political power is the fount of all other powers. Therefore, the persons of different classes are busy making maximum exertions to win and comer the political power. The amount of power and prestige enjoyed by the political leaders in modern India are unmatched by the leaders in science, culture and arts. The political leader is welcome everywhere. The people throng in large number wherever he goes; he is hailed by them and processions are taken out in his honour, his death results in national mourning. All this excites the envy of the educated men and women. In no other progressive and developed country, the politician is accorded so much honour and importance. The inordinate importance given to the political leaders in India goes to prove that the pursuit of cultural goals does not have the same importance as the political power. The circulation of newspapers is progressively going up. With the introduction of radios in the remote corners of the country the people are becoming interested in the political news. The interest in the political news clearly exhibits the tendency towards politicization.

Politicization in Social Sphere

The politics dominates various aspects of our social life today. In India, the evil of casteism has weakened on account of social and cultural changes; but the political factors have given it a fresh lease of life and it is once again raising its ugly head. The politicians are exploiting the sentiment of casteism for their nefarious end not for the genuine welfare of the caste. Similarly, communalism, linguism and regionalism are being exploited by the politicians not for the interest of any community, language on religion but for selfish political ends. Not only, the castes but marriage and family have also been affected by politics. In urban areas the capitalists after acquiring lot of wealth make it a point to corner political power. In municipalities and corporations the elections are fought with selfish political motives. After success in elections grinding of one's own axes and not commonweal is their real purpose.

Politicization in Government Services

The political considerations seem to prevail in appointments to government services. The top politicians try to fill up top government with men loyal to them. In administrative and police forces, the chief ministers and other members of this cabinet try to have men of their confidence at key posts.

Politicization in Education

In the field of education even a number of appointments are made not according to merit but due to political considerations. The appointment of vice-chancellors is usually a political appointment. Even school and college managements are befouled by politics. The academic atmosphere today is befouled by politics. The politicians are busy using students as tools for their nefarious ends. This is resulting in progressive deterioration in the academic standards.

Politicization in Economic Sphere

In both private and public sectors, the politics dominates economic activity. In the private sectors, the top posts in big industrial houses are occupied by the relatives of the management. The welfare of the labour is not the primary consideration with them; they are more concerned with subserving their private ends. But the maximum politicization is to be found in the public sector. In the recent past, there have been demonstrations to get the steel industry established in the particular areas. At places these demonstrations have been violent. The people in various states want maximum number of industries in their areas, because this enhances the opportunities of employment. However, some industries cannot be started in some areas because of adverse economic factors, for example, undeveloped means of communications. But political pressure is exerted to bypass economic and rational factors. The politicians know best how to swim in troubled waters. They grind their own axes without national consideration. Thus, reason is excluded from their thinking. This adversely affects national life.

Boundary Disputes

After independence, the boundaries of the states have been realigned, a number of times. The areas of some states have been lopped off and added to other states. A number of new states have been carved out. Punjab has been split into Haryana and West Punjab. A new state of Nagaland has been created. There is now demand for divisions of U. P. and M.P. into smaller units. While there may be some merit behind these demands, these are by and large politically motivated. More the states, more are the posts of political incumbents. Therefore, behind the creation of new states is the factor of political motivation and selfish interests.

Politicization in Culture

There is so much politicization in India that even the cultural field is not free from its influence. Many a time the selection of all-India sports team is made not on the basis of merit but on political considerations. In Olympic games, the number of officials sometimes exceeds the number of players. The same thing is also true with regard to cultural troupes sent out of this country. The artistes who are able to carry favour with politicians get included in these troupes. The government grants to cultural associations are frequently made on political considerations.

The above survey of politicization in various fields clearly brings out the urgency of stemming this rot. The foreign observers are surprised to see that an Indian attaches so much importance to the political leaders and discusses the political news with so much avidity and ignores the cultural and artistic activities. The evil of politicization can only be removed if the elitist class of industrialists, professors, doctors, engineers, artists and literatures stop attaching too much importance to the political news and politicians. They should realize the importance of their professions and assert their worth. For example, they should not brook interference of politicians in their respective fields.

QUESTION FOR EXERCISE

1. Write an essay on Politicization in India.

26

Democratization

Abraham Lincoln's definition of democracy as a government of the people, by the people and for the people is the most appropriate. Though, there are many definitions, none is so complete as Lincoln's definition. Democracy is a people's government in which the persons elected by the people run the affairs of the state. The ideals of democracy are Liberty, Equality and Fraternity. In democracy, an attempt is made to establish political and economic equality. In democracy, a person has the freedom to express his opinions, from associations and to engage in any valid or constitutional activity. The ultimate aim of democracy is not the efficiency of government but to promote a sense of brotherhood among people. Democracy provides an opportunity in which a man can make maximum growth of his personality.

Though, democracy is a government by the majority group, but the protection of the interests of minorities also is a crucial element of democracy. In view of this, Robert Dahl has written, "If there is anything to be said for the processes that actually distinguish democracy (or polyarchy) from dictatorship, it is not discoverable in the clearest distinction between government by majority and government by a minority. The distinction comes much closer to being one between government by a minority and government by minorities." Indeed democracy is not an end but a means. According to Wm. David "...democracy is a from of government wherein the will of the people is promptly and accurately executed."

Is India Fit for Democracy?

British did not consider India to be fit for democracy. According to them, India needed the support of British empire for its protection. According to J.S. Mill, India is so populous a country that direct elections are unthinkable. Elections even for the municipalities will have to be indirect. From Duffrin to Montague the British men thought India unfit for the parliamentary form of government. But, the Indian experiment with democracy has belied all the fears. Indeed, India has had a long tradition of democracy. Eminent Indian thinkers like M.G. Ranade,

Dadabhoy Naoroji and G.K. Gokhle showed that there was a grassroot democracy in India and that it was not a new concept. The Indian leaders were well conversant with the various forms of government and by consensus they chose parliamentary form of democracy for India.

Characteristics of Indian Democracy

The Indian Constitution has quite clearly fixed the form of Indian democracy. Its chief characteristics are:

1. Parliamentary Form. Instead of being a republican from of government India has chosen to be a parliamentary form of government. Under it the representatives of people constituting the parliament are the supreme.

2. Federal. Another feature of Indian democracy is its federal character. Lord Bryce has characterized U.S.A. as 'republic of republics'. The same thing holds true in the case of India. The Article I of Indian Constitution describes India as a Union of States. According to our Constitution, the states are autonomous. They have full freedom in certain spheres but in others they are dependent upon the centre. Though, it is true that in India the centre has wider powers than the states, this is correct in view of the fact that a newly emergent nation requires a strong centre to curb the fissiparous tendencies. There are a number of matters even then in which the states enjoy full freedom and unless there is total constitutional breakdown the centre does not interfere in their internal matters.

3. Dual Government. Because there is central and state administrations in simultaneous operation in India, there is a dual government in India. In the centre also there are three independent governmental wings, *viz.*, Legislature, Executive and Judiciary.

4. Collective Responsibility. In the Indian democracy, the Councils of Ministers both in states and centre are collectively responsible to their respective legislatures. Therefore, even when one minister resigns it is an occasion for the resignation of the entire government. No minister is singly responsible for any act of the government. The entire Council of Ministers is responsible for each act.

5. Triple List of Administrative Subjects. There are three lists of administrative subjects: the Central, the State and Concurrent. In the central list there are 97 subjects. These are exclusively under the jurisdiction of the centre. In the state list, there are 66 subjects; legislation on these matters is the sole jurisdiction of the states. In the concurrent list, there are 47 subjects, both centre and states can legislate on these matters.

Democratization by Indian Constitution

The freedoms guaranteed by the Indian Constitution provide a sound basis for the democratization of Indian society. In the chapter III, articles 12 to 35 of the Constitution guarantee fundamental rights to the Indian people. The intent of these rights is to respect the human personality. By article 32 of the Constitution, a citizen has the right to approach the Supreme Court for the enforcement of the fundamental rights. The Supreme Court is empowered to strike down any legislation or act of government which curtails these rights. The personal freedom is the comer stone of the true democracy. Besides equality and fraternity, freedom is the most essential constituent of democracy. This freedom is established and guaranteed by the rule of law and the judiciary is its protector. The articles 14, 19, 21, 22, and 32 guarantee freedom to the Indian citizen. According to article 14, every citizen is equal before law. According to article 19, every citizen has freedom of speech and expression. No society can afford to give indefinite freedom to its members. Therefore, the Indian Constitution has defined these freedoms and also made certain provisions about their restriction. According to article 21, no one can be deprived of any freedom except through a valid process of law. Article 22 empowers a citizen to move Supreme Court against his arrest etc. During emergency, of course, some of these freedoms can be suspended.

Decentralization of Power

Another basis of democratization in India is the decentralization of power. By establishing the panchayats in villages and investing them with wide powers, India has decentralized the political power and attempted to restore the ancient rural democracy. This helps to appraise people with the administrative problems and participate directly in the task of governing. Even the Britishers were impressed by the role of rural panchayat. It is undoubtedly a very creditable institution and speaks volumes for the political wisdom of our ancients. However, in the recent past, the institution of panchayat has been infected by a host of evils. The maximum politicization can be seen in panchayats. In modern panchayats, the common interests of village are sacrificed at the altar of sectarian gains. The elections to the Panchayats are fought on a political basis and these are used to subserve the ends of their political masters. Thus, the evil of politicization can be seen at every step. The politicization of rural India has encouraged casteism and now elections to the Panchayats are fought openly on the basis of caste alignments. After elections in order to keep themselves in power they subserve the interests of their respective castes. The various problems like communalism, regionalism, linguism and parochialism are the direct outcome of politicization. The dream of village self-rule visualised by M.K. Gandhi may not materialize if this politicization continues. The chances of its reversal are almost nil. The main reason for this state of affairs is the lack of proper education. The decentralization no doubt helps the process of democratization, but it can prove beneficial only if the power goes to deserving hands.

Factors of Success

The present government favours not political democratization but economic democratization also. It aims at the establishment of democratic socialism in India. In the absence of economic progress there can be no real democracy. Without economic equality the political equality is meaningless. In order to achieve economic equality India has undertaken planned development. The following are the important factors for the success of democracy:

1. Election. The freedom to elect one's representatives in the government is the fundamental basis of democracy. For the proper use of this freedom the citizens must be well educated. The elections must be free and fair and there should be no element of fear or intimidation in them. If any person employs unlawful means to secure his election, it should be set aside. There is such a provision in India. The elections can be challenged in the court of law.

2. Political Freedom. For the success of democracy the freedom of speech, expression and association is most essential.

3. Education. Without education there can be no democracy. A democracy of illiterates is a contradiction in terms. In the absence of sufficient education elections become a farce. In this respect the situation in India is not satisfactory.

4. Development of Means of Communication In order to educate the public the means of communication must be well developed. The newspapers, radio, cinema and television helped to educate the public. The development of rails and motor service are also necessary for democracy.

5. Independent Judiciary. For the success of democracy an independent judiciary is a must. Only an independent judiciary can ensure that there are no abridgement of rights of the citizens In India, the judiciary is independent of both executive and legislature. During his presidency. Shri V.V. Giri appeared before the Supreme Court and thus vindicated its honour.

6. Accountable Administration. In democracy, the government is responsible to the people because it is they who elected their representatives. Therefore, in a democracy, administrative machinery and the police must be accountable to people. In India, our administration is not truly responsive to people. There is on the one hand, undue interference by the politicians in the administration and, on the other hand, the British rule hangover continues in which administration was unresponsive. Now, that the people are becoming aware of their rights and privileges the administrator reversal are almost nil. The main reason for this state of affairs is becoming more cooperative. But, for a healthy democracy we must have an administration that is fully responsive to people's needs and aspirations.

7. Growth of Middle Class. For the success of democracy a powerful middle class is necessary. It is the middle class which is responsible for maintaining and sustaining the healthy growth of the democratic institutions.

8. Freedom to form Political Parties. Last, but not the least, requirement for the growth of democracy is the freedom to put forth one's political demands and to form a political party to accomplish them. In India, people enjoy this freedom. There is no bar on political activity. In modern India, political parties of all hues and shades are in the arena, competing for people's patronage. So many parties merged to form a single party. They succeeded in capturing power at centre. The Congress has faced split. In border states regional parties are to the fore. All this goes to prove that in India there is no bar on political activity. However, a party which wants dismemberment of India or owes open loyalty to some foreign powers is not allowed. This restriction of course is most rational, because no country can allow its own liquidation.

Problem of Adult Franchise

The critics of Indian democracy find fault with it because under it every adult, irrespective of his educational or financial qualifications, has a right to vote. A university professor and a peasant wholly illiterate have same political value. Both have one vote each. Before independence only a limited group of persons had this right. After independence everyone got the voting right. The rich and poor, educated and uneducated were brought on the same level. As we have referred earlier, education is an essential ingredient of democracy. By endowing everyone with the voting right, the sanctity of political choice is lost, because an uneducated person cannot exercise his choice freely. Moreover, the better off people lose interest in elections because in India votes are weighed but not counted. There is a tendency of block voting. All this has given rise to indiscipline. Money and muscle power are more important in winning elections than moral stature or brain power.

But the advocates of adult franchise consider it to be a wise step. According to them this checks leftism and thus helps democracy. The voting right is a powerful instrument of political and social education. Because of voting right there is political awakening among the masses and they participate in the political gatherings and listen to various viewpoints. This is a fine source of their education. Though, the need of proper education is not derived for the success of democracy, withdrawal of the adult franchise is no remedy.

Obstacles in Democracy

The obstacles in the path of democracy have been discussed below:

1. Illiteracy. As we referred earlier, without education there can be no democracy. Without education people do not know their rights and duties and cannot conduct themselves properly as citizens.

2. Poverty. The poor people have no time or leisure for anything. They are not aware of their rights. They are easily exploited by others. Therefore, poverty is a great hinderance in the way of democracy.

3. Pressure of Population. India is a country of teeming millions. In spite of all attempts to check it is growing very fast. In 1976, it had crossed the 60 crores mark. The fast growing population call offset all our plans and even the best brains and most efficient planning cannot check economic deterioration if the population grows unchecked. Therefore, for the success of democracy population must be checked.

4. Low Capital. Because of low rate of investment the progress of industrialization is not satisfactory. A poor country obviously cannot save much.

5. Low Productivity. Both in agriculture and industry our productivity is low and this comes in the way of satisfactory economic progress.

6. Problem of Foreign Investment. It is not possible to get foreign aid without political strings. The donor of aid tries to impose its own condition. This constitutes a threat to democracy.

7. Moral Crisis. In the past decades the moral standards, have fallen steeply and this is posing serious threat to the integrity of our social fabric. Our political leadership is thoroughly discredited. Their sense of moral values is conspicuous by absence. There is all round corruption. The caste considerations and not merit compel the choice of political candidates. Even educational institutions are thoroughly infected with corruption. This must be reversed if democracy has to have any future.

8. Disintegrating Forces. Today a number of disintegrating forces have come to the fore. The problem of language has become very thorny. It may lead to serious rift between South and North. The virus of communalism is still with us. The regionalism is raising its head. All these disintegrating forces, if allowed to go unchecked, will spell national ruin.

9. Foreign Threat. Indian democracy, besides internal problems, is faced with foreign threats. We have long borders. The border states are vulnerable to foreign influences, the problems of Nagaland, Mizoram etc., clearly show that the Indian democracy is facing real foreign threat.

QUESTIONS FOR EXERCISE

1. What do you understand by democracy? How far do you think it is suitable to Indian society?
2. Discuss the pattern of social growth and progress in modern India since 1947. Analyse the reasons for and against them.
3. Discuss the salient features of Indian democracy bringing out its weakness and strong points.
4. "Democracy in India is in danger". Discuss.

27

National Emotional Integration

Need for National Integration

The unity of a nation depends upon the extent to which its various members look upon themselves as members of the same group. National Unity or integration does not automatically follow upon living within the same geographical boundaries. Emotional integration is necessary for this unity. As is evident from the term itself emotional integration is the unity, identity or similarity of emotions. If it exists, then individuals feel related to and concerned with each other, despite any external differences. It is emotional integration is generated through various community programmes. It promotes a sense of community and impedes the progress of disorganizing tendencies.

In India, one finds marked differences in the living standards, dress, customs, religion, culture, etc., of the various people existing in different parts. India's large size is emphasized by these differences, but one result of this is that when a person goes from one part of the country to another, he is almost a foreigner there. This had led to regionalism, expressed in the desire of people of one region to promote their own regional interests at the expense of the interests of other regions. Regionalism has gained tremendous momentum because it has been linked with linguism. Linguism is the prejudice of the speakers of a particular language to develop their language, to the detriment of any and all other languages spoken in different parts of the country. Casteism or racial distinction between the Hindus and Muslims has led to deterioration of social organisation in the country. Untouchability is an offshoot of casteism. Religious communities have been known to come into violent conflict with each other, thus leading to considerable damage to public and private property, and bloodshed on a large scale. Communalism is responsible for the hatred which one religious group fosters for another. Putting it briefly, regionalism, linguism, casteism, communalism, etc., are the disruptive and disorganising influences which have divided Indian society into various groups. It is impossible to hope for a solution of these problems in the absence of emotional integration. And, if these problems remain unsolved, democracy will also remain a dream.

Unity in Diversity

Generally speaking, the extent of diversity found in India trends to create the impression that it is not a country but a sub-continent. But this does not imply that unity or integration is impossible in such a situation. One finds distinct and different racial characteristics among the inhabitants of different parts of the country, because differences of complexion, size, shape, etc., are clearly evident. It can be clearly seen that there is a gradual decline in the physical stature of the inhabitants as one moves from Punjab to Assam. If other examples are necessary, it can be seen that there are all kinds of complexions in this country. In the north complexion varies from darkly wheatish, dark, yellow to red and even runs into mixtures of these colours. Inhabitants of the Andamans are jet black while those of the South Dravidians is a shining black, in direct contrast is the rosy white complexion of the Kashmiris. Turning to languages, one finds that the Indian Constitution has granted recognition of Urdu, Bengali, Assamese, Oriya, Punjabi, Gujarati, Marathi, Sindhi and numerous other languages, in addition to Hindi. Besides, Telugu, Kannada, Tamil and Malayalam have been accepted as the four Dravid languages. Sanskrit has also been given special consideration, as the original Aryan language. Differences exist not only at the level of language but also in respect of dress, religion, culture, etc. Tribes of the north, east, central districts and the south differ from each other in their modes of life, their social and psychological characteristics, etc., to such a great extent that one can find among them different cultural and social regions. If one travels from east to west, and then back again, one will find clearly perceptible differences in complexion, dress, customs, modes of life, dietary habits and other aspects of culture, even at very short distances. But despite these differences of region, race, language, tribe, etc., the existence of a national unity cannot be questioned. One finds this inner unity or integration in all the people spread over the landmass limited by Himalayas on the one side and the Indian Ocean on the other, the Burma Hill on the east and Pakistan on the west. This inner unity is the basis of emotional integration. Despite the more obvious and superficial differences, there is inalienable underlying unity. It is this inner unity which Sir Herbert Rizley described when he commented that, at the root of the apparent diversity of physical and social type, language, custom and religion that immediately strikes the observer coming to India, is a definite similarity or identity or inner unity of life from the Himalayas to Cape Comorin. This inner integration or unity is the basis of Indian culture. All the saints of the past were aware of this unity, although they were no less aware of the obvious differences. It is for this reason that India has always been treated as a single unit, even in the remote past. It has been customary to refer to all the people residing in different parts of the country as Indians, even though one could see the differences of religion, culture, languages, etc. In fact, the very name Bharatvarsha denotes not merely geographical boundaries but actually the ideal of a cultural unity. During the Middle Ages, India was always treated as one unit. That India is accepted as the mother by all Indians is only due to a feeling of oneness and identity.

Efforts at Increasing Emotional Integration

It was this question of emotional integration which inspired the Central Education Ministry in 1961 to organise a committee for emotional integration under the chairmanship of Dr. Sampurnanand. This campaign to increase emotional integration had the solid foundation of belief in the principle of unity in diversity. All that is needed is that the younger generation should be educated in this direction through various kinds of programmes. Speaking at the inauguration of the Indian Integration Committee, Shri K.L. Shrimali, explained the significance of education and commented that if we want to generate a national consciousness in our people, we will have to plan our education accordingly. Education must be so designed as to encourage each participant to think of himself as a responsible part of the Indian nation. Education must take upon itself the responsibility of awakening the younger generation to the truth that, despite obvious external differences, all Indians are the same, emotionally.

Keeping in mind the objective outlined above, the Emotional Integration Committee gave the following suggestions:

1. Reorganization of Syllabi. In order to reorganise and reshape the syllabi of colleges and universities to accord with the needs of the nation, the committee made the following suggestions:

(1) At the primary stage, stress should be laid upon nationalistic stories, poems, songs, etc.

(2) At the secondary stage, in addition to the other subjects being taught, special attention should be given to the study of national literature, social studies, moral and religious guidance and extra-curricular activities.

(3) At the university level, the syllabi should include the various social sciences, languages, literatures, cultures and arts. Teachers and students should be given facilities to travel to various parts of the country.

2. Encouragement to Extra-Curricular Activities. Besides imparting formal knowledge to the students, the teachers must provide them with the opportunity to take part in such extra-curricular activities which are important from the standpoint of emotional integration. Besides, such programmes, must also represent the entire nation. Such programmes help in the development of 'we' feeling, a feeling of unity and sympathy. One example of such programmes is the Inter University cultural festivals in which teachers and students participate from all parts of the country.

3. Improvement of Textbooks. It is desirable that textbooks on various subjects, and especially on history, should be amended and improved. They should be designed to encourage a sense of emotional unity with people living in other parts of the country. This will also help to check the growth of communal feelings. But it should also be remembered that such amendments should not be made at the cost of truth because such violence to truth is counterproductive. That the country is one is an undeniable truth. What is required is an expression of this truth.

4. Improvements concerning Language and Script. In this connection the Committee on Emotional Integration made the following recommendations:

(1) The use of the roman script should be permitted to increase knowledge of Hindi in certain areas.

(2) International numerals should be used in every part of the country.

(3) Arrangements should be made to teach the Devanagri script where it is not known.

(4) Hindi textbooks should also be provided in the regional scripts. Dictionaries using both Hindi and the regional languages should also be prepared.

(5) At the university level, study of Hindi and English literatures should be encouraged so that integration is encouraged and divisive forces checked.

(6) The rights of the minorities should be protected in formulating a language policy.

In addition to the above list of suggestions, the Committee for Emotional Integration also made certain other suggestions. In schools the daily programme should be started after a community prayer and a ten minute talk, either by the principal or by some respected persons, on some subject which may encourage emotional integration. Another way of encouraging emotional integration is to organise a mass meeting of the school once a year and asking the students to take an oath to increase emotional integration. Besides, all subjects and activities likely to lower awareness of differences should be encouraged. In this manner it is possible to create a climate in which all people feel that they are members of one nation. On the negative side, all efforts must be made to destroy all elements which tend to obstruct the growth of emotional integration.

Suggestions for Improving Emotional Integration

Apart from the suggestions outlined above, education can be used in the following suggested ways for improving emotional integration in the country:

1. Development of an All-India Language. The first condition for increasing emotional integration in the country is that an All-India language should be evolved. Hindi is the only language capable of performing this role. Hence, it is desirable that knowledge of this language be made compulsory for every citizen. Government should extend every facility for developing Hindi literature. The development of a national language will not prejudice their interests of regional languages. They should be allowed to pursue their own course. But all communications between the Centre and the States should be conducted in the all India language. Applicants for administrative jobs in the government should be required to know Hindi, although they may be allowed to take the examination in their regional language.

2. An All-India Educational Policy. Education is the most effective tool for spreading emotional and national integration. For this reason a national educational plan should be devised. The plan should aim at providing every child with knowledge of the ideas of great men, poets, leaders, religious thinkers, etc. Textbooks should be prepared under the supervision of the Central Government and provided by it, so that the younger generation may be brought up in an atmosphere of nationalistic fervour. Rules for the appointment of teachers, their pay scales and their conditions of working should be common all over the country The same syllabi should be applicable to all institutions in the country at the primary, secondary and university levels. All-India organisations like the N.C.C., Scouting, Girl Guides, etc., should be given appropriate encouragement. University education should be through the medium of the national language, even if the students are permitted to answer questions in their mother tongues. In this manner, the objective of national unity or integration can be achieved by evolving an All-India educational plan.

3. Programmes for Increasing National Unity. Many kinds of programmes can be devised for increasing national unity. For example, the cinema can be used to spread the feeling of national unity. Radio and television can also be used equally effectively. All-India competitions and meetings can be organised in various parts of the country to increase national unity. Such programmes help people living in different parts of the country to meet residents of other parts and learn their ideas and understand them. Travel facilities should be made more common and delegations and tours encouraged. During the last few years special trains made up of farmers of different areas, students and members of parliament toured the entire country. The helped the cause of national integration. Other programmes similar to these can be organised.

4. Development of Intercultural Understanding. In all the programmes outlined above, intercultural understanding will be promoted. This helps people to achieve liberality of attitudes to other cultures, an essential precondition of national unity in a country in which there are many cultures.

5. Efforts by Teachers. Success of most of these programmes for increasing national unity depends upon teachers. As long as the teachers themselves do not rise above their petty narrowmindedness and create ideals, there is little hope of the students developing any emotional unity. Hence, it is desirable that national consciousness should first be stirred in the students. For this, teachers from various parts of the country should be encouraged to meet each other. This can be done through the All India Teachers organisation. Even otherwise, most of the problems of teachers are common all over the country, and when they meet each other they will get an opportunity to think over these problems and exchange ideas At the same time, a national consciousness will awaken in them. Yet, attention must be paid to forestalling the development of a class consciousness among the teachers. The government can make a positive contribution in this direction by organizing lectures from time to time and distributing literature of this kind.

6. Governmental Efforts. Governmental effort is essential for bringing success to all the projects outlines above, because without official blessing, there is little that education can achieve. This cannot be doubted because there are many agencies which are working against the development of emotional integration. So long as the government fails to check agencies which encourage linguism, communalism, religious bigotry, and other disruptive forces, education will not be able to achieve the goal. One of the first steps in this direction is control over destructive political parties. In every part of the country laws should be enacted to prevent any individual from giving expression to linguism, communalism, regionalism, casteism, untouchability, etc. This should be followed up by a strict application of these laws.

It is evident from the foregoing description of the measures for increasing emotional integration that these measures must be both positive and negative. Adoption of all these measures would be a positive step. The negative step of destroying all obstacles in the way of emotional integration is not less important. For this, teachers, administrators and guardians will have to work collectively.

QUESTION FOR EXERCISE

1. Discuss the problems which Indian Nationalism is facing now-a-days and assess how emotional integration of Indian people be achieved by state action in India.

Bibliography

Arrian, History of Alexander and Indica, tr. E. Itiff Robson, London, New York, 1833.

Majumdar, R.C., *The Classical Accounts of India*, Calcutta, 1960.

McCrindle, J.W., *Ancient India as Described in Classical Literature*, Westminster, 1901, reprinted, New Delhi, 1979.

———, *Ancient India as Described by Megasthenes and Arrian*, Calcutta, 1926.

Aiyangar, K.V.R., *Rajadharma,* Madras, 1941.

———, *Aspects of Social and Political Systems of Manusmriti*, Lucknow, 1949.

———, *Some Aspects of Hindu View of Life According to Dharmasastra*, Baroda, 1953.

Altekar, A.S., *State and Government in Ancient India*, Delhi, 1955.

Apte, V.M., *Social and Religious Life in the Grhyasutras*, Bombay, 1956.

Auboyer, L., Daily Life in Ancient India, Delhi, 1965.

Banerjee, S.C., *Dharma Sutra: A Study in their Origin and Development*, Calcutta, 1962.

Basham, A.L., *The Wonder that was India,* London, 1974.

Beteille, Andre, *Castes: Old and New,* Bombay, 1969.

Bhandarkar, D.R., *Carmichael Lectures,* Calcutta, 1919.

———, *Some Aspects of Ancient Hindu Polity*, Benaras, 1929.

Bhargava, P.L., *India in the Vedic Age,* Lucknow, 1971.

Bhattacharya, Haridas etc., *The Cultural Heritage of India,* 4 Vols., reprint, Calcutta, 1970.

Bhattacharya, J.N., *Hindu Castes and Sects,* reprint, Calcutta, 1968.

Bhattacharya, Tarapada, *The Canons of Indian Art,* Calcutta, 1963.

Blunt, E.A.H., *The Caste System of Northern India,* reprint, Delhi, 1969.

Bongard-Levin, G.M., *Studies in Ancient India and Central Asia*, Calcutta, 1971.

Bose, A. N., *Social and Rural Economy of Northern India,* Vol. I, Calcutta, 1961, Vol. II, Calcutta, 1945.

Bose, N.K., *Cultural Anthropology and Other Essays*. Calcutta, 1953.

Bose, N.K., *The Structure of Hindu Society*. Delhi. 1975.

Brough, J., *Early Brahmanical System of Gotra and Pravara*, Cambridge, 1953.

———, *Aspects of Indian History and Civilization*, Agra, 1965.

Chakladar, H.C., *Social Life in Ancient India,* Calcutta, 1929.

Chanana, Devraj, *Slavery in Ancient India,* Delhi, 1960.

Chattopadhyaya, S., *Social Life in Ancient India* (in the background of the *Yajnavalkyasmriti),* Calcutta, 1965.

Chattopadhyaya, B., *The Age of the Kushanas: A Numismatic Study*, Calcutta, 1967.

———, *Kushana State and Indian Society*, Calcutta, 1975.

Choudhary, Radhakrishna, *Vratyas in Ancient India,* Varanasi, 1964.

Dass, M.M., *Women in Manu and His Seven Commentators,* Varanasi, 1961.

Das, S.K., Economic History of Ancient India, Calcutta, 1925.

Dasgupta, S.N. and De, S.K., *A History of Sanskrit Literature,* Vol. I, Calcutta, 1947.

De Bary, T.W., *et al.*, ed., *Sources of Indian Tradition*, Varanasi, 1963.

Derrett, J.D.M., *Religion Law and the State in India,* London, 1968.

Desai, A.R., *Social Background of Indian Nationalism,* Bombay, 1948.

Dikshitar, V.R.R., *War in Ancient India,* Madras, 1948.

Drekmeier, Charles, *Kingship and Community in Early India*, Bombay, 1962.

Dutt, N.K., *Origin and Growth of Caste in India*, Vol. I., London, 1931.

Dutta, B.K., *Studies in Indian Social Polity*, Calcutta, 1944.

Fick, Richard, *The Social Organisation in North-East India in Buddha's Time*, tr. S.K. Maitra, Calcutta, 1920.

Ghoshal, U.N., *Contributions to the History of Hindu Revenue System*, Calcutta, 1929.

———, *The Agrarian System in Ancient India*, Calcutta, 1930.

———, *History of Hindu Public Life*, Vol. I, Calcutta, 1945.

———, *A History of Indian Political Ideas*, Bombay, 1959.

———, *Studies in Indian History and Culture,* Calcutta, 1965, originally published as *The Beginnings of Indian Historiography and Other Essays*, Calcutta, 1949.

———, *A History of Indian Public Life*, Vol. II, Bombay, 1966.

Ghurye, G.S., *Indian Costume,* Bombay, 1951.

———, *Caste, Class and Occupation*, Bombay, 1961.

———, *Family and Kin in Indo-European Culture*, Bombay, 1962.

Gopal, Lallanji, *The Economic Life of Northern India, c. A.D., 700-1200*, Delhi, 1965.

Hazra, R.C., *Puranic Records on Hindu Rites and Customs*, Dacca, 1940. Hocart, A M., Caste: A Comparative Study, London, 1950.

Hopkins, E.W., *The Religions of India,* New Delhi, 1978.

———, *The Great Epic of India*, New York, 1901.

———, *India: Old and New,* New York, 1902.

Hutton, J.H., *Caste in India,* Bombay, 1963.

Jain, J.C., *Life in Ancient India as Depicted in the Jain Canons*, Bombay, 1947.
Jain, P.C., *Labour in Ancient India*, New Delhi, 1971.
Jayaswal, K.P., *Manu and Yajnavalkva: A Basic History of Hindu Law*, Calcutta, 1930.
———, *Hindu Polity*, Bangalore, 1943.
Jha, C., *Hindu Law in its Sources*, Allahabad, 1930.
Kane, P.V., *History of the Dharmasastra*, Poona, 1930.
———, *Hindu Customs and Modern Law*, Bombay, 1950.
Kangle, R.P., *The Kautilya Arthasastra: A Study*, Bombay, 1965.
Karve, I., *Hindu Society: An Interpretation*, Poona, 1961.
———, *Kinship Organisation in India*, Bombay, 1965.
Ketkar, S.V., *History of Caste in India*, New York, 1909.
Kosambi, D.D., *Introduction to the Study of Indian History*, Bombay, 1956.
———, *The Culture and Civilization of Ancient India in Historical Outline*, London, 1965.
Law, B.C., *Some Kshatria Tribes of Ancient India*, Calcutta, 1924.
———, *India as Described in the Early Texts of Buddhism and Jainism*, London, 1941.
———, *Tribes in Ancient India*, Poona, 1943.
Law, N.N., *Studies in Indian History and Culture*, London, 1925.
———, *Aspects of Ancient Indian Policy*, Calcutta, 1961.
MacDonell, A.A. and Keith, A.B., *Vedic Index*, London, 1912.
Majumdar, B.K., *The Military System in Ancient India*, Calcutta, 1955.
Majumdar, R.C., *Corporate Life in Ancient India*, Calcutta, 1922.
———, ed., *The Vedic Age*, London, 1951.
———, ed., *The Age of Imperial Unity*, Bombay, 1951.
Mandelbaum, D.G., *Society in India*, Bombay, 1972.
Mehta, R.N., *Pre-Buddhist India*, Bombay, 1939.
Metraux, Guy S. and Francois Courzet, ed., *Studies in the Cultural History of India*, Agra, 1965.
Mookerji, R.K., *Chandragupta Maurya and His Times*, Madras, 1943.
———, *Ancient Indian Education*, Delhi, 1960.
Mudgal, B.S., *Political Economy in Ancient India*, Kanpur, 1960.
Nesfield, J.C., *Brief View of the Caste System of the North-West Provinces and Oudh*, Allahabad, 1885.
Pandey, R.B., *Hindu Samskaras*, Delhi, 1969.
Pant, A.D., *A Critical Study of the Arthasastra Tradition in Ancient Political Thought*, unpublished D. Litt. thesis, Allahabad University, 1967.
Patil, D.R., *Cultural History from the Vayu Purana*, Poona, 1946.
Prabhu, P.N., *Hindu Social Organisation*, Bombay, 1954.
Rai, Jaimal, *Rural-Urban Economy and Social Changes in Ancient India*, Varanasi, 1974.

Rhys Davids, T.W., *Buddhist India,* London, 1903.
Risley, H.H., *The People of India,* reprint, Delhi, 1969.
Roy, U.N., *City and City Life in Ancient India* (Hindi), Allahabad.
Saran, K.M., *Labour in Ancient India,* Bombay, 1957.
Sarkar, B.K., *Political Institutions and Theories of the Hindus*, Leipzig, 1922.
Sarvadhikari, R., *The Principles of the Hindu Law of Inheritance*, Madras, 1922.
Senart, E., *Caste in India,* tr. E.D., Ross, London, 1930.
Sengupta, Nilakshi, *Evolution of Hindu Marriage,* Bombay, 1965.
Sengupta, N.C., *Evolution of Ancient Indian Law,* Calcutta, 1953.
Sharma, Brijnarain, *Social Life in Northern India,* Delhi, 1966.
Sharma, G.R., *Kusana Studies,* Allahabad, 1968.
Sharma, R.N., *Contemporary Indian Philosophy,* Atlantic, New Delhi, 1994.
——, *Indian Ethics,* Surjeet Publications, New Delhi, 1994.
——, *Social Philosophy of Sri Aurobindo*, Vineet, Meerut, 1978.
Sharma, R.S., *Sudras in Ancient India,* Varanasi, 1958.
——, *Indian Feudalism, c. 300-1200*, Calcutta, 1965.
——, *Light on Early Indian Society and Economy*, Bombay, 1966.
——, *Aspects of Political Ideas and Institutions in Ancient India*, Varanasi, 1968.
——, ed., *Indian Society: Historical Probings*, New Delhi, 1974.
Shastri, D.R., *Origin and Development of the Rituals of Ancestor Worship in India*, Calcutta, 1963.
Silson, J., *Indian Caste,* 1877.
Singer, Milton, ed., *Traditional India: Structure and Change*, Philadelphia, 1959.
——, and Cohn, B.S., ed., *Structure and Change in Indian Society*, Chicago, 1968.
Singh, Mohinder, *The Depressed Classes,* Bombay, 1947.
Sinha, H.N., *Sovereignty in Ancient India*, London, 1938.
Sircar, D.C., *Indian Epigraphical Glossary*, Delhi.
——, *Studies in the Political and Administrative Systems in Ancient and Medieval India*, Delhi, 1974.
Sorokin, P.A., *Social and Cultural Mobility,* New York, 1959.
Spellman, J.W., *Political Theory of Ancient India*, Oxford, 1964.
Srinivasa, M.N., *et al., Caste in Modern India and Other Essays*, Bombay, 1962.
——, ed., *India's Villages*, Bombay, 1960.
Srivastava, Balram, *Trade and Commerce in Ancient India*, Benaras, 1968. Stembach, L., *Juridical Studieṣ in Ancient Indian Law*, Vol. I, Delhi, 1965. Sukthankar, V.S., *On the Meaning of the Mahabharata*, Bombay, 1957. Trautman, T.R., Kautilva and the Arthasastra, Leiden, 1972.
Upadhyaya, B.S., *India in Kalidasa,* Allahabad, 1947.
Wagle, Narendra, *Society at the Time of the Buddha*, Bombay, 1966.
Weber, Max, *The Religion of India,* tr. H. Gerth and D. Mertindale, Illinois, 1960.
Yadava, B.N.S., *Society and Culture in Northern India in the Twelfth Century*, Allahabad, 1973.